A CELEBRATION OF POETS

WEST
GRADES K-6
SPRING 2016

creativeCOMMUNICATION
A CELEBRATION OF TODAY'S WRITERS

A CELEBRATION OF POETS
WEST
GRADES K-6
SPRING 2016

AN ANTHOLOGY COMPILED BY CREATIVE COMMUNICATION, INC.

Published by:

PO BOX 303 · SMITHFIELD, UTAH 84335
TEL. 435-713-4411 · WWW.POETICPOWER.COM

Copyright © 2016 by Creative Communication, Inc.
Printed in the United States of America

Thank you to our student artists whose work is featured on the cover:
Sayo Watanabe, Grade 11; Wancheng Lin, Grade 11; Ethan Oh, Grade 7; Grace Gerber, Grade 9; Yekaterina Kaydash, Grade 12; Linnea Fraser, Grade 12; Maggie Yang, Grade 8; Alexandra Mosomillo, Grade 8; Mary Wang, Grade 10; Priya Goel, Grade 8; Stephanie Qie, Grade 9; Anita Zhang, Grade 10.
To have your art considered for our next book cover, go to www.celebratingart.com.

ISBN: 978-1-60050-749-6

FOREWORD

Dear Reader:

In the forward to the anthology last spring, I mentioned one of my favorite writers, John Tobias, whose most famous poem, "Reflections On a Gift of Watermelon Pickle Received From a Friend Called Felicity," featured in the book by the same title, has been published well over a million times. As a writer he has been published by numerous magazines including *The New Yorker*, and had had his plays produced in 15 countries. I shared with him a copy of the Spring 2015 edition and wanted to share with you, our readers, his comments.

> *Thank you for sharing your "Celebration" anthology. A Celebration indeed – I find its mix of young voices expressing their yearnings, self-discoveries, responses to nature, to change, to death, and all other outer and inner forces that strongly affect them a fascinating window into the future of writing as they explore the power of language linked to metaphor, counterpointed imagery, rhythm, music, and tough minded insights.*

> *It is you who have given them and their teachers the impetus and courage to try their wings and risk disappointment…to fall down and get up again and keep at it…to accept the need to re-write and improve and simplify and learn when less is more, and how to create a synergy that stays with the reader long after the piece has been read.*

> *Thank you again for all you do and have done to keep writing alive and flourishing.*

No, John. Thank you.

I am a teacher and have been the Editor at Creative Communication for over 20 years. I firmly believe in what we do in promoting writing in our schools. But when an accomplished, professional writer validates my belief in our mission, then all is well.

Sincerely,

Thomas Worthen, Ph.D.
Editor
Creative Communication

WRITING CONTESTS!

Enter our next POETRY contest!
Enter our next ESSAY contest!

Why should I enter?
Win prizes and get published! Each year thousands of dollars in prizes are awarded throughout North America. The top writers in each division receive a monetary award and a free book that includes their published poem or essay. Entries of merit are also selected to be published in our anthology.

Who may enter?
There are four divisions in the poetry contest. The poetry divisions are grades K-3, 4-6, 7-9, and 10-12. There are three divisions in the essay contest. The essay divisions are grades 4-6, 7-9, and 10-12.

What is needed to enter the contest?
To enter the poetry contest send in one original poem, 21 lines or less. To enter the essay contest send in one original non-fiction essay, 100-250 words, on any topic. Please submit each poem and essay with a title, and the following information clearly printed: the writer's name, current grade, home address (optional), school name, school address, teacher's name and teacher's email address (optional). Contact information will only be used to provide information about the contest. For complete contest information go to www.poeticpower.com.

How do I enter?

Enter a poem online at:
www.poeticpower.com
or
Mail your poem to:
Poetry Contest
PO Box 303
Smithfield, UT 84335

Enter an essay online at:
www.poeticpower.com
or
Mail your essay to:
Essay Contest
PO Box 303
Smithfield, UT 84335

When is the deadline?
Poetry contest deadlines are August 18th, December 1st and April 6th. Essay contest deadlines are October 13th, February 16th and July 13th. Students can enter one poem and one essay for each spring, summer, and fall contest deadline.

Are there benefits for my teacher?
Yes. Teachers with five or more students published receive a free anthology that includes their students' writing. Teachers may also earn points in our Classroom Rewards program to use towards supplies in their classroom.

For more information please go to our website at **www.poeticpower.com**, email us at editor@poeticpower.com or call 435-713-4411.

TABLE OF CONTENTS

STATES INCLUDED IN THIS EDITION:

ALASKA
ARIZONA
CALIFORNIA
HAWAII
IDAHO
MONTANA
NEVADA
NEW MEXICO
OREGON
TEXAS
WASHINGTON
WYOMING

Spring 2016 Poetic Achievement Honor Schools

*Teachers who had fifteen or more poets accepted to be published

The following schools are recognized as receiving a "Poetic Achievement Award." This award is given to schools who have a large number of entries of which over fifty percent are accepted for publication. With hundreds of schools entering our contest, only a small percent of these schools are honored with this award. The purpose of this award is to recognize schools with excellent Language Arts programs. This award qualifies these schools to receive a complimentary copy of this anthology.

A E Arnold Elementary School
Cypress, CA
Candice Earley*
Janice Wright*

Annunciation Orthodox School
Houston, TX
Adam Flores
Mrs. Hopper
Ms Kiki*
Kiki Przewlocki
Amy Williams

Archer City Elementary School
Archer City, TX
Miriam Knobloch*

Ascension Episcopal School
Houston, TX
Valerie Varhaug
Pam Ziegenbein

Austin International School
Austin, TX
Shachon Leaf

Beckendorff Jr High School
Katy, TX
Lee Gabel*

Big Springs Elementary School
Simi Valley, CA
Mrs. Adamski
Robin Boswell-Thomas
Annmarie Ingram
Mrs. O'Leary-Fisher

Cokeville Elementary School
Cokeville, WY
Roger Warner*

Dallas International School
Dallas, TX
Patty De Villiers*

Dingeman Elementary School
San Diego, CA
Leigh Morioka*

Duchesne Academy of the Sacred Heart
Houston, TX
Christy Casagil
Susan Knizner
Mrs. Petree
Melanie Rhode

Eastwood Elementary School
Westminster, CA
Kym Slingerland*

Elk Ridge Elementary School
Buckley, WA
Anne-Marie Allpress*
Morgan Johnson

Farmersville Intermediate School
Farmersville, TX
Alicia Farrar
Angelia Moses
Cyndi Rudd*

Fort Worth Christian School
North Richland Hills, TX
Nancy Hart*
Kelly Tenery*
Ginger Wetter

Fort Worth Country Day School
Fort Worth, TX
Kim Davis
Karen Davis
Mark Martin*
Joan Massey*
Mary Kay Varley*

French Elementary School
Spring, TX
Julie Drouillard*

Harmony Science Academy
Austin, TX
Abby Deshazo*

Heritage Middle School
Meridian, ID
Donna Castillo*

Hope Elementary School
Carlsbad, CA
Syndi Lyon*

International Leadership of Texas Garland K-8
Garland, TX
Rachel Schurman*
Irene Villalobos*
April Whitstone

Irma Marsh Middle School
Fort Worth, TX
Rebecca George*

Islamic School of Muslim Educational Trust
Portland, OR
Kim Carter*
Vi Pham
Youssef Ziari

Itasca Elementary School
Itasca, TX
Kim Abbott*

John Muir Elementary School
Stockton, CA
Beth Pelley*

Khalsa Montessori Elementary School
Phoenix, AZ
Lindsay Caglio*

Kleb Intermediate School
Spring, TX
Connie Braziel
Susan Collier*

Laurence School
Van Nuys, CA
Sharon Green
Kim Milman
Steve Nairin

Learning Foundation and Performing Arts
Charter School-Warner
Gilbert, AZ
Kimberly Marin*

Lookout Mountain School
Phoenix, AZ
Grace Manno*

M D Betts Elementary School
Edinburg, TX
Ada Mendoza*

McDowell Mountain Elementary School
Fountain Hills, AZ
Lynette Gross
Talia Houseal
Linda Ness*

Montessori Learning Institute
Houston, TX
MyLe Nguyen Vo
Jo Ann Turner
Lekha Worah

National University Academy 1001
San Diego, CA
Aisha Boulil*

Neblett Elementary School
Sherman, TX
Rebecca Mullendore*
Kathleen Wilcott*

Notre Dame School
Chico, CA
Stephanie Beyers*

Outley Elementary School
Houston, TX
Jayati Sengupta*

Pasadena Rosebud Academy
Altadena, CA
Sonia Anand*

Peach Springs School
Peach Springs, AZ
Cameron Shepherd*

Robert L Stevens Elementary School
Santa Rosa, CA
Amber Lesset*

Rolling Hills Country Day School
Rolling Hills Estates, CA
Debby Corette*

Scholars Academy
San Jose, CA
Rosy Pahwa
Rina Roy
Natalie To
Catherine Wong*
Ms. Zanub

Sierra Vista Elementary School
Perris, CA
Abigail Gonzalez
Brenda Lamph*
Channeal Payton*

Sonoma Charter School
Sonoma, CA
Bob Edmondson*

South Lake Middle School
Irvine, CA
Azadeh Estrada*
Danielle Jones*
Sandra Lee
Allison Neser*
Vincent Rico

South/West Park Elementary School
Tracy, CA
Jennifer Kassel
Sherry Martinho

St John's Episcopal School
McAllen, TX
Ashley Moore*
Maria Peña
Lindsay Wernecke

St Joseph Catholic School
Auburn, CA
Dede Gottlieb
Don Marsolais
Kristen Mendonsa
Jamie Zalud

St Louis De Montfort School
Santa Maria, CA
Cindy Hubbard*

St Mary's School
Fredericksburg, TX
Donna Itz*

St Raphael School
Santa Barbara, CA
Diane McClenathen*

St Thomas More Parish School
Houston, TX
Naomi Mannino
Beth Strausser

Sugar Land Middle School
Sugar Land, TX
Kristi Person*

Sunnyside Christian Elementary School
Sunnyside, WA
Diane Groenewold*

Teeland Middle School
Wasilla, AK
Colin Boyden*

The Mirman School
Los Angeles, CA
Lisa Barba
Wendy Samson*
Marjorie Zinman

Trailside Elementary School
Anchorage, AK
Mark Miner
Carleen Ulbrich

Washington Elementary School
Sandpoint, ID
Ann Dickinson*

White Oak Middle School
White Oak, TX
Monica Floyd*

Wilchester Elementary School
Houston, TX
Mrs. Belcher
Erica Finley*
Kristie Shankles*

Woodland Park Middle School
San Marcos, CA
Patricia Browning*
Maritza Witmer*

Top Ten Winners

List of Top Ten Winners for Spring 2016; listed alphabetically

Lily Banks	Grade 5	Khalsa Montessori Elementary School	AZ
John Beaupre	Grade 3	Fort Beaupre Academy	ME
Miriam Bloom	Grade 5	Isthmus Montessori Academy	WI
Magdalena Gonzalez	Grade 4	Neblett Elementary School	TX
Sophie Jaeckel	Grade 2	Stormonth Elementary School	WI
Anabel Klein*	Grade 6	Central Public School	ON
Erica Kretz	Grade 6	Pine View School for the Gifted	FL
Lily McBride	Grade 5	Christ the King Regional School	NJ
Zara Motan	Grade 5	Oliver Hoover Elementary School	FL
Maxwell Nickel	Grade 3	K B Sutton Elementary School	GA
Grace Palumbo	Grade 2	Sacred Heart Academy	OH
Isobel Sample*	Grade 6	Central Public School	ON
Serena Stefanek	Grade 1	St Stephen Lutheran School	CA
Branna Sundy	Grade 6	Diablo View Middle School	CA
Katie Treadon	Grade 5	Forcey Christian School	MD
Emma Treber	Grade 2	Ramsay Elementary School	PA
Isabel Vilensky	Grade 3	Public School 205	NY
Abigail Villatoro	Grade 3	Grant Elementary School	IA
Makenna Walko	Grade 5	Villa Maria Academy Lower School	PA
Bellatrix Willets	Kindergarten	Gibbs Elementary School	TN
Milo Willets	Grade 3	Gibbs Elementary School	TN

*Co-Authors

All Top Ten Winners may also be seen at www.poeticpower.com

Sweet Africa

The buffalo picks insects off its fur at sundown
As the zebras travel in packs at noon
Far from the pyramids of Egypt
To the sun-baked beaches of Madagascar and its islands
The inhabitants of sweet Africa roam

The giraffe sways its long neck in the morning
And as the wild pigs lie in the puddles of mud
the wildlife of sweet Africa thrives

And though it thrives,
I ask myself,
will we still have it tomorrow?
For it thrives, for it thrives!
But the hunters and the fishers,
and their brothers and their sisters,
might someday take our beauties away

So the next time you go visit the Nile
or the outbacks of the Sahara
just enjoy it
for it might be gone, sometime soon

Maxwell Nickel, Grade 3

Francis Marion

Marion watched from behind a tree,
As the Redcoats made their final flee,
From the mud and waters of Lynches Creek.
They could not find the man they tried to seek.
Marion rode back to his camp,
Then made the plans by the light of the lamp,
He'd move his men up to the Upper Santee.
Reinforcements should come soon from Lee.
They surrounded the British camp pretty soon,
And took them by surprise in the light of the moon.
The officers being taken by surprise,
Gave up to save their lives.
He freed one hundred and fifty men,
And one hundred and forty-seven men left then.
At Snow's Island two weeks they were idle,
And at the end they put on the bridle.
And in six months and two years,
The Bluecoats had filled the enemy with fears,
And Cornwallis handed over his sword,
As the new united people cheered and roared.

John Beaupre, Grade 3

Fall

The leaves get ready to leave
The cold night with snow
And delight.

Although there is a blanket
So smooth and light,
The leaves give up their hearts
For their loved ones to come back later in spring.

Red, yellow, orange, and pink —
They turn colors so slow
With the feelings they get
From the winter.

They let it into their hearts

As they get so frozen tonight —
In the cold winter nightfall

Abigail Villatoro, Grade 3

Clouds

A cloud is a sorrowful soul,
raining into the sea.
The wonderful fluff soothes the sky.
Birds rush by the wonderful misty air.
It can't be touched.
It's a ghost.
Clouds turn into fog.
It takes a trip down to the earth.
It's the king of the sky.
And it evaporates.

Serena Stefanek, Grade 1

Outside Music

Rain falls down from the sky
Bloop, bloop, pitter patter
Drumming the beat

Flowers bloom like loud horns
Trumpets, Trombones, and Tubas
Toot, toot, honk, beep beep

Wind flies through the trees
Invisible air rolls around
branches dance and sway

Spring is here
Nature comes alive
It's a magical musical day

Bellatrix Willets, Kindergarten

April Showers

April showers bring May flowers, or so they seem to say,
All I know is that when it is raining, I can't go out to play.
I'm stuck inside now with all my indoor toys,
Listening to my mom yell at me if I make too much noise.
I pass by the window and it is still coming down,
I sit with a book to read and all I do is frown.
I'm not sure how much time goes by, but wait, I perk up and strain hard with my ears,
Could it be, could it be, that the end is finally here?
I take one last peek out that window, and yes, yes, the rain has stopped,
I feel excitement stirring and my heart feels like it has dropped.
I open up the door, and the best thing that I see,
Is that April showers also bring puddles to play in with my friends and me!

Emma Treber, Grade 2

The Rain

Grey shadows bring clouds,
They cover the sky.
Sheets of rain bursting,
The lightning shall fly.

A defining clap of thunder
Is heard from far above.
Suddenly, there is wonder
The plants seem to show love.

The whole land rejoices
As stormy clouds leave.
Now, nature is beautiful,
The whole land looks so pleased.

Isabel Vilensky, Grade 3

My Mother

Mothers are sweet, mothers are fine,
My mother is one-of-a-kind.
Mothers are loving, mothers are caring,
My mother is known for her sharing.
Mothers are awesome, mothers are great,
My mother loves to make cake.
Mothers are nice, mothers are cool,
My mother teaches me school.
Without my mother, I would be heartbroken,
When we are together, no words need be spoken.
My mother is perfect, the very best,
Because of my mother, I'm very blessed.
She takes care of me, loves me, puts me to bed,
She teaches me, helps me, keeps me fed.
I'm thankful for my mother; she means so much to me,
I love my mother and my mother loves me!

Grace Palumbo, Grade 2

Dinosaurs

If dinosaurs still roamed the Earth,
Who would be in charge?
Massive bodies with razor teeth,
Or brains that are very large?

Would we be pets?
Would they be friends?
Or would we all run and scream?

Would we be food?
Would they be food?
Or would surviving be the theme?

If time went on and we died out,
And dinosaurs took our place.
Would they talk about the distant past,
and the extinct human race?

Milo Willets, Grade 3

Night

Approaching as the sun's fire dies down,
The stars make her cloak and the moon is her crown.
She brings out the cold with a flick of her wrists,
And often her breath turns into damp mist.
Her hair's glossy black and her skin is quite pale,
Wherever she walks turns into a frosty veil.
Thin and mysterious, with sharp features, too,
Her shoes made of snow and her eyes icy blue.
Dark, flowing dress concealing small feet,
Scaring some children hiding under their sheets.
Deep red lips on her sad, perfect face,
And at dawn she sneaks off to a faraway place.

Branna Sundy, Grade 6

Rosemary's Fire

Death had been eating away at her like a hungry lion
Roaring and thrashing, draining her life
At first she was running, escaping
But the lion was catching up

She gave up on fighting, she fell into the abyss of despair
She put on a wry smile to cover the truth
She knew the truth would hurt the most for her loved ones, the truth she had already accepted
No one wanted to think about the future, but the future wasn't far away

They had to deal with the stress of her state already
Lots of tears and last goodbyes, she wasn't as they remembered, cancer does that to people
Shriveled and pale, she had lost her color and hope they remembered
And then she was gone, just a memory

All except her flame red hair, even after the fire left her soul
Her red locks remind us of her burning love
I only met her once, in her last stage
But I like to image her before cancer as a happy young beautiful woman

Bright hair blowing in the wind, dancing without a care
That's how we will remember Rosemary

Erica Kretz, Grade 6

The Depths of the Ocean

The ocean depths act like a mystery
Where blue whales dance through schools of minnows
Just like a church full of people
Each unique and different

The sun peeks through the surface
sending a shade of sapphire throughout the water
Boisterous sounds fill the miles of the ocean
Like a buzzing sensation of gaiety in a New York train station

But no longer may I hold my breath
I tread towards the fresh air above
A deep breath in, a deep breath out
And a chill rolls down my spine while gazing at the horizon

The odor of salt water fills my nostrils
I stare out along the shoreline so peaceful, almost too peaceful
The silence aggravates my ears
Like a bee stinging the tip of my finger

I hear the soft melody of the waves crashing onto the shore
Sending an incessant drop of sea water to slip into my mouth
I breathe in fresh air and dive into the depths of the ocean
I glide through the water like an eel, with my lithe body
Dodging peculiar sea creatures to the harmony silence

Lily McBride, Grade 5

Italian Grapes

The secreted, vineyards of Bologna Italy,
the sun glows brightly on a massive gazebo.
A gazebo-like housing to luscious grapes.
Grapes wind, coiled springs, fixed on the poles
A special bunch of red succulent grapes.
Forming, winding around a rusty fixture
in an intertwining spider web clinging to a wall
cascading to human reach.
Sweetened perfection are the plump red grapes
ripened, juicy insides contained by one thin barrier,
the surface is a smooth, magenta-dyed silk,
the grapes as rotund as a crystal ball.
The sun reflects off their sweet surface
and they glow and radiate like polished amethysts,
dark green leaves patiently grow,
rich, pure like shining emeralds.
The delectable grapes are at their best,
plucked with care and tucked in a basket,
brought to the fresh market with cherries and apples,
sold to nomads, neighbors, friends and family.
Savored by the Italian families.

Lily Banks, Grade 5

Change

The winter wind stings my face, I trudge, slowly but surely.
Soon the snow will disappear, as if by magic
Flowers emerge from their winter cabins
And show the world their never-ending beauty

Hot days and cold nights, never-ending mosquitoes
"School's out!"
Days of lounge ahead
Back to school shopping
Visiting Grandma

Soon an artist paints the leaves
Red, green, orange they turn, showing their true selves
Before they tumble to the ground.
Sandals come off and the boots come on

Then the winter wind arrives from vacation
Blows powder onto the bare ground
Naked trees dot the streets
Jack Frost painted pictures on the window
Isobel Sample and Anabel Klein, Grade 6

The Flying Jewel

A small small bird is floating through the light
On visible waves ready for flight.
Radiant, like an emerald in the sky,
Floating swiftly, going up so high.
Indescribable colors of blue, purple, green,
Gently fluttering, never unseen.
Fluffy like a cushion in its nest so small,
Everything to the bird may seem so tall,
Gracefully sailing from flower to flower
Rain or shine, or a chance of showers.
Examining all the sweet smelling blooms,
Peeping a sound, one small tune.
Humming softly, though other birds bellow
Over the ground, hovering over a meadow.
Peeking into petals, nectar on its beak,
Drinking from flowers, blossoms they seek.
Communicating through humming not using a word,
Composing a noise: the humming bird.
Katie Treadon, Grade 5

The Northern Lights

The great Northern Lights
Dance over a frozen tundra
Like glowing crystal bulbs
Grandstanding their unblemished beauty.

The palace beneath it shines
In the vast, dazzling ocean
As the moon crawls
Across the sky.

A plethora of stars
Illuminate the emerald ceiling
In the open waves
That ripple by.

The aurora of colors
Sit proudly on their thrones
As all lies still
On top of the world.
Zara Motan, Grade 5

Life Is a Mountain

Life can be hard, but not all the time.
Life is a mountain and you just have to climb.
Just be patient, take your time,
Wait for tomorrow and you'll feel alive.
Everyone is special, don't you see?
I feel great — be like me!
Do I get sad?
Yes, I do.
But people say,
"No one can be as good as you."
So play around and have some fun.
Try to be kind to everyone.
Yes, life is unfair
But kindness is somewhere in the air!
Tomorrow is a new day,
So goof off and play.
Life is hard, yes all the time,
But life is a mountain you just need to climb.
Just be patient, take your time,
Wait for tomorrow and you'll be fine.
Magdalena Gonzalez, Grade 4

I Have Seen the Seasons Change
I have seen the seasons change: leaves turning from the glorious greens of life
to the rusty colors of the earth, memories scattered on the floor
and left victim to the ever-devouring face of time.

I have seen flowers, with petals of every hue and scent,
cover the fields and meadows, bringing the rainbows from the heavens
and spreading them out across the countryside, like laundry hung out to dry.

I have seen the icy swirls of winter, lace the frozen ground,
pirouetting across the sky, in a race of immortal grace,
blanketing the world in a quilt of silence and peace, a single note of glorious relief
in a world constantly caught in the music of life.

And I have seen the sun. Shining in the east,
fiery in its magenta robes of heat and inhuman power,
as it both scorches life from the world, leaving it barren and dry,
dusty in the embers of what could have been, and as it revives Mother Nature…
Sending blessings of cradling beams, and enveloping gentleness to wash away its grip of fear.
Yes, I have seen the sun.

Makenna Walko, Grade 5

Fireflies
Sometimes beauty is not something you see.
Sometimes it's the feeling rising up in your chest;
Bare feet, warm room, full moon.
Sometimes it's the kind of silence that settles over you like a blanket;
Dragonfly, Mason jar, fingers stained with blackberries.
Sometimes it's the wonder that comes from a flight;
July is the time for staying late in the night air,
        old car down a gravel road,
        smiling hushed smiles of painted-moon laughter.

My eyes are aglow with fireflies:
when the snow has fallen, lulled the earth into slumber, softening all the edges
I remember when there was no numbness once.
When I was cartwheeling through thick waves of freedom,
The beauty of that night.

Miriam Bloom, Grade 5

Hello and Goodbye
Hello, shiny dewdrops, hanging from a thread,
Goodbye, warm hot cocoas that send you off to bed.
Hello, loud bees that hover by the flowers,
Goodbye, gentle voices while taking steaming showers.
Hello, sunny picnics where you can run and play,
Goodbye, enormous snow hills where you sled and ski all day.
Hello, green hills, green grass, green trees, sprouting more green leaves,
Goodbye, great blizzards falling where and whenever they please.

Sophie Jaeckel, Grade 2

Grades K-1-2-3
High Merit Poems

Howler Monkey

A Howler Monkey's black coat is as dark as the midnight sky.
A Howler Monkey's voice is as flat as a screaming baby.
A Howler Monkey's tail is a long as a third grader's desk.
A Howler Monkey's claws are as sharp as a pocket knife.
A Howler Monkey is as big as a three year old little child.
A Howler Monkey can swoop on the vines like Tarzan.
A Howler Monkey is as fast as a predator.

Lillie Harper, Grade 3

My Mom Loves Me

My mom loves me.
She takes me everywhere I want to go.
She always picks me up from school.
Mom cooks yummy dinner.
She is beautiful!
She makes me feel happy.
And when she puts on perfume, she smells like a flower!

Spoorthi Gowda, Kindergarten

Too Much Homework

I've got so much homework tonight.
The light needs to stay on very, very bright.
I'll be doing my homework day and night,
If I don't get it done I'll get in trouble
And my mother will shove me into a bubble.
My homework will double and double.

Margaret Touma, Grade 2

Golden Poison Arrow Frog

The golden poison arrow frog is as sticky as slime.
The golden poison arrow frog is as fast as a cheetah.
The golden poison arrow frog is as bright as the sun.
The golden poison arrow frog is as toxic as toxic waste.
The golden poison arrow frog is as still as a sloth.
The golden poison arrow frog can jump as high as the sky.

Eli VanBeek, Grade 3

I'd Rather Be Fishing

I'd rather be fishing because it's the best.
I have a break from school not to be stressed.
On the bay I wait and wait with my hook and bait.
I wait and wait until the fish is caught, great!
I'd like to be fishing because it's the best.
I know not to be worried because it's not a test.

Connor Vodebnal, Grade 2

Love

Love is the color red
Love smells like the lovely roses in my grandma's garden
Love sounds like my sister singing a beautiful song
Love tastes like my grandma's yummy spaghetti
Love looks like my mom's big heart
Love feels like my caring and loving family

Kanoa Arzaga, Grade 2

Spring

Spring is in the air!
You can smell it in the blooming roses field.
You can see it in the beautiful sun set.
You can hear it in blue jays singing in a red wood tree.
You can feel it in the shining trees at your backyard.

Damian Avalos, Grade 3

Spring

Spring is in the air!
You can smell it in the blooming roses.
You can see it in the beautiful sun set.
You can hear it in robins nest in a redwood tree.
You can feel it in the cold breeze.

Andrew Urban, Grade 3

I Am a Child of God

I feel happy when God is happy,
I feel really sad that my Lola died,
I feel excited when I play Star Wars Battle Front,
I feel mad when my dad is mad,
Because I am a child of God.

Dominic Mendoza, Grade 1

My Mamma

Mom, you are as pretty as a butterfly.
As smart as a princess,
As sweet as a strawberry,
I like it when you play the "Frozen" puzzle with me.
I love you!

Saesha Bargal, Kindergarten

Tiger

A tiger's eyes look like a bright light.
The orange fur on a tiger looks like lava.
The color white on the tiger is like the clouds.
The roar of a tiger is like screams at a horror movie.
A tiger is as scary as a zombie.

Justin Jibben, Grade 3

Blue

B lue is the color of the sky and the ocean.
L ots of things are blue even birds are too.
U nder, over, left, and right there is blue everywhere.
E ven the emotion sadness is blue.

Danielle Josephine Fuentes, Grade 1

The Old

The old need teeth and dentures
The old need lifelong love
The old are something that should not be forgotten
The old are something we become

Anika Pathak, Grade 1

Color

I pick up my pencil, draw my mind.
I step into my picture and say what a great way to be me
I take a look around and put my head down knowing someday I'll be someone else
I step out of my mind and find me in a different galaxy. I pick up my jump rope skip my way home
I loan my pencil to my best friend
I wake up and find myself in Heaven even though I'm only 7
I look up pick up my pencil stare at my stencil and start color.
Forever I stay clam, hold my palm and see the sky blooming
Doing my things that I love. COLOR

Iris Hanszen, Grade 3

My Sister, My First Friend

My sister, my first friend loving and caring always by my side makes me feel better when I cry,
That love is sister love that sisters only enjoy, that love is impossible to destroy,
she is like an angel from above,
and she is calm like a dove,
sometimes mean but mostly nice she has my back without even trying,
she is the best sister in the world,
Jasmine
My sister, my first friend

Kayla Evans, Grade 2

The Beach

I love the beach,
So sunny and bright.
I adore the beach,
I wish I could go every night.

The warmth of the sand rubbing my tan toes,
The frigid water splashes at me, this is how it goes.
As the freezing, blue waves soak me,
Some green, wet seaweed gets stuck on my ankles and knees.

The majestic, yellow star's sparkling golden beams hitting me,
There is a lot of relaxation and action to see.
My beautiful, creative sandcastle glimmer in the sun,
I'm just having too much fun!

The shrewd eagles in the turquoise sky,
So way up high.
I hear the gulls shrieking out aloud,
Their old, rusty voices are so loud!

My fondness for the beach will never stop
Even when I grow up to be a strict cop!

Ananya Niranjan, Grade 3

My Toucan

A toucan's beak is as bright as fireworks.
A toucan's noises are as loud as a little girl's screams.
A toucan's legs are as strong as Hulk.
A toucan flying is as bad as a clumsy kid trying to do karate.
A toucan's body is as black and white as an Oreo.
A toucan's eye is as blue as the sky on a sunny day.
A toucan's feet are as pointy as a sewing needle.

Hailey Adkins, Grade 3

I Am Krish

I am smart and sporty.
I wonder if there is life on another planet.
I hear a drum that is playing nice and loud.
I see a tiger eating its prey.
I want to be good for my whole life.
I am smart and sporty.

I pretend to be in war.
I feel the fluffy clouds in the sky.
I touch a shark's sharp tooth.
I worry about people that don't have any food.
I cry when old people die.
I am smart and sporty.

I understand people make mistakes.
I say "God is real".
I dream that I shoot webs like Spiderman.
I try to be a good student.
I hope people get a second life.
I am smart and sporty.

Krish Reddi, Grade 2

All About My Mom

My mom plays with me with my cars.
I'm going to buy my mom a BMW M6.
I help my mom cook mac and cheese on the stove.
I love my mom because she hugs me.
My mom drives me to school.
My mom cooks the best mac and cheese.
My mom likes jewelry on her ears.
My mom is as sweet as me.
I'm going to buy my mom a bike.

Amit Biligiri, Kindergarten

Love

Love is the color light green
Love smells like cotton candy being made
Love sounds like my daddy and mommy kissing me
Love tastes like a baked apple
Love looks like hearts
Love feels like big hugs

Brooke Sato, Grade 2

Love

Love is the color violet
Love smells like roses in my mom's garden
Love sounds like happiness when the birds chirp
Love tastes like my mom's special sugar cookies
Love looks like my family's smiles
Love feels like kisses are everywhere

Ailene Lim, Grade 2

My Science Fair Project

My science fair project has a good presentation
I will show it to the whole nation
My project is very creative
It is about plants that are native
The judges think it is very impressive,
Because I am so obsessive.

Jack George-Womack, Grade 3

Tennis

T hankful for your new Grand Slam win
E asy shots make you win
N ice serves make an extra point
N o wins make you a rank 1,000 or 999, it's ok
I njuries are bad, that you might retire
S elf-control you might lose and break your racket

Johann Lee, Grade 3

Spring

Spring is in the air!
You can smell it in field of roses
with nectar and a gentle breeze.
You can see it in the sunset.
You can hear it in singing birds in an oak tree.
You can feel it in smooth grass.

Albert Hernandez, Grade 3

Christmas

I can see my beautiful glowing Christmas tree
The delicious Christmas cookies
Laughter from people
Delicious ginger bread cookies
And the noisy wrapping paper
Christmas

Ethan Lee, Grade 3

Leaf

A leaf is blowing in the sky and only I saw the glories in its awe
And oh so to have a beauty to yourself
But I simply know that to and fro
Oh no you will never ever see a leaf like this.

Sloane Crocker, Grade 2

I Am a Child of God

I feel happy to laugh with my family,
I feel excited when I go to volleyball and basketball,
I feel mad when my brother pushes me,
Because I am a child of God.

Isabella Espinosa, Grade 1

Far Away*

Far away
Is the day when I saw you last
I am depressed as I think back.

The rain was dripping as I was crying.

You and I
Miles and miles away.

I might see you
In a better place.
Someday but that
Seems so far away…

You left me…
How could you?

I didn't know the last time
I saw you, would be the
last time!

I barely even knew you,
But I still care!

But I remember…
That your spirit is always inside

Me!!!

Ledia Chombe, Grade 3
*To Grandpa from Ledia

Grandma's Glory

She sings a lot.
She loves to dance to music.
She likes to play instruments.
She is nice.
I like to play with her.
Grandma is soothing.
Her voice is loud sometimes not.
We always cook together.
Our cinnamon rolls are the best.

Shawn Mack, Grade 3

A Poem of Poems

Poetry is fun.
Although it is short,
Possibilities are endless.

You could write about animals,
You could write about cars,
You could write about anything,
Oh boy, what fun!

Who doesn't like poetry?
Oh poetry is so fun.

With so many types of poetry,
A sharp pencil, eraser,
And a good imagination.
The possibilities are endless.
Oh who doesn't like poetry?

Ideas are easy,
With a sharp imagination.
Write away, again and again

Oh who doesn't like poetry?
Griffin Ferguson, Grade 3

Packages

Mail keeps coming to the house.
We can't find my mom's blouse.
It's on top of every single table.
It's even on my Auntie Mabel.
Uncle Bill has not been happy.
He's really been quite snappy.
It's on the floor, blocking the door.
We've tried to shout for the mailman
It hasn't worked.
The mail just keeps on coming.
There is no stopping it.
We do not know who it's from.
We haven't ordered anything
From any place like Amazon.
The people there might just be generous.
Who knows, they might be mean.
But anyway, we can't live properly.
Our cat can't eat, and we can't either.
We're getting very slim.
Wait. You know what.
I think it's probably bills.
Garrett Lewis, Grade 3

Pizza/Cheesy

Pizza
Delicious, good
Eating, pizza, party
Tasty, yummy in the tummy
Cheesy
Vincent Larson, Grade 2

Earth

The Earth has done so much
for all of us,
we've got to be nice
to the world around us.
We litter,
the Earth stays calm.
She doesn't get mad
but forgives us,
hoping one day
we'd come around,
even care
about the world;
she helps us,
lives with us,
and most importantly of all
provides the environment
for all of us.
Morgan Suman, Grade 3

Brain Storm

There's a storm in my brain
and I can't get it out,
what should I do
should I shout should I pout?
There's a hurricane going
on inside my head
should I ignore it instead?
There is a tornado
whooshing in my brain,
it feels like
it is starting to rain.
So you can see
there is a storm
in my head so
please tell me what
to do instead.
Camden Hopper, Grade 3

Spring Fever

Spring fever,
I have spring fever
I got the blues

Wet rags, Tylenol.
Sick day, smoothies,
soap too!

Spring fever, spring fever,
I have spring fever
I've got attitude

Whining, towels, hygiene,
fluids, other too!
I'll tell ya I've got the blues
Morgan Swearer, Grade 3

All About Me

K ind to kids
O ften outside
Y ellow hair
E yes that are blue

M ad sometimes
A lways smiling
R eaches for the stars
I mportant to my family
E xcited for school

D reams of being a doctor
Koye Dennett, Grade 2

The Storm

BOOM!
CRASH!
What?
Again?
What's that booming sound again?
It's trembling.
It's crying.
It's shaking.
It's shouting.
It's angry.
Did I do something wrong?
How do you make a storm feel better?
Ella Coker, Grade 3

The Ocean

Dark, blue water,
Waves going slowly back and forth,
Dolphins playing in the water,
Swimming all over,
All day long,
Smart, very smart,
Dolphins call out
To each other
To play.
Loves to jump up
Then drops down to
The ocean.
Alexa Galvan, Grade 2

Christmas Is in the Air

You can smell it in the
gingerbread cookies.
You can taste it in the spicy
peppermint candy canes.
You can hear it in Santa
riding his sleigh.
You can see it in the tree and
nice ornaments jingling to me.
You can feel it in the proudness
of being good all year.
Nitin Kumar, Grade 3

Sea Days
Swimming in the sea, free as can be.

I wish, I wish, that I was a fish.
I'd swim in the sea and always be free.

I know a fish that's named Swish.
Oh he would swim in the sea free as can be.
I always wished I was a fish.

Oh I know all the places I'll go in the water,
Flipping and swishing in that cold shimmering sea.

The sea, the sea, it's a wonderful place to be.
The fish swim free as can be,
Swimming in that cold shimmering sea.
Kate Wagers, Grade 2

Pebble, Pebble
Pebble, Pebble
nice and sweet, having you is such a treat.
Pebble, Pebble
come with me, fun it will be.
Pebble, Pebble
you're so neat, you're way smaller than my feet.
Pebble, Pebble
nice and rough, I hope you'll be really tough.
Pebble, Pebble
you're so red, it's time to go to bed.
Pebble, Pebble
just small, I wish you were tall.
Pebble, Pebble
you're my rock, tick tock goes the clock.
Kaiden Dallas, Grade 2

If I Had a Magic Wand
If I had a magic wand
I would turn my lazy dog into a tap dancing dog

If I had a magic wand
I would turn my homework into an apple pie

If I had a magic wand
I would turn my old oak tree into a money tree

But I know I can't
because I have to be
happy with what I have
Breanne Blaylock, Grade 3

Mr. Season
I like Mr. Season for a special reason.
Warm, cool, hot, and cold. Your mood is always changing.
At least, that's what I am told.
Mr. Season, Mr. Season, I will meet you soon.
With your warm weather, and sun made of gold.
Nabila Khan, Grade 2

I Am Charlotte
I am a nice and loving girl.
I wonder if winged wolves are real.
I hear wolves howling in the night.
I see wolves flying over my head.
I want the ability to transform into a wolf.
I am a nice and loving girl.

I pretend that I am a wolf.
I feel a winged wolf perched on top of my head.
I touched a winged wolf's wing.
I worry about when wolves go extinct.
I cry if wolves go extinct.
I am a nice and loving girl.

I understand wolves are not close to going extinct.
I say wolves are awesome.
I dream I can turn into a wolf.
I try my best to be nice to wildlife.
I hope my dream comes true.
I am a nice and loving girl.
Charlotte Kennard, Grade 2

Martin Luther King, Jr.
I am an American
I wonder about equality and justice for all
I hear about the laws that need to change
I see violence and people that want to change
I want no more discrimination
I am an American

I pretend to change the world
I feel happy about the future of the world
I touch the hands of the people
I worry about the world
I cry when I see discrimination
I am an American

I understand our problems
I say freedom and justice for all
I dream that everybody will be equal
I try to respect everyone
I hope for a better world
I am Martin Luther King, Jr.
Eduardo Pastor, Grade 3

Yosemite
Y ou can go and see Yosemite Falls.
O ctober 1, 1890, President Benjamin Harrison
          signed legislation that created Yosemite.
S equoia trees are HUGE.
E xciting places like water falls.
M arvelous gift shops.
I nteresting views of nature.
T errific sights like Half Dome.
E l Captain is a giant granite rock.
Jaclyn Stone, Grade 3

Sunset

The wind,
the birds,
the soft pitter-patter
of a light rain.
I stand outside,
watching the day
turn to night,
as the sun
sinks behind
the mountains.
Sadie Bankhead, Grade 3

Hello Kitty

Hello Kitty is a cat,
She has many kinds of hats.
She also has many friends,
So the adventures never end.
She can be anything she wants to,
And can dress in pink, purple, or blue.
Her books are cool and funny,
And make my world so sunny!
She likes to play, rain or shine.
You can play with her anytime!
Wanisa Suwannakinthorn, Grade 2

Myself

Zi Shan Chew is me,
I am nice and helpful,
Soon I will be in third grade,
Hope third grade is fun,
At home I get sleepy,
Not cool to be the only child,
Cool to be myself,
Happy to be home,
Excellent me,
Way to go!
Zi Shan Chew, Grade 2

Spring

Spring is in the air!
You can smell it in the bloomed
    cherry blossom flowers.
You can see it when animals
    wake up looking for food.
You can hear it in the rustling leaves
    as a light breeze goes by.
You can feel it when a gentle wind
    circles flower petals around you.
Sophia Park, Grade 3

Earth with All Its Wonder

Volcanoes galore…boom!
Many of its plants are gone.
Earth's oceans, plants and life.
It's our father, it's our home.
Rylee Holmes, Grade 3

The Dark Night

One night
As the city fell asleep
The sky darkened
And
Mr. Moon
Came out
To brighten the night.
Mason Story, Grade 3

War/Peace

War
Dangerous, scary
Shooting, winning, killing
People, countries, love, family
Loving, hugging, caring
Quiet, peaceful
Peace
Briana Isavet Maldonado, Grade 2

The Beautiful Blowing Wind

The leaves are falling.
Hollow trees lose leaves.
Animals are hibernating.
Leaves turn brown.
Beautiful winds blow.
Winds are blowing.
Nature gets calm.
Isabella Kolmel-Vieira, Grade 2

Rain

Rain
Cold, wet
Flowing, boring, flooding
Worms, slugs, hot, dry
Scorching, sweating, drying
Warm, dry
Sunny
Mahdi Bhuiyan, Grade 3

The Garden

Walking peacefully into a grassy plain.
Flowers bloom.
The sun shines. Birds sing.
My heart fills with joy
as butterflies flutter and
humming birds hum.
No enemies at all.
Malachi Smith, Grade 1

The Waves!

Waves are big they make a splash,
they go on shore and then go back
I wonder how they get so big?
The waves seem so fun when I go in.
And that is the poem of waves.
Daniella Aweidah, Grade 3

Yellow Is

Yellow is a charming banana,
And a bursting lemon.

Yellow tastes lemon sour,
And banana sweet.

Yellow smells sweet daffodils,
And lemon bad.

Yellow hears popping
Loud and quiet.

Yellow sees sweet corn,
And the flaming sun.
Chase Duncan, Grade 3

Jaguar

Roar!
What is that?
Is it a lion?
What is it?
ROAR!
We don't know!
Yet it has sharp claws
And sharp teeth
It hunts
It purrs
I am terrified!
I know what it is now!
It's a jaguar!
ROAR!
Canila Ruiz, Grade 2

Soccer

Two teams against each other
For the championship
This team
They hear the whistle
They pass
The ball
One
By
One
To
Each Other
They hear the whistle
Whoosh!
They score!
Jayden Moncivais, Grade 2

My Dog

My dog is fluffy
My dog is big
My dog is nice
My dog is mine
Hiddekel Davis, Grade 1

I Am Amber

I am a wonderful sweet girl.
I am a dreaming girl.
I feel like I'm touching the blue sky.
I'm curious about the world.
I like to imagine about the stars.
I am a wonderful sweet girl.

I love marshmallows.
I hear the stars in the sky talking to me.
I wonder if I'm doing the wrong thing.
I see the clouds looking at me.
I feel like I'm up in space.
I am a wonderful sweet girl.

I am always full of energy.
I worry if I do not get good grades.
I like my life.
I do not like to worry.
I like math and books.
I am a wonderful sweet girl.
Amber Huff, Grade 2

I Am

I am fast and focused
I wonder how fast the other guy is
I hear the coach yelling
I see the lights on the field
I want to be the best
I am fast and focused

I pretend to be the ball
I feel everyone's eyes on me
I touch the sweat on my forehead
I worry that they'll catch up to me
I cry after a tough loss
I am fast and focused

I understand what I need to do
I say "good game!"
I dream of being the next Babe Ruth
I try to hit the ball
I hope to win the game
I am a baseball player
Joseph Raudel Garza, Grade 2

I Like Sports

K aden plays a lot of sports
A wesome athlete I am
D o help me coach
E ver lasting player I am
N othing can help me

J ust don't get in my way

H orton I am and the game I will play
Kaden Horton, Grade 3

The Rainbow

The rainbow is so high,
It shines in the sky!

As the sun rays shine bright,
A raindrop touches it
…and
It makes a pretty rainbow.

It's like a crayon collection,

So bright and colorful!
Teresa Tran, Grade 3

Blue

Blue is the ocean,
Bright like the sky.
Blue is like a jelly bean,
But cotton candy sweet.
Blue can feel like water,
And like a bird.
Blue can smell sweet,
And refreshing too.
Blue sounds like the night sky,
And like a whale.
I see blue as a beautiful color.
Camryn Morris, Grade 3

Puppies

Puppies, puppies, so cute and fluffy.
Puppies, puppies, always in a hurry.

Puppies, puppies, always looking cute,
Puppies, puppies, chewing on your shoe.

Puppies, puppies, looking for scraps,
Puppies, puppies, always smelling bad

Puppies, puppies, jumping on your bed.
Puppies, puppies, they beg and beg.
Anna Hardig, Grade 3

Softball

We are softball!
We wear maroon and white.
We may look like a doll,
but we have a lot of fight.
We win tournaments.
We like the sound
of the ball hitting the bat.
We love our teammates.
We enjoy playing the game
we love.
Softball.
Jerra Spahr, Grade 3

Best Friends No Matter What

Even though you moved away
I'll still be there
for you!
Even though we don't see
each other anymore
…
I'll still be there
for you!
Even though we don't
talk to each other
anymore
…
I'll still be there
for you!
Because we're best friends
…
No matter what.
Valerie Luciano, Grade 3

Good

Good is good
It's good to be good
There are good things
and good people
Good is good to be

Good is nice
It's good to be nice
There are nice things
and nice people
Nice is good to be

Good is kind
It's good to be kind
There are kind things
and kind people
Kind is good to be.
Luke Pine, Grade 3

Basketball

Dribble, dribble, shoot, shoot
Score!
Basketball rocks!
You can play it every where you go.
Balls bouncing everywhere
People running everywhere to get the ball.

Dribble, dribble, shoot, shoot,
Score!
The crowds roar when you score.
Dribble, dribble, penalty!?
The other team gets the ball.

Then dribble, dribble, shoot, score!
You win!
Caden Bush, Grade 3

Cleopatra

I am beautiful and can speak different languages
I wonder why I wanted to be queen
I hear the voices of the past pharaohs
I see the sunset
I want my brother and sister
I am beautiful and can speak different languages

I pretend to rule the world
I feel the hot sun on my face
I touch a golden throne
I worry that I will not become a queen
I cry that I won't be queen
I am beautiful and can speak different languages

I understand how to run a country
I say I am queen
I dream of sailing down the Nile River
I try to win the heart of Rome
I hope to be queen of Rome
I am Cleopatra

Sofia Aguilar, Grade 3

The Living Nightmare

I went to bed thinking I would have a dream,
But instead I had
A NIGHTMARE!
I closed my eyes,
Going deeper and deeper,
Until
I hit the floor of a dark deep world.
Every second I was in there,
The more it hurt,
Like one million monsters digging into my skin.
I tried to escape,
But the monsters wouldn't let go.
I saw the way out,
But it closed before I could get there.
And
I never stopped having the living
NIGHTMARE!

Parker Browning, Grade 3

Sofia

It means courage, caring, funny
It is like the color of the beautiful ocean
It is like going to the lake with my family
It is the memory of my older sister —
Who taught me to be myself no matter what people say,
and to have courage.
When she stood up for herself,
When people said she wasn't good at basketball,
She also had courage.
My name is Sofia.
It means to try your hardest
and never give up.

Sofia Zendejas, Grade 3

The Sun

I love the shine so very bright,
Giving the Earth a lovely sight

I hide at night, and come out during the day
When people wake up, they say "hooray!"

I love to keep everyone warm,
It is hard to see me during a storm.

Ryan Dopp, Grade 2

The Green Anaconda

The green anaconda is as dark green as a shimmering green pond.
The green anaconda's eyes are as yellow as the sun.
The green anaconda is as long as the Mississippi River.
The green anaconda is as wide as a computer.
The green anaconda squeezes harder than a belt around your waist.
The green anaconda has teeth as sharp as needles.
The green anaconda has a varied diet like a human.
The green anaconda is as smooth as the skin on an apple.

Vincent Allison-Dice, Grade 3

A Mountain

A mountain! A mountain! I have nothing to do,
A mountain! A mountain! I'll take my friend too,
A mountain! A mountain! Where is the end?
A mountain! A mountain! To climb it is tough!
A mountain! A mountain! We've got the right stuff!
A mountain! A mountain! We're almost through!
A mountain! A mountain! We're up! Yahoo!

Katelyn Segura, Grade 3

My Mom Loves Me

My mom plays with me.
She plays with my doll.
She braids my doll's hair.
My mom and I sometimes bake a blue Elsa cake.
My mom is as beautiful as a butterfly.
My mom's favorite color is golden.
My mom loves me!

Poongodi Chidambaram, Kindergarten

My Awesome Mom

My mom is the nicest mom ever.
She is the best I could have.
I will miss her forever, without her I'm sad.
She was nice to our brother.
When I saw her I was glad.
She was a good mother.
She's gone, but she's the best that I ever had.

Erick Romero Tamez, Grade 3

Trees

When a tree was a seed do you think a tree remembers?
It is very creative when its leaves change color!
It is impressive how tall it is or it wants to be!

Samuel Fitch, Grade 3

Life
Life is great,
Life is full of great things.
Life will end.
Life is treasure,
Life is precious.
Love life.
Sophie Bernadac, Grade 3

Lion
ROAR!
Large legs
And orange hair
Hunting in the day
A lion is diurnal
A kingly lion
Brisa Cortez, Grade 2

Alabama
The Heart of Dixie
Biggest Product is cotton
Harper Lee, Author
Twenty-Second State
Home of Coretta Scott King
Yellowhammer flies
Lucy Walker, Grade 3

Jaguar
Sharp claws, sharp teeth, and black fur
It naps, it hunts, and purrs
I hear a loud ROAR!
I'm nervous and terrified!
GULP!!
Now I know what a jaguar eats!
Arely Vela, Grade 2

Mom
Mom
She is kind
She is loving
She helps a lot
She reads to me
Mom
Zoie Starkey, Grade 2

Spring
The sun shines brightly in the sky.
The grass is green like emeralds.
The water in the river is like sapphires.
The sky is blue like bluebonnets.
The air is crisp like an apple.
Spring is the best time of the year.
Angela Nguyen, Grade 2

I Am a Child of God
I feel happy to laugh with my dad,
I feel sad when I am hurt,
I feel excited to play basketball,
I feel mad when somebody hits me,
Because I am a child of God.
Matthew Jumalon, Grade 1

Sleepy
There once was a man named Fred
One night he was in his bed
He saw a big bug
he grabbed his white mug
and squished it until it was dead
Carson Smith, Grade 3

I Am a Child of God
I feel happy with my mom,
I feel sad when I get hurt,
I feel excited to play basketball,
I feel mad when my dog bites me,
Because I am a child of God.
Esteban Larrahona, Grade 1

I Am a Child of God
I feel happy to laugh with my Dad,
I feel sad when I fall down,
I feel excited to go to the show,
I feel mad when I make a mistake,
Because I am a child of God.
Lucia Blackwood, Grade 1

Heart
H elpful friend
E xtremely kind
A bout to be blessed by God
R emain to love
T emper is never lost
Isabella Diaz, Grade 2

My Mama
Mom, you are as pretty as a flower.
As smart as a cat,
As sweet as Nutella,
I like it when you play race cars with me.
I love you!
Sujay Kankipati, Kindergarten

All About Juliette
Juliette
Funny, fun, friendly
Play, run
I love my family.
Juliette
Juliette Romero, Grade 1

Mom/Dad
Mom
Funny, cuddly
Loving, demanding, caring
Pretty, cook — handsome, hard-working
Sleeping, snoring, interesting
Happy, joyful
Dad
Amy Sakshi Sparks, Grade 3

Me
My hair is dark like the night
My eyes are round as a circle
My nose sharp like a needle
My mouth is quiet as a mouse
My face is smooth as silk
My body is soft like rabbit fur
My hands are strong like wolves
Bilal Ibrahim, Grade 3

All About Me
All about me
Love, glad, helpful
Be funny
Swim
Run
I love my family.
Harper
Harper Smith, Grade 1

Ruby
Ruby
Expensive, beautiful
Shining, sparkling, glaring
Mountains, rocks, soil, minerals
Growing, blowing, blooming
Dirty, brown
Dirt
Rania Kramer, Grade 3

Teacher
T eaching
E xcellent
A mazing
C aring
H elping
E ducating
R e-teaching
Gurshaan Thukral, Grade 3

Balloons/Bright Red
Balloons
Rubber, floaty
Flies and floats in the air
Happy balloon lifts off to sky
Bright red
Violet Bertrand, Grade 2

Basketball
Stephen Curry
Cool, great
Fast jumping running
Makes me feel good
Warriors
Simon Zapien III, Grade 3

All About Jamie
Jamie
Cute, soccer
Happy, love
I love you.
Jamie
Jamie Brown, Grade 1

Sister
I love my sister
Sister plays with me
Sister loves me
Sister is the
Best sister ever
Elizabeth Bitson, Grade 2

All About Ethan
Ethan
Cute, happy, nice
Play fight
I love my family.
Ethan
Ethan Winchell, Grade 1

Windy
W hy is the wind so cold
I n winter and in spring?
N obody knows what it will do.
D on't you wish that it would stop?
Y es, I do!
Lucas Ramirez, Grade 3

Dogs
I love my dogs
My dogs are playful
My dogs are
Abby, Vixen, Havikhexs
I love my dogs
Zach Howard, Grade 2

Snowflake
Snowflake
Blue, white
Falling all down
Makes me feel happy
Cold
Eileen Flores, Grade 3

The Ring Tailed Lemur
The ring tailed lemur is as black and white as an olden-day movie.
The ring tailed lemur is as funny as a monkey that swings around in the jungle.
The ring tailed lemur is as jumpy as a frog in a puddle.
The ring tailed lemur has a tail as long as a giraffe's neck.
The ring tailed lemur is as cute as a dog in a dog show.
The ring tailed lemur is as smart as Einstein.
Cheyenne Bush, Grade 3

My Mom
You are as sweet as a cupcake.
You have the smile of an angel.
You bring joy to the world.
You have always been there to help me out and make me feel at home.
You do so much for me when I do so little for you.
You have been my mom from the day I was born.
Noah Kassner, Grade 3

I Am Ava
I am a doll that is nice.
I wonder if Florida is ever cold.
I hear books talking to you.
I see people kissing.
I want new clothes.
I am a doll that is nice.

I pretend to clean up the house.
I feel like touching the sky.
I touch a dream.
I worry about me.
I cry for not seeing my parents.
I am a doll that is nice.

I understand math.
I say "go away".
I dream being in a dream.
I try to do better in ballet class.
I hope to see my sister and brother.
I am a doll that is nice.
Ava LaChiusa, Grade 2

I Am Pikachu
I am yellow and electrifying
I wonder why I don't evolve
I hear my friend Charmander
I see my trainer Ash
I want to evolve someday
I am yellow and electrifying

I pretend I am strong
I feel cool
I touch the sky
I worry about Leaf Pokemon
I cry when Ash is not with me
I am yellow and electrifying

I understand my trainer's lessons
I say I can touch the sky
I dream to evolve
I try to win
I hope to get bigger
I am yellow and electrifying
Roberto Roux, Grade 2

Cats
Cats, cats
They're wonderful pets
They catch the rats,
And go to vets.

Cats, cats
They sleep all day
They always scat,
And always play.

Cats, cats
They get food now
They like sweet pats,
And say meow.
Beth Tenney, Grade 3

My Friend's House
We play board games and video games
We play hide and seek

We eat popcorn
We eat cookies
We eat cereal

We play on the computer
We do homework

We are as loud as elephants
We are as quiet as a mouse

I'm so glad I go to my friend's house
Angel Garcia, Grade 2

Trying
Why do I always cry
When I TRY
And TRY
And TRY.
I always try my best
on those silly tests
SO JUST TRY!
Kendall Parker, Grade 3

Kitten/Cat
Kitten
Baby, fluffy
Loving, snuggling, playing
Kind, sweet — obeys, runs
Tearing, clawing, protecting
Adult, purring
Cat
Liliana Bitner, Grade 3

Spring/Fall
Spring
Pretty, colorful
Playing, drinking, watering
Outside, drawing — rainy, fun
Praying, sleeping, coloring
Wet, leafless
Fall
Katie Kilcullen, Grade 3

Puppy/Dog
Puppy
Cuddly, sleepy
Playing, whining, running
Funny, cute — fast, jumping
Sleeping, barking, playing
Naughty, shiny
Dog
Chloe Sankey, Grade 3

Sun/Moon
Sun
Hot, round
Blinding, burning, moving
Bright, orange — craters, white
Lighting, circling, shining
Smaller, paler
Moon
Mahayla Smith, Grade 3

Love
Love,
gentle kind,
easy to lose,
hard to find,
love, love, love, love.
Alyssa Ngo, Grade 3

Cheetos
Hot Cheetos
Spicy, crunchy
Crunching, chewing, flaming
Sour, red, brown, small
Chewing, disgusting, sickening
Soft, squishy
Beans
Umar Alyajouri, Grade 3

Winter and Summer
Winter
Fun, white
Sledding, skiing, fighting
Sled, snow, sun, beach
Swimming, tanning, cooling
Hot, sunny
Summer
Addison Palacios, Grade 3

Fire and Ice
Fire
Hot, red
Burning, flaming, sparkling
Fire, wood, water, ice pieces
Freezing, melting, reflecting
Cold, blue
Ice
Landon Vatran, Grade 3

Me
My hair is light brown like caramel
My eyes are as round as a circle
My nose is smooth like paper
My mouth is pink like lipstick
My face is soft like whipped cream
My body is clean like soap
My hands are creative like artists
Jenna Fahmy, Grade 3

Windy Wind
Windy wind, come play with me.
Fly my kite up high.
If I climb up into a tree,
I can feel you passing by.
The dandelions you puff away.
Come on wind, I want to play!
Tigerlily Taylor, Grade 2

Movies
Popcorn, candy
Big screen
I see people on cozy seats.
The lights go off,
Some are dim.
Now it's time for the movie to begin.
Jesus Ivan Perez, Grade 2

Guru – My Angel
I look up to God so good
Whenever black turns my mood
To give me hope and light the way
On which I must walk every day.

And in Guruji I did find
A voice that is so kind
That tells me with such warmth
Which I feel in every breath.

"Love is above all
In its might we rise, not fall
In its light, our life stays bright
There is no dark, no night."

His hands that hold me tight
Make me do everything right.
When I am lost and I am sad
It is Guruji who makes me glad.

For all the happiness he gifts me
For all the blessings he showers me
Thank you God for showing me
An angel so beautiful as he.
Sumena Nair, Grade 2

My Passions
Handstands, forward rolls
Cartwheels, round offs
Leaping, kicking, flipping, arching
Gymnastics

Freestyle, backstroke
Diving, jumping
Laps, fins, rings, kicks
Swimming

Scoring, stealing
Running, missing
Teamwork, hard work, goal, sweat
Soccer

Upstage, downstage
Twirling, skipping
Plié, jeté, chassé, piqué
Ballet

Quarter note, whole note
Crescendos, rest
High, low, fast, slow
Music
Sara Rajpathak, Grade 1

I Am Haley Larios
I am a good and loving person.
I wonder if God is real.
I hear puddles splash all day.
I see marshmallows swim.
I want for everybody to have food.
I am a good and loving person.

I pretend to be a lion roaring.
I feel sad when my mom gets mad.
I touch happiness floating in the sky.
I worry in the dark.
I cry when I fall down.
I am a good and loving person.

I understand when my mom says no.
I say "never say never".
I dream of running so so fast.
I try to do my best.
I hope nobody gets sick.
I am a good and loving person.
Haley Larios, Grade 2

I Am Natalia
I am a sweet and smart girl.
I wonder if I am going to be an artist.
I hear footsteps from outside the building.
I see a desk and a computer walking.
I want all people to believe in God.
I am a sweet and smart girl.

I pretend to have wings and fly like a bird.
I feel sticks tapping on me.
I touch a happy face dancing in the sky.
I worry if someone is sad.
I cry if I hurt myself.
I am a sweet and smart girl.

I understand people fight.
I say "flying horses are real".
I dream I am an Engineer.
I try to make my Mom and Dad smile.
I hope everyone has a good life.
I am a sweet and smart girl.
Natalia Charvel, Grade 2

Valentines
Valentines
are fun.
Valentines
are pretty.
Valentines
will be
friendly.
And Valentines
are love.
Lyndzie Reed, Grade 1

The Wind
The wind has a high pitched voice,
When it goes away, we rejoice!
At times it blows off our hat,
Sending it to the ground with a splat!
It blows and blows and cools us off,
Until we sneeze and get a cough!
Alex Ordaz, Grade 3

Icicle
Icicle
frosty, triangle
falling, freezing, shattering
feeling cold and sad
clear.
Jacob Esparza, Grade 3

Cats Like
Cats like jumping over a fence.
Cats like walking.
Cats like cat food.
Cats like string.
Cats don't like water
Christopher Bryan, Kindergarten

Swimming
I swim, I swim with a big force
I swim, I swim faster than a horse
I like to swim in round and rounds
I dive and I swim
But I don't like to lounge
Omer Yavuz, Grade 2

I Am a Child of God
I feel happy to play with my dad,
I feel sad when I am hurt,
I feel good when I go to Mass,
I feel excited to play basketball,
Because I am a child of God.
Karel McMayon, Grade 1

I Am a Child of God
I am happy to laugh with my Dad,
I feel sad when I get sick,
I feel excited to go to second grade,
I feel mad when someone takes my pencil,
Because I am child of God.
Amelia Janoe, Grade 1

Love
Love is the color blue
Love smells like candy
Love tastes like Valentine cookies
Love looks like a red heart
Love feels like kindness
Justin Yoo, Grade 2

Christmas Is in the Air
You can smell it in the spicy
peppermint candy cane.
You can taste it in the
marshmallow in hot cocoa.
You can hear it in the carolers
singing Christmas songs.
You can see it in the presents
under the tree.
You can feel it in the joy
and hugs on Christmas.
Kaleb Hurtado, Grade 3

Girls Can Do It
Lots of men
As president.
Hundreds of years of just men.
TIRED,
Disappointed, frustrated
From it!
Not fair,
Not fair.
It's time for a woman to be
The president of the United States!
Mia Garcia, Grade 2

The Colors
Red as a beautiful rose,
Green as the waving grass,
Blue as the bright sky,
Pink as a used eraser,
Yellow as the warm sun,
Orange as a romantic sunset,
White as the cold snow,
Black as the dark night,
Gold as a shiny necklace.
My heart is full with colors!
Ilany Graham, Grade 2

Cheetah
Cheetahs run faster than tigers.
Large feet and long tail.
Cheetahs are amazing.
They live in the jungle
They live in the zoo
And in the grass lands of Africa, too.
They sleep at night
And hunt in the day.
I love the cheetah's
Kingly ways.
Daniel Moreno, Grade 2

Family
Brothers are awesome
Mom is an enormous help
My brothers are great
Brandon Blanken, Grade 3

Snow

Snow is so breezy
Snow is so freezy
Snow is so cold
So if you go outside
you will be bold
stay inside
have hot cocoa.
Andrew Mathis, Grade 3

Snakes

Bumpy skin,
Scary faces everywhere,
Frightening me where ever I go,
Seeing snakes slither around,
With their forked-tongues,
Flying as fast as a dart.
Feeling nervous when I sleep.
Semere Tesfay, Grade 2

I Am…

I am gymnastics
I am candy
I am friends
I am music
I am outside
I am books
I am Charlotte.
Charlotte Bell, Grade 3

Fire and Water

Fire
Orange, hot
Flicking, burning, cooking
Rocks, lighter, tricks, rocks
Swimming, skipping, cooling
Blue, wet
Water
Joel De Anda Ramirez, Grade 3

Emma/Wyatt

Emma
Pretty, sassy
Funny, laughing, inviting
Goofy, happy — loving, kind
Focusing, calming, visiting
Boy, honest
Wyatt
Emma Tubbs, Grade 3

Wolf

Awroo!
Long legs, big paws,
Powerful jaws;
Roaming for miles —
The noble wolf.
Jacklinn Gonzalez, Grade 2

Basketball

Dribble! Dribble! Dribble!
We start to play
Excited and glad
To start the game
Pass the ball
To the person
That's next to you
Shoot and score!
Briana Hernandez, Grade 2

Black Tiger

ROAR!
A loud sound
The black tiger
Licks his lips.
I'm so nervous!
But the only thing —
I hope
He doesn't eat me!
Maddison Marquez, Grade 2

If You Need a Cat

If you need a cat,
I've got one right here,
It's soft and cuddly and has fuzzy ears.
It likes to play,
It likes to sleep,
It likes to snuggle at my feet.
It's time to go, it's time to sleep,
But tomorrow it can snuggle at your feet!
Madeline Gage, Grade 3

I will Always Remember You Kristaf

I will always remember you.
When I played with you,
I loved you more than ever.
I cared for you.
Why did you have to leave?
When I kissed you, you licked my face.
When you left me I cried.
Why did you leave me?
Trinity Campos, Kindergarten

Butterflies

Butterflies
are pretty
as a flower.
Butterflies
have colorful
wings.
And butterflies
can fly.
Haylee Lackey, Grade 1

The Wind

The wind blows softly through the trees
It also likes to tickle my knees.
It blows across my garden swing
Then off it goes to happily sing.
When I'm asleep it comes through the door,
It comes closer, more and more.
I can feel the wind go by
It helps me to fly my kite up high.
Eliana Beckett, Grade 2

The March Wind

The wind loves to push and pull
He works day and night.
Of energy and strength, he's full.
He blows with all his might.
I wonder if sometimes
The wind gets tired.
Maybe he really wants
To be retired?
Meridel Spence, Grade 3

God Made the Wind

God made the wind
When it's gentle or it's strong.
A soft breeze on my face,
Or a storm that's wild and long.
Wind blows my hair so fresh,
And often sings a sweet song.
It wiggles the leaves and waves the grass,
Then wind gently moves along.
Case Porter, Grade 2

The Sun

The sun is a fire that burns in your heart.
Until it goes down.
Then your heart is broken.
You see the shadows turn around.
See the sun rise up.
See the sun fall.
It must rise and fall.
Now you know all!
Victoria Carter, Grade 3

Lion

I am a Lion.
I'm tan as a speck of sand.
I hunt my prey.
I also sit in the hot sun,
staying still so no one will see me.
I can bite down hard on my kill.
I can jump and bite real good.
I am a Lion.
Skyla Samples, Grade 3

Fish

Fish move like waves in the water,
Sucking in their cheeks,
Orange and silver,
Like a boat floating in the sea.
Really sensitive creatures,
Can die with
The wrong food.
Give them fresh water,
Check on them after school.
When the fish die,
I will still love them.
Adriell Bermudez, Grade 2

The Ocean

Salty, cold, blue water,
Little waves, moving back and forth,
Full of animals.
Find them deep down in the sea.
Sharks, octopus, sting rays,
Sounds like nothing,
down, down,
All the way down
To the
Bottom
Of the ocean floor.
Luke Gomes, Grade 2

Musical WrArt Beginning to End

The music stops then grows,
I'm happy in a river of candy,
Happy pink,
Slate gray,
A bush full of berries,
Rapunzel when she is
Free,
Feeling alone in
The dark.
Then,
A summer waterfall
Laela Aboudaher, Grade 2

In the Musical WrArt

Tunnels and drills,
Mud,
Winter's dark,
Cold, dull,
The grey and white
Of a stone wall,
Pencil lead,
A marching band,
Whirlpools in the Pacific Ocean,
Anger —
Losing all your money.
Henry Caputo, Grade 2

Little Sunrise

Sunrise comes,
for everyone.
Birds chirping,
They are blue,
But now it's cool.
2, 3, 50 days later,
still I love my little little sunrise.
But now again about
50 years later,
I still see my little sunrise.
Austin Queal, Grade 3

Christmas is in the Air

You can smell it in the
fresh cut trees.
You can taste it in the inside
of my favorite chocolate chip cookies.
You can hear it in the
bells jingling.
You can see it in the people
that they are happy.
You can feel it in the wrapping
of Christmas presents.
Guillermo Murrieta, Grade 3

Baseball!!!

I play with heart all day long
I hit the ball like a dart
It soared and soared over the wall
Not one mitt had the ball
My team went wild when it soared
My bat had a dent after the hit
The score was 15-16
I made us win with that hit
We threw our mitts and celebrated
That was the best day ever!
Cole Adam, Grade 3

Christmas is in the Air

You can smell it in the cookies
baking in the oven.
You can taste it in the
marshmallow melting in the fire.
You can hear it in the
laughter in the houses.
You can see it in the Christmas
tree with beautiful ornaments.
You can feel it in the hugs,
love, and joy.
Charis Choi, Grade 3

Summer

I hear birds tweeting
I like the season summer
I feel the sun's heat
Logan Poling, Grade 3

Butterfly

B right butterfly
U nique and colorful you are
T iny and fragile, you stand on a
T ree
E ating and
R esting
F lying and fluttering
L ooking for a flower to pollinate
Y ou make the world happy!
Galilea Prieto, Grade 3

Mr. Jankens

Mr. Jankens is very nice
Mr. Jankens has pet mice
Mr. Jankens lives down the street
Mr. Jankens has big feet

Mr. Jankens has cool hair
Mr. Jankens really cares
Mr. Jankens has no place to go
But I still love him so
Addison Beyer, Grade 3

Our Family

Your family and my family
Are friends to the end

Forever for me and you

We hand together
We laugh together

We are stuck together like glue
Catherine Perez, Grade 3

The Beach

I stood on a
cold,
dark,
beach.
I looked out on the beach.
I saw the glare of the beautiful water.
The wind picked up
and tossed the sand around.
I felt free.

Billy Jones, Grade 3

If I Was Only One Inch Tall

If I was only one inch tall-
Humans would be GIANTS!
Bugs would be HUGE!
When I go out,
A "Hot Wheels" would be my car.
Dirt would be the ground.
If I were only one inch tall.
Aiden Irvin, Grade 3

Baseball
Baseball baseball the sport for you
Baseball baseball hit a home run
Baseball baseball hit a double
Baseball baseball the sport for you
Trevor Suter, Grade 3

My Favorite Animal
My favorite animal is a cat.
He likes to wear a hat.
He would also wear a dress,
when he wants to look his best.
Juliana Hamati, Kindergarten

Apples
Green apples are sour,
Red apples are sweet,
No matter what,
They're always good to eat!
Tilly Morrison, Grade 3

Space
Space, space, always in a race.
So large I can't chase!
Vast and beautiful,
Like a bottomless case!
Sabir Mohamed, Grade 2

Waves
Rolling back and forth
Pushing rocks away
So soothing
Takes your fears away.
Morfoula Barbatsis, Grade 2

Birds
They are majestic
Amazing fliers, soaring
Swoop then a twirl loop
Sam Barnard, Grade 3

Bunnies Can
Bunnies can hop.
Bunnies can jump.
They are so fluffy and soft.
Renesmee Figueroa, Kindergarten

Spring
Flowers bloom in spring
Happiness spreads everywhere
I like spring so much.
Skyler Marich, Grade 2

Spring in Japan
Think about spring in Japan,
Sakura trees bloom, as well as all the pretty flowers there,
Drizzling of blossoms fill the moment with the magic of spring,
Luscious green grass, new green trees instead of bare old winter trees,
Butterflies and ladybugs state super fancy spring for you and me!
Spring has a glaze of pretty flowers for pollination,
Pink and white cherry blossoms will turn to cherries,
Yum, yum, yum!
Now it's pink and white Japan!!!
Amrita Arun, Grade 2

Kapok
The kapok tree is as tall as the Eiffel Tower.
There are as many animals that live in the kapok tree as there are bones in your body.
The kapok tree's bark is as thick as a dictionary.
The kapok tree's flowers are as beautiful as a rainbow.
The kapok tree is as tall as a skyscraper.
The kapok tree is as big around as an elephant's hug.
The leaves of the kapok tree are as big as a binder of poems.
The kapok tree protects the animals of the rain forest as a house protects people.
Racine Homyak, Grade 3

Earthquake in Nepal
Boom, there it was – an earthquake.
The shaking of the ground destroyed Hindu temples and broke the ground.
It made many people poor.
Some people survived even being trapped under cement.
It came without warning.
You need to hide.
Boom – one more time.
Brendan Mooney, Grade 3

The Ocean
The ocean air is like the crisp moon in the dark midnight sky.
The small ocean wave sounds like a soft lullaby.
The ocean's tide is like a soft blanket being pulled over your shoulders.
The ocean's scents are like a new lavender candle.
The ocean palm trees are like a nice companion.
And that's why I love the ocean!
Katherine Hampton, Grade 3

My Mom Is Pretty
I cook some chocolate brownies with my mom.
My mom takes me to the park so I can play on the swing.
My mom takes me to my friend's house so I could play with my friend.
Sometimes my mom sleeps in my room with me.
When my mom picks me up from school, she smiles, hugs, and kisses me.
My mom is pretty.
Avni Nayak, Kindergarten

Winter
Winter is cold.
Winter is windy.
And winter is frosty.
Winter is fun!
Jaiden Peel, Grade 1

Wind
W onderful wind
I think you're best
N ice you feel on my face
D on't you ever get tired?
Trinity Kelley, Grade 2

My Beach Vacation

Ocean waves are my favorite, the sandy beach, not a far reach.
The sun on the horizon, shiny and bright, Oh! A perfect beach day. What a delight!

The place we'll stay, not too far away, with beautiful palms, that swing and sway.
To the ocean breeze, what a nice feel! And the colorful birds give such an appeal.

What perfect hotels with colorful beds! There are many couches with small pouches.
The kitchen smells so very well. "Welcome everyone!" greeted the Maitre d'hotel.

I've got sunscreen, towels, and toys, oh what a joy! And my swimming suit packed in a little loop.
The tropical ocean breeze calling out, "Come join us please!" It's time to hit the beach, come on, and say cheese!

Warm beach sand and crisp sun rays reflecting and dancing to the blue ocean waves.
Kids run, kites fly, guitars play, oh how I wish I was here on all days.

Dad is taking a warm dip, while Mom is relaxing with her favorite tea to sip.
Dad sees some bright fish along the shore as Mom picks some seashells that she adores.

I build my sand castle tall and firm. And make some designs that twist and turn.
"Look what I made!" I exclaimed. "A masterpiece indeed," said Ma and Pa pleased.

I'm now hungry for lunch. I can't wait for grilled cheese and pineapple punch.
"Care for some watermelon or ice-cream?" Mom said. But I wish I could have both instead.

I want to go for a swim before the day gets dim.
With my snorkel gear and paddle feet. Here I come for a visual treat.

So many colorful fish swimming together in a swish. Rainbow fish, clown fish, and manta rays, moving in an array.

It's time to head back. Toys, towels, and gears in a sack.
What a fun day we had! I wish we could do this all over again, Mom and Dad.

Sanika Datar, Grade 3

I Am Maya

I am a kind girl. I love who I am. I am smart at reading. I like butterflies. I get over my fears.
I like to play with my friend at school. I worry about my Mom and my Dad. I love to learn more in class.
I wonder what is in Palm Spring. I like to ride my scooter. I touch piece in the sky. I like to go to the park.
I dream about having a dog. I listen to my Mom and my Dad. I do my homework at home. I am good at dance.
I love to try my best at school. I love to go to Texas and make snowballs.

Maya Maldonado, Grade 2

Life

The beauty you see
The birds flying in the air
The breeze in your hair
The trees swaying in the wind
The grass in moist air
And the sun in space
And the big blue sea you see
The giant moon appears in the sky
And you see me
The roses and the daffodils grow by the stream
And the water flows

Aidan Osmonbekov, Grade 3

I'd Rather be Fishing

I'd rather be fishing, I wish I could.
I want to go fishing, please I should.
You should let me go.
Have I told you, I'm a pro!
I caught fifty fish in one trip.
All it took was a good grip.
Now people say fish is a fine dish.
It would be nice to have a dish of fish.

Cooper Peery, Grade 2

My Sister

Sister,
Kind woman,
Laughs a lot,
Sweet as candy,
Helps me with my reading.
But one day
She had to move to L.A.
I cried.
Sad,
So, sad
to see her go.
Heart pounding fast,
My body
Was shaking terribly
When I saw
Her leave.
In my heart,
She will always be by my side,
Never forget her,
Always love her
In my mind and heart!

Kendall Gonzalez, Grade 2

I Am Evan

I am a very good friend that cares.
I wonder if my friend likes me.
I hear my friend calling me.
I see a crow in the sky.
I want me and my friend to marry.
I am a very good friend that cares.

I pretend I am a girl dancing.
I feel sad without my friend.
I touch the flowers blooming.
I worry for my step-mom.
I cry because my grandma is dead.
I am a very good friend that cares.

I understand some people don't get food.
I say "I believe in God".
I dream I have long hair.
I try to be good.
I hope my step-mom feels better.
I am a very good friend that cares.

Evan Zevenbergen, Grade 2

The Wind

Whirling the leaves down on the ground
That's the wind all around.
He swings your door open wide
Then he whistles back outside.
He briskly takes off your hat
Like he's just being a brat.
He can make your hair so wild
That it looks quite un-styled.

Ezekiel Walker, Grade 3

Orca

I am an orca
I am black as a chalkboard
I swim in the water
I can swim really fast, too
I can catch fish blindfolded
I am an orca

Dominick McCallister, Grade 3

Wonder

As I look up in the sky
I see an angel passing by.
A shooting star flying by,
Its gleaming and so bright
As it gets closer and closer
I realized it is my imagination.

Whitney Bui, Grade 3

Crystal Blue Water

The crystal blue water
of a glistening waterfall.
The roaring fills my heart
with joy. A stream flowing
in my heart; a never ending
waterfall of joy.

Kaia Knudson, Grade 2

The Sun

Sun is power.
The sun is light.
The sun lights up,
The glamorous sky.
The sun is setting.
It is night.

Amir Gharaibeh, Grade 3

A Day at the Beach

The beach is fun.
I like the sand.
I like to run in the sun.
My skin got tanned.
The sun is hot.
I love the beach a lot.

Emmanuel Lobrin, Grade 2

Love

Love is the color indigo red
Love smells like an ocean of roses
Love sounds like an indescribable harp
Love tastes like delicate marshmallows
Love looks like a worthy painting
Love feels like a cozy hug

Catelyn Kellogg, Grade 2

Spring Time

Spring is time for play.
All the snow melts away.
You don't have to be stuck in snow
that is like clay!
The sun comes out
and the fun begins.
"Hooray!" We all say.
Time for tank tops.
Town becomes a bang bop!
Ice times end.
Spring is nice.

Avery Schmidt, Grade 2

My Dog

Tan and black
Soft as a blanket
Lots of energy
Bouncing up and down
Long walks in the park
Enjoys walking with me
Licks me after sports
Jumps on me when I'm sleeping
My dog
Coco.

Damian Carranza, Grade 2

Christmas Is in the Air

You can smell it in the cinnamon
in the Christmas tree.
You can taste it in the hot
chocolate and marshmallows.
You can hear it in the Christmas
carols that sing for you.
You can see it in the
snowy weather.
You can feel it in the happy
Christmas joy.

Zoey Pena, Grade 3

My Grandma

When I go in
my grandma's house
I see grandma's happy face
I hug her
and kiss her
I love my grandma!

Rodrigo Enriquez, Grade 2

Moko Sharks

Moko Sharks
Are as fast as a zooming car,
Gray, orange, black and blue.
Smart, smooth skin.
Teeth sharp as a chainsaw.
Moko sharks are as strong as Batman.

Leonardo Zamora, Grade 2

Christmas
Christmas
Fat, jolly
Santa eats cookies
Makes me feel good
Magic
Angel Martinez, Grade 3

All About Guillermo
Guillermo
Fun, nice, good
Games, play outside
I love my mom.
Guillermo
Guillermo Gaona, Grade 1

Dr. Seuss
Dr. Seuss
funny, artistic
creates, makes books, draws
Dr. Seuss made funny books.
Author.
Ryker Norwood, Grade 3

Halloween
Halloween
Black, orange
Trick or treat
Makes me feel scared
Monster
Christian Jacobo, Grade 3

Love
I love mom
I love dad
I love brother
I love friends
I love Easter bunnies
Jaime Gonzalez, Grade 1

My Mamma
Mom! You are as pretty as a princess,
As smart as a spelling girl,
As sweet as jalebi,
I like it when you hug me.
I love you!
Aneira Fernandes, Kindergarten

Dr. Seuss
Author
funny, cool
smart, fun, silly
Dr. Seuss is a good author
Dr. Seuss.
Brooke Kimball, Grade 3

Scary, Mean Monster
Creak
What was that?
Creak
Where is that coming from?
I toss and turn in bed.
I think there is a monster in the closet. I am very scared.
I try shutting the closet
But I feel scared that the door will open and the monster will come out.
Big, ferocious,
Eating, roaring, stomping,
Always scaring little kids,
Mean
Raine Wen, Grade 3

Weather, Rethought
Rap-a-tap-tap, goes the rain as it hits the window.
Crackle-snap-snap, goes the snow under your feet.
Whir-whir, goes the hurricane, outside.
Stir-stir, goes the twister as it roars down the cornfield.
Screech-bam goes the car as it slides off the icy road.
Flash-crash goes the thunderstorm as it rolls toward town.
Crumble-grumble goes the earthquake as it makes the ground shiver and shake.
Splash-crash goes the tsunami as it topples a skyscraper.
This is
Weather, rethought.
Tristan Walton, Grade 3

How to Write a Story
When I am stuck with a blank sheet of paper and don't know what to write
I just stop and think about what I had dreamt that night
Writing is all about the imaginations in your head
And it helps see way more than real when you are laying in your bed
Make believe and fiction give many an addiction
But non fiction and real stuff might have more connection
Writing is a message from one's heart to another
A true demonstration of mystery and power
So always remember, every single word counts
And you will soon be writing in leaps and bounds
Hansa Giridhar, Grade 3

Birds
Birds love to fly, up so high.
with their wings, in the big blue sky.
Always lay eggs, in their nests.
Such good animals, they're the best!
Awesome wings and feathers, and cool colors too!
Some are big, and some are small, and take care of their young ones too.
Always flying in the sky in all sorts of weather,
flapping their wings up and down with their feathers.
Sometimes they can be such a pest,
Just because they don't have enough rest.
Nalina Devadoss, Grade 2

Amethyst

A mazing sight.
M ade of minerals.
E veryone loves amethyst.
T ruly beautiful.
H appy color.
Y ou can use it for jewelry.
S hiny like a star.
T ruly purple.

Kylie Forrester, Grade 3

Rocio

Rocio
It means kind, loving, smart
It is like a rose
It is like a flower
It is the memory of going to California
When my mom helped me speak Spanish
My name is Rocio
It means keep your day happy!

Rocio Soto, Grade 3

Baseball

B ases loaded
A wesome Astros
S mash hit
E asy homer
B aseball on fire
A ll people screaming
L oud noses in the crowd
L osing team, going home

Tyler Davis, Grade 3

Country

The breeze blows
While you're riding your horse.
Cleaning stalls that smell
like dirty socks after playing
all day and rotten eggs.
Seeing the sunset every night,
being with your family,
is the best.

Hannah Ryan, Grade 3

Plaid Is So Bad

I wish our school's uniform was not plaid.
It looks so bad, it makes me sad.
I wish it was pink,
But the teenagers will think it stinks.
Why do we have to wear green shirts?
To change the rules it will not hurt.
I wish our school's uniform was not plaid.
It looks bad, it makes me sad.

Kessia Kurian, Grade 2

Spring

Birds chirping,
bees buzzing,
flowers blooming,
waving grass,
bright sky,
rattling leaves on trees
sprouting plants,
blue skies,
sunny days,
sprinkling rain,

Spring makes me feel
like I am the only person in the world.

Tristan Thompson, Grade 2

The Red Ravens

BOOM!
It was Halloween night.
I was alone.
Fear was everywhere.
"Caw, caw, caw,"
Came a sound from the distance.
Red clouds circled around me.
The noise became
Louder
And
Louder.
I felt in my bones
Something was not right.

Kylie West, Grade 3

Electric Eel

E lectric
L arge
E el
C old blooded
T iny
R eal
I nsect eater
C ool

E pic
E arth living
L eopard like

Jack Boersma, Grade 3

Thanksgiving

I am thankful for the yummy food
that my parents make me.
I am also thankful for my mom
because she always takes time with me.
I am really thankful for my family
they make good choices.
Most of all, I am thankful for the trees
they help us breathe.

Leena Adem, Grade 3

Rabbits

Rabbits are fluffy,
Soft, white and gentle.
They like to hop
hop
hop!
Gray fur,
Small round eyes,
staring up at me.
Fun to play with,
Fun for a pet.
Likes to twitch
twitch
twitch!
Soft, white and gentle.
Rabbits are fluffy.

Joscalyn Martinez, Grade 2

Spring

The tree has green leaves
Falling leaves all drifting down
Birds chirp and fly high.

The spring breeze feels cold
As it rustles through the tree
I need a jacket.

Gloomy is the sky
Clouds hang low from the hillside
Rains fall through the clouds.

Flowers growing wild
Orange, red, pink, and purple
Oh! They are pretty!

Pranav Sajith, Grade 3

Winter and Summer

Winter
Cold, lonely
Fighting, sledding, running
Snowball, snow, beach, pool
Cooling, swimming, tanning
Sunny, hot
Summer

Elisa Galli, Grade 3

Hawaii

volcano eruptions
they have luaus
it's the biggest island
they eat poi
it's a pretty island
they are nice people
island made of volcanoes
so much water
Have fun in Hawaii and relax!

Emily Chenh, Grade 3

In a Fantasy
If we lived in a fantasy
And all the world kind,
Instead of people causing mischief,
Or being deaf or blind.
If only people would stop and think,
The world would be perfect in just one blink.
But we don't, we're rude and sarcastic,
We destroy nature for things like plastic.
Each blade of grass has a story to tell,
But the thing is, we don't listen too well.
If the world was a fantasy things would change,
And we would have a better range.

Isabela Iglesias, Grade 3

Blank Mind
I have nothing in my mind…
My mind now is just a blank
piece of paper waiting for ideas
I might just go crazy
if I don't get ideas
there's nothing in my mind
no one single idea.
Nothing to write.
It's like my hand is growing roots in my pencil.
No ideas, no ideas.
Seriously, I have no
ideas.

Addison Durnell, Grade 3

Mountaintop
It was April
When I sat on the mountaintop
Waiting for the sun to rise
Like gold in the sky,
So beautiful and so bright.

But while I waited
The wind blew by,
And made the trees sway
While the leaves flew
To the sun that was peaking over the mountains

Shamayin Nally, Grade 2

Arctic
Snowflakes, snowflakes fall all day
in the arctic far away
one penguin hops in the water
it comes back with a fish
for its family, seals wait for penguins
to hop in and pounce on them
like cats pouncing on lizards.
Sharks wait for seals to come just close enough
and tackle it like a lion tackling a zebra.
Everything in the arctic is very different.

William Edwards, Grade 3

Pi
I love sweet
sour
preserved
pi. I am astonished
with
it when the smells of cinnamon
Fill the air, the sweet smell of cinnamon fills
the air.
The sweet smell of honey and
lemon juice creeps upon my skin.
My mouth waters
with saliva and air. A
frantic feeling tells me to get it. I
must be patient and tell myself don't do it.
The preserved pi in the fridge was
telling me "Get me" "Get me."

Jack Bowden, Grade 3

Minecraft, Minecraft
Minecraft, Minecraft monsters at night,
and during the day they cannot fight.
Minecraft, Minecraft blocks and blocks,
wool blocks, brick blocks, even a clock.
Minecraft, Minecraft portals to the Nether,
you might not survive and come back never.
Minecraft, Minecraft there's a block,
it is strong you can even turn on a song.
Minecraft, Minecraft different dimensions,
can you create and make an invention?
Minecraft, Minecraft day and night,
Minecraft is a really good sight.
Minecraft, Minecraft you can tame,
get a pet, and also make a name.
Minecraft, Minecraft time to get this game,
love *Minecraft* and create your game.

Cade Tullis, Grade 2

Dream
Once upon a midnight cloudy
A big old guy said "Howdy, Howdy!"
He looked at a lemon next to the sink,
It was a juicy one, I think.
The lemon rolled away from there,
Straight out the country into a lion lair.
Soon, the earth started to rumble
And he slowly felt a little mumble.
He looked around, he thought he said,
I'd rather be in my awesome bed.
Soon he woke up by a loud "Moooo".
But he could have swore his dream was true.
He looked outside for a minute or two,
Everything was crazy, and I thought so too.
Even at a fast pace,
You couldn't leave that mixed-up place.

Levon Melkonyan, Grade 3

Kitty

Kitties are nice and mean
I love cats
terrific cats are cool for me
tricks are good for cats
yarn is fun for cats to play with.
Megan Sloan, Grade 2

Games

G ames can be hiding in the trees
A nimals can be playing games
M y games can be on the TV
E ither they can be inside or outside
S ome games are scary.
Courtney Whittaker, Grade 2

Goddess Stephanie Kass

Mom, you are as pretty as a goddess.
As smart as wonder woman,
As sweet as a mom can be,
I like it when you play race cars with me.
I love you!
Alexandra Kass, Kindergarten

All About Ke'Rion

Ke'Rion
Happy, kind, glad
I like basketball and baseball.
I love my mom.
Ke'Rion
Ke'Rion Green, Grade 1

Puppy

Puppy
Black, brown
Run, sleep, walk
It makes me happy
Soft
Hanna Diaz, Grade 3

Pablo

P eace liker
A mazing
B rother
L oving
O ptimist
Pablo Gonzalez, Grade 3

The Park

I like to go to the park
In the month of March.
I like to swing,
While swinging, I sing.
Brayden Tsang, Grade 1

A Dream

As soon as my head
touches my pillow,
I travel to a land,
that nobody knows
except for me,
a place,
where anything can happen
where you live in a castle
on a cloud,
where there is a law,
that you have to be happy
and nothing bad can happen
in,
a dream.
Savera Karia, Grade 3

All Alone

All alone at home,
Watching TV.
Left me.
Parents on vacation
To the beach.
Left me at home,
Left me alone
With the dog.
Left me
Reading a book,
Alone in the
Night,
In the dark,
In my bed.
Zoe Segura, Grade 2

Boo

Boo!
Do you hear that sound?
It matches with the beat.
Boo!
Does that scare you?
That's the word you scare with.
Boo!
You can say it
Over
And
Over again.
Boo!
Boo!
Boo!
Cace Mouton, Grade 3

You

You are so cutie
And so am I
You are so sweet
And so is candy
Cameron Feliciano, Grade 1

Love

Love is the color red, pink and purple
Love smells like cupcakes
Love sounds like my dog's kisses
Love tastes like cookies
Love looks like puppies
Love feels like swimming
Isaiah Campbell, Grade 2

My Dog

My dog is love
I love my dog
My dog is a cutie
I love my cute dog
My dog is fluffy
I love my fluffy dog
Tristan Veith, Grade 2

I Am a Child of God

I feel happy to laugh with my Dad,
I feel good with my family,
I feel sad when I am hurt,
I feel excited about first grade,
I feel mad when someone is mean,
Because I am a child of God.
Micaela Lim, Grade 1

Kevyn

I love daddy
I love mommy
Daddy loves Kevyn
Mommy loves Kevyn
Grandma loves Kevyn
I love Kevyn
Kevyn Throngard, Grade 1

Dreams

Dreams come true
Oh yes they do
I have dreams
Sometimes they are blue
I love dreams
Oh yes I do
Alondra Cartegena, Grade 1

Thomas

T hinking before talking.
H andsome young man.
O pportunity to explore.
M adness at home.
A sking for help at school.
S adness in my head.
Thomas Cowardin, Grade 2

Thunder Storms
Thunder is so loud.
Thunder, Thunder makes cool sounds.
Thunder does damage.
Parker Johnson, Grade 3

Cats
Cats like to eat birds
They like to talk in cat language
They are very calm
Liberty Fontaine, Grade 3

Bird
A bird flies and sings.
Birds pick seeds and worms to eat
And feed their babies.
Jaidev Pathak, Grade 2

Bug
I am a red bug
I have small black beady eyes
I am colorful
Delonda Ponciano-Wathogoma, Grade 3

Rain
Get your umbrella.
Step outside before your eyes.
Is a big puddle
Evelyn Coles, Grade 2

Puppy
A little puppy
So cute you want to pet it
Sweetest in the world
Karli Latona, Grade 3

Wind
Wind blows in the trees
Blowing pollen into the air
Wind gives me a breeze
Jordan Marsello, Grade 3

Lion
Mean but beautiful
Soft like a cat on their mane
Pouncing on its prey
Jake Markel, Grade 3

Snow
The snow starts falling
Fluffy and soft on the ground
It makes me feel cold
Tyler Griggs, Grade 3

Let's Stop Stereotypes
When you stereotype someone, you put them in a box.
Come on, let's not treat people like a pair of socks
They have to go together.
We're not talking about birds of a feather

Why can't boys wear nail polish? Why can't girls have short hair?
The answer to your question is, Why should we care?

Why can't women be president? Why can't ladies and girls be strong?
If you feel like stereotyping someone, you should know it is very wrong!

Why don't boys pass the ball to girls?
Girls can do it too, let girls try and give it a whirl,
Be fair. Pass the ball to everyone.
Without stereotypes, games would be so much fun!

Look at Wilma Rudolph who over came polio, and ran like lightning
Malala Yousufzai, who conquered all things frightening
Marie Curie, the eminent scientist, Mother Teresa, the epitome of love
All these women have risen above, and shattered stereotypes that hang in the air
Doing good everywhere

Don't make assumptions, girls are smart too
Don't stereotype people, it is the wrong thing to do
Try to stop stereotypes in this school.
Without stereotypes, games would be more fun and cool
Mehr Grewal, Grade 3

I Am Grady
I am a soccer player and an active person.
I wonder how Abraham became president.
I hear voices of a wolf.
I see a dark shadowy place.
I want an RC car.
I am a soccer player and an active person.

I pretend to be chased by somebody.
I feel the pain of my worn out ankle.
I touch the worn out ankle.
I worry about the new bully in school.
I cry when I get bullied.
I am a soccer player and an active person.

I understand that a square is a rectangle, but a rectangle isn't a square.
I say that God is real.
I dream of being in heaven.
I hope that I get to play video games.
I am a soccer player and an active person.
Grady Kunoth, Grade 2

A Day Ago
A day ago it was bright and colorful
I played with friends that are sweet and beautiful
A day ago it bloomed on a summer day, it was more beautiful than ever
A day ago I wish happened again, I love a day ago
Anna Simonich, Grade 3

Wings

If I had wings I would
glide in the sky,
flying while the world goes by.
It would be a pretty moment for the time.
For all my life that's
all I wish,
and the water of the ocean
would swish.
Flowing down the waterfall ways,
I remember those days.
My wings would be pink in delight.
I'd fly with them day and night.
Oh, it would be such a pretty sight!
Gianna Valdovinos, Grade 1

Cars

I love cars,
Red, black, golden, blue,
Shiny, fancy, fast and cool,
Takes you places.
Magnificent tricks,
Riding on three wheels,
Flipping on ramps,
Smoky engines,
Showing off,
Loud sounds,
Vroomm.
Vroomm.
Awesome cars.
Alexander Perez, Grade 2

Me

When I close
my eyes I
feel like I'm
a bird in the
sky like a
stray cat as
lonely as the
moon sky. As
calm as the
beach. And as
lazy as a
lizard in the
rain forest.
Sophie Chavez, Grade 3

Firefly

F irefly
I n the sky
R eady to fly
E ver so high
F irefly, up so high
L ight up the sky
Y ou're ever so bright.
Colt Horlacher, Grade 3

LuLu Has a Tutu

LuLu has a tutu,
Like feathers in blue.
After she puts it on,
She can do something new.

To play with a wood uke,
To drink some warm soup,
To read a funny book,
To look at a green newt.

And so she sang a song,
And played all day long.
The sun was going down,
With her on the ground.

She ate a big pie,
And took out her bun.
She closed her eyes,
And the day was done.
Vivian Stone, Kindergarten

I Am Chance

I am smart and happy.
I wonder if there will be world peace.
I hear bells ringing.
I see a volcano.
I want no wars.
I am smart and happy.

I pretend that there are 100 dollar bills.
I feel the sun burning.
I touch the stars shining.
I worry that I will get hurt.
I cry when I get hurt.
I am smart and happy.

I understand that people get hurt.
I say everybody should try their best.
I dream about world peace.
I am smart and happy.
Chance Alfred, Grade 2

Elephant

I saw an elephant
and I played with him.
Now, we were at the zoo
with other elephants.
We went back home and played.
He is my pet elephant
big and grey.
I feed him
and love him.
At night we sleep
in a huge king bed
because he is huge.
Elijah Woodworth, Kindergarten

Easter

Easter is…
love
and
peace
of God.
It is not about getting candy.
It is about
rebirth.
Tristan Ackerman, Grade 3

Godzilla

Destroyer of Japan,
big scaly back,
fire breathing monster,
big sharp claws,
humongous creature,
stomping all over,
breaking buildings,
crushing the town.
Alonzo Martinez, Grade 2

Wind, Why?

Wind, why do you give us a good breeze,
And why are you so wild?
Why do you blow down the trees,
And why are you so mild?
If you are mild,
It makes me glad.
But when you're wild
I do feel sad.
Henry Schmies, Grade 2

I'd Rather Be Fishing

I'd rather be fishing
And not be wishing.
I really want to have fun.
Fishing in the sun.
The water feels cool in the pool.
I like when we sit on a boat.
I like when we float.
Karnell James Jr., Grade 2

The Sun Will Get Your Heart

The sun will get your heart.
It will make you feel pleasant.
Why does the sun get your heart?
Because when you are kind,
The sun gives you more kindness.
Sarah Mohammed, Grade 3

Snow

So fun and so white,
you can eat while it comes from the sky
you can be creative with snow,
snow is wonderful for you.
Patrick Harris Murphy, Grade 3

Sierra Nevada Waterfall
It is a sunny day next to a waterfall in Sierra Nevada
Mountains miles away,
Tall pine trees, plunging waterfall, blue sky, tall rocks
The waterfall surrounded by giants
It's as pretty as a wedding veil
Trees stand high like skyscrapers
Sky as blue as a lake
The rainbow sits happy over the waterfall
Beautiful, white water really, really wet
The day is over, beautiful sunset behind the waterfall.
Hannah Harston, Grade 3

Dinosaurs
A big dinosaur is walking in the scary woods
B rontosaurus was one of the feared
C ausing trouble all the time
D oing what they have to do to survive
E veryone ran away from him
F ear was his weapon
G igantic dinosaurs fought each other for food
H iding in the shadows at night
I slands full of them
Andrew Tucker, Grade 3

I Would Name This
The magical land of winding roads
Is what I would name this art,
It reminds me of a river,
A stampeded of wildebeests running through
The grass.
I hear a scratching kind of loud
Music.
I want to be in my cozy, soft
Bed.
Gemma Huang, Grade 2

Mama's Glory
Mama's voice as soothing as a bird chirping.
Tells us in demand what to do.
Sometimes angry and sometimes happy.
She'll always be with you.
Off on a walk.
Peaceful with her.
In my bed.
She'll read you a story.
In the night sleeping with glory.
Bailey Seaholm, Grade 3

The Ribbon
The ribbon is dark blue.
It tastes like victory.
It sounds like loud cheering from the crowd.
It smells like the blue sky.
It looks like the deep blue ocean.
It makes me feel victorious.
Adam Bolline, Grade 3

Animals
They are beautiful, full of nature, full of power.
Lions care and defend,
Koalas relax,
Tigers sneak and hunt,
Cheetahs do the same thing
But as fast as the speed of light,
All of them as caring as moms,
No matter what I love humans
And animals the same.
Steven Mendoza-Diaz, Grade 3

Before Morning
When night dawns my hands float off,
open doors, grab the car's wheel and drive off.
They go to the field and play catch.
They grow hands and wings.
They fly higher than a skyscraper.
They dive down into the trees.
They land on a branch then fly home.
They land back on my wrists.
Right before morning.
David Wong, Grade 2

Spring
Spring is in the air!
You can smell it in the countertop
with thirty cookies baked.
You can see it in the willow trees
dancing slowly in the park.
You can hear it in the gentle wind floating by.
You can feel it in the leaves falling
on your head and hand at the park.
Kyle Lim, Grade 3

Thanksgiving
I am thankful for my dad when he makes
my brother and I laugh and have fun.
I am also thankful for my little sister
when I play peek-a-boo with her.
I am really thankful for my grandma
because we're kind of like sisters going shopping,
Most of all, I'm thankful for my loving family,
they're very kind and sweet.
Malia Sutton, Grade 3

Vivid Lime Green
Vivid lime green is the beauty of a garden's gaze.
Vivid lime green is the color of spring and covers summer fields.
The taste of lime,
The color of life.
Every field or garden on nature's face,
Vivid lime green is in the place.
Covering mountains or grassy hills,
It's always there, under your heels.
Ethan Johnson, Grade 3

The Fall
The wind was whistling.
The ground was rumbling.
I was almost gone,
four fingers hanging on.
One minute left to spare.
Then
I fell.
The roots pulled out.
I was over.
Grant Slanker, Grade 3

Spring
Spring showers
May flowers
April is blue rain
May is green plants
Grass is green
Everything is clean
The birds are singing
Blossoms are blooming
Everybody is treating plants like a pet.
Cian Pullan, Grade 1

Musical Writing and Art
The magical world of an ocean
green, white, blue.
A beautiful green tree with a touch
of yellow in fall.
I feel the sadness of winter in the lines.
The music is slow,
soothing,
with colors
like a lullaby.
Ella Utterson, Grade 2

Dragonfly
D ragonfly
R ed
A nd
G reen
O n my
N ose
F ly away
L ike
Y ou're an eagle
LauraJo Moulton, Grade 3

I Am a Child of God
I feel happy to laugh with my Dad,
When God saved us,
I feel sad when my grandmother died,
When I get hurt,
I feel good when I play games,
I fell sad when someone is mean to me,
Because I am a child of God.
Leighton Gregory Carnes, Grade 1

Panther
I am dark as night
Pouncing like a big black cat
I have big sharp claws
Aslan Sanchez-Acevedo, Grade 3

Spring
Spring is in the air!
You can smell it in the scent of
blooming white daisies.
You can see it in pure green leaves
growing from a tree.
You can hear it in the crickets buzzing
around the new grown sunflowers.
You can feel it in soft and delicate
petals falling on your hand.
Aditya Desai, Grade 3

Mom and Dad
I love mom
I love dad
My dad loves me
My mom loves me
I love my brother
I love my sisters
My brother loves me
My sisters love me
Ryan Sebring, Grade 1

Butterfly
Butterfly
Up in the sky
Take flight
To a flower
Eat nectar from a
Red flower
Lay in the
Yellow sun.
Riley Stubbs, Grade 3

Starving
S nack none
T ummy rumbling
A t snack, I had none
R umbling stomach
V ibrating stomach growling with hunger
I am starving
N o food at all
G urgling with hunger
Rohan Sharma, Grade 3

Grades 4-5-6
High Merit Poems

Alone

I'm alone
In the winter cold
Everyone sees something bright
But all I see fright
I'm alone in the winter cold
With no presents to enjoy
Miguel Federico, Grade 6

Oops!

I meant to finish my math problem today,
But I wanted to play with my dad,
And it was time for dinner,
And I had to get ready for bed,
I meant to finish my math problem today,
But school day things got in my way.
Jamie Fong, Grade 4

My Blue Personality

Blue describes me
Like the ocean breeze calm and relaxing
And like the downpour loud and restless
But like the sky nice to look at
But like ocean water flooding over a city
But always nice and mean
Vincent Reyes, Grade 6

Christmas

Green Christmas tree
Breakfast being made
Christmas songs like "Jingle Bells"
Tasty cookies
Wrapping paper being opened
Christmas
O'Lisia Banks, Grade 5

Snowmen

The snowman is a funny guy,
He looks like he needs a pie,
We named him Joe then thought of Glow,
But none of those quite fit,
Now he melts to run his course,
So maybe next year we'll make a horse.
Kathryn Watson, Grade 5

Dragons

Dragons soaring through the air
Dragons darting towards the world
Dragons flying through the wind
Dragons searching high and low
Dragons hiding away in caves
In a group set off to save the world
Sarah Sims, Grade 4

Kindness

"No act of kindness, no matter how small, is ever wasted."
— Aesop

No act of kindness,
No matter how small,
No matter how large,
No matter how tall.
No matter the size,
The same it will be.
A small act of kindness,
From you to me.

I think that even if it's just a smile, you should always be kind to others.
You never know what people are going through,
So they could really appreciate it.
Aubrie Fuller, Grade 4

Where I'm From

I am from the cold, sleeting rain that lashes down on the roof
From the soft, fluffy snow spiraling down from the sky
The rare, sunny, shining days where it's still cold.

I am from tall black hats and bayonets, and trumpets announcing the Changing
From the towering poles sporting the Union Jack
The smart black cars carrying the royal family.

I am from the delicious, soft sticks of Cadbury Fudge
From the amazing Christmas lunches, followed by heated games of Nefarious
The salty boxes of fish and chips by the ocean.

I am from enormous clocks, sharpened axes resting, waiting for another
From small cages containing spines, scales, fur
The underground, with its steel snakes flying through tunnels.
Milo Moffitt, Grade 5

I Am No One

I am no one
I am nothing that they can compare to
They take one look at the surface,
But they don't dive in to really get to know me as a person.
They basically see me as my own species, a parasite
I just get in the way.
I'm like an apple at the top of a tree,
No one wants to climb that high to be with me,
They just get the lower ones, the easy ones to reach,
And I think something is wrong with them,
But I know that one person will climb to the top, and see the girl on the inside.
Makayla Clendening, Grade 6

Embarrassment

Embarrassment is blood rushing to your cheeks.
It sounds like a thousand tiny voices laughing at your every move, every thought.
It smells like lead while your mind is trying to process what just happened.
It tastes like saltwater, fresh from the ocean.
Embarrassment feels like every person knows your faults and will never forget them.
Elizabeth Murphy, Grade 5

If I Were in Charge of the World

If I were in charge of the world,
I'd remove asparagus
Cancel grounding from parents and
Get rid of tests in school

If I were in charge of the world,
There'd be longer summers,
Dancing pet penguins
And ice creams sundaes for everyone

If I were in charge of the world,
You wouldn't have empty cookie jars
You wouldn't have homework
You wouldn't have bad luck

If I were in charge of the world,
Kids would be able to stay up all night and
Watch TV all they want
And a person who sometimes talks back
And sometimes doesn't brush at night
Would still be allowed to be
In charge of the world
                    Younhah Kang, Grade 5

Brian Michael Thompson

B asketball Player
R ight Handed
I mprints on you
A thletic
N ever gives up

M ad Man
I nspiring
C lothes
H ats
Al l Stars
E ncouraging
L oves Sports

T eam Mate
H unter
O utgoing
M indful
P oint Guard
S econd Basemen
O utstanding
N ice
            Brian Thompson, Grade 5

Greek Gods

Greek mythology
Zeus, Hades, and Poseidon.
Hera, Demeter
Hestia, Dionysus,
Artemis Apollo too
            Ana Deny, Grade 4

Ode to My Papa

Papa, O Papa
I love how you help me
To learn my spelling words
You're like a busy bee

Papa, O Papa
You're strong, but kind
Being with you
Blows my mind

Papa, O Papa
Magnificent you are
You help me with my vocabulary words
you are the most loving by far
            Margaret Maloney, Grade 5

Ooh Ooh Ahh

My monkey little brother
ooh ooh ahhs so annoyingly.
He also ooh ooh ahhs with
a mouthful of ABC peas.
He ooh ooh ahhs like
he doesn't like me.
He ooh ooh ahhs when
he pulls my hair.
He ooh ooh ahhs like
he doesn't even care.
He ooh ooh ahhs in
his underwear.
He ooh ooh ahhs out
of nowhere!
            Sarah Jordan, Grade 4

The Night Stalker

The woolly beast
Is ready for a feast
Snarling teeth
He's silent underneath
Luminous eyes, frightening
Ululating through the night
Roaming in a pack
Always on the hunt
But not for a runt
They're out for your sheep
Watch out little Bo Peep!
The night stalkers
Ululating and prowling
Through the night
            Noah Squires, Grade 6

My Puppy

My fluffy brown puppy is my best friend.
He will be there until the end.
We will be together at the park.
But on my shoes he will leave a mark.
            Valeria Eureste, Grade 5

Mahatma Gandhi

Mahatma Gandhi
Born in Porbandar in Gujarat, India
Child of Karamchand and Putlibai Gandhi
Lived in Porbandar, India and South Africa
Studied at University College London
Overcame British rule
Worked as a lawyer and freedom fighter
Challenged by British rule
Personal traits for peace and freedom
Always fought with words not weapons
Never gave up
Best known for getting India independence.
            Shyam Sundar, Grade 4

Road to Freedom

I have running been for so long.
My feet are cut and sore.
The patrollers are not far behind me.
I hear the dogs howling for me.
It is so dark.
But I can still make out the North Star.
My heart is beating very loud.
I see a house ahead of me.
There is a quilt hanging on the fence.
I tap on the door.
Friendly faces invite me in.
I know that I am on my way to freedom.
            Adela Campo, Grade 4

Ode to Pie

Pie,
Oh pie!
Yummy, yummy, pie.
Nothing so sweet as thee
Yummy, yummy, pie.
I eat you,
Then you are me,
Yummy, yummy, pie.
You're so,
So yummy
In my tummy,
Yummy, yummy, pie.
            Kayla Nutter, Grade 5

Eraser

I feel so cold just sitting in there
It's not that fun being me I'm
Getting down days by days
It's not fun cause one day
I'll be all alone and one day
Someone will just use me
And I'll be gone but there's
One thing my shavings will
Still be there in memory of me
I Hope…
            Cassandra Casillas, Grade 6

Yellow
Yellow describes me.
It reminds me of pizza or a poster.
Yellow is my favorite color.
That is the reason why I chose it.
It also reminds me of cheese.
Do you like cheese?
Yellow is always around me.
Yellow is love.
Not really but to me it is.
Why?
Because yellow is life.
Or to me it is.
Daniel De Lara, Grade 6

Jackson Odom (Amazing!)
J umping Jellybeans (It's a pun)
A wesome at gaming
C ool beans
K ing of drawing
S mart dude (maybe)
O n top of the universe
N o one can be just like me

O ver joy every day
D ino man all the way
O h my friends love my drawings
M LG pro (major league gaming)
Jackson Odom, Grade 5

Nature's Song
Tweet, tweet goes a bird
the most wonderful thing I have heard
Snap, crack, goes the squirrels
still exploring the world
a river flowing near by
fish jumping as if they can fly
deer roaming all around
as a few stop to lie down
bunnies hopping here and there
now appearing everywhere
this place only one has heard
but I mustn't say a single word
Karol-Anne Cook, Grade 6

My Shadow Wears…
My shadow wears
The jacket that keeps me warm in winter
The shirt that is too big for me
The sneakers that cover my feet
Her hair is like a horse's tail
Sleek and soft
My shadow is a cheetah
Ready to pounce
Swift and speedy
Racing day by day
Roocha Thatte, Grade 5

Kentucky Fried Chicken
Well, I go walk down the sidewalk,
With my mouth watering and licking,
Then I found,
Kentucky Fried Chicken!!!
I went in the store,
With a guy, hair of white,
He had glasses,
So he lost his sight,
Before he gave my food,
He said,
Its finger licking good,
Then I asked him,
Do you like panthers?
He said no,
But he was Colonel Sanders,
Then he left,
Without a dread
Then I remembered,
He was dead
Andie Ngo, Grade 4

Seasons
Summer
The sun is scorching
Chilling in the treehouse
Swimming in the sun

Winter
The window is frosty
Snowy flakes fall on the frozen lake
It's freezing outside

Spring
Bees buzz around blossoms
Cool water runs over rocks
New life is around

Fall
Leaves are falling free
It is cold but we are warm
Fall is beautiful
Zander Roe, Grade 6

The Heart in an Ocean
The ocean is like my beating heart,
crashing and picking itself up.
Every time, the moon fueling the
waves like happiness carving my
heart's shape.
The ocean's creatures being moved
and moving inside the waves,
like people coming and going.
The lighthouse searching and searching,
like my very own soul searching for
more of His word.
Alexis Huddleston, Grade 6

My Piano
When you come,
It sings with joy,
With all your fingers,
Pinky to thumb,
Tickle it and tickle it,
And you shall see,
It singing louder,
With wonder and glee.
Jennifer Le, Grade 5

My Friend Moon
I have friend,
Around the bend,
His name is Moon,
He's coming soon,
In the day,
He goes away,
But at night,
He's quite a sight!
Michael Williams, Grade 5

Football
The QB throws the ball.
I can only catch them if they're small.
I don't want to be popped,
Cause that's worse than getting chopped.
Every time I see my dad,
I try my best to make him glad,
Even though the game was fun,
I have to go cause it is done.
Saul Treviño Jr., Grade 5

Nature Hike
All those trees
All those bees
Leaves grow on branches
Why, yes they're green
Grass so thin
Water so deep
Nature so fun
Then we go off to sleep
Beau Caldwell, Grade 4

The Arrow
The arrow is brave
It travels a long way
Discovering the future
And lets go of the past
It goes fast, but decides slowly
The arrow is thrown by the bow
But in the end, it gets farther
And hits the target.
Ella Fathi, Grade 6

50 Years Later

50 years later, will anything exist?
50 years later, is humanity just mist?
50 years later, will sinks be self-unclogging?
50 years later, will people have stopped logging?
50 years later, what's the state of the environment?
50 years later, will we be free of tirement?
50 years later, will we have new dinosaurs?
50 years later, is there anything that roars?
And how could I know?
It is where I cannot go.
I truly cannot see,
50 years ahead of me.

Owen Griffith, Grade 6

If I Were in Charge of the World

If I were in charge of the world,
I'd make school two days only,
and make the school year 6 months,
and we also get our own lounge in school.
If I were in charge of the world,
there'd be candy stores in every neighborhood,
and donut shops, and pizza places.
If I were in charge of the world,
you wouldn't drop bombs,
and you wouldn't use guns,
you wouldn't use any weapons.
If I were in charge of the world.

Omair Siddiqui, Grade 6

Lost

Sometimes you can find yourself alone
trapped in a forest as dense as the abyss.
Sounds swallowed whole in the blinding mist.
You may think of yourself as invisible, gone.
But you aren't.
You are there.
You can lift the fog,
you can feel the sun.
You are there.
You still have a voice.
You can change the world.
You are not lost.

Alex West, Grade 6

I Remember

I remember tubing on the lake
I remember swimming in the creek with friends
I remember sledding on the hills
And going for a hike in the woods
I remember grilling on the grill
I remember fishing on the lake
I remember looking up at the sky and seeing all the stars
Even though it was a cold night
I remember meeting my first best friend
But my favorite memories are yet to come

Layton Tucek, Grade 6

If I Were

If I were a star in the night sky
I would be full of wishes people make
I would taste like glitter
I would like to make people's wishes come true
I would want to see people having a good life

If I were a star in the night sky
I would shimmer when I am happy
I would wish to be a person
I would love to explore space
I would watch spaceships go by
I would never wish to be in another galaxy

Sheena Gandhi, Grade 4

A Fun Day at the Beach

The salty sand touches my toes
Whoosh! Whoosh!
Waves crash on the shore
The sun slamming down on me
I am excited as I run to the sea
but I take a step back because the water is cold
"into the water", he told me his daughter
I go in and do as I'm told
We're starting to get tired and now it's time to pack
So I go back
As the sun sets on this beautiful day
And now I am going on my way

Karla Morales, Grade 6

The Immense Desert

It is clear as water
Stripes like tiger skin
Hot as the sun
The cold night with stars
Like snow falling
Walking with a sense of death and admiration
The vastness of the Mojave
Makes me feel small
Like an ant
Beautiful life on this earth exists
Hidden
Like shadows

Angel Tostado, Grade 5

Remember the Dust Storm

I remember it was spring, was April
I remember my father went to buy food
I remember I said we should go to church
And church was 6 miles away
I remember then I saw a wave of dust
I remember the birds were falling out of the sky
I remember a blizzard of dust was coming at us
Even I was paralyzed in fear
I remember the whole town was wiped out
But my favorite memory's yet to come

Amr Ayed, Grade 4

Happiness

The world is filled with happiness.
People are loving and caring.
People are cheering.
Everybody is at peace with each other.
Gentle music fills the air.
Even though there is war,
There is happiness all around us.
No more fighting, stealing, and lying.
God has forgiven our sins.
The world is at peace.
There's life and hope everywhere.
The forgiven lives a peaceful life.

Everywhere you go,
Even with tragedy and death,
There is still hope.
Oh, shall the world be filled with happiness
And the world be forgiven!
There's joy even though the world is dark.
Leif Inocian, Grade 4

Madison Kay McNeely

M onkey
A wesome
D azzling
I ncredible
S uper
O utgoing
N osy

K ind
A rgumentative
Y oung

M iss. Piggy
C razy
N ice
E asy going
E veryone's friend
L oud
Y eller
Madison McNeely, Grade 6

A Quiet Revolution

a single soul
of strength, bravery
one who dares
to speak out
a quiet declaration
without hopes of glory
a voice from the oppressed
to bring forth a deluge of reconciliation
the birth of freedom
a tide of beauty
overwhelming the world
Clea Caddell, Grade 6

A True Friend

A true friend will always be there
No matter what I do
Standing by my side
laughing loudly and crying softly

A true friend will never leave me
Even when times are bad
We may not always agree
But we never leave each other mad

I am so happy that you are my friend
You really are a true friend
as long as we stick together like glue
our friendship will have no end
Victoria Rankin, Grade 6

Weather

The rain is very wet,
It comes down as fast as a jet,
It also gets very cloudy,
The rain drops hit very loudly,

I extremely like the snow,
It makes the water really show,
The snow whispered to the people below,
Come and play I am not just for show,

I run as fast as the wind,
Come by me you will get spun,
As the wind goes swoosh,
It will give me an extra push.
Jayden Haywood, Grade 6

The Open Man

I receive the pass
Find the open shot
My knees bend
And I start to jump
I'm about to flick my wrist
And send the ball arcing
Into the hoop
But something catches my eye
The open man
A wide open player
With an even clearer shot
Change of plans
I pass
Christopher Granberry, Grade 6

Eating Bacon

Bacon
It's amazing
Bacon is my favorite
Bacon goes good with anything
Good pigs
Liam Cox, Grade 6

Make-Up

As colorful as it is
it's only a pretty mask on your face
It can break easily
"crack" it goes as it falls down

How to fix it? I don't know
let's go to the mall and buy more
as I look around the store
I see lipsticks as red as cherry's

"ooh" I say I want them all
Bright as the sun I see pigments of gold
I look at the price and say
"oh no"
Kaylie Calderon, Grade 6

Planets

As they travel along the Heliosphere,
they shine and look quite clear,
some are big and some are small,
but all are in the shape of a ball.

With different mixed color variations,
they were beautiful creations,
also with extremely intense pressure,
it took centuries to measure.

Some travel fast and some travel slow,
those travel slow as a rhino,
and some travel fast as a zap,
but all travel around the same path!
Alan Gutierrez, Grade 6

Ocean

Whoosh
It is big as the sky
You can find it all over the earth
Dark blue with living things

Big waves knock you down
The salty water
Which is huge and blue
The peacefulness of the waves

The nasty blue water
Coming back with sand in my hair all wet
Soft sand on my feet
It is almost bigger than earth
Ariana Berumen, Grade 6

Candy

Candy is so sweet,
I eat with glee!
It is so tasty
And I eat it daily!
Leanna Espinoza, Grade 5

Bad Kitty

I once had a cat named Sniffles Mc'Gee
who peed on a mat, and then on my knee
I put her outside,
and took it in stride
until she climbed up a 100 foot tree

Aidan Aitchison, Grade 6

The Square Ball

There once was a square soccer ball,
That poor ball could not roll at all,
The kids could not kick it,
So they threw a big fit,
That square ball was no good at all!

Kenny Orsatti, Grade 6

The Library

It is quiet.
It is full of books.
It is sometimes full of kids.
At last you can hear a story
read by the teacher in the library.

Veronica Nava, Grade 4

Tornado

Tornado
Humongous, terrifying
Twirls, kills, destroys
Alarmed, frightened
Tornado

Kayla Wilkinson, Grade 4

The Fox Facts

Fox
Furry, soft
Grabbing, hunting, eating
Enjoys catching the fish
Fox

Alyssa Upton, Grade 4

Chinese Zodiac

Monkey
Intelligent, clever
Guarding, distrusting, active
A witty, trustful animal
Ape

Ethan Strubbe, Grade 6

The Mill

An old man works in that mill,
Up on the green little hill.

The old man grinds some wheat,
To give to someone to eat.

Amelia Richardson, Grade 4

Unstoppable

The boy with his brushed bright hair sweeping against his face
and his drum freely pulsing to the beat of his heart
He climbs up the lush green hillside
With every thumping step he takes, other children come following
They journey through both whispering rain and the smiling sunshine
Unstoppable
Knowing only good will come
They don't care about the problems that lay ahead
The boys and girls just keep on walking, without a care in the world
Their smiles light up their faces
With their sense of freedom and rebellion
Nothing can stop them when they soar
High above the clouds, beaming and as free as a bird
Unstoppable

Ava Fattahi, Grade 5

August Luhnow — The Story About a Group of Mysterious Children — US1

To fly or not to fly is the question that most birds ponder,
Or should they stay rooted to the earthy ground?
These mystifying children on an island ponder that too
And with the encouragement of a mighty drum, up up and away they go
Except for the tiny pale one who just couldn't believe in his ability
So he watched, and on, on his jolly friends embarked, to the freedom of other islands
Leaving everything they've known to go somewhere unknown
The danger provided them courage to keep going on
Along with the guidance of the whispering winds
To not tumble into the vast ocean beyond
But what follows for these jubilant children?
Nobody knows, but anyone can imagine
One day, somewhere, somehow, on a rocky island beyond
They might land in their new and happy lives

August Luhnow, Grade 6

Love Is

Love is a diamond, sparking in the sunlight with a rainbow reflection
Its value so rare it is priceless
Love is a photo hanging up on the wall
Its memories captured in time with you and your loved ones
Love is a wooden table, sturdy, polished, hard
Each fiber is a developed friendship promised to last a lifetime
Love is a bouquet of roses, oh, so red and beautiful
Their petals grow and flourish just as love does
Love is a piano, its enchanted sounds soothe my ears
The keys playing gently tickling it,
As it laughs an affectionate giggle
Love is a white sheet of paper,
Starting over with forgiveness and a clean slate

Shayna Bresnick, Grade 5

Blizzard of Black

The dust storm roars across the prairie
It fills the houses with dust
The Great Plains are rampaged by the dust storm
The wind picks up loose dirt like a hurricane and destroys everything in its path
The winds die down and the dust settles

Jaden Ip, Grade 4

The World
The world is a beautiful place
So when you're bored go out
And take a
Stroll

Find something unusual to
Brighten up your day

The world is a beautiful place so
When you're bored go
Outside and take a
Stroll

The world is an unusual place
And the things to discover are just one
Secret
Between you and me
Reece Tveter, Grade 4

Basketball
Bouncing the ball bravely high
Seeing defenders running by

Shooting free throws at a line
Took the ball now it's mine

Shooting the ball with a twist
I feel a sweat, like a liquid mist

Then I look up at the score
My team is up by way more

Then I took a big look at the time
Now I have a lot of decisions on my mind

Made a shot with a win
The victories our finishing up by ten
Tiffany Wynne, Grade 6

Friends Forever
F riendly
R espectful to each other
I ntelligent companions when together
E ncouraging self-growth
N ever mean or degrading
D elightful to be around
S uprising in a nice way

F unny
O pen to feelings
R esponsible
E xtremely nice to each other
V aliantly defending our sacred friendship
E xcellent counselor
R estless to make you happy
Miriam Coria, Grade 6

My Mom
See there is this lady
I think I drive her crazy

She is always on the run
Never letting me miss the fun

She is always by my side
This woman is my greatest pride

She helps me grow and improve
Putting up with my attitude

She helps me learn right from wrong
Telling us all to get along

See there is this lady, she is the bomb
I'm glad I get to call her my mom
Alejandra Velazquez, Grade 6

Spring
Spring is where the flowers come,
where blossoms start to bloom.
It's where the sun comes out,
it's sunshine makes everyone smile.

Spring is where kids play outside
with happiness everyday.
The children all come out and say,
"Sun, I'm glad you're here to stay."

I see flowers here to there.
I see beautiful flowers everywhere.
Flowers from pink to red.
They play with their dog Fred.

Spring, I am glad you're here,
From now on I'll have no fear.
Rachel Maynes, Grade 4

Home
I miss I miss
My home that I love.
I miss
I miss
My brother so dear to me
He will love me
I miss
I miss
The sea I don't see
The waves that crash
The way I would splash
The way we would dash
Home
My home
My home
Makayla Lord, Grade 6

Street Performer
I am a street performer
no house, no warm place to go

I'm on the street sidewalk
cold winter season air

My wish is to be famous
though right now my passion is to juggle

From my perspective,
people look at my juggling,
my tangled hair in knots
I feel like running away from their
cold
crushing
stare
I am a street performer
no house, no warm place to go.
Craig Yujuico Chiu, Grade 6

Gold
I soar through the golden sky
High in the sky
Wondering why,
Just why
The world is like this now
I am forced to the back,
But warriors don't cry
Justice, we lack
Why is it just I
Just I, the black woman
Who is treated like that?
Like a felon, fettered in chains?
I know in my heart
In years, mere years
The world shall be
As good as gold
Help make this world
Gold!
Lauren Zaidel, Grade 5

Blueberry Pie
B aking wonder
L icious taste
U ltimate flavor
E xtremely good
B ound to be great
E ngage in eating it
R eally wonderful
R elish
Y ummy!

P erfect
I ncredible zest
E verlasting savory
Amita Manjunath, Grade 6

I Am…MyKayla

I am unique and loving
I wonder what's at the bottom of the ocean
I hear the beautiful blue bird songs outside my window
I see circus clouds filling the sky
I want a big bushy long haired Maltese

I am unique and loving
I pretend I am as fast as a jaguar
I feel sad when I see a homeless person with no family
I touch a hairy monster in one of my nightmares
I worry if a natural disaster is coming to California
I cry when my family gets hurt and I can't help them

I am unique and loving
I understand that life is unfair
I say old sayings that can inspire others
I dream about a new world where there is no violence, just love
I try to treat people nicely and help them get better
I hope I will live a long peaceful life
I am unique and loving

Mykayla Collier, Grade 4

Ten Little Racecars

Ten little race cars that are mine
One lost a wheel, now there are nine
Nine little race cars found a crate
One got lost now there are eight
Eight little race cars talked of heaven
One got stepped on now there are seven
Seven little race cars, one got lost in the mix
Now there are six
Six little race cars learned to skydive
One race car's parachute did not work now there are five
Five little race cars began to snore
One didn't wake up now there are four
Four little race cars learned to ski
One got lost, now there are three
Three little race cars looking blue
One did not make it, now there are two
Two little race cars had some fun
One fell off a cliff now there is one
One little race car began to run
The poor little race car crashed and, now there are none

Quade Meckel, Grade 5

Snakes

Whenever I catch a snake,
When my mom sees me with a snake she gets in a panic
Then she says, "Drake."
Then she makes me put the snake in a jar in the attic.

I found one in Mexico.
My mom said not to pick it up.
She said, "Let it go."
The snake wasn't a grown up.

Drake Plowman, Grade 4

Charge of the World

If I were in charge of the world,
I'd end all problems between different countries,
invent more desserts, and
end world hunger.
If I were in charge of the world,
there'd be less homework for good kids,
more homework for bad kids, and
NO DONALD TRUMP!
If I were in charge of the world,
you wouldn't ever be bored.
You wouldn't have to deal with bullies.
You wouldn't have to eat healthy all the time,
or wouldn't have to eat just one dessert.
If I were in charge of the world.

Afaf Asad, Grade 6

Little Do You Know

Little do you know
how I'm dying inside while everyone sleeps
Many problems I have but you can't see
and I need someone to help me out
Little do you know
I'd be there wondering myself to sleep
I wish someone would see through me
and how I wish someone could help save me
Little do you know
I wouldn't want to hurt anyone
I try to fix everything step by step
I've been awakened by another side of me
Or I'm trying my best to help myself
Little do you know

Victoria Wright, Grade 6

Green

Green is the color of the Earth in the universe.
Green is the color of grass.
Green is the color of the trees outdoors.
Green smells like apple.
Green tastes like my mom's apple pie.
Green sounds like peace and quiet.
Green looks like everyone is quiet.
Green feels like cold rain on my hair.
Green makes me want to rest for so long.
Green is my sister's favorite color.

Na'kibria Summerling, Grade 4

The Sun

The sun is so big and bright
Although we cannot see it at night
Helium and hydrogen make up the sun
Don't look at it, that wouldn't be fun
The sun is only a medium sized star
Especially from Neptune the sun is far
The sun gives us vitamin D
If it was gone, Earth is one place we wouldn't be

Savannah McVey, Grade 5

Hello Goodbye
Hello to bikes
Goodbye to skate boards

Hello to two wheels
Goodbye to four wheels

Hello to sitting
Goodbye to standing

Hello to pumping
Goodbye to pushing

Hello to chains
Goodbye to board

Hello to the road
Goodbye to the sidewalk
Axel Giron Rayas, Grade 4

Carrot
I am a
Carrot I live in the
Ground. My favorite
Colors are orange
And green.
I wear lumpy orange
Coats. My job is to be
Eaten and my friends
Are potatoes.
My mom is a
Smoothie
Now, the
Farmer
Brings
Me to
The store
Brayden Brockelman, Grade 4

Walking in the Darkness
Crickets singing in the night,
The moon, as white as the snow,
The scent of lemons,
Hanging on the tree,
The cool, night air,
in my face,
Toads croaking at one another,
The orange, setting sun,
Sitting on the horizon,
Complementing the rising moonlight,
The sweet aroma of eucalyptus trees,
Swaying in the wind,
Wind whistling, whistling, whistling,
My own,
    quiet,
      breathing.
Aaron Power, Grade 5

Can You Hear Me?
Hello?
Can you hear me?
I'm going under a bridge.
There is very bad reception
Right above me is a ridge
But don't worry; I'm still here
Although I'm lost and filled with fear
But soon I'll find my way
Through all the pretenses of the day
But when I come you'll shout "Hurray!"
And as the light comes and fades away
I am still lost
Struggling through the frost, alas
Peering through the glass
Almost home at last
Yet home seems so far off still
But shivering through the chill
I will make it back in time
Hopeless but alive
Because I came to say goodbye
Frances Altes, Grade 6

When the Winter Wind Blows
When the winter wind blows,
the sun hides.

It's cold again,
and it starts to snow.

Flakes dancing,
children playing,
and lakes freezing to ice.

Then comes the time of giving
when our families gather 'round.
We give and get gifts
wrapped in bright red ribbons.

When winter is finished,
we can still be entertained.
Spring's on it's way.
Let's just enjoy the moment
as we wait for winter again.
Keira Barry, Grade 4

Dreams
Dreams
Love, escape
Inspiring, welcoming, interesting

But not always

Scaring, terrifying, saddening
Tears, sorrow
Nightmares
Corbin Young, Grade 6

Oh Earth
Oh Earth, Oh Earth
So round and blue
With sister sun, and brother moon
Oh Earth, Oh Earth
I see you too
With Neil and Buzz
Just guess…

We're on the moon.

Oh Earth, Oh Earth
We're going down
There's something wrong
With Houston's sound
They can't contact

The first men to walk
on the moon

I think there's something wrong
I'm worried
And you look so far away
Well goodbye
I think I know one of us has to stay

Goodbye
Elijah Braide, Grade 5

Waiting
There he was,
Standing,
Waiting,
In the damp spot.

Many stems,
And many others,
All had teeth like claws,
And stood as patient as a hunter.

In wet area,
Standing,
Waiting,
In the swampy area.

Fly in search of food,
Lands in sticky spot.

Finally,
It finally landed,
The wait is over.

The sky grown dark,
Stars spread like broken glass hidden,
The plant stands,
Waiting.
Jenner Arriaga, Grade 6

What Happens to a Dream Deferred?*

What happens to a dream deferred?
Does it swim away
Like a great white shark?
Or leap like a dolphin out of your mind
and then fade like a forgotten memory?
Does it soar away like a bird?
Or burn
like a fire on a house.
Maybe it just shines
like a brand new penny.
Or does it float up to the sky and disappear?
Ryan Salinel, Grade 6
*Inspired by Langston Hughes

Small

I am the smallest person in the world,
but it's not always fun
I'm too small to do my big homework
then I can't get it done
There is more than one thing to say
Like my bed is just too big for me,
so I take naps on the floor all day
and my food is just too tall
that I can't finish it at all
That's all I have to tell
Oh, and how do I throw the
coin into the magical wishing well?
Monamari Presto, Grade 5

The Moon

She comes every night
And shines her bright light.
She's pretty with her star friends
All around her.
She's big and round
And I wonder if she makes a sound.
She is beautiful in her form,
Even in a storm.
She is my biggest love.
It is hard to let go of
Because she is my friend
Until the very end.
Jimena Marquez, Grade 5

I Am

I am pink like a happy little kitten
I am Christian and kind
I am Christmas and Easter
I am all four seasons happy and cheerful
I am morning and night like moon and sun
I am pretending that cats speak English
I am soft like a fluffy bunny
I am happy endings
I am artistic and creative
I am Brooke Lydia Baldwin
Brooke Baldwin, Grade 4

A Day at the Track

A clear sky with few clouds
One cloud was a fluffy pillow
Tires crying cause of so much spinning
Engines roaring like angry lions
"Vroom, vroom, vroom"
Lights switching from
Red
Yellow
Yellow
GREEN
Could hear the roaring down the track
Fastest always wins the championship.
Omar Alvarez, Grade 6

Our Musical Atmosphere

Music is everywhere
Just like air
It is expressive
It is unique
Music has a special taste
Better than your favorite delicacy
It expresses itself in the form of nature
It expresses itself by a violin
A flute, a piano
In the form of singing
Singing expresses your feelings,
Like notes express your thoughts
Stuti Shelat, Grade 5

Ode to Love

The birds are singing,
Bathing in water,
All the fun,
Is starting in the sun.
Then he left and walked right out,
Tears run my face drop by drop
Puddle by puddle
One by one, my heart breaks to pieces.
Love, hope, prayer tears away piece by piece
My heart drowning in sorrow,
Laughter and love flew away.
My eyes see nothing but all gray.
Jade Williams, Grade 6

Spelling Bee Champion

Nerves were really shaking
Heart was beating
Loud as a bell,
But I heard the word
Loud as a lion.

Nerves were a tad shaky,
But my smile filled the air.

I won the Spelling Bee.
Arfan Hossain, Grade 4

The Perfect Person

He stands up tall
Hovering over us all
He is bigger than an Ox
More clever than a Fox
We hide in his shadows
Not daring to look up
Not knowing who he is
But knowing he's a wiz
To some people he is royalty
Nothing less than perfection
Because we are his collection
Giving him our heart
Now we'll never be apart
Payton Dorris, Grade 6

Humanity

Death.
The drive of all humanity
Yet, humanity's greatest fear.
The thought of immortality
is relief.
Relief
But to some, anger
The thought of defying death.
Only for humans
Lives would be saved
but only for humans
Humanity would live through all.
All.
Isabel Matos, Grade 4

Fire Red

Red is just like me
It is nice
Red is the color of love
It is spicy
Everybody is friends with Red
Red is my friend
Red is Valentine's Day
But Red is also violence
And the color of blood
Red can punch you in the
Boxing ring and make you bleed
Red is not everyone's color,
But it's mine.
Alissea Huff, Grade 6

Dance

Dance
Hard, emotional
Technical, graceful, entertaining
Lovely, pointe shoes, teammates, goals
Cleats, medals, winning
Enjoyable, amusing
Soccer
Evigene Draper, Grade 5

August

A ll of us want to
U ndo something we have done.
G et rid of the negativity.
U nique people do the right thing
S o that others won't get hurt.
T rust and forgive those who have hurt you,
    and they will do no wrong.
Victoria Tighe, Grade 6

The World

Wind blows a soft summer breeze.
Soft splashes come wet and dry.
Caves echo loud and low.
Vines swing and flowers bloom.
Bees buzz and frogs croak.
The clouds don't block the sun
And then a warm feeling comes to you.
Adam Su, Grade 4

Wackiness

Wackiness seems psychedelic
Like rainbow popcorn.
I see glitter glue.
I hear honking horns and ringing bells.
I smell scented highlighters.
I touch swirly designs.
I taste pink, bubble gum flavored ice cream.
Savannah Johnson, Grade 4

Man's Best Friend

Ranger
slobbery, playing
barking, wondering, licking
leash, colorless, whiskers, fur
scratching, purring, meowing
gentle, sleepy
Leo
Evan Dickinson, Grade 5

Happiness

Happiness seems neon yellow
Like the cheerful sun in the sky.
I see puffy bunnies.
I hear enjoyable kids.
I smell beautiful yellow roses.
I touch chocolate ice cream.
I taste joy.
Diana G. Alvarado, Grade 4

The Ocean

Last Sunday we went to the ocean
Making sure to grab our suntan lotion
We then grabbed our snacks
And our computer Macs
To take pictures of waves in motion
Alondra Aguilera, Grade 5

Remember Me

I remember when I was your only.
I guess you opened your eyes and found someone else.
You left me alone in the rain while you danced in the sunlight.
My imagination so big I actually thought we would be forever.
I guess it was for the best, I saw a huge future with you.
Remember that time you said I was your only,
Remember that time you lied but I forgave you
and gave you a second chance,
Remember the time I asked you if I could trust you and you said,
yes of course, I would never hurt you.
Remember the time you expected a goodbye hug but it didn't happen,
Remember the time you said, okay bye, and I left you on "read."
Remember all those goodnight texts we would send each other,
they all just seemed to fade away,
but why did you have to lie again?
I don't understand.
Remember me.
Regina Sarinana-Perlasca, Grade 6

The Thunderstorm

While I was watching T.V. I heard a loud "BEEP, BEEP, BEEP"
On the screen it warned of a thunderstorm coming,
Then I knew, I wouldn't be able to sleep,
"CLAP" went the thunder as I walked into the kitchen humming,
"BANG" went the thunder again which made me "LEAP,"
"FLASH" the bolt of lightning streaked, oh how I knew the next big
"BOOM" was coming,
The tree branch went "CRACK," oh how the sound was so numbing

Once again "CLASH" the lightning "HOWLED"
I jumped into bed with a loud "CLANG" and hid under the sheets
Oh how I couldn't sleep, because of the loud thunders "GROWL"
"CRACKLE" went it once more, oh how much I wanted to retreat,
Another "SNAP" went the branches on the tree, I thought this was foul
I finally went to sleep but to only hear the thunder on repeat
There it was sunshine, in the morning thank goodness for I would not scowl
The sound of birds, the thunder was gone it was just plain sweet
Bryan Ly, Grade 6

The Wonderful Outdoors

Dwarf cotton tree,
found soft enclosed in pods.
Still hanging on, abounded in every direction,
indeed discovered this valuable plant.
A great journey, crossing a pretty wooded hill.
Luxuriant grass stretched down the hillside,
below lies the rich green forest.
What better situation to find our shelter pitched and situated.
The trunks served as far advanced most comfortable beds,
prepared for us to our purpose.
From the ground, the greatest cut deep trunks formed beams for making a roof.
While cleaning up other rubbish,
I picked up the bark, and to my greatest surprise,
the terebinth tree said to me,
look forward for the journey is still among you.
Joshua Carpentier, Grade 6

Night

The night is quiet and still
The sky is a black blanket
That is wrapped around the Earth
But little stars
Shine through this blanket
And make the night a little bit brighter
And the moon
Is a giant ball that is like the sun
Shining at night
The night is beautiful
And no one can ever change that
Alice Connolly, Grade 5

Summer

Barbecues grilling
Ice cream dripping
These are the sounds of summer.

Kids diving
People laughing
These are the sounds of summer.

Postcards mailing
Waves splashing
These are the sounds of summer.
Belle Xu, Grade 4

Baseball

Fans cheering,
Vendors shouting.
These are the sounds of baseball.

Ball and glove hitting,
Umpires yelling,
These are the sounds of baseball.

Walkup music playing,
Ball and bat hitting,
These are the sounds of baseball.
Jack Bradford, Grade 4

Horse Barn

Horses neighing,
Metal clanking,
These are the sounds of the horse barn.

Hooves stomping,
Flies buzzing,
These are the sounds of the horse barn.

Kicking,
Chomping,
These are the sounds of the horse barn.
Addie Miller, Grade 4

Ode to Cookies

Cookies,
I would literally die,
If I could not eat you.

Long before I can even see you,
Your incredible smell
Just takes my breath away.

I already know what you're saying,
"Eat me! You know you want to eat me."

And then, when I put you in my mouth,
My mouth explodes with delicious delight!

I feel like I'm dreaming.
How can one bite be so splendid?
Where is the milk?

I am so ashamed at my weakness.
But, you're to blame.
Shame on you!
Carly Walker, Grade 4

The Ocean

As the water glistens
So beautiful and wonderful
The place takes time to glow
In your heart and soul

The ripples are going small to BIG
Sparkling water
Then the ocean starts to grow
With feelings and life
The water seems to
Live and work all over again

Time rises before the water
Gets pollution and trashed
So making a difference in
The world and the community

So cleaning the ocean can change
A lot and a whole lifetime
Of pollution
Everywhere
Emma Araujo, Grade 4

Friends

Flipping with joy
Radiant and fashionistas
I like them a lot
Elegant and very friendly
Neat and organized in work
Duh they are like sisters
Sometimes they are mean
Tara Kodukula, Grade 4

I Am

I am friendly and funny
I wonder what life means
I hear voices and sounds of my memory
I see things from my past when I sleep
I want to be a famous actor
I am friendly and funny

I pretend to be an almighty god
I feel things going down my spine
I touch things no humans have touched
I worry that I will get robbed
I cry when people talk about my dad
I am friendly and funny

I understand why kids go to school
I say God is real
I dream that I will get a new dad
I try not to think about my dad
I hope I will have a good life

I am friendly and nice
Kenneth Soto, Grade 5

Both People

You say I'm disabled,
In a way, so are you,
We are no different.
I love to hear music,
I bet you do, too,
We are no different.
I want to express myself,
You do it all day,
We are no different.
I want to be normal,
You struggle to, too,
We are no different.
I have potential,
I see it in you,
We are no different.
I am imperfect,
You know you are, too,
We are no different.
We are both people,
You know it is true,
We are no different.
Emma Raney, Grade 6

Cupcake

C ontagious with its scent,
U pright or stacked perfectly,
P assionate with its taste,
C onvenient,
A ny topping will do,
K eep enjoying this tasty treat,
E dible with heavenly sweetness.
Maha Rehman, Grade 4

Broken Bones

My first break
Was at the age of three,
When I was with my dad,
Climbing a tree.

My second bone to break
Was at the age of five;
I jumped off the climbing structure
While trying to dive.

Next came the leg
In the summer of 2009;
We vacationed on Balboa,
And it turned out fine.

For my most recent break,
I fell on my wrist,
My bright red cast no one can miss,
You get the gist.
Reese Tillson, Grade 6

Is This Love

Music is my passion
I really love the captions
I love the song, what do you mean
It makes my dog dance like a teen

Boom goes my heart in the air
But it is like a fair
My heart has a good tone
But it's heavy as a stone

I wrote your name in the sky
And when we fly we go so high
I wrote your name in my heart
But then again it fell apart

when I dive into these pages
I may not come back for ages
But do not worry, and do not fear
I am happy here.
Jazmine Hernandez, Grade 6

Leader

The world needs a leader,
Someone

L earning
E ducated
A mazing
D aring
E nduring
R esponsible

Now go on, be that leader.
Claire Jensen, Grade 4

The Sound of Silence

My ear catches the sound of silence,
I take in the scent of fresh Downey,
The smooth texture of my sheets,
I gaze at the sunset,
Through the window pane,
My bed is as quiet as a mouse,
Bed, why are you so comfortable?
Sound of silence,
   Sound of silence,
      Sound of silence.
Wyatt Baker, Grade 5

Football

Running down the field
Quarterback dropping back
I'm running toward the end zone
And I catch the ball on the 40
Feeling fast and powerful
Touchdown!
I'm feeling strong
I'm feeling happy
I walk off the field
Pumped up
Brayden Hinton, Grade 4

It's Game Time

Before the game I'm ready.
But when I play a game,
   It's a little scary.
I get ready and throw the ball.
Can you guess what game it is?
   It's football!
My friend catches the ball
   and runs it all the way.
      Yes!
We won the game.
Nicholas Gonzalez, Grade 4

The Water's Injury

Water runs away from our sand,
   And oil infiltrates the water's base.
Leaving seagulls with nowhere to land,
   Now no life is safe.
   Grief fills the sea,
And as suffering spreads far and wide,
   Sadness grows within me.
We will stand by nature's side,
   Helping it up as it starts to crawl.
Soon it will once again stand tall.
Serena Lee, Grade 6

Stream

Beautiful colors flow
Roaring rapids down river
When will the stream end?
Gavin Derman, Grade 4

Adam and Eve

Long after the world was made,
There came a man to lay.
His name would be Adam,
And Eve would be his madam.

In Heaven there was a fraud.
One of the angles wanted to be like God;
So He cast him down to Earth,
Which would lead to a curse.

He slithers down the tree of life,
And meets Adam's wife.
Eve takes a bit,
Which could lead to a fright.

But then Adam takes a bite,
Then both re in fright.
They hide and hide.
But inside a spirit dies.

They confess everything;
But soon they have to go,
And find a new home.
Soul Barbosa, Grade 6

Sounds of Horseback Riding

Hooves thumping,
Horses neighing,
These are the sounds of horseback riding.

Dogs barking,
Harnesses clicking,
These are the sounds of horseback riding.

Trees swaying,
Twigs breaking,
These are the sounds of horseback riding.

The password beeping,
The gate creaking,
These are the sounds of horseback riding.

Kids talking,
Instructors yelling,
These are the sounds of horseback riding.

Whips slapping,
The rain pounding,
These are the sounds of horseback riding.
Brynn Nesslein, Grade 4

Surfing

Whooshing through the wave,
the warm breeze brushes my face,
lights shine on palm trees
Cassidee McDermott, Grade 5

Help

I come home with my homework,
I sit down in a chair.
It takes me an hour or two,
Until my father's there.
He explains it to me,
Word by word, but when,
I'm done sometimes,
I forget to say Thank You,
But the next day, he doesn't care,
He is still going to help me
Because he is always going to be there.
Charlotte Zachary, Grade 4

I Don't Mind

I scream, you scream
We all scream for ice cream.
We can eat by the pool or inside.
As long as you're happy,
I don't mind.

Let's go to the swing.
We can go there or maybe the trampoline.
I don't mind.
As long as you're happy,
I don't mind.
Hali Holder, Grade 4

Moon

Shining
bright as
can be
from the
sun rotating
around the
Earth
going back
from over
there to
over here
Emma Chiasson, Grade 4

Bird Feathers

Life
is like a
bird's feather
Frail and fragile
but when we say we can do
things we really can't just to
IMPRESS
someone
. . .
we
Fall
Cyndah Lacy, Grade 5

Go to the Zoo

See the lions roar
The cheetah run at its top speed
The majestic vulture
The smart lemurs and parrots
The flying sugar glider
The butterfly with its glimmering glory
The gazelle munching blazing green grass
The rhino with that big glorious horn and
The giraffes beautiful long patterned neck
I truly hope you have a wonderful time
At this magical zoo
Abdulhadi El-Najjar, Grade 6

Tony (Rip 2003-2015)

You're in my mind
Your life is over
We all cried
Can't wait to see you
In Heaven
The day I die
Will never forget that smile, that laugh
And the happiness in his eyes
I can't forget,
I won't forget
Tony
Meadow Roberts, Grade 6

Dust Bowl

I remember a big scary storm
I remember everyone running
I remember everyone looking for cover
And the dirt killing you
I remember the dirt eating me up
I remember the storm killing animals
I remember birds flying scared
Even after that killing day I was alive
I remember all those best things gone
But my favorite memory's yet to come
Brian Rivera, Grade 4

Invitation from a Bunny

Come on down
  I live in a burrow
    Smell the sweet fresh spring air
      Tasty carrots I have
        Nice hideout in the field
          Close your eyes
            Wrap yourself in nice fur
              Hear foxes coming by…HIDE!!!
                See what you're missing on this
                  Cool spring night
Emma Bleckov, Grade 4

I Am From…

I am from a home
where we worship God and
we eat at our table and
where we have, our red leather couch
and brown recliner.

I am from a yard
where we have a green coiled hose
and trees that differ from each other,
and a wooden fence to block out animals.

I am from a family
where we have many traditions
for many things, one is for food
it is twice baked potatoes. And a saying is
it's not my fault

I am from a neighborhood
where there are houses
in a row and many
trees that differ
Henry Toon, Grade 5

Pink

Looks like my favorite shoes
The popped bubblegum on my face
The pink butterflies flying around flowers

Sounds like the pigs oinking
Flamingos honking
Pink dolphins laughing

Tastes like drinking a strawberry smoothie
A juicy grapefruit
A pink velvet birthday cake

Smells like the cotton candy at the circus
The fragrant roses in my backyard
The raspberry sorbet

Feels like my soft blanket
The bumpy starfish in the ocean
My rosy cheeks blushing

Pink can bring happiness to everyone
Jena Leia Hernandez, Grade 6

Best Friends

They have each other's back
They always keep secrets safe
Never making fun of each other
Solving problems together
Helping when they need it the most
Best friends, always, and forever,
Together we are strong
Paris Amaro, Grade 5

Growth with a Helmet

I wore a small helmet on my head.
Lost every game when I was young.
All my teammates teased me for my lack of skill.
But the hate that was made to get me down, only lifted me up.
Hour after hour I worked hard.
I trained until my idols were my rivals.
Through all the pain and rejections,
I now stood on the field where many legends once stood.
Then only did I realize, I was an inspiration;
At which people look up to.

Aaron Bhattachan, Grade 6

Happy Birthday, Mama

Mamá, you're such an extraordinary person
and I'm just…ordinary.
I can't count how many things
you do in my life.
It's like counting how many stars are in the sky.
You're like a star in my life.
You shine in my darkest times.
That's why I'd like to say, "thank you
and have a happy birthday," Mamá.
I love you!

Mikey Campos, Grade 6

Friendship

F unny in numerous ways
R espectful to feelings
I ncludes you in secret conversations
E nergetically encouraging
N eeds you for who you are
D ependable like a soft fuzzy blanket
S tands up for each other
H elps each other in times of stress
I nspire each other with words of encouragement
P ositively a best friend.

Anai Madrigal, Grade 6

My House

My house is brown with pops of color.
It tastes like a home-cooked meal.
It sounds like a bird chirping and dogs barking.
It smells like food cooking in the oven or delicious smelling candles.
It looks like a well-decorated zoo with lots of animals.
It makes me feel like I have the best family in the whole world.

Gracie Johnson, Grade 6

Joy

Joy seems sunflower yellow
Like the sun on a hot summer day.
I see a light bolting in a dark cave.
I hear kids playing in the park.
I smell the wind warming the Earth's surface.
I touch the soft grass beneath my bare feet.
I taste the melting ice cream dripping through my fingers.

Melissa Hernandez, Grade 4

My Extraordinary Sister

My sister is pretty ordinary
But to me she is extraordinary
She likes to draw amazing pictures
And creates crazy color mixtures
Outside we like to bike and play
And when she catches me she likes to say "Got you!"

As I declared she's really fun
But sometimes we don't always play in the sun
Sometimes we fight with swords
And we pretend to be lords
We call each other by code names sometimes
When we fight pretend crimes

Oftentimes we don't get along
Like when choosing which is the best song
We yell and fight
But later we see forgiveness in the light
No matter what, we love each other
I'm starting to sound like our mother
I think she's really extraordinary
Even if she's a bit ordinary

Noah Salazar Perez, Grade 4

I Am From…

I am from a family
Where my Aunt Christine and
Aunt Mary Linda teach me to
make balish and chicken paprikash
in the cold winter months

I am from a house
Where it is warm and I miss it when I'm gone
Where we gather around the dinner table
to say grace

I am from a class
Where we laugh and play
Where we share secrets when we go on field trips
Where we all are like brothers and sisters
so we never make fun of each other

I am from Myself
Where I'm blossoming into wonderful creations
Where I don't know where life is going to take me

All of these things make me who I am

Rebecca Digmon, Grade 5

The Beautiful Lily

There once was an athletic boy named Billy
His favorite thing to eat was chili
His mom served him a bowl
It helped him score a goal
So after the game he brought her a beautiful lily

Noah Carrillo, Grade 5

I Am Melody
I am the one
I smell no different
I am visible
Not invisible
I am smart
I am funny
On the inside
I am Melody
I am like a tree
Everyone wants me to leave
I am Melody
I am friendless
Except for one
Rose is my friend
The only one
I am Melody
I have a tornado
When I get mad
I Am Melody
Azhure Landers, Grade 6

Who Am I?
They say I'm as fast as a cheetah
That like a lion, I am strong
But what they don't realize
Is that I really don't belong

They say I've got eyes
As clever, as sharp as a hawk's
But what they don't realize
Is that they're in for some shocks

They say I'm as mean as a leopard
That I don't give anyone a chance
But what they don't realize
I see the demons in their eyes as they dance

All these things they say I am
But why can't they see?
I don't need to be described
Why can't I simply be me?
Eden McDowell, Grade 6

Ode to Dreams
Oh, my deal illusions in the night!
How you keep my fantasies alive,
and help me revive.
Yet you still frustrate me as I
awake from my slumber, and wonder
why, oh, why did I awake?
You drag my wishes back from
the Underworld so they can live
in the limelight again.
How I adore my sweet visions of
my own imagination.
Italia Jahmeek, Grade 6

If I Were in Charge of the World
If I were in charge of the world,
I'd get rid of gross green vegetables
And slow down time

If I were in charge of the world
There'd be cake for dinner,
And you'd still get dessert
And all friends would stay friends forever

If I were in charge of the world
You wouldn't have dares
You wouldn't have competition
You wouldn't have homework
Or poky wires on your braces
You wouldn't even have braces

If I were in charge of the world
You would have immortal pets
And no one would betray you
And a person who sometimes screams
when she sees a spider
And sometimes forgets to brush her teeth
Would still be allowed
to be in charge of the world.
Lillian Laatz, Grade 5

A Very Terrible Baseball Player
I swing
I miss
until I get out
just like every time.

The crowd sighs
as I slowly walk back to the dugout
my team says nice try
as I wait till my next at bat.

All my at bats go the same
I have no hits
for the whole season
for I am the worst in the league.

I practice and practice
I practice day after day
until I get better
but I never do.

Every day I get the same results
I swing
I miss
just like every time.
Colin Brown, Grade 6

War
Someone going, someone leaving.
Hope forgotten.
They leave behind what was,
what will be.
An empty room, empty home
With little hope.

While on the other side,
In another world;
Guns fire.
Knives clash.
Death hangs like a fog.
Bodies lie on the ground,
slowly rotting.

So many dead, so many lost.
An empty home.
An empty world.
Was left behind.

An endless tragedy called war.
Ariana Casillas, Grade 6

Forgiveness
When all you say is sorry
Was that sorry good enough?
Whether you feel guilty or remorse
Was that good enough?

When all you get is nothing
Is nothing all you want?
But it isn't
Was that sorry good enough

Forgiveness is accepting a mistake
Washing away your sea of regrets
It's like freeing a bird from it's cage
A weight lifted off your chest
Was that sorry enough?

Then you start to question everything
Am I bad or am I good?
Then when you realize what I've done
Shame on me
Was that sorry good enough?
Merflor Hernando, Grade 6

Monster
M ean
O dd
N asty
S tealthy
T oxic
E at meat
R oar
Wyatt Beam, Grade 4

The Game of Life
This life that we live,
It is a game.
If you don't believe me!
Then I will tell you why.
Don't we gain experience?
Don't we only have one life?
Don't we try our best?
Trying with all our might.
We enjoy life, like a game.
Think about it,
It might gain you experience,
Or a level.
Christina Orlowski, Grade 6

Mother
I miss my mom every day
I wish she were here to say
Dear Brooklyn child
Don't you cry
I wish I was able to stay a while

But dear mother, why can't you stay
My mother said in the kindest way,
I will see you again someday
Goodbye mother, I will miss you so
I will miss you too
But we will meet again someday
Brooklyn Camach, Grade 4

Locks of Love
I like to donate my hair
Because I care
My hair flows in the air
Like a leaf at the fair
I donate my hair to people
Because I am equal
She looks like a butterfly
When she tried it on she wasn't shy
She was happy as the sun
When she looked in the mirror
Ever since she had my hair
I've been grateful
Jailyn Trevino, Grade 6

Fluffy, Furry Friend
I love my dog more than I can express,
So I will give her a nice big compress
There is no word to define
This creature that is so fine
She walks like a tiger even through fire
As she marches higher and higher
The day she dies you will hear my cries
Which will rise and rise till the end of times
But for now she is full of love
Just like a dove that flies high above
Chloe Serna, Grade 6

Ocean
Cool, clear, blue sea
calm and colorful
coral reefs dotted here and there
fish swim fast
streaks of color everywhere
bioluminescent plants and fish
pink, orange, green, red, and yellow
habitat for all.
Ellison Albright, Grade 4

She Had a Dog
She had a dog that was great to her.
She had a dog that protected her.
She had a dog that was white and black.
She had a dog that she loved so much.

Until one day the dog that she had
The one she loved so much
Ran away and was never found.
Hannah Pickett, Grade 4

The Girl
There is a girl
She is friendly
She is crazy
She is unique
She is smart
She is encouraging
That girl is me
Kaylee
Kaylee Brand, Grade 4

Blue
Blue is the color of the sky without a cloud
The winter is blue, misty and proud
Blue is the feeling way down low
There might be even blue playdough
Blue is the wind yelling at you
You better listen what to do
Fresh blueberries on your plate
Blue is very great
Abbie Arbogast, Grade 4

Blue
What is blue?
The Ukraine flag has blue.
Blue is the ocean that waves
    Are crashing into each other.
    Blue smells like the fresh air in the sky.
I feel excited in the airplane in the blue sky
    Going to my homeland Ukraine.
Blueberries are blue and the great blue sky.
Mykola Aleksiychuk, Grade 4

Fear
If fear were an action,
it would be
outside alone
in the pitch black

If fear were an image,
it would be
hundreds of creepy dolls
staring at you while you sleep

If fear were a sound,
it would be
a teeth chattering
unearthly shrieking

If fear were a feeling,
it would be
a brush of
cold down your spine

Fear is
terror
and
despair
Emily Seo, Grade 5

Transformations
I had long wings,
They felt like silk
I flew through the sky,
With fast dips and slow tilts

I landed in water,
And swam with the fish
I had gills like a mermaid,
Like I had always wished

I transformed into a dog,
Everything in black and white
I heard noises I've never heard before,
And I howled through the night

When I turned back into a human
I could move things with my mind
I could play the guitar with no hands,
And all my lyrics rhymed

But then I woke up,
Tucked into bed
I guess all that imagination,
Was inside my head
Vivian Oxley, Grade 6

A Silly Mouse

There once was a black and white mouse
Who lived in the wall of a house
He ate lots of cheese
And always said please
Once he got tangled up in a blouse
Jenna Balboa, Grade 5

Gymnastics

When your talent is being a gymnast
You could do a layout full twist
Bars, floor, vault, and beam
You'll compete with your team
But be careful not to hurt your wrist
Braque Looper, Grade 6

Spy Dog

There once was a spy dog in space
Who flew down to Earth in a race
He fought a mean robber
And saved his own daughter
Who thanked him for solving the case
Pierson Cazalas, Grade 5

Ode to the River

River, you are so nice.
I can splash and swim.
It is very fun.
But when I have to go I feel sad.
And when I come back, I am glad.
Kate Heestand, Grade 5

Ode to Life

Life,
Life is a good thing to live in.
Life can have sports.
Life is about having good times.
Don't let anyone bring you down.
Riley Reeves, Grade 4

Jacob

Jake is my nickname
A happy boy
Can play any sport
Outside when I can
But always sporty.
Jacob Thomas, Grade 4

Golden State

Curry is the best,
Because he makes all the shots.
In the game, he's faster than the rest.
When shooting, he makes lots
of three pointers.
Noel Serna, Grade 5

Black Bully*

I remember you, so big and mean
We ran away from you feeling like you were going to end the world
My mind used to be colorful, but now it's just black
He was pitch black, he bulldozed the land and houses
He was made out of contagious pneumonia that took you to the clouds and up with the sky
That is one big bully, my pop said
Never have we seen you, but have you trampled us
To see such a sight, caused a fright

After our fright we were calm and steady
Not knowing what's after us
The sky, you were so blue and free
Watching down at us, patrolling the sky and land
But just when everything was still, you saw something off the horizon
YOU TRIED TO WARN US BUT…then it was too late
He came after us with his knights in dust armor as hard as bones

Faster than stampeding horses
You came after us, and when you hit us we could tell who you were
He was made out of contagious pneumonia that took you to the clouds and up with the sky
He forced people to be dry and cold, to heaven and up they go
Catherine Blackstock, Grade 4
*Inspired by the events of the Dust Bowl

It Was Just a Dream

It was just a dream
Anything is possible in my dream
I spoke my own language
I was flying
I was free, a free flying spirit with no limits
No rules, just me and my dreams
My dream had trees that could speak birds with weird beaks
Music that never stopped playing, the drums bum dom bum dom bum
It was the happiest place for me
I would not want anything more but my dream
It went on for hours and never stopped
When I was tired I slept on a bed that was in my palace

I woke up and realized where I was, to the sound of screams and pain
In a place of all black
Gates blocked me from getting out
A place of sadness and anger, hatred was all over
The guards with no hearts
People with no smiles, people sent on a train and never returned
I was trapped with no hope, no drums and no music
I could not go back to my dreams, I was stuck
It was just a dream
Isabella Quaife, Grade 6

Embarrassment

Embarrassment is the laughter of pain.
It sounds like people laughing at you when you mess up.
It smells like the hate coming from the people laughing.
It tastes like the salty tears running down your cheeks.
Embarrassment feels like you want to fade away to never appear again.
Jeremiah Steib, Grade 5

Meow-Meow the Adventurer

Running in vast halls,
As if he broke the laws.

Wonder why he's running around,
Like he's on a merry-go-round.

Who is this crazy cat,
That will lay on any mat?

He loves to catch some Z's,
Hey, catch him before he leaves!

It's my pet cat Meow-Meow,
Who won't even say 'me-ow'!

Loves to chase pom-poms on the floor,
He sometimes gets them stuck under a door!

If you hear him cry,
Don't wonder why.

Don't give him food,
If he's being rude.

Natalya Garavito, Grade 6

Idaho

Idaho is a land of beauty,
Its communities are warm and inviting,
Full of mountains and forests and meadows,
The adventures are exciting.

The gem state is definitely a jewel,
Its beauty is beyond compare,
During the day the lakes and forests gleam,
While at night the stars sparkle like diamonds so rare.

New York has Lady Liberty,
Pennsylvania has Independence Hall,
But Idaho is full of natural beauty,
And that makes it the best of all.

Nathan Edvalson, Grade 6

Scissors

If I were scissors,
I would taste like metal.
I would be full of old cuts of paper.
I would like to be something else, like glue.
I'd want to see your projects that you have made with me.

If I were scissors,
I would make clean cuts.
I would wish for your forgiveness when I accidentally cut you.
I would love for you to keep me up straight.
I would listen to your ideas all day long.
I would never let you down.

Kate Daly, Grade 4

Family

Family is crazy, but nice to see
But being nice to family is always the key
They can be nice, funny, or mean
But you can be the one that can be the
positive one in the group

But won't you be grateful for who you have?
They might surprise you in the long run
There are people that understand you
So just give them a chance they're your family
Family is the most important thing in the world

You can go on family trips
Even for your birthday they will be there too
My cousins and I have so much fun together
Doing many things like
Drawing, playing, and having parties for no reason

Once you are with family
You will have a great time
Have fun and you will be fine
And be grateful for all your
Happy family

Katelhyn Garcia, Grade 4

An Invitation from a Wolf

Come on over

Come run with us
Taste
The fresh air
On your big panting tongue
Feel
The dirt between your toes as you run
Listen
To the birds chirping and the grass go crunch
Smell
The moose that is eating the grass, it's your lunch
See
The wonderful world, because you are missing out

Marianne Cliff, Grade 4

Those Feelings You Have

I'm happy you see.
I'm excited for lots of things.
I'm proud of everybody in my family.
Sometimes I'm anxious to get what I want.
I get mad at people, sound, or things that get on my nerves.
I get hungry when I don't get fed.
I get sad when people pass away, but I get over it anyway.
I get playful for when people play with me.
I get scared when people scare me.
I get greedy with the things I like.
I love people who love me back.
Aren't those the feelings you have?

Xavier Marsh, Grade 5

Summer Sun

Under summer sun
Our feet dance
On yellow sand
Sounds of waves
Break
Silence
As sunset begins
Fun ends
Only beginning another day
Over again
Arrive home
Laying in bed
Imagining
Stars dancing in my head
Isabella Pope, Grade 6

My Aussie Shepherd

My Aussie is so cute.
Possibly the cutest one in Butte.
He is six months old.
He's probably worth more than gold!

I love my dog to death.
But he sure does have stinky breath!
My dog's name is Charlie.
Sometimes his fur is a little snarly.

Great Falls is his birthplace.
He likes to lick your face.
One time Charlie caught a groundhog.
I sure do love my dog!
Meredith Varady, Grade 5

The Super

Superman our hero
the man of steel
soaring like a bird in the sky
flies at the speed of sound

Lex Luther foe not friend
made this green crystal
kryptonite bright, glowing, powerful subject
he uses this to weaken him

but with his friends
the justice league, lives in the watchtower
they protect and serve the world
as they fight crime
Evan Michel, Grade 6

Zombies

Zombies are scary
Diseases they carry
Because they are undead
They need to be fed.
Alejandro Cedillo, Grade 5

The Ocean

The summer breeze
Gently fingers my hair.
I look at the ocean; what do I see?
Only you and only me.
I get my board, wetsuit and all.
Then run to the beach
On this lovely, lovely day.
Paddling out to the deep,
A wave chases me like thunder.
Whoosh, I dive under,
Where all is silent.
Then come back to try again
And ride this one in.
My eyes close and open.
The ocean is what I see.
It's a joy for you and a joy for me.
Matthew Hamel, Grade 6

A Special Place

Sometimes I close my eyes
And think of a place,
Not just any place,
My place.
Somewhere far away
Where no stress,
Or negativity,
Can find me.
Somewhere where no matter what,
Nothing is impossible.
So, when I feel sad,
Or hurt,
I think of this place,
Because in my place,
Sadness doesn't exist.
This is my happy place.
Katie Mitchell, Grade 6

Happiness Is the Little Things

Happiness is fruit and whipped cream,
A fresh picked apple,
Caramelized fruit.

Happiness is something that gleams,
Being on stage for the very first time.

Happiness is writing a poem,
Saying "I know him",
Reading a book.

Happiness is a choice,
A choice you make,
So use your voice.

Happiness is the little things!
Brittany Birmingham, Grade 6

Oh the Sky

Oh the sky,
It's so big,
It's so high
Oh the sky,
Can you fit it
in your arms?
Can you fly?
Oh the sky,
Let your angels fly,
from the heaven,
to the sky,
on to beautiful earth
Oh the sky,
It's so high
Can you fit it
in your arms?
Can you fly?
Oh the sky
Sarah Golovey, Grade 5

Ode to Beauty

Beauty, perfection, to be lovely
all long for you
those who have it want more,
those who desire you
will do anything
to achieve their perfection

Few will covet you
while you last
many try to preserve you
but beauty is random,
lucky,
blessed upon
in any way seem fit

Beauty
is ever changing
never lasting
Teah LeBlanc, Grade 6

My Lovely Mother

You mean so much to me
That I can see
I'm so lucky to have you
As my mother
Offering me good advice
Keeping me on the right track
You have always been there for me
Throughout all of my hardships and strife
You have taught me so much
About getting through my daily life
You mean so much to me
That I thought you should always know
I love you so much!!!
Huda Ahmed, Grade 6

The Wanderer

Wandering,
Like a seed from a puffy dandelion
Blowing in the wind

Like a lazy shepherd in clover fields,
Meandering in the sun

Like a green glass bottle pushed by foamy waters
Bobbing in the sea

I am a wandering soul, leaving footprints in the hills,
Where grass grows green and eyes grow dull

I never stop to rest, roaming wild and free,
As unbridled ponies on desert shores,
Their manes rippling in the breeze

I have walked to the ends of the Earth and back
And have seen the Dawns and Twilights
Of another life

I could play Hide and Seek
With Purposes and Answers;
Yet I will choose to be content with the arts of wonder and wander.

Xi An Niles, Grade 6

Life

Life is like a river
It flows by slowly sometimes and other times it speeds up
You never know what's around the next corner
It may be calm or it could be rocky
Once you pass one point you can't go back

Life is like a game
Making memories is the prize
While playing is all of your life
Once it ends you look back and see all you have done
Good or bad its all ours

Life is all about letting bad things go by
And letting good things last
If you are mean, people are going to remember
And it's going to come right back to you
Just like a boomerang

If you let time fly by and be moody you'll be gone in a flash
Just like lighting, it stays in a flash like how you let your life end
Savor the moments and don't waste it
Do all the fun things
Before it ends
And there's no coming back

Cayden Murphy, Grade 4

Fox

Foxes living in the woodlands
Why don't you live near the beaches' sands?
With your fur so very bright
Why do your eyes glitter and gleam in the night?

Moving as fast as a flash
Why are your paws as black as ash?
Why do you sometimes not even show?
How come your tail's tip is as white as snow?

Why do you frolic near the trees?
How hard do you try to avoid honey bees?
Why are you so very shy?
How are you so wise and sly?

Why are you up so late at night?
How long do you wait for something to bite?
Why do you frolic then suddenly leap?
Is it to catch your prey as they are asleep?

How long are you with your kits?
Do you feed them little animal bits?
Why are you as quiet as a mouse?
Are there ever times where you wander around the house?

Larissa Aul, Grade 4

Heaven Is for Real

When you get old, you go somewhere.
Whether you're good or bad,
You will go, young or old.
When you go, you might be sad.

You may ask why…
Why is it me?
People will miss you,
But when you find the man upstairs you will see.

There will be people,
Just waiting there for you,
But you will wait for people too.
Your life must have been through.

It is OK to go,
You can cry.
Because you love people and they love you,
You can be an angel and you will fly.

One day you will find,
You will go to the light,
God is waiting for you,
He is waiting for you to take flight.

Sean Mathews, Grade 5

Ponds

Ponds have small and big fish.
Some are even shaped like a dish.
Silently the wind blows by.
As fast as lightning flies a dragonfly.
Even ducks flying with their wings.
Brown and green feathers in the air.
They just fly without a care.
Some animals like to jump and leap.
While others prefer to stay in the deep.
Ethan Shaw, Grade 6

Yellow Wave

She appears very bright,
as the sunset nears night.
She feels very mellow,
Dressed in waves of yellow.

Light like a butterfly,
yet she won't fly quite as high.
Presented as decoration,
all across the American nation.
Thobe Moeller, Grade 6

A Black Day

It was a blue day.
Smiles on everyone's face.

And before you know it,
The wind was coming to you.
It was like the a tornado with dust.
No one can see the darkness coming.
People were shocked.
We could not see it.
Jisselle Williams, Grade 4

Sad

Why am I here?
I feel like I don't belong.
I try to look deep inside,
But there's nothing there.

I never feel good about myself
I wish my dad would walk,
Then I would smile.
Olivia Johnson, Grade 4

The Lion

Prowling in the moonlight
Thy mane shining bright
Creatures scared of the king
Opening his mouth of blades
Is the king close to the kitten?
Curling up to go to sleep
Purring in the moonlight
For this moment is to keep.
Mimi Clot de Broissia, Grade 6

Every Poem Has a Hand

Every poem has a hand,
That reaches out towards me.
Some twist my lips into a smile
And some just make me sob.
Yet others reach right to my mind
And inspire me to do more.
When I am feeling down,
They pick me up and lift me high.
Most poems' hands do all of these,
But they also do much more.
They reach their fingers right
Through me, and
Warm my heart with their gentle touch.
Ishika Bhasin, Grade 6

Life

A mystery it is
But beautiful
As we live it through
No matter what
It always comes
And never leaves
It stays with us
Through dark and light
Like it or not
It stays with you, until you die
Then it is
Your soul
Life
Morgan Christopherson, Grade 5

Haunted House

There is a haunted house you see,
And it is very frightening to me.
Every day I hear a scream
And ghosts fly out the window and sing.
The house is very old,
And painted red which is very bold.
The windows are cracked,
And the doors are stacked.
It is always cold,
The walls are covered with mold
There is a haunted house you see,
And it is very frightening to me.
Grace Henry, Grade 4

Wishes for Riches

I wish, I dream, and my wishes and
dreams gleam.
I wish for gold.
I dream for silver.
I wish I had a golden silver.

Wishing is good, and dreaming is great, but
having is awesome. It's really first rate!
Kayla Bryant, Grade 4

Her...

She
walks by
like nothing,
always keeping
the feelings
inside her,
even though
she's not
feeling it today.
I can feel
her tantrums
from miles away.
I don't know
What's stopping
her from
coming home,
hopefully she'll
make it out there
and we won't
end up at another
funeral home.
Samantha Gomez, Grade 6

Stars

Little white lights
High in the sky
Glistening and slowly migrating
Across the ocean of darkness.
Whispering from above,
They lure you in their charm
And dance with you
And sing with you
And you forget your worries,
All your losses,
All your failures.
You're just happy.
Perfectly happy,
And you spend the night that way.
Leaping, running underneath the stars.
The stars that charm you, enchant you,
Change you.
The constellations that rotate your life.
The stars
That are so far
And yet so close.
Varya Buben, Grade 6

Light Will Not Always Shine

Light
Bright, great
Guiding, helping, cleaning
Light will not always shine
Depressing, dream-crushing, saddening
Dark, scary
Darkness
Julian Delorme, Grade 6

Trees

Trees all around
the green forest
rain falls everyday
vines all around
the trees.

One odd plant around
flies are caught in this plant
chomped down like
an alligator, it makes
the fly into paste

A smoothie like
paste is what
they eat
raw meat is one of their colors

It is a living plant
flies caught in a
sticky mess
they can be tall
Julian Beresky, Grade 4

Believe in Yourself

Everyone was looking
At me I was so frightened
So I just said something

"Ding" the judges
Hit the bell
It was right
I was so surprised
My mouth dropped
And that meant
We were in the finals

No one knew our team
Would make it this far
But I believed

I was so excited
But I wouldn't
Get my hopes
Up but I still believed
We would win
Mark Koehler, Grade 6

Free

With the wind in my hair, I knew I was free.
I swam in the ocean, as happy as I could be.
I swat away bugs as I trek through the rain.
My heart beating, I struggle with strain.
As I crawl with despairity through the desert.
With mud up my shirt, I spit out dirt.
    Maybe it's not so good to be free.
Jack Bengston, Grade 6

The Ocean

Splish, splash
Water
Crashing onto the
Sandy shore

Feet climbing
Into the
Blazing water

Creating sand castles
Out of wet
Sand

Munch, munch
Eating freezing cold
Ice cream
On a scorching
Hot day
Hear that
That's the sound of
fun!
Maya Warner, Grade 4

Life Hurts

Life hurts
You ruin my smile
Just with one word
It hurts me inside
Even though I'm disabled
Doesn't mean I'm not smart
It offends me
Tears run down my cheeks
Don't laugh at me
Treat people just like
You would want to be treated
Don't try to make my smile disappear
You don't bother me anymore
I've learned
I'm one of a kind
Special and intelligent
I am who I am
God created me this way
I'm God's creation
That makes me special
In many ways
Breanna Watson, Grade 6

Birds

Chirp, chirp, what's that sound?
It's a bird, looking for food on the ground
Their colors are red, yellow, and blue
Some are bold
Others are old
Some are new
Just for you
Micah Miramontes-Taylor, Grade 4

Nature During the Night

As the wind was blowing,
Fireflies were glowing.
Where there stood a big oak tree,
It had smiled with glee.

As the bear was asleep,
A bird made a peep.
When the fish would swim,
The night's light would be dim.

When the mouse was small as a toy block,
It stood on a gray rock.
As a spider hunted for prey,
It was almost turning day.
Marisol Chamberlain, Grade 6

My World

If I were in charge of the world,
I'd eat
ice cream and
junk food.
If I were in charge of the world,
there's be unicorns,
fairies, and
minions.
If I were in charge of the world,
you wouldn't be bored.
You wouldn't be bullied.
you wouldn't be sad
or get scared.
If I were in charge of the world.
Rebecca Nguyen, Grade 6

Spring

Oh Spring, Oh Spring
you have flowers to bring.
You're always so fun
to play with under the sun.

Oh Spring, Oh Spring
What do you have to bring?
Roses and Lilies
You're so silly.

On the last day of spring
I will want you to bring
laughter, love, and joy
next year I will be much more.
Isabella Suseno, Grade 4

Dogs

I have a dog
That plays in the fog.
He likes to chase our car,
But not too far.
Angel Hernandez, Grade 5

Game vs Family
In my house I am the odd duck
I am the one that is stuck
While they're playing games
I wait until dinner because
That's the time we're together.
Linus Scheibmeir, Grade 4

Free
The wind is like hair
Waving gracefully
Back and forth
Then it dies down
Like the end of the world
Daniel Valle, Grade 4

Soccer
Soccer
Fast, slow
Kicking, running, walking
Kick that ball so hard
Sphere
Hallie Taylor, Grade 4

Hummingbirds
Hungry hummingbirds hurry, flashing fast
Twittering tongues, tiny wings zipping past
Finding nectar so sweet
Buzzing in speedy beat
Bird watchers are spying in a mass
Alexis Alaniz, Grade 6

The Night!
There once was a bright light
Shimmering in the dark night
Then there was a bang
That sounded like a clang
And everyone woke with such a fright
Aracely Salazar, Grade 5

Chess
Chess is fun
Chess is challenging
Chess is a thinking game
Chess is a game for you
Chess is a great sport
Gavin Rios, Grade 4

Pears
Pears are all sorts of colors…
green, yellow, any color
that come into your imagination.
They taste so good when you eat them,
your taste buds begin to have a party.
Jesus Lerma, Grade 4

K-9s
Dogs, showing their love when you are sad
At your side whenever you start to feel alone
Always there when you need someone to hug
Always glad to treasure you with licks of love

All they want is your love, a little attention, and protection
Throw a ball, give them a pet, or even a talk
Dogs seem to listen, understand, and know your thoughts
If people are so smart, why can't they be more like dogs

There are all kinds of dogs, fit for each owner's personality
How did I get my dog Bonsai
She loves running, playing, and being with our family
My brothers are different, she loves us in different ways

My hope is that everybody will be able to have their own dog
We are lucky because when we are sad, lonely and happy
We always have what's called man's best friend
My wish is for everybody to have a dog never mind I'll just keep my dog

I LOVE MY DOG
Lorenzo Tamez, Grade 5

The Delight Song
I am the farthest branch on the tree in the fall
I am a blue dog that runs around in the fields
I am the lion that roars when he's angry in the world
I am the bird that follows the sun, I am the day, the light of the sun
I am a mouse playing with the cheese
I am a cluster of a wolf's head
I am the farthest star
I am the cold of the wind
I am the whistle of the forest
I am the glitter of the ice
I am the long snake of the forest in the light side
I am the peacock of four colors, I am a hyena that laughs away in the wild
I am a field of grass and trees
I am a group of wolves of night in the dark forest
I am the hunger of a sad child, I am the whole myself of these things
You see, I am alive, I am alive
I stand in good relation to my family
I stand in good relation to my friends
I stand in good relation to my God
I stand in good relation to myself
You see, I am alive, I am alive
Omar Tovar, Grade 6

Poems
A poem is something you read
It can be something to lift your spirits
They can be short like baby's finger
Some can be long like the highway you drive on all night long
Some can be sad and others just downright depressing
Some can be happy and fill your day with joy
But one thing they all have in common is that they are written to be read
Emilee Sirdoreus, Grade 4

Summertime

S ports are great fun
U ntil summer ends I am happy
M ight go hiking
M ud is wet and sticky
E very day we have fun
R iding dirt bikes is my favorite thing to do
T rack and field begins
I gloos are all melted
M owing grass is not fun
E very day we have to do chores

Hayden Rector, Grade 5

New School

N obody knows me
E ntertaining games outside
W indy River Elementary School

S trangers walking through the halls
C rossing roads to go to school
H earing students learn
O bjectives that impress me
O ther new students coming in
L oud bell that scares you when it rings.

Lizbeth Rios, Grade 6

Dylan Dann–Me

D ecently smart
Y eller of stuff
L iar (not)
A wesome
N ice

D ying a shirt
A mazing
N uts for nuts
N eed for speed

Dylan Dann, Grade 5

The World

The curve of the world,
the rock on the ground,
the waters in the oceans,
and the sky of blue.
The chatter of humans,
the buzz of electricity,
the rumble of thunder,
and the crack of lighting.
These things are the world,
and that is very pleasant.

Brady Stroud, Grade 6

Horses

Strong but sweet they are
Their manes flowing in the wind
Large hooves leaving tracks

Karly Trupiano, Grade 6

Ode to Sleep

I'm Asleep
I'm in your trance

That trance you're making, is my dreams
Dreams become my imagination

My imagination becomes whatever I want
I'm still sleeping
I'm still in your trance, until my body tells me to wake up.

I'm thinking about my dreams,
Wishing I was still there.

Once I'm back in my bed,
My dreams are waiting for me.
I go back to sleep, I'm so close I can feel it!
I'm back in that trance, I feel my imagination getting overpowered.
It's working! I'm back to sleep.

Those dreams of mine are so opalescent,
Sometimes I make those vibrant colors feel onyx, like the blanket of night in the sky.
It makes me feel like I'm camping. I like that feeling. My dreams change.

Dreams become more vibrant than before, not onyx like the blanket in the night sky,
It's almost morning, I can feel the bright sunshine through the blankets of my bed.
My face feels warm. I'm waking up. I open my eyes and see my wonderful room.

It feels good to be back in the real world, sometimes.

Chase Weiss, Grade 6

Energy Wheel

Surprised
Surprised is yellow like the sun rising out in the morning.
It runs in my room like a monster coming to eat you.
It reminds me of the time when I had to put my hands over my head
To shield the bright sun.
It makes me want to get up in the morning.

Excited
Excited is blue like the ocean water.
It pumps me up when I am in the finals in a soccer tournament.
It reminds me of the time when I got epically barreled in an awesome wave.
It makes me want to live at the beach.

Furious
Furious is red like a fire coming out of the earth.
It hits my stomach like a punch coming at me.
It makes me feel very mad and angry.
It makes me want to pull out my hair.

Calm
Calm is green like the grass in the middle of the day.
It drifts over me like wind over me.
It makes me feel like I'm a floating wave.
It reminds me of a beautiful sunset.

Harris Feinman, Grade 5

The World
The sky has lost his color.
The streets have faded away.
Nobody has color in their faces.
It's a black and white movie.
For some reason I remember this jewel in the sky smiling at me.
It's color was gold, but since then I've long forgotten what the color gold was.
I remember the beach, oh, it was so wonderful.
The water was so steady and so calm, just like a stream.
It was cool and crystal blue.
The sky has lost his color.
The streets have faded away.
The Ferris wheel has no more color.
It used to be as bright as the sun.
But now its bright eyes have closed for now, for good.
But every time my head hits the pillow and I close my eyes, I see this place bright and colorful.
I have to walk many miles to get to this place, but every time I reach this place, I wake up to a world of gray.
The sky has lost his color.
The streets have faded away.

Veronica Guzman, Grade 6

The Gloomy Sights
I am the mountain, serene and ecstatic.
Seeing all my sisters and the creatures rouse from the beaming sun.
It's Spring,
Humans dig their grappling hooks on my rocks, trees, cliffs and even on my noggin.
Newborn fawns with white, speckled blotches getting the hang of walking, not wobbling.
All is well, until thunder awakens.
Mortals tumble onto my rigid base and take off into the clouds.
Anteaters, porcupines, and gorillas, all tremor, hoping to find shelter or anything to ensconce under from the almighty Zeus.
Although this terrifies my younger siblings, I have experienced this rare occasion and appear to be satisfied.
Suddenly, . . . CRASH! BOOM! CRACKLE! . . .
Trees and animals devoured by the rapid oxidation lit by the Heavens.
I savor scorched minerals flying in the air.
At last, this war between destruction and my fellow citizens end.
After all this, there's no change with my innovation with the deaths of these souls because I knew this day would
eventually come and that I cannot do anything about it, just like how my day would soon come.
For I have been existing for millions of years, observing the idea of life and death is common,
so I will always be beaming on the inside knowing that they would come again soon.
I am the mountain, serene and ecstatic.

Yuna Song, Grade 6

Winter
Winter is a beautiful time of year.
Snow is like angels falling from the sky.
It is also when Christmas comes around.
Red and green decorations all over the city.
Snuggling on the couch with family watching a Christmas movie eating gingerbread cookies and drinking hot chocolate.
Snowball fights with your friends.
Making snowmen and dressing them up, going to bed on Christmas Eve.
Waking up in the morning knowing that Santa came.
Going to your parents room and waking them up, opening presents after eating breakfast.
Watching movies and playing with your presents.
This is why I love winter.
HO HO HO and Merry Christmas!

Madelynn Arvizu Arvizu, Grade 5

Tuukka

Tuukka my sweet dog
You want to hug him a ton
He will snuggle you all night
You will play with him
Forever you will love him
Tuukka will miss you so much
Margaret Miller, Grade 4

Winter Snow

Watching children play outside,
Looking at them slip and slide,
Frosty, icy, gentle snow,
It can be friendly, and also a foe,
Looking at children sled down hills,
Snow drifting down like dollar bills.
Jack Cimo, Grade 4

Nature

N ever leave a campfire burning
A tiger hunts
T he hawks that fight in flight
U nderwater there are sea creatures
R emember there's animals every where
E very animal does its part in nature
Kevin Sanderson, Grade 4

Sprite

S uper
P owerful
R efreshing
I ntense
T ough
E xotic
Joe Weaver, Grade 4

Family

With all the hurt and pain,
The family came together.
With all the stress,
The family came together.
Everyone is different,
But they all come together.
Aleena Martinez, Grade 4

Wesley

Wesley likes to run but needs to speed
Wesley speeds for a need
When he gets there he sees Mrs. Sneed

She gives him a potion for speed
He drinks the potion for the speed he needs
Wesley Stinemetze, Grade 4

Aqua

Aqua is a happy, calm beach in Hawaii that I see while riding a cruise
Aqua is the cold, arctic snow in the large iceberg floating and bobbing in the bay
Aqua is the coral underneath the shore of Casablanca, Morocco
Aqua is the summit high above the earth, around the peak of Everest
Aqua smells like a blooming blue bell flowering the spring
Aqua tastes like sticky cotton candy at the county carnival fair
Aqua sounds like a serene, gentle breeze on a cool night
Aqua looks like the Australian waters at sunset
Aqua feels like a bright, blue day at the beach
Aqua makes me want to take a swim in the pool at the resort
Aqua is a shining, sparkling topaz gemstone in a case at the museum
Aqua is my favorite color
Hafsa Erfan, Grade 5

Friendship

Friendship is a word that can't be explained in many ways.
It has an impact on you like no other feeling.
Some people don't have a bond that goes as deep as a friend.
But if you do have a friend that you trust you know that special feeling.
Friendship is one of those things you think keeps the world at peace.
Friendship can be as deep as the ocean.
This is how special this bond can be!
It has the power to change something in another person's life!
If everyone made friends, there would be harmony in the world.
Now that's a powerful thing!
This bond has some struggles, but in the end you can resolve it.
And that's true friendship.
Marcus Ragin, Grade 6

Brothers

Brothers.
Brothers little or big will follow in your footsteps.
Brothers.
Brothers little or big look at you for advice.
Brothers.
Brothers little or big play with you.
Brothers.
Brothers little or big will take care of you.
Brothers.
Brothers little or big will bully you but all in all you love your brothers.
It may be hard to not fight but all in all you love your brother.
Gabriel Hart, Grade 5

Happiness Unhappiness

Happiness is seeing your grandpa.
Unhappiness is hearing your grandpa snore all night.

Happiness is eating ice cream.
Unhappiness is going to the bathroom and coming back to find it melted.

Happiness is reading.
Unhappiness is someone telling you the end of the book.

Happiness is getting a new house.
Unhappiness is it's too big for me.
Emma Jean Hepworth, Grade 4

Roses

Little Red
Sitting in the vase
I watch you walk down the aisle
Bees fly around the bush I live in
Pink and white too
I am never blue
I hope you like me too
Darian Keeney, Grade 5

Fear

Fear seems midnight black
Like the dark shadows of wolves.
I see the ghosts across the forest.
I hear Mother Nature's animals screeching.
I smell the smoke ripping through the sky.
I touch the thorny branches.
I taste the black fog.
Teely Manor, Grade 4

Happiness

Happiness seems bubble gum pink.
Like kids in a candy store.
I see children playing tag.
I hear creaking swings.
I smell delicious milk chocolate.
I touch Milky Ways.
I taste joy.
Eli DelaFuente, Grade 4

My Parents on Christmas

My
Parents
work too hard
for one thing and
it is to make me happy
All I want this Christmas is
happiness.
Bryana Balderas, Grade 6

Kittens

Kittens are as sweet as cupcakes.
There as funny as a dog chasing it's tail.
There as soft as a puffy jacket.
Kittens are as energetic like a wild child.
Kittens are as sneaky as a spy.
Kittens are as charming as a diamond.
They're like a big heart.
Marcie Dumont, Grade 4

Super Pals

There once was a boy named Mark
Who was friends with a man from the park
Who lived in a tower
And was rich with power
They called him Tony Stark
Gavin Nunez, Grade 5

Come to the Lake, Come

Come to the lake, come. Look at the cool, blue, clear water.
Come see the trout hiding in the seaweed,
Go behind the bubble curtain to get a gulp of oxygen,
Look as the fallen tree branches fall into the lake.
The current washes away the trout eggshells,
See dead logs resting in the water making a safe place for fish to hide.

Come to the lake, come. Look at the eyed eggs laying on the lake bed.
Come see the alevins with their yolk sacs hanging from their belly,
See the alevins button up and turn into fry.
See the fry swim as fast as lightning, look at fry turn into big trout.
See the big trout jump as high as the sky.

Come to the lake, come. See the kingfisher fishing for trout,
Look at the trout jumping high in the air catching dragonflies in their mouth.
Go under water and see otters chasing trout.
Look at big trout devour smaller trout. See the water scorpion snatching trout.
Look at trout eating spiders.
See the trout spawn.
Come to the lake, come.
Jordan Camacho Mora, Grade 4

I Am From...

I am from a house
with an electric keyboard sitting peacefully in the study room
with a simple and ordinary closet full of coats
with a wooden table with framed pictures

I am from a yard
where there is a wooden fence to protect us from outsiders
where there are trees with green leaves and living plant life

I am from a neighborhood
that has Karen's beat up white Camry
Conner's tangled up swing
Raya's basketball hoop

I am from a family
of Uncle John who mends bones
of Grandma Ruth who visits me from the Windy City
of Grandma Kathryn and Grandpa Ray who watch over me peacefully in heaven

These are the places where I am From.
Ryan Olenyn, Grade 5

As the Wind Turned Ahead

As the wind turned ahead all the people fled in fear.
Then came a whoosh and none were near.
Two came out and gave a shout.
So they all turned their heads, looked and said
the wind has gone ahead.
The pets howled, the children sang and all must not be near.
For all the men and all the women stopped and sang again.
For they were at last,
The breaths and sorrows still borrowed from the wind that turned ahead.
Kira Rose, Grade 5

Spring

As I walk outside
It starts to rain above me
I see a rainbow
Lis De Sa Fonseca, Grade 5

Grandma

Grandma you're so sweet
The most fun times I ever had
Hope you rest in peace
Brayden Sparks, Grade 5

Dolphins

Dolphins swimming far
So baby blue in water
Coming up to play
Flora Eldredge, Grade 5

Turks and Caicos

Waves crash against me
Standing on the beach
I breathe in calm air
Anna Reinink, Grade 5

The Bird

The bird soars overhead
Its shadow ripples on lakes
As it glides softly
Emily Ballard, Grade 5

Ladybug

Ladybug in spring
Beautiful colorful wings
Are colorful too
Jonathan Bernal, Grade 4

Horses

Galloping horses
Racing to the apple trees
To get juicy snacks
Matthew York, Grade 4

Polar Bears

In the freezing wind
Polar bears play on the ice
Happily sliding
Adrian Rojas, Grade 4

Fish

Across the ocean
Deep in the water fish swim
Around the old boat
Yenis Ramirez, Grade 4

How to Write a Regular Poem

This is my poem, a poem about poems,
on how to properly write a regular poem.

When you write your poems, if you follow my directions,
they will be surprisingly fabulous!

First get a paragraph down, get it flying out of your mouth,
and get those words to sit on a paper or a doc.

Make sure it has figurative language, like idioms,
or similes or metaphors or personification.

Edit your paragraph to make it nice and neat, and go beyond the limits,
so that it can't be beat!

Then make the words rhyme, in a catchy catchy time,
with synonyms and reworded sentences.

Then transform your paragraph into stanzas, so it's truly a poem,
and now it has qualification!

So read over it to make sure you're done, and now you're done!
Turn it in, take your time, and just wait 'till you WIN!

That's how you win using my steps, originally written by me,
and since this poem zoomed through these directions itself...

The End!
Aishvarya Dhamodharan, Grade 4

A Journey Across the Atlantic

The engine grew louder and louder,
The wind blew my hair and whipped my cheeks.
My face turned redder as I flew,
Across the Atlantic Ocean.

I looked back down at the world beneath,
I had faith,
And this time, it won't escape me.
My faith and belief grew stronger and stronger as I crossed the Atlantic Ocean.

At first when I started the adventure,
I was filled with determination,
But now that I've tried,
I know how great it is,
To finally be set free across the Atlantic Ocean.

No one can stop me, nor change my mind,
I will do this only once, I should remember
The journey across the Atlantic Ocean.

It was a one of a kind adventure. Oh, it was quite grand.

Can you guess who I am?
I am Amelia Earhart.
Anais Sobrier, Grade 4

From Korea to America

I'm from Korea to America
through vast oceans and seas
a world of difference

I'm from books to the library
J.K. Rowling, James Patterson, and Rick Riordan
From classics to fairy tales, I read them all

I'm from music to concertos
Beethoven, Taylor Swift, and Bach
a harmonious melody all mashed together

I'm from sibling rivalry
to fights and forts
with my sisters gentle smile and my brothers laugh

I'm from swimming and the pool
with chlorine smelling hair, friends, and practices galore

I'm from delicious foods to restaurants
miso soup, cheeseburgers, and stew
All combined into a glorious heaven of delicious food

I have my past
but what is in the future I cannot tell
I'm looking at the road
waiting to see what life has carved for me

Yelin Tahk, Grade 6

Ice Skating

If this moment were to last forever, skating on the ice,
I would gladly spend it with you, paying any sort of price.
The silver blades are gleaming,
Sparkling hair is streaming,
Everyone is beaming as they slide across the ice.

Everyone is zipping in a blurry flash of tint,
Hoping for some hot cocoa, with a hint of peppermint.
Beanies, long socks, mittens too,
Without my coat I would turn blue.
Scarves, gloves, hats and boots,
Our love for winter is absolute.

Boys play rowdily with their pucks and hockey sticks,
While the girls are cautious, making sure the ice is thick.
Parents sipping cider as they watched the children play,
Whoever could have dreamed of a more beautiful day?
Everything is perfect, like a Christmas window on display.

And now I'm regretting leaving a time such as that,
While I'm staring at a photograph with ice skating acrobats.
Ah, the ice was like a gigantic mirror for everyone to see,
And everyone was holding hands as they skated with endless glee.
Yes, you have to agree,
The rink is just the perfect place for a girl like me.

Sarah Carr, Grade 6

Decisions

Life is a menu
You see all the choices
You see the opportunities on the page
You just have to go out and CHOOSE what looks good
What you think you can succeed at
What you think you can handle
You just have to make the CHOICE

Life is a menu
Just CHOOSE
And pray it works out for the best
Because you know you'll end up paying for your
DECISIONS
It's just a matter of how much

Because Life is a menu
Just CHOOSE
And pray that what happens
Will be for the best

Daniel Creager, Grade 6

Bullies

Bullies are mean and bad
and sometimes very mad
they'll kick and punch
and normally do it at lunch

Some kids are afraid to stand up
so when you see one don't close up
go over and yell, "stop!"
stop being mean and stop being a swamp

Bullies can be nice in some ways
they have their good and their bad days
do you know what makes a bully a bully?
Maybe it happens at home with family

If you see a bully coming your way
go toward don't hide away
today is the day to stand up, it's the day
once it's all over you're free to play, play, play

Ella Heitmeyer, Grade 5

Stormy Beach

Whoosh, the wind blows calmly in my face.
Swoosh, the water gently ripples onto the beach.
Crash, the waves smash into each other.
Rumble, the thunder sounds.
Smack, the lightening hits.
Splash, the waves hit me hard.
Crash, splash, smack, rumble.
Blub, blub, blub silence.
I see a bright light.
Angels singing songs.
I see God's loving face.

Ashley Holcomb, Grade 6

Life

Life is everything
Life is what's outside your door
Life is you and me
Mia Grasse, Grade 5

Summer

The summer sun beats
Down on the dead, blue flower
Until it blossoms.
Aidan Jensen, Grade 6

Paper Crane

I make the last fold.
The paper crane spreads its wings,
Preparing for flight.
Annalisa King, Grade 6

Meadow

Cherry blossoms bud
Ants raid the picnic's great food
Meadows full of life
Aharon Suri, Grade 4

Mountains

Breathtaking views,
Climbing high into the sun,
Majestic wonders.
Pooja Rajaram, Grade 5

Cherry Tree

Big, red, ripe, cherry
Hanging on the tree so high
Waiting to be picked
Alejandro Ramos, Grade 6

Nature's Beauty

The iris is white
Its petals are very soft
It's a lovely scene.
Sugopi Palakala, Grade 6

Snowflake

Flowing gently down
Creating shadows in snow
Soft, small, beautiful
Addison Mitchell, Grade 4

Cheetah

Quick and graceful strides
Beware, going for the kill
Creeps up on its prey
Arin Budhiraja, Grade 4

Springtime

The temperature is rising,
Snow is melting,
Birds are chirping,
Flowers are blooming,
And leaves are turning green.

Children are playing,
Bears are awaking,
And songbirds are singing,
As joy fills the air.

The beautiful flowers glisten after early morning showers,
With dew drops like pearls running down stems.
The beautiful flowers flourish in large clusters bigger than bouquets,
Spreading their lovely fragrance.

The days are longer,
And there's a light, warm breeze.
The seasons are definitely changing,
Springtime is finally here.
Nico Martinez, Grade 6

Hidden Gems

I look at these plastic women —
Why am I not like them?
Come at me with your worst!
They are talented and
I am not a hero.
People suffer, differ from the rest.
I was not born a hero —
I was born my mom's child and
She is my hero.
I will grow to my full potential. That is who I am.
I suffer but I differ and
I cry and time passes by.
These women are not real —
They are just here to steal the spotlight from the hidden gems.
Pretty hurts but we still live.
Men and women share the same strength but men are given more faith.
Black or white, Mexican or Asian, man or woman
My looks don't define me.
I am a sparkling gem —
Too bad for them.
Alexandra Lewis, Grade 5

White

White is the color of snowflakes falling from the sky
White is arctic fox in the winter
White is snowshoe bunnies hopping in the woods
White is snow shining on the ground on a winter's eve
White is a marshmallow melting in your mouth, one piece by one piece
White is the sound of a snowy owl hooting
While is a pearl that you wear on your wrist or your neck
White is a sparkler lighting the way on the Fourth of July
White is the noise of a waterfall tumbling down a mountain.
Emily Sanchez Malagon, Grade 4

Winter

Winter, cold as ice,
Cold, cold as ice, frigid cold,
Do you like winter?
Shreya Gupta, Grade 6

Snow Fall

Little dots of cold
Falling from the bright blue sky
Kids coming to play
Valerie Negrete, Grade 6

Oceans

All oceans are deep
Oceans go on for miles
Fish have their homes there
Paris Leverett, Grade 6

Succeed

The sun
The sea,
They'll guide you to succeed.
James Cruz, Grade 6

Springtime

Sun shines on your face
Time that the flowers can bloom
Bright blue sky above
Kaydence Mayse, Grade 6

My Dog Lyric

Running in the snow,
using your nose as a plow,
and sniffing the fire!
Ryan Whitten, Grade 6

The Woods

The trees are pretty
All the trees look different
The wind is howling
Dani Hammond, Grade 6

Life

Death is the Road
Life is the Traveler
Our Soul is our Guide
Delaney Matthews, Grade 6

Fire and Water

With its pure gold flames
Blue matches red with full force
Fire or water wins
Morgan Day, Grade 4

Delight Song

I am a book on the shelf
I am a black wolf that cares for its pups on the grassy meadow
I am the wolf that roars the night away
I am the evil that follows the good
I am the midnight, the darkest spot in the sky
I am the dragon playing with the people
I am a group of good books
I am the farthest book on the shelf, I am the coldness of the snow
I am the howling of the wolf, I am the glitter on the snow
I am the long wave of the ocean on the sea, I am the flame of four colors
I am a bunny hopping away through the meadow
I am a field of darkness and dragons
I am a pack of wolves on the coldest snow of Alaska
I have the hunger of flames from a dragon
I am the whole darkness of these things

You see, I am alive, I am alive
I stand in good relation with my comrades
I stand in good relation with lovely nature
I stand in good relation with all animals
I stand in good relation with my family
You see, I am alive, I am alive
Melanie Salazar, Grade 6

I Am Abby

I am a sensitive and playful girl.
I wonder what he world would be like if there was no technology.
I hear footsteps in the hallway in the middle of the night, but it's my sister.
I see when I come home, my mom is cleaning and making dinner.
I want to be a successful actress.
I am a sensitive and playful girl.

I pretend when I'm performing that I'm on Broadway.
I feel that I should try harder to school.
I touch people's souls.
I worry that someday my family and I won't keep in touch.
I cry when someone else is hurt.
I am a sensitive and playful girl.

I understand when life gets tough, it's hard to deal with it.
I say be positive anyway, because no matter what, life will get better.
I dream one day that I can change the world with my performing talent.
I try to fit in, but I realized I don't have to try.
I hope that I'll be successful someday.
I hoe that I'll be successful someday.
I am a sensitive and playful girl.
Abigail Allen, Grade 6

Sisterhood

T o have a sister is like having a friend
H aving a cool sister knows how to connect
A sister knows how you feel even if you don't tell her
N ice sisters show love
K eeping secrets from a sister is like keeping a secret from your life or future
S isterhood is what I love in life
Diamond Densby, Grade 4

What Lies Behind the Siren's Voice?

What lies behind the clear glass pond?
Water that glitters, shimmers and shines like diamonds —
I can't seem to see beyond
Let me see what lies behind.

What lies behind the fancy walls?
Warm fireplaces and extravagance —
An abundance of laughter down the halls
Let me see what lies behind.

What lies behind the Siren's Voice?
Joyful parties with great love,
Rejoice,
Enchanting music —
Whispers for me to come,
I see the shore, I hear the beauty
As I stretch out to the rocky shores, I succumb —
To the song's glory and power
I finally see what lies behind.

The muddy rocks,
The ghost that haunts mankind.
And the sirens —
Are not who you think they are.

Victoria Peng, Grade 5

The Four Seasons

Grass of rich green, on it, the sun gleams.
Not a single flake of snow, just the warm sun's glow.
Flowers bloom, butterflies emerge from their cocoons.
How high birds fly, in the sky,
And how beautifully they sing…It is spring!

Then comes the heat, smoldering, burning, stinging.
Only the cicadas in the trees are singing,
And you think, "Won't a cool drink be nice?"
Then relief, because at the pool you splash in water as cold as ice.
School is out, so there is no need to pout…It is summer!

Leaves, no longer green, Turn to orange, brown, and yellow.
All the colors calming and mellow.
Then they fall, leaving trees bare and tall…It is fall!

After fall, the weather turns icy and cold.
To go out in this weather, you've got to be bold!
The temperatures are low, and it might snow…It is winter!

The seasons change, four times each year,
So great and magnificent, Let's give a cheer!
Oh what happiness the seasons bring…
As they rotate from summer, fall, then winter; and back to spring!

Aliya Alidaee, Grade 6

Little Things

We all are proud of the big things,
ones we achieve through struggle and strife.
But we need to stop and appreciate,
all the little things in life.

We push through for the big things,
to achieve something new.
But think, what factors help us?
That's right, the little things push us through.

Little things are simple,
something anyone can do.
you become friends with someone,
or just simply say thank you.

These little things leave an impact,
like simply being kind.
This could encourage someone,
pushing them through along the ride.

Now that you come to think of it,
they're more important than they seemed.
For it's the little things in life,
That help you row down life's stream.

Adam McCall, Grade 6

Ode to Hot Dogs

When I smell you fresh from the microwave,
I almost faint in happiness,
And, when it comes time to eat you,
I sink my teeth into you,
and your good old cousin "Bun."

The juice that you have
Is the best lotion ever invented,
I wish I could use it as soap,
But my mom won't let me.

Oh, hot dog
When you speak to my in that sizzling sound,
I rejoice in sheer exhilaration,
It's a thrill when I calmly say,
"I'M GONNA EAT YOU!"
You always taste that much better.

You know,
I don't care that you are full of artificial junk,
Or that you are extremely horrible for me,
Just remember this one thing,
I will always eat you,
Ketchup or not.

Oliver Brown, Grade 4

Life
Friends are
like bird feathers
they will float off
and start a new life
Mackenzie Sonnenberg, Grade 5

Winter Snow
Snowmen being built
Ice skating in the snow
Sipping some hot chocolate
In the winter we go
Savanah Evins, Grade 5

Winter
We have snow
Everywhere we go
We like to play
In the snow all day
Karine Arredondo, Grade 5

Angel Island
This was hard
for me
Terrible sickness
Immigration wait
Isac Ortega, Grade 5

Winter
Sledding down the mountain side
looking for somewhere to hide.
Snow falling on the ground
pounding lightly all around.
Caleb Davis, Grade 5

The Breeze
The breeze blows by,
Giving a warm gust from the spring sky.
Blowing flowers way up high,
Once again the breeze will fly.
Marissa Valenzuela, Grade 5

Under the Sun
Having fun under the sun
Playing basketball or volleyball
Playing all day until it's night
Until the moon comes and lights, the night
Adriana Hinojosa, Grade 6

The Sparkling Sun
Waking up
the sun is too beautiful
beaming like sparkling stars
in the sky
Jacquelyn Alcantara, Grade 4

That Old Willow Tree
I saw her walking in the meadow.
She was obviously in a hurry,
For I have no clue why.
She was singing that pretty song of hers,
With her pretty thick black hair,
Swaying in the wind and she skipped off of the plantation.
The girl turned left at the gravel,
Heading straight for me.
It was very dark now, too dark to even be outside, too dangerous,
She climbed me all the way up to the coziest branch.
As my long branches and leaves covered her,
Protected her from the slave catchers,
She fell into a deep sleep awakening to a strong wind as the sun rose.
I kept her warm, kept her safe on her journey to freedom.
As she started her decent down me in the morning,
I said to her "You be careful now, I don't want you to get caught."
The pretty dark-skinned girl wondered who said that.
"Me," I said, "The big willow tree that kept you safe for the night."
She thanked me but said she should be off on her way.
I hope she made it to freedom.
Caitlan McHugh, Grade 6

Christmas in Ardennes, 1944
Shots ring out in the distance and chants bounce off the snow,
Of "I'll be Home for Christmas," and other tunes you surely know.

Shells launch out like rockets, exploding on the ground,
Sending bits of soil and debris everywhere around.

A Tiger appears in the background, pushing trees down as it goes,
Firing its machine gun, its shots hit my companion's toes.

He winces in his pain, but still he remains silent.
For I carry a rocket launcher to use against the tyrant.

The Tiger still progresses, leaving tracks deep in the snow.
It's coming nearer and nearer, I pull the trigger to strike the blow.

The Tiger explodes a second later, with flames rushing to the ground.
I have just saved many lives, by firing my compound.

Oh! How many dream of home while lying on cots or in the snow,
Fighting off the enemies' forces, this Christmas Eve long ago.
Matthew Leone, Grade 4

Dust Bowl
Dust Bowl
deadly, strong, powerful, dangerous,
Relative of storms
Possessor of destruction, droughts, and objects
Who feeds on dirt, objects, and lives
Who reproduces destruction, pain, and suffering
Who is noted for regeneration, destruction of environment, and torture
Inhabitant of land
not known
Sayed H. Habib, Grade 4

She Is an Angel
She is an Angel
There is an angel that watches over me.
She kisses my forehead and helps me forget pain.
"She is an angel" is what I sang.
There is an angel that watches over me.
She tucks me into bed and puts a pillow under my head.
"She is an angel" is what I said.
There is an angel that watches over me.
She has curly brown hair and pretty like any other angel out there.
She is my mom and will always care.
Lillian Mueller, Grade 5

The Sound of the Ocean
Have you ever heard the sound of the ocean?
The water moves calmly in gentle motion.
Not nearly as loud as a graceful bird.
The waters splash against the rocks
During the thunderstorm.
Though afterwards the sun shines
Showing the oceans jagged but pretty lines.
The ocean's beauty
Is something quite different
Because nothing can quite compare to it.
Sanvi Joshi, Grade 4

The Dust Bowl
The Dust Bowl was called the black blizzard.
The Dust Bowl damaged everything.
It killed many people.
It ruined all the crops.
Family and farms were lost.
The area affected the Panhandle.
Their crops and land blew away.
People all over the state were hurt.
The severe hurt the cattle and other animals.
I am the Dust Bowl
Abby Price, Grade 4

Banana Split Yellow
Banana split yellow,
She's perky and likes to play.
Did you know she was once part of a 1950's television parade?
Banana split,
She's a classic, she's fantastic.
And she will always be the most delicious of the bunch.
Jane Shelton, Grade 4

Happiness
Happiness seems carnation pink
Like the sky when the sun is setting.
I see sunflowers filled with joy.
I hear kids playing volleyball.
I smell melted chocolate ice cream flowing down my hands.
I touch my dog's white, fluffy ears.
I taste delicious, blue cotton candy.
Ruby Patino, Grade 4

Sky Blue
Sky blue is my favorite color
Sky blue is like a light
Sky blue is a color that gives energy
Sky blue smells like the ocean during the summer
Sky blue tastes like the beach
Sky blue sounds like a summertime
Sky blue looks like a blue-eye cockatoo
Sky blue feels like the wetness of the ocean
Sky blue makes me feel excited
Sky blue is alive!
Malak Ali, Grade 5

Just Believe*
Penny is free to do whatever
like put on a sweater
Melody can't even do something that simple
She is like a caged animal
Waiting to be freed
starting to lose hope
Still waiting to be freed
Learning to believe
Now she knows if she believes she will be forever free.
Tommy Covington, Grade 6
*Inspired by "Out of My Mind" by Sharon M. Draper

Sun and Waves
I stand upon the cliff
The sun glistens on the water
The sun is an altered rainbow, fading behind the earth
The sun glows with warmth like a crackling fire
The ocean: moving, dancing, moving calming the graceful wind,
The waves splash on the shore.
Orange sand, yielding to the waves, so bravely
The sun is almost down now
The sky suddenly is orange
I'm still standing
Eli Derr, Grade 6

Colors
Colors are fun
They taste like Skittles pouring from a waterfall
They sound like spring flowers blowing in the breeze
They smell like leaves falling down from a tree
They look like the pot of gold that you find at the end of a rainbow
They make me feel happy
Zuha Murad, Grade 4

Sadness
Sadness seems dark blue
Like the midnight sky.
I see tears rolling down rosy-red cheeks.
I hear screams of sorrow.
I smell wet, salty raindrops from humans.
I touch the dread of a tiger leaping onto a zebra.
I taste depression.
Mackenzie Strecker, Grade 4

White Day

Slipping sliding all the way.
Hot chocolate at the end of the day.
Oh what fun is the snow!
Shaking, shivering in the white glow!
Stella Raynor, Grade 4

Food

Cheesy, white
Eating, biting, laughing
A whole plate of…
Pizza!
Katelyn Casillas, Grade 4

Bear

Starts to roar
Is too hairy
Eats more
And more berries
Monserrat Lara, Grade 5

Betts

My school is the best
When I achieve my graduation
It means to have a great destination
Not convinced, go ask the rest
Jennifer Martinez, Grade 5

Singing

I hear it on the radio
I sing in the car
It makes me happy
Because I feel like a star
Nayeli Hernandez, Grade 5

Gamer

I love to play *Back Ops*
Because I save the day
By being cops
In the bay.
Sabian Salinas, Grade 5

Soccer

I like to play soccer
Because it is fun!
We run, kick
And score in the sun.
Bryan Escobedo, Grade 5

Mint

M outh watering flavor
I dea filling smell
N ice soothing breeze
T inted with sight
Kendal Gerick, Grade 4

I Am Colorful

I am colorful like the shining rainbow.
I wonder how the flowers bloom in time for the spring.
I hear the chirping birds in the trees.
I want to touch the sky and fly.

I am colorful like the shining rainbow.
I pretend to fight evil monsters coming my way.
I feel loved like the feeling of warmth in the winter.
I touch the grass, while I lay down to see the clouds.
I worry that all my feelings, like the sun, will burn away.

I am colorful like the shining rainbow.
I understand the sounds of nature like music.
I say never give up in times of trouble.
I dream that I am living in a pillow of clouds.
I try to love as God loves us.
I hope that all our dreams will come true, so we can shine like the sun.

I am colorful like the shining rainbow.
Eunice Bae, Grade 6

Unconditional Love

"I am alone for no one is to be trusted"
That's the lesson I learned the hard way
As my classmates huddle and chat, I sit contentedly in the corner
Because I was once naive like that and opened my heart to the disguised blades
That ripped it to pieces, now still broken
They were lying from the start, their words and promises all fake
My world turned bleak, I lost all emotion
I was all by myself
My love for them ended in vain
For they betrayed me and never cared
I am alone
A presence steps out and hugs me tight, like it is afraid I'll disappear
I tilt my head and turn
A face similar to mine is reflected in my eyes
And then that's when I realize that I was not alone
For there was already someone who loved me all this time
People call it unconditional love
The one who was always by my side
Has always been my sister
Stella Koh, Grade 6

What Happens to a Dream Deferred?*

What happens to a dream deferred?
Does it slowly melt away
like a cone of caramel on a hot summer's day?
Or shrivel up
and then crumble like a dead flower on an icy winter's night?
Does it elude you
like an upset friend?
Maybe it just slips and tumbles into an endless abyss
like a forgotten memory?
Or does it linger and eventually vanish into the giant black hole that is modern society?
Steven Cook, Grade 6
*Inspired by Langston Hughes

America

Blue is the color of the flag on the wall.
White stars are in the middle, 50 in all

Red stripes are on the side
for all the people who died.

White behind red
for the innocent people that bled

Grey is the color of the pole where it hang.
Representing the sound of the gun going bang.

They cover the caskets with dirt that is brown.
Where the caskets are buried way underground.
Jacob Pritchard, Grade 6

Fourth of July

Black is the color of sky, way up in height.
BANG! Is the sound of the soft gleaming light.

Yellow and orange are beams in the sky.
While we watch in awe of the fun of July.

Red is the color of the fuse ever shortening
Following a line to the sky, which is darkening.

Gold is the color of sparks that are flying.
Toward the crowd who is outlying.

Silver is the color of the sparkling lights.
While we sit back with all our delights.
Andy Mihills, Grade 6

What Is Green?

Green is the color for the Seahawks team.
Green is the color for the grasshoppers hopping in the grass.

Green is the smell of granny smith apples.
Green is the feeling when you get sick.

Green is the food avocados.
Green is the sound of waving grass.

Green is green.

Michael Morgan, Grade 4

Sea of Green

In the meadow of green
Where insects are seen
A soft wind blows
Down the hill below
In the soft dirt patch
Where the shacks open latch
Under below is where the treasure is in hold
Only a true descendant will ever take possession of the gold.
Vivianne Medina, Grade 5

Ode to Buster Pawsy Miller

Buster Pawsy Miller,
You are my happiness,
my entertainment,
my light in the darkness,

Your silky fur is like a soft blankie,
I would do anything to understand you,
and what you are saying,

We are like two chew toys in a crate,
waiting to be chewed,
If you run away I would run day and night,
to find you wherever you are,

When I am sad you give me a kiss,
and you let me lean on you so I can get up,
When you are sad I give you a hug and make you feel
better so you can rest and be the happiest dog ever,

Buster Pawsy Miller,
You are my happiness,
my entertainment,
my light in the darkness
Christopher Miller, Grade 6

Turtles

Turtles are so cute.
But I do not think they live in Butte.
Their kingdom is Animalia.
Their class is Reptilia.

I would like a turtle for a pet.
I would get it plenty wet.
Most turtles spend most of their lives on land.
I wonder what they like the best, dirt or sand.

They love to eat plenty of sea plants.
Or they might like ants.
They probably do not like the zoo.
But some animals do.
Ashlyn Burnett, Grade 5

Love

Love is sweet
Love is great
Love is wherever you look
Parents love
Brothers love, too
And sisters love even if they don't talk to you
Family loves
Friends love
Teachers love
Love is in your heart
You just have to believe in
LOVE
Mia Espinoza, Grade 4

Technology

Technology is tech
Tech is inventive
Inventive means smart minds
Great tech, Great Minds

One great invention, the Phone
Connections, calls, texts, apps
There are even some maps.
On the go, it's a great mobile invention!

Click, click, it's the TV!
From the old to the new.
It's all about size, quality, and shows!
Need to go? Click a button and it's off!

Vroom, vroom, let's go in a Car!
You can go places a far,
You can go in an old or a new car, it doesn't matter!
You can even go to Canada!

If you make something new,
You might be a great inventor
Like Franklin or Einstein!
Brain is the real factor!

Tuan Le, Grade 4

Butterflies

Butterflies flying so high,
flying till they reach the sky.
It would be fought,
but the wings are very tough.

Butterflies are great creatures with many types of colors.
One butterfly has different trails than another.
Sighting beautiful colors in the sky.
Can't see camouflage but to try.

Many will migrate in the winter so,
Mexico they will go.
Sleeping in the warm sun.
Although dying is not so fun.

Then butterflies do the laying.
Many caterpillars are born in the spring.
Sadly the butterflies have died,
but new babies have risen.

They will go back to where they came from.
They will eat well at their homes.
They turn into a cocoon,
and become a butterfly soon.

Brendon Nguyen, Grade 4

Yosemite's Soul

El Capitan towered above us
At Tunnel View
Nearby Bridal Veil roared
Into a large lake

Beside great Half Dome
Dominating the amazing area like the finishing touch,
Final beautiful brush strokes, completing the painting
Opposite the rushing Bridal Veil
Birds sang out their happiness
Never again will they forget the feeling
Of such freedom

With much resistance, we left
But our presence still was in that moment to stay
Never once did I peel
My soul's eyes away from such beauty

The picture of art
A picture of life in the making
A life that will never
Not in a million years
Back down to fear,
Or back down to destruction

Fanna Seman, Grade 5

The Queen of the World

If I were in charge of the world
I'd end brushing your teeth two times a day
Cancel eating all your vegetables
Get rid of Sunday evenings

If I were in charge of the world
There'd be no end to eating ice cream
No end to my birthday
And no mean brothers

If I were in charge of the world
You wouldn't have to wake up early
You wouldn't have to clean
You wouldn't have to go to school
Or go to the dentist

If I were in charge of the world
You wouldn't have to brush your hair and
All the stuff in stores would be free
And a person
who sometimes
Forgets to do your homework
And sometimes forgets to be a good friend
Would still be allowed to be in charge of the world

Nikita Gupta, Grade 5

The Best Friend
Wagging his tail, he always receives his friends.
Winston my old pal always playful and comical
My company he appreciates and he can say it by licking my face

He is a member of our family and takes his role so naturally
He wakes up every morning to enjoy the rising sun
He won't sleep until the home is quiet as a stone

He loves long walks and watching squirrels run
Winston loves to take long naps, when you tuck him in his sack
There is no other best friend you would want guarding your back
Bella Chavarria, Grade 4

Who Am I
I am blue like a cool breeze in the sky.
I am Christmas full of giving and joy.
I am night like the owl's hoot,
and that one lone light glowing in the window.
I am a fantasy cat with wings,
and I fly magically in the sky.
I am loud, funny, and laughing.
I am like Tex-Mex mixed with flavor.

Who am I?
I am Will Martin
Will Martin, Grade 4

Ode to Hazel, My Puppy
Hazel,
You have earned all your treats for being the good dog you are.
Now, you're the best dog in the whole world!
I'm proud of how you smell after your coconut shampoo bath,
And how a few days later you smell only of your dog breath.
I'm amazed how you can sit and leave sticks alone,
When I tell you to.
When I touch you, you're a fluffy fuzz ball,
That I wish I could squeeze.
Hazel,
You are the best dog ever.
Emily Klein, Grade 4

Who Am I?
Aisha
Smart, funny, sporty, respectful
Daughter of Abukar and Sacadiya
Lover of baseball, jokes, and writing
Who feels happy, energetic, scared, and sad
Who needs life, friends, and electronics
Who gives help, food, and patience
Who fears God, trouble, and parents
Who likes to see the sunset, happiness, and beach waves
Resident of King City
Basharow
Aisha Basharow, Grade 4

Cesar Chavez
Cesar Chavez was born in Arizona
He was child of Mr. and Mrs. Chavez
They lived in a small town
He studied civil rights
He overcame hunger and fasting
He also worked as a farmer
Also challenged by the farmworker bosses
His personal traits are bravery, courage, and hard work
He never gave up
He is best known marching for equal rights
Thank You Cesar Chavez!
Andrea Carreras, Grade 4

If I Was a Bird
If I was a bird,
I would taste the soothing fresh air.
I would be full of warmth and joy.
I would like to soar and look at the beautiful view.
I would want to feel the breeze ruffling my feathers.

If I was a bird,
I would dive down and catch worms in my beak.
I would wish to glide around the whole world.
I would whistle everywhere I go.
I would listen for the beautiful sound of other birds.
Gavin Spikes, Grade 4

Spring
Spring is a time for the sun to shine
Spring is a time where no one whines
Where flowers bloom and people loom around the streets
Spring is a time where it also rains
Spring is a time where everyone is drained
But unlike winter and fall, spring is the time for all
So no one is grumpy and no one is sad
No one even has the strength to get mad
Because we all know that spring is fab
So let's all cheer
For spring is here!
Chloe Wilson, Grade 4

Hamsters
Hamsters are sweet,
Hamsters are cute,
They will cuddle right up to you.
They run and they run all day on their wheel,
And when they bury themselves you can hear them squeal!
You can feed them seeds out of your hand,
And when they fall asleep on top of you,
You won't leave until someone makes you.
They will be loyal to you all the time,
And one thing you know for certain,
Is that your friendship together will never end!
Brielle Burns, Grade 4

I Used To

I used to play *Roblox* on the computer a lot
But now I play *MineCraft* on the PC a lot
I always trick in the Kickstart Room
But I never use the Rubik's cube 24/7
I once knew how to back handspring
But now I do my back handspring sideways
If I could fly
I would fly to Japan, Nigeria and Asia
I never did my B-Twist right
But I might attempt it
I can't do a ninja into a swipe
But I can do a back flip, aerial, front flip, and back handspring
I won't attempt a double backflip
But I might attempt a wheelie on my BMX bike
I used to know how to Parkour horribly bad
But now I'm a Parkour master

Bryan Mba, Grade 6

Rainbow

Ah the rainbow
Such a beautiful thing
We thank Mother Nature for an enlightening thing
Oh how it glimmers and shines
Up high in the sky
Smiling down at us
Blessing us with kindness
Sitting up high on its throne up in the sky
The kids look up with excitement
They yell and scream, "Look, Mommy, it's a rainbow."
Oh how happy they make me feel
They can't offend anyone or anything
They have all of the colors
Violet, indigo, blue, green, yellow, orange and red
Everything is in the rainbow
What a blessing!

Ana Castellanos Velasco, Grade 6

If I Ruled the World

If I ruled the world everyone would have money.
I'd make the economy better
have less school and more weekends

If I ruled the world,
there'd be less homeless people
free food, free shoes

If I ruled the world,
you wouldn't have Saturday detention,
you wouldn't have lunch detention,
you wouldn't have semester exams
or have to do this poem

If I ruled the world,
everything would be better

Emad El-Refaei, Grade 6

You Don't Have to Try

I used to let people push me down
But now I get back up
I always worried about myself
But I never had anxiety over others
I once believed what people said
But now I change the conversation
If I could fly back then
I would have flown away and never come back
I never could do that
But I might have tried
I can't be who everyone wants me to be
But I can be myself
I won't change who I am or was
But I might have wanted to be someone else
I used to let people push me down
But now I get back up

Isra Malik, Grade 6

I Remember You

I remember the way that we would
laugh and smile
I remember running with my friends
around the wild
I remember climbing trees like there was
no tomorrow
And the way we would roll down the hills like a ball down
a mountain
I remember playing the piano with my friend
next door
I remember the way we would tap dance on
the floor
I remember every single day going by
Even though we are older now
I remember the way that we would laugh and smile
But I will always remember you

Kyra Reid, Grade 6

I Am Unique

I am
unique because I
will
always believe that magic is
real, even
if people say
it is not. They say there's no
Santa or fairies.
In my opinion, they are wrong. It's only my
opinion. They don't have to believe it.
Just like how I don't have to believe their opinion.
They don't have to believe for it to be true.
You have to believe hard enough for your dreams to come true.
They don't believe me because they don't see the
way I see the world. Start believing in the way
you see the world, though.

Paulina Warren, Grade 6

Diamond

The rare crystal
diamond found
in the mining of
the caves

Once you found
the diamond
bring it to the
museum for people to see
the bright shiny diamond

But be aware for
robbers to steal
at night the
expensive diamond

Don't worry security is
there to protect the
diamond
Arturo Gutierrez, Grade 4

Red Roses

Roses grow from a seed,
they become red beauty,
but with petals so delicate,
not firm or strong, they are
graceful and peaceful.
When water falls from the sky,
the droplets drizzle down the petals,
and to
the ground.
Red roses are truly beautiful
pieces of art.
Just on a green, thorny stem
with not much beauty
to spare
but just above that stem
is beauty the color of
a precious ruby
and it's called
a red rose.
Simone Peppel, Grade 4

I Don't Understand

I don't understand why grandfather left me.
Why did he go to the next life?
Why did he go without me?
Why did I not at least see him once?
But most of all,
Why is he gone too soon?
Why am I not crying?
What I understand most is
Why he is gone.
Why he is in a better place.
Why he is there, and I will see him again.
Catherine Chi, Grade 4

Ode to My Friend

Friend, friend
Beautiful and brave
Strong and kind
You're like a crystal in a cave

Friend, friend
You stand up for me when I'm in trouble
You make me happy when I'm sad
It is almost like we're in a bubble

Friend, friend
Magnificent with a gold heart
I know I will always need you
I know we will never be apart
Ashlee Cleary, Grade 5

Ode to a Veteran

Veteran, Veteran
Strong and brave
You made a choice, to serve our country
You could even be a guy named Dave

Veteran, Veteran
You follow orders
Strong, like a tank
You sleep in quarters

Veteran, Veteran
You protect us all
You have the country's heart
May you stand very tall and never fall
Stella Ptacek, Grade 5

Daddy, Oh Father

Daddy, oh father
You're oh so faithful
I love the way,
You're also so grateful

Daddy, oh father
You're oh so shiny and bright
In my darkness,
You are my light

Daddy, oh father
You're oh so kind
You're on my mind
Like all the time
Christina Stanfield, Grade 5

Sky High

I dreamt I could fly,
I believed I could try.
I flew with glee,
And soared as if I was free!
Chloe Moreno, Grade 5

Winter

Snowflakes fall at the dimmest light.
Santa may come,
yes, he might.

He will be coming very soon.
At the time
of the moon.

Sitting down beside the fire.
The lovely view
you admire.

Icicles hang like bats.
You hear
lots of chats

As you hear everyone cheer,
you know
winter is here.
Diya Vakil, Grade 5

Skiing

As I soar past the speeding trees,
I feel the frost in my fingers.
Excitement rushes through my body.
It's pure joy.

Giant forests of trees engulf me,
Treat me to quiet, and
Snow falls from heaven,
Creating a paradise for skiing.

I soar to the bottom, and
Race up again,
Jump off of the chairlift,
And let my adventure begin.

I whizz past trees,
Do a trick, and
Challenge myself,
To conquer the mountain.
Tyler McBride, Grade 6

The Storm

The pitter-patter of the rain
Sounds like a lullaby
The slishity-slosh of the rain
Is like a boat on the rolling waves
That resembles the ones that fill my dreams
The crash of the thunder
Sounds like the alarm clock
That wakes me up in the morning
The bright lightning
Looks like rays of sunlight
That floods my room
Crawford Arnow, Grade 5

The Sky

Oh! the great sky is blue.
The breezy wind that blew.
The blue sky, puffy clouds, and the bright sun.
The outside sky, extremely relaxing fun.
The yellow flowers bloom.
Flowers will bloom, very soon.
The warm weather from the heat.
The breezy winds that leap.
The birds will bawk!
And rabbits will hop.
The blue sky is the best
And also, it's not a mess.
When it's summer, it's better.
I just feel like writing a letter.
Now, the sky is dark and black.
I won't worry, it'll be back.

Vincent Nguyen, Grade 4

Love

Love —
a wonder-filled power.
Happening to
All
good people.
Through massive, wet storms and frightening, red tornadoes
Love will
find a way.
Through depressing losses and
nervous moments,
love will find a way.
With all your loving family
and all your caring friends
love will shine through the crying, angry, gray clouds.
Every person in the world share the same thing.
Love.

Dominique Mallo, Grade 6

Summer

Finally, summer is here!
This is the time when school is not near!
I can go to the beach with all my friends,
School has finally come to an end.
I get to sleep in late every morning
And my parents don't give me a time warning.
I don't have to worry about any work
The ocean is clear and not filled with murk
I get to ride my bike.
And eat a bunch of foods that I like
Swim trunks and sandals is all I will need
It's a time when I will not need to read
Boy do I love summer!
When it ends, it will be a bummer.
The sun will always be out,
And all my friends will be about!

Liam Heinz, Grade 6

A Lake

As the branches swayed in a quiet breeze
The water lazily lapped to the lake
The lake teemed with life
The bees buzzed
While the deer bent down to take a drink
The fish splashed in the water
And the people looked lazily
At nature's beauty
The children splashed, waded, and
Played hide and seek.
But as soon the sun dripped down as night came
And the lake was a quiet paradise
Moonlight danced on the water
A lone wolf howled
Life rises in the light
But also streams at night

Taein Shim, Grade 6

Shadow

My shadow wears,
A dark cloak that hides who I am,
A hat that hides my true feelings,
A glove that hides my monstrous look.
His hair is like ice
Crunchy and hard,
My shadow is a vampire
Hiding from the sun
Feeding off darkness
Hiding in shade,
My shadow is like a monster waiting to strike,
My shadow follows me everywhere,
waiting for the perfect time to pounce
Only leaving my side when I hide in shade,
I have tried to escape but escape is nowhere
Shadows they are your follower

Owen Hadley, Grade 6

Winter Aura

The brisk wind blows through the pine trees,
Rain beats on the roof like a drum.
I sit inside with my family
Drinking hot chocolate.

The furious fire crackles in the fireplace.
And clouds are a mask, covering the sun.
The delicious smell of gingerbread floats through the air.
The taste of a grand holiday meal fills my mouth.
A velvety texture of a warm blanket dances around my fingers.
The merry songs of carolers fill the atmosphere.

The aura of winter is everywhere,
Outside on trees,
Inside near the fireplace,
And everywhere with family.

Isabella Barragan, Grade 6

Red

The color red is as bright as a rose
Red tastes like fruit punch
It sounds like kids laughing
It smells like cherries
It looks like apples
It makes me smile for joy
Cooper Rawlins, Grade 4

The Bride

There once was a bride
Who cried and cried
Until she could find her way
Back to her house
Where she had pride and pride
And was happier yesterday
Ava Godfredsen, Grade 4

Salena

S trong, silly, skinny
A ppealing, athletic, artistic
L oud, likeable, lovely
E xcitable, energetic, encouraging
N ice, nifty, neat
A dventuress, active, aggressive
Salena Kilgore, Grade 5

Pain

Pain is seeing a family member die.
It sounds like someone screeching for help.
It smells like a hospital with ill people.
It tastes like metal in your mouth.
It feels like a knife cutting flesh.
Isabella Lopez, Grade 5

Sly's Prayer

There once was a boy named Sly
Who felt that he wanted to fly
Until in May
He prayed all day
And now he can fly in the sky
Dante Fidel, Grade 5

Hot Chocolate

Hot chocolate is the best
Especially on winter days
I love hot chocolate
It is warm and toasty
With marshmallows
Taylor Farless, Grade 4

Baseball

Players hit the ball.
A referee says "Out!"
This baseball is small.
Losing was my only doubt.
Mia Checa, Grade 5

Galaxy Girl

One twilight, I looked up to the sky, and I was surprised by what I saw.
A girl's face made of galaxies, without a single flaw.

Her eyes made of stars, and her smile bright.
And though the sky was dark, her personality shone light.

I was mesmerized by the glow of her face,
The swirling colors, and her beautiful grace.

We talked, we laughed, and she danced for me.
She was the answer — she was the key.

And softly she spoke of what she saw from the skies.
Good things, and bad things, people that fly.

She saw the ups and saw the downs.
She saw the smiles, and the frowns.

She saw the losses and saw the gains.
She saw the healing, and the pains.

She saw the weak and saw the proud.
She saw the quiet, and the loud.

She saw the death and saw the life,
She saw the peace, and the strife.

And she said that from above,
Through it all, she could still see the
Love.
Kaissa Doichev, Grade 6

Rising to the Heavens

Listen to the birds chirping sweet melodies,
The rustle of emerald leaves,
Bees buzzing,
Faint whistling of the wind,
Eavesdrop on the low tones of crashing waves,
Inhale the sweet aroma of flowers,
Fresh dew,
Tantalizing fragrance of honey,
Run your hands along the rough bark,
Pull on green vines,
Ivy creeping up the trunk,
Sap dripping down branches,
As you watch from a limb,
The sun shines creating spotted patterns along your back,
The sunset screams vivid colors of orange, pink, fiery red, and yellow,
Amber, crimson, gold,
Amethyst, brass, copper,
It shines on your face,
So touch the sky,
Touch the sky,
Touch the sky,
And spread your wings and soar.
Jevin Lim, Grade 5

The Earth

I love you…who knew?
You are so beautiful…and blue!
Your grass is so green,
Your air is so clean.
Your mountains are so high,
They reach up and touch the sky.
Together, the Earth and I will be
Like a doorknob and a key.
Carson Carpentieri-Asbury, Grade 5

Movies

Late at night
The movie starts,
but then comes a fright.
Look out he's coming for you!
We all run away,
Then all of a sudden
we have forgotten
we had 3D glasses on!
Saul Cohete, Grade 4

Soccer Is My Favorite Sport

On a Saturday morning
With my friends and coach
On the soccer field
Among the opponents
About to kick
Toward the goal
Through the net
Onto the winner's circle
Johnny Walls, Grade 4

Fear

Fear seems frost blue
Like the chill that covers your body.
I see the trembling of the people next to me.
I hear the screeching screams.
I smell the terror in the air.
I touch the gloominess of the dark.
I taste the teardrops trickling down my face.
Madison Hornbuckle, Grade 4

Butterfly

Butterfly
Delicate, beautiful
Flying, flapping, hiding
Makes me feel calm
Beautiful day moth
Raigh Kitowski, Grade 4

My Dog Toby

My dog likes to hide
under my bed.
He likes to fight
and plays dead.
Erick Rossette, Grade 5

16 Wonderful Facts About Me

I used to like fat cats, but now I enjoy only fluffy cats.
I used to unlike hippos, but know I like how cute they are.
I used to drink unhealthy soda, but now I prefer juice and water.
I used to like yellow bananas, but now I enjoy juicy peaches.
I used to like green apples, but now I prefer red delicious apples.
I did not like reading, but now I read most of the time.
I used to see animated movies, but now I like action packed movies.
I used prefer cute, kind dogs, but now I enjoy nice cats too.
I used to love good, creamy villain cake, but now I prefer creamy cheesecake.
I used to enjoy rough hard soccer, but now I prefer nice fun baseball.
I used to adore the color blue, now I enjoy the color bright red.
I once loved good hot dogs, but now I prefer mouth watering hamburgers.
I used to want to be a cool vet, instead I prefer to be a doctor.
I used to love big animals, now I savor very small pets.
I used to enjoy being 5 and shy, but now I love being 10 years old.
Long ago I was in 1st grade, but now I am going to middle school.
Alexis Bitnar, Grade 5

My New Lifestyle

I used to favor food, now I love going to the gym.
I used to favor food, now I favor basketball.
I used to drink orange soda, now I prefer Gatorade.
I used to get mad, now I choose not to get mad.
I used to like RiffRaff, now I like The Weekend.
I used to never go outside, now I always play basketball.
I once read Green Eggs and Ham, now I read long chapter books.
I used to be six years old, now I'm eleven years old.
I used to weigh 150 pounds, now I weigh 143 pounds.
I used to be lonely, now I have a lot of exciting friends.
I used to watch humorous cartoons, now I prefer NBA Game Time.
I used to like wealthy Chris Bosh, now I like famous LeBron James.
I used to live with my lovely grandma, now I live with my great mom.
My mom used to have a red car, now she has a white car.
I used to like cars, now I like Transformers.
I used to like amazing WWE wrestling, now I like great Lucha Underground.
James Copeland, Grade 5

Say Goodbye

Five years old, too young to know what was going on
All I knew was that you were gone
I never got to say goodbye
I didn't want to let go, you made me
You picked the worst way to leave
With a loud boom and not saying a word
Why did you leave me
Anger filled my body, tears fallen on my face
"There was nothing we could do" are the words that I could never shake from memory
A couple days passed, the time came to send you to the clouds
I knew you were safe, up there
My father said, with tears welling up in his eyes "Heaven got another angel"
You were strong, I know you tried to fight the pain
I understand it was too much
Remembering our times together, sometimes makes it better
I'll see you again, that I'm sure of
Erminia Garcia, Grade 5

Dragons
Dragon
Scaly, spiny
Fly, eat, climb
Fire-breathing house destroyers
Monsters
Samuel Steffon, Grade 6

My Family
I like to see my family.
My family is loud and noisy.

They jump, sing, and play.
They're like a group of blue jays.
Savannah Bell, Grade 4

Chinese Zodiac
Snake
Slithery, scaly
Fast, hissing, striking
Vicious, cruel, deadly, stealthy
Salamander
Hannah Tipton, Grade 6

Storm
Thunk, thunk
Rain trickles down on the house
It is a sleepless night
And the howling wolves are coming out
Scary!
Jamie Varga, Grade 4

Swimming
I like to swim in the deep blue
I don't like to swim very fast
You may see my big fin
And you might run away
Maybe because I am a shark
Summer Ruedy, Grade 6

Jerry
There once was a guy named Jerry
His friend Larry choked on a berry
He jumped on his back
And gave it a good smack
Then everything was fine and merry
Hannah Runyan, Grade 6

Tree
My special tree
Is my favorite place to be.
And even though it's fresh
I can never seem to rest.
Christopher Rodriguez, Grade 5

Misconceptions
The knife is cunning and lethal.
Its razor sharp blades cut at the most precise points.
An enticing concoction of ingredients are placed carefully in the center.
A ceremonial stick is jabbed into the object.
The people gather around it.
It is lit on fire.
They chant out a song indigenous to their land.
Flames burn the stick until it crumbles down.
A gray, foul-smelling wisp of smoke fills the room.
The jagged knife carves out big, thick chunks.
Chunks are distributed around the room.
Afterwards, offerings are given to a specific person.
Many compete to give the best offering.
The person rips, tears, and shreds them apart with all their might.
Pieces are flung across the room.
The crowd eagerly awaits the reaction.
The person yells and shrieks. "Ahhhhh!"
A year later, the events will repeat.
Happy Birthday!
Lee Fontanares, Grade 6

Legacy
I swirl and spin like the wind,
Knowing each step I take is making history.
I did not have advantages like other ballerinas.
I was disregarded for my skin color, but then I proved my potential to the world.
I am Misty Copeland.

I will not get off this bus,
I will stay right were I am.
My skin tone makes me an outcast.
But I will not give up my seat.
I am making history, even when I do get arrested.
I am still Rosa Parks.

I have a dream, my famous speech.
I want everyone to be equal.
After all, we are just human, when you strip down all the layers.
I am Martin Luther King Jr., And we will all make history,
And one day be free.
Audry Carruth, Grade 6

My Brother
Take a spoonful of kindness, a teaspoon of caring, and a pinch of anger.
Put a spoonful of kindness, and a pinch of anger into a teaspoon of caring.
Mix all the ingredients
Until you get brown, thick luscious hair.
Throw it on the window,
And let it dry for an hour.
At 350 degrees Fahrenheit.
You can tell it's done when it forms into a sixteen year old boy.
Let it stand for about an hour.
Sprinkle some love.
Serve with a brother, sister, mother, and father.
Lastly, taste a loving brother named Paiton.
Landri Felker, Grade 6

Gone

When the World
Becomes difficult
  And cocoons you;

    you're gone.

When conflict disturbs
  Your cool
    Self-esteem;

    you're gone.

When someone finally
  succeeds in breaking
your walls of solitude;

    you're gone.

Oh, how I dreamed
  I could be like
    you, to learn,

But I can't,
Because every time I try;

    you're gone
        Aine McElroy, Grade 6

Lightning

BOOM!
Goes the lightning
You dash away as fast as a cheetah

BAM!
Goes the Lightning
You get frightened to death

CRACK!
Goes the lightning
It creates a fire that spreads like a virus

KABOOM!
Goes the lightning
The water explodes like a nuke

BANG!
Goes the lightning
The power goes out

ZAP!
Goes the lightning
You get shocked by electricity

Lighting is full of tremendous power
Lightning is an assassin
        Michael Rees, Grade 4

Cats

A lways by your side
B engal tigers beautiful and fierce
C uddly and cute
D ogs are their enemies
E ats like a queen
F ights fiercely
G oing as fast as a car
H eart as soft as gold
I n your heart they stay
J umping from branch to branch
K illing birds
L oving you back
M ice stand no chance
N o birds either
O celots roaming freely
P urring perfectly
Q uiet at night
R ough tongues to clean their fur
S till and ready to pounce
T o me cats are beautiful and deadly
        Catherine Petty, Grade 4

Deployment

Out the house
On a plane
Up in the air
Past America
Off a plane
Into Kuwait
Near trouble
In a building
Far from home
At work
By many soldiers
From the U.S.
In a helicopter
Into armed fire
Left the war
Near safety
Above Kuwait
Back to America
In El Paso
To me
        Reign Fakih, Grade 5

Trapped

You used to ignore me
  Leaving me behind
    I gave up
No one was by my side
Sitting alone was hard to do
But now it doesn't bother me
    I'm smart
I am special in my own way
  I'm the girl on the inside
    Lyndsey Cubine, Grade 6

I Am Peter

I am Peter
I wonder about life
I hear other people
I want to go to heaven

I am Peter
I pretend I'm rich
I feel good
I touch my iPhone to play games
I worry about my life

I am Peter
I say I'm nice sometimes
I dream I'm cool
I try to be nice
I hope I'm nice to other people

I Am Peter
        Peter Dadinis, Grade 6

A Day at the Beach

Come to the beach
Where the ocean is blue
And little white waves
Run after me
A wave is splashing
Over my toes
I stand in the sand
And see it go
I build sand castles
Down by the sea
And look for sand dollars
When my friends come with me
Standing by the lifeguard tower
I feel the ocean breeze
I see pearly white shells
And hear the palm trees
Come to the beach
Where the ocean is blue
        Lena Campbell, Grade 6

She Loves Me!

Smart as can be
Talks me through things
Is there for me
Will guide me
Won't let go
Will talk to me
Won't make fun of me
She is nice to me
She means the world to me
She is helpful to me
If I am down she will pick me up
But the most important thing is that
SHE LOVES ME!
        Kaylee Wilkinson, Grade 6

Aquamarine
Aquamarine describes me
It's light like the sea
Underwater I could live
Sea life lives here
Aquamarine is my color
It's my mood a positive color
Lived in my heart
Aquamarine is my sight
All joy and nothing left behind
Aquamarine is my soul, my life and
My friend she loves me as I
Love her too and I'll never stop
Loving her as she does to me in
My life.
Katia Cuevas, Grade 6

Best Friends
A friend is like a owl,
so beautiful and calm…

Or maybe like a key chain,
that rattles all day long…

A friend is like a teddy bear,
you keep it by your side…

Or maybe like a statue,
the never ever lies…

A friend is like a sibling,
that you never ever forget!
Victoria Hix, Grade 6

Sundown
The frog makes its last hop,
The lumberjack takes his final chop.

The child finishes his bedtime story,
not heard by his father, nor he.

The bee pollinates its final flower,
The sun is running out of power.

Now all of the tiny workers of space,
Work silently, each at their own pace.

Quickly, quietly repairing the sun,
to the eternal light, the greatest one.
Calvin Rutledge, Grade 6

Puppies
Puppies are so cute and fluffy,
They are rough and kind of puffy.
They fall and run and play,
Outside on a sunny day.
Braydee Millard, Grade 4

Why?
I feel as invisible as the air,
no one understands.
I try to talk and just be normal,
Why?

I scream, I shout, I let it all out,
it's all so hard.
People are so rude, so crude,
Why?

I'm smart, I'm kind,
so why do you judge me?
We all have flaws,
and yet you pull out mine.
Why?

I'm disabled,
so what.
We're all different,
Me, just a little more than you.
So I ask you,
Why?
Abby Quesenberry, Grade 6

A Moment by the Sea
The clouds are turning
An exquisite
Orange and pink

It Illuminates
The sky
All the colors dance
In my mind

The sun glows like
A sizzling fire as it
Glistens over the ocean

The waves look as if
They are pulling us in and
Wanting us to stay

The rich light
Touches our faces
For the last time as it

Fades behind the sea
Reese Ingram, Grade 6

Disneyland
Visiting Disneyland is so very fun
And you ride each ride one by one
It would be such a thrill
And it will give you a chill
After you are done you had so much fun.
Steven Pallan, Grade 5

Ninjas of Light
Sneaky, stealthy, as they creep,
Maneuvering smoothly without a peep.
They disappear in the night,
These Ninjas of Light.

As colors peek over the clouds,
Shadows begin to arouse.
They're fast, they're quick,
Tracking you in a tail flick.

They show no fear,
They're always near.
They feel at home.
When you start to roam.

I must confess,
They're are bland and colorless.
They have no feature,
To be your favorite creature.

Yet, when night falls,
They stop roaming walls.
Even they go night-night,
These famous Ninjas of Light.
Parveen Udawala, Grade 6

I Am Not Afraid
Walking in the dark.
Seeing a shark.
Strangers at the park.
I am not afraid.

Bees that like to sting.
People with a nose ring.
Pulling a hamstring.
I am not afraid.

People who throw pie.
Shampoo in my eye.
Parents saying their last bye.
I am not afraid.

Long, slimy, snakes.
Cars with no brakes.
Vampires with wooden stakes.
I am not afraid.

Ok,
I'll admit.
I might be a little frightened.
A lot frightened.
Karlie Tenery, Grade 6

Video Games

In video games you have to read.
And then win for the lead.
You fly,
All the way to the sky.
When I lose I feel bad,
And then I feel sad.
Avdiel Garza, Grade 5

Chubby

My dog is black.
His house is next to a shack.
It feels like he's double,
Because he is full of trouble.
I tell my parents to let him be,
Because to me it's only him and me.
Belen Hernandez, Grade 5

Cats

Cats
graceful, furry
purring, hunting, sleeping
paws, claws, collar, crown
royal, queenly
Tabby
Kora Converse, Grade 5

Earth

Amid the solar system
With a green and blue mass
Beneath the bright stars
At number three
From the sun
Within the universe
Amon Odom, Grade 4

Texas

Texas is like a red volcano
It tastes like barbecue
It sounds like rock music
It smells like barbecue
It looks sunny
It makes me feel happy
Travis Griffiths, Grade 4

Mr. Frankenstein

Mr. Frankenstein is mean
He is green
He is really tall
That makes me look small
With bolts on his head
He was able to wake from the dead
Emmanuel Carbarin, Grade 5

I Feel as Silly As…

I feel as limp as a snake
I feel as happy as a hyper dog
I feel as strong as a gorilla
I feel as silly as a cartoon character
I feel as sad as Prince Charming when Snow White went to sleep for a long time
I feel as angry as a monster
I feel as excited as a monkey getting a treat
I feel as frightened as a deer being hunted
I feel as light as a bird
I feel as grumpy as Grumpy the dwarf
I feel as slow as a sloth
I feel as hungry as an elephant staring at peanuts
I feel as sleepy as Sleeping Beauty
Kolbie Berkowitz, Grade 4

Blue

Blue is the color of the sky
Just as dinner comes in my house
Blueberries, Jolly Ranchers, jelly, and Gatorade
The smell of berry smoothies when they get
mixed in the blender…blend blend blend
There are waves crashing against a lighthouse with a really bright light

The color blue is the river with lots of water with its bright shine.
Alle Klemkow, Grade 4

Darkness

When darkness comes farther to closer,
Don't let it fill you, don't let it in.
Increasing the fright, sometimes at night, you don't want it there but there it comes.
Don't let it know you're about to let the light go.
Those who wish to take the light's place will be embraced.
It is dark, like the bottom of the ocean.
It will come and snatch you when you open your eyes.
Darkness may be your final break.
You might scream or shiver when darkness comes.
When you let the light go, there is something that lurks in the dark.
It grabs you and you scream.
When you finally see who it is, you scream even more.
To those who know and those who don't, it's your worst nightmare and never before.
Jonathan Aggar, Grade 5

Hope

If hope could be a color, it would be yellow as bright as the Heaven gates.
If hope could be a taste, it would taste just like an ice cream sundae on a summer afternoon.
If hope could be a smell, it would be a vanilla bean fragrance.
If hope could be a sound, it would be the sound of friends hanging out.
If hope could be a feeling, it would be like being baptized.
If hope could be an animal, it would be a swimming baby duckling.
Reagan McFarland, Grade 6

Music
A way to free yourself
from the darkness.
Thump thump, following the beat,
It will show you the way.

Finally found the funny one.
Lyrics of a song that
touches your soul and
understands you.

Feeling like another world
that nobody understands
but you and
your beating soul.
Angel Herrera, Grade 6

Alone
Alone frightened worried
I travel in the darkness
Looking for a light
I get closer and closer
But then it disappears
I try over and over again
When ever I get closer
The light goes further
I start running, as fast as I can
I feel the cold breeze of the air
No matter how hard I try
Nothing could get me to the end
I give up
The darkness has won
Finnian Vogelpohl, Grade 6

Fire, Fire
Fire, fire burning bright,
Dancing, prancing through the night.

Sparking, lighting, flames anew,
Starting, catching, fires too.

Sparks and flames, calming, slowing,
Embers and ashes softly glowing.

Dark and black, silent, cold,
Flames erupt from the old.

Fire, fire burning bright,
Dancing, prancing, through the night.
Amberly Brice, Grade 6

Perfect Princess
I am a queen
I have a crown
It's very clean
I wear it with my gown
Aracelia Moreno, Grade 5

Friends Are Beyond Boundaries
There are no boundaries,
No mountain too high
Nothing can stop me
I can't say goodbye

Wherever you come from
No matter where
Whatever you go through
I'll always be there

See, appearance doesn't matter
Eternally I'm your friend
Because I know you'll be awesome
Until time's end
Elizabeth Owens, Grade 6

That's Me
Yes, that's me
Look and you'll see
My hair dirty blond
My eyes brown
My hands are so very pink
My heart knows what it wants
I'm very special to my mom
I never wear too short of a dress
My friends are very special to me
I live in a good town
I hope to live in Hollywood
I dream of being a singer
It's clear as can be
That's positively, absolutely me
Jadalynn Baugh, Grade 4

The Night
I was walking in the night,
Then I saw a bright light.
I was driving in my car,
Then I saw a shooting star.

Late at night when the fires are out,
why does he gallop and gallop about.
I went down a path that was long,
Then I wrote a song.

The night is a beautiful sight,
for me a source of delight.
Sleeping in the night without your face,
I just miss your darling grace.
Denisse Gonzales, Grade 6

Chameleons
Chameleons change colors
And cost so many dollars.
They eat flies
And spy with their eyes.
Andres Barrientes, Grade 5

Eagles
An eagle
A bird of prey
Flies like an arrow
Through the
Big blue sky
It is as ferocious as a lion
As graceful as a deer
The bird is majestic
When you watch it fly
You are watching pure
Majesty
The eagle is beautiful
It is glorious
It is epic

The eagle is
Awesome.
Riley Roderick, Grade 6

Emotion
Sadness, love
Happiness, anger
All of these and we ask
Ourselves…
Is it worth it?
Is it not?
Why we do it?
Why we don't?
Where it is?
Where it's not?
Do it?
Don't do it?
Whether we like it?
Whether we don't?
And we ask again,
Is it worth it?
Is it not?
Lily Marie McConnell, Grade 6

Sun
Rain
Pops out
Colors,
Personalities,
And
Perspectives.
The crystal drops fall
From above.
Listen.
Can you hear?
Listen closely.
A sound
Grows louder
Find the rain in your life,
And make it sunshine.
Logan Wickman-Hudnut, Grade 6

Horses

Brown, black, white, and bay
They romp and play all day
They nicker and neigh

Grab a horse from the stable block
Gallop, canter, trot, then walk
If you want to slow down it helps if you talk

If you watch them while they graze
You might catch a look at the stripe or the blaze
Horses. You cannot look away, you just gaze

Horses are agile and able creatures
They have easily noticed and beautiful features
Everyone stares in awe from the bleachers

Kathryn Eastman Curry, Grade 4

The Beach

The sun shines across the sandy beach
Bright
The sand is
As the sun shines on it
The ocean's waves crash onto the sandy shore
As the ocean sparkles
The waves carry lost seashells from the Gulf
Lost and forgotten forever
Kites soar through the air
Gracefully dancing through the sky
Flying
Like the birds do
The sand is soft on my feet
Relaxing, soothing
Just like the beach itself

Anna Adkison, Grade 6

Aahil

Yes that's me
Look and you'll see
My hair is black
My eyes are really dark brown
My arms are long
My hands are large
My heart is always positive
I'm always laughing
I never betray my friends
My friends are always supporting me
I live because I have a family who cares about me
I hope to live happily
My dream is to go to Stanford
It's all clever as can be
That's positively absolutely me.

Aahil Syed, Grade 5

Epic

See, life is too short…
One minute you're happy, the next you're sad.
One minute you're here, the next you're there.
One minute you're walking your fist baby steps,
    the next you're getting ready to die.
See, life is too short…

Tamana Fakhri, Grade 6

Easter

Easter is a special time of year,
To remember what Jesus Christ did for us.
He saved us from our sins,
So we were welcomed into the gates of Heaven.
God our Lord gave up His son,
For humanity because He loves us and everyone.

Judson Beard, Grade 6

Easter

E aster is a time for family to reunite.
A re you faithful?
S ome people like to take pictures in the bluebonnets.
T oday is Easter!
E veryone loves eggs.
R ight now people are hunting for eggs.

Brennan Vollmar, Grade 6

Spring

S ucculent green grass
P ecan trees, never stop growing
R ow boats, across the water, floating with sass
I gnoring our electric devices
N obody complains, just happiness
G leaming meadows, never I thought, could be so nice.

Justine Neely, Grade 4

Soccer

Soccer is green.
It tastes like chocolate chip ice cream
It sounds like the ball hitting the net of the goal.
It smells like snacks being sold at the concessions stand.
It looks like the arena full of audience members.
It makes me feel energetic.

Rifet Rizvic, Grade 5

Blackout

The day came, dust, wind, dirt blowing on your face. You
start running, screaming, grabbing your family members
to keep them safe, but there is nowhere to hide. If you
survived, there was no point because there was nothing to
eat, all the crops were covered in dirt.

Viviana Alday, Grade 4

Dust Bowl

I am the dust bowl
black as a dark sky
devouring people with dust
scooping over 100 degrees
a hard dark blizzard
destroying homes and animals around me
chasing birds away with fear
hurting people with my dust and dirt
I am the dust bowl
Tiffany Nguyen, Grade 4

Free Birds

Hear them sing
Watch them soar through the sky
Such a beautiful song
Loved by all
They bring peace and love
As they soar so high
With a passion to be free
To touch the sky
Fly free birds fly, and sing your happy song
Carolinn Dukes, Grade 5

Hawaii

the huge volcano
part of archipelago
lava rocks
thirteen alphabet letters
luau, festival party
hula, native dance
they eat poi
fiftieth state
The paradise, Hawaii
Kaede Chung, Grade 5

My Newfoundd Twin

She follows me around,
together we are bound.
Whatever action I may do,
she imitates behind me, too.

When the sun is out,
it's like I've found my twin no doubt.
So clouds stay away,
I want to see my shady shape stay.
Callie Donaldson, Grade 5

Follow the Swirl

Dance with the swirl on top of
a cinnamon roll following a
path to another word.

View a small maple leaf and
climb to the top of a pine
tree and snack on salami.
Lara Ibrahim, Grade 4

Yellow

Yellow is the hot sun beating down on me while walking through Hollywood
Yellow is the lemon used for ice cold lemonade
Yellow is butter melting on the burning pan ready for the vegetables
Yellow is the beautiful daffodils sitting in the sun
Yellow smells like freshly made mac and cheese
Yellow tastes like the cold sour lemon drops
Yellow sounds like the shimmering stars in the sky
Yellow looks like the sand blowing in the bright light of day
Yellow feels like fire from blazing flames
Yellow makes me see bees buzzing wildly around their hives
Yellow is the lightning illuminating the windows during a storm
Hana Wali, Grade 5

My Dusty Shadow

My shadow wears
His beautiful dusty green coat hovering over his torso because of the wind.
His blue jeans and brown belt floating calmly.
His shoes carrying dust from the dust storm.
His hair is like a beautiful black cloud.
The hair blows with the gust of wind.
My shadow is a victim in the dust bowl.
A terrified victim.
A survivor.
A shadow…
Norman Catalano, Grade 4

Ahlam Ali Shido

Ahlam
Funny, punctual, smart, organized
Daughter of Ali Farah and Fadumo Hassan
Lover of "Best Friends Whenever," rice, and Oaks Park
Who feels nervous about singing in front of people,
Glad after turning in homework, and happy when she gets good grades
Who fears dogs/puppies, staying home alone, and being on top of Ferris wheels
Who would like to see world peace, stop pollution, and go to Cairo, Egypt
Resident of Hillsboro
Shido
Ahlam Shido, Grade 4

Amazing Amira

Amira
Smart, well-mannered, and loves others
Sister of Dania and Abukar
Lover of adventurer, the beach, and Great Wolf Lodge
Who feels shy around strangers and embarrassed in front of others
Who fears nightmares, scary movies, and death
Who wants to see everyone get along, no more wars and everyone is kind to one another
Resident of Beaverton
Mohamed
Amira Mohamed, Grade 4

Baby Bunny

Bye baby bunny
It's now time for me to leave
I promise to come again
Analicia Leal, Grade 4

Worry

misuse of the mind
you should never have to worry
it is never right
Spencer Gertz, Grade 4

Camping

Camping is something I don't like to do
My little brother, Jayden, doesn't enjoy it, too
We have to set up a really big tent
No matter how hard we twist and turn
It always turn out all crooked and bent

Late at night
We always have a fight
With our mom and dad and cousins, too
It's usually no biggie, but we don't realize that
We sometimes make up when Jayden yells, "Boo!"

At twelve noon, we each eat a s'more
We sit on logs, not on the floor
S'mores are always super yummy
Jayden would always make up words to describe them
Like great, tasty, and really crumby

The next day
We don't continue to play
Camping outside is done
We pack up and go home
But we'll go again because it was lots of fun!

Eileen Phung, Grade 4

Henry Harrison III

Henry Harrison the 3rd
was a boy who could fly like a bird.
Every day he'd spread his wings
then eat an extraordinary amount of dumplings.
His magic would begin to work
he'd fly above the clouds and smirk.
One day as he swooped down low
Henry began to create a big show.
The neighbors started to stop and stare,
people came from everywhere!
But Henry was extremely shy
all he could do was weep and cry.
Until his wings just would not flap
he fell like a bomb, and landed with a WHAP!
However, Henry wasn't finished just yet
back to the sky, his mind was set!
He conjured his magic, with all his might
using his courage, he gained back flight.
Suddenly, his arms went wild
crowds began to cheer on the child.
Floating mystically, up towards the sun
out to have a little more fun!

Dante Sbarbaro, Grade 6

The Way Things Whoosh, Sway, and Sing

Waterfalls spit and splash and slide,
Trees whistle in the night time,
The birds sing to me,
Now the sand rushes against my feet

Madison Martinez, Grade 4

Drumming Heart

I miss the chill that bit my nose,
The wind that would always freeze my toes.
My hands were red as they thawed,
While icicles dripped, never flawed.
I would stick out my tongue to catch the snow,
But now that seems so long ago.
Now I'm in a place that's always on fire,
I left behind people that I will always admire.
A friend that's like a sister,
Teachers that I would call Miss and Mister.
I miss the pines that I would climb,
And the sap that ran down the trunks like slime.
My heart was a drum as it beated,
My energy not just yet depleted.
I climbed the trees just to show
The world how far I could really go.
I snatched a star and held it close,
Telling myself not to boast.
My heart was a drum as it beated,
But still my energy is not just yet depleted.

Ljiljana Parker, Grade 6

I Think My Biggest Mistake Was

I need to snap back into reality
I've gotta find my inner peace
It's like my life is on a leash
But before I hit distraction
I've gotta to decide to make my actions
Less of a chain reaction
Made up of mixed up fractions

I need to take back my lost and wasted time
I need to make up for my life of crime
But how can I achieve this in the matter of just a clock chime
I need to analyze it
Sometime it'll become a bigger problem
And I wouldn't mind it,
if the time, it
just slowed down I might have plenty
of things to firelight it.
The problems with myself, my personality
I've gotta do this ASAP.
I need to snap back into reality.

Alexus Morrison, Grade 6

Goal Keeping

The diving, the sliding and saving
The stress that burdens your shoulders
No one is behind you to keep them from scoring
The dribbling of the strikers pounding in your ears
The sound of the kick resounding on the field
Is it going in?
I stretch my body across the goal to get a hand on the ball
Then I hear the crack of the net
And it's in for them.

Logan Toé, Grade 6

Ode to Cheese Balls
Oh, great and powerful Cheese Balls,
your cheesy smell enchants me.

When I look at you,
I just want to eat that crunchy delicious ball of flavor.

I can envision you saying, "Eat more cheese balls!"
(but with a girly enticing Texas accent)

If you ever want to continue to live,
I would recommend running!

My lips are smacking already,
just thinking about you.

Run, Cheese Balls!
Run, you orangey ball of delightfulness!

I don't know any stronger power of food,
you've captured me,
Oh, great powerful Cheese Balls.
Marshall Lehman, Grade 4

I Am
I am kind and brave
I wonder if I'll see my brother again
I hear angels singing
I see God taking me to heaven
I want to feel my brother again

I am kind and brave
I pretend I am in the military
I feel wetness
I touch clouds
I worry that I will lose my other brother
I cry when I remember the day my brother died

I am kind and brave
I understand why God loves me for who I am
I say that I will see Ms. Solarzano when I grown up
I dream to be in the military
I try to get my grades up
I hope I have a German Shepherd

I am kind and brave
Melanie Solares, Grade 5

The Sun
T he sun medium sized is a star
H uge ball of very hot gas that gives off energy so very far
E arth is our planet that orbits the sun, you can't go there in a car

S atellites orbiting objects in space
U ranus also orbits the sun, a very hot place
N eptune is the last planet that orbits the sun, a very long lace
Jacque Schwarz, Grade 5

I Am
I am joyful and friendly
I wonder if my dad will come back
I hear my name
I see my brother that's dead
I want my relatives to come back alive

I am joyful and friendly
I pretend to be an investigator
I feel scared that something will happen to me
I touch the sky
I worry that my mom might die
I cry when I think of my dad

I am joyful and friendly
I understand why Jehovah is real
I say that Jehovah is our creator
I dream to be a veterinarian
I try to be a nice little sister
I hope my mom gets better

I am joyful and friendly
Angelica Perez, Grade 4

Ode to Crockett, My Puppy
Crockett,
you've earned a Ph.D. in craziness.
Now you're a scholar among cuteness,

I love your warm and fuzzy messed up fur,
and the way you come inside and greet me with
your wiggly tail.

I love you,
because you comfort me when I'm sad,
your wet slobbery licks warm my heart.

Crockett,
I love it when you come home from a walk,
and you are wet from jumping into the lake.

Just one request,
please stop shaking it off around me.
You soak me.

I love you Crockett!
Reagan Hall, Grade 4

Happiness
Happiness seems bright yellow
Like the sun shining on a pleasant day.
I see a rainbow as colorful as a box of crayons.
I hear people cheering with glee.
I smell pollen from a sweet sunflower.
I touch the color splash of the water.
I taste joy.
Abigail Ruiz, Grade 4

Art

Paintings are all different
Some made of dots
Others made with streaks
They all blaze with brilliance

The image made with paint
Telling a story of life
One might be of the Southwest
Another of Paris, France

Sculptors make art with clay
Sculpting 'till it's perfect
Nothing is left out

Coming form all around
Art is pure
Glowing with joy
Drenched in sorrow

Time is tranquil
Life is soothing
if art is
In your world
Afrin Momin, Grade 4

Rabbits

As they jump up
they're quick in running
so, they can escape
from you when you catch them
so, they might run and run
but others might catch them

As they go in their burrows
they will escape from enemies
but then again they'll go outside
you will feed them a carrot
but they might not fall for it

So as the rabbits go find food
danger will be there
they will have to watch out
for wolves and much more

But some arctic rabbits
can camouflage with the snow
so the arctic rabbits can
survive better than regular rabbits
so every rabbit needs to be careful
Jaquelin Don, Grade 4

Traveling

Long time in the car
You see a long stretch of road
Finally see home
Chloe Mahurien, Grade 5

The Perfect Melody

Lost and alone
afraid and scared
Enclosed for too long
Different

Like a melody

Abandoned and lonely
Upset mad at myself
Cold in the darkness
Confused I have no clue where to go

Like a melody

Forgotten and betrayed
Left to rot
Falling apart
Used
Unbeautiful
A nobody

Like a broken melody
left to fight to fight for myself
Like a lion roaring in my face
Tear shed from my face

Like a perfect melody
Austin Moss, Grade 6

I Am Passionate

You try to hold it
it always slips,
chasing after
again you trip.

As darkness eats you
it swallows you whole,
pushing through
your pure soul.

Last one standing
won't let it go,
the depths of darkness
your passion will grow.

The light shines brighter
you can see the end,
feeling much closer
you're hopeful again.

Forever longing
your heart turns to dust,
blowing away
collects as it must.
London Lack, Grade 5

Light Lavender

Lavender flowers blow in
the gentle breeze.
She danced gracefully
with the lavender fairy
she found in the flowers.
Her house was quaint,
and she could even walk lightly
on the creaking, noisy stairs.
Lavender and Tickle Me Pink
share secrets in her room.
She giggles while wearing
lace clothing and smelling
like her name.

Lavender is sweet,
and loves vanilla ice cream.
She screamed excitedly
as soon as she found out
there was a mystery to be solved.
As soon as she went to sleep,
she dreamed of
sugarplums, cupcakes, and lollipops.
Elizabeth Askin, Grade 4

This Cruel World

The world is so cruel
To people like me.
When we ride the bus to school
We're separated.
We have our own rusted fountains-
Separated.
We have our own restaurants,
Separated.
Because black goes with black
And white goes with white.
When they see us, they turn their backs —
Why don't we have the same rights?

We must change this!
It's a vicious world we live in —
We must fix this injustice!
This world is cruel like theft
Cruel like war
Cruel like death!
Let's stop running from whites,
And give us blacks justice
Once and for all!
Jocelyn Shek, Grade 5

Bob the Hog

There once was a pig named Bob
who was actually a very big hog
he climbed up a tree
and fell down on me
and it felt like a hundred pound log
Henry Harrison, Grade 5

Kind Ruler

If I were in charge of the world
I'd get rid of cake prices, and
Any prices for sweets!
Onions, too!
If I were in charge of the world
There'd be dancing doggies
Kittens in mittens
And hamsters on Broadway!
If I were in charge of the world
You wouldn't have angry parents
You wouldn't have uncomfortable shoes
You wouldn't get splinters
You wouldn't even have rotten wood.
If I were in charge of the world
Everyone could go anywhere free
Everyone will smile forever
And a person who sometimes forgets homework
And forgets everything
Would still be allowed
To be in charge of the world

Tiffany Enering, Grade 5

I Am

I am loving and kind
I wonder what I will be when I'm older
I hear my great grandparents when I'm sleeping
I see God when I'm daydreaming
I want to grow up and be a great person

I am loving and kind
I pretend I'm a teacher when I play with my sister and brother
I feel excited for Saturday
I touch the clouds when I'm happy
I worry if I will get bad grades when I'm older
I cry when I think of sad things

I am loving and kind
I understand why my cousin is different
I say I love my family
I dream to have a good future
I try to be a good example for my younger siblings
I hope I have a good rest of my life
I am loving and kind

Sajdel Romero, Grade 4

Soccer

I like to play soccer in the rain,
Because that's when I have all my fame.
When I'm on the field I feel like I'm faster than a train,
And that's when everyone starts to recognize my name.

The fields are green and full of hills,
While the wind brings lots of chills.
I like the breeze and like to sing,
To the beauty of the spring.

Marisol Pacheco, Grade 6

I Am Justin

I am a boy who misses his uncle.
I wonder will everything be ok?
I hear the voice of my uncle's words of wisdom.
I see him in my dreams.
I want him to come back.
I am a boy who misses his uncle.

I pretend he is still alive
I feel he is watching over me.
I touch my belt buckle from him.
I worry about people dying.
I cry when I see pictures of him.
I am a boy who misses his uncle.

I understand one day everyone dies.
I say nothing is wrong.
I dream about him at night.
I try to remember our good memories.
I hope one day I can be with him.
I am a boy who misses his uncle.

Justin Bradley, Grade 6

Tomorrow

Tomorrow
The world will be perfect
Tomorrow
There is hope and people are kind
Tomorrow
People are content with themselves and the world
Tomorrow
You can feel joy abundant in the air
But tomorrow is just a dream
Because tomorrow
Always becomes today
And today
The world is dying
Today
People hate themselves
And everything else they see
Today
Joy is gone and isn't coming back
Leaving us to wonder
Will it ever be tomorrow?

Ireland Griffin, Grade 6

Basketball

The important thing about basketball is
that it works you out on every part of your body.
You use your brain.
You run and shoot with your arms,
and you sweat and it makes your arms and legs strong.
and it proves your sportsmanship,
and you can get a scholarship if you try.
But the important thing about basketball is
that it works you out on every part of your body.

Alay Ledezma, Grade 4

Clouds

Clouds
White fluffy things
Moving and pouring down
Like cotton candy in the sky
Fluffy
Camille Gaffney, Grade 5

Mountain Lion

A mountain lion is peeky,
But also sneaky.
When it finds something to hunt.
It starts to run.
It eats it until it is done.
Alfonso Rodriguez, Grade 5

Smiles

Smiles always cheer people up,
And keep the happiness going.
I love it when someone smiles at me,
Because I feel fair and swell.
Smiles, keep going!
Suhyeon Emelie Kim, Grade 4

Pet Snake

There was a kid named Jake
He had a pet snake
He slithered around
On the ground
Which made his whole body ache
Jake Wallingford, Grade 5

Sleep

Sleep
Peaceful silence
Dreaming, smiling, resting
Regain energy and strength
Slumber
Isa Barajas, Grade 5

Florida

It sounds like waves crashing on the rocks,
It tastes like good seafood,
It smells like salty beaches,
It looks like birds and surfers,
It makes me feel happy and cozy.
Luc Brown, Grade 5

Prayer

Genuine prayer is often silent
Conversing with God, a blessed event
Pray the Divine Mercy
Or Holy Rosary
It's as beautiful as a diamond
Madison Janachovsky, Grade 6

The Dust Storm

It was a sunny day.
My family and I were able to breathe again like we were able to do.
I was happy because I was positive thinking no more dust bowls.
My family and I were driving, we were some miles away from our house.
Until a frown came along my face.
Looking at the blue sky turn into black and a white cloud turning into black.
It looked like if it automatically turned into the night.
It was coming toward us, it was really fast.
We drove back home as fast as we can, knowing that it was following us.
We were back home. We took shelter. It hit us.
When I woke up I was not at my house.
I kept on wondering where I was.
I was lost, frightened and covered in dust, and dirt.
I looked around, houses were destroyed there were no people, I think they died.
I felt like I was choking to death, if I had dirt or dust in my lungs.
By the time I knew it I was in the ground.
All I saw was darkness and the world fading. I was alone and terrified.
Jennifer Turrubiartes, Grade 4

Old Davy Jones

To sail the great big blue
Oh, how I wish for it to come true

The endless discoveries to find
This one, no this one, I can't make up my mind

And oh the plain beauty of the seaway
From the whales to the magnificent manta ray

With the mesmerizing coral reef and the treacherous midnight zone
The powerful waves where an elephant can be blown

But people who understand the importance of the sea are rare
You know, it does produce 93 percent of our air

So come on, let's go sail the uncontrollable tide
With it's elegance, I'm sure you will be mesmerized
Arturo Marquez, Grade 6

Mission San Luis Obispo de Tolosa

S an Luis Obispo de Tolosa was established in 1772
A t the mission there is a fountain showing a Chumash Indian child sitting by a bear
N umber of neophytes in 1804 reached a peak of

L ife at the mission presented difficulties for everyone living there
U nlike other missions it is shaped like an "L"
I t was the 5th mission
S an Luis of Toulouse is the patron saint of mission San Luis Obispo de Tolosa

O n the church are the numbers 1772
B ecause of the amount of bears Saint Junipero Serra built a mission there
I n 1776 non mission Natives attacked the mission San Luis Obispo
S unrise was the time when the residents woke to the sounds of bells
P edro Fages accompanied Serra to choose the spot for the mission
O utspoken criticism by the Padres led to difficulty with the governor
Tessa Johansen, Grade 4

Lost My Heart

I knew I had lost her
I knew as she spoke
Because my heart collapsed
My heart had broke

Into a million pieces
They fell on the ground
Every beat hurt more
I hated the sound

My legs had no power
They couldn't hold me up anymore
They gave out
And I fell on the floor

I thought of her last words
They popped in my brain
She told me find the sun
When you're in the rain

I stood up
Wiped my tears away
Because I knew she'd always be there
In my heart she'd stay
Satvi Sheth, Grade 6

We're All the Same

Around the world
There are so many races,
We started from one place
We have the same traces.

We scattered across the globe
And we learned different things,
We were people who cared
Yet we acted like kings.

We spread our hatred
To a particular race,
Saying they're inferior
Though that's not the case.

Whites and Blacks
Latinos and Asians,
We're all the same
From different nations.

We're all the same
We're all the same,
Shame or no shame
We're all the same.
Tarun Yendrapati, Grade 6

I Am Marcus

I am cool and smart.
I wonder if there was no politics.
I hear people talking.
I see my puppy sleeping.
I want to see the Empire State Building.
I am cool and smart.

I pretend to be a police officer.
I feel someone hugging me.
I touch a castle door.
I worry about my grandpa.
I cry when my older brother picks on me.
I am cool and smart.

I understand I can't do certain things.
I say it's going to be ok.
I dream about being in the military.
I try to do good in school.
I hope to see my grandma in heaven.
I am cool and smart.
Marcus Hernandez, Grade 6

Seasons

Summer
It is always hot
All you want to do is swim
The beach is the best

Winter
Winter is freezing
I love skiing down big hills
Skiing is the best

Spring
Bees buzz around buds
Flowers will look colorful
Flowers are pretty

Fall
Fall is colorful
All the leaves are different
Thanksgiving is fun
Angelo Piziali, Grade 6

In My Mind

In my mind I have thoughts
and words. In my mind I
always have different things
floating around. In my mind it is
like a giant puzzle made of what's
inside. In my mind I can do anything.
In my mind I can conquer the world.
In my mind you can be anything you
want to. I know what's inside my mind, but
what's in yours?
Erin Rolfe, Grade 4

Seafood

A series of fish going to my mouth
Salty sticks, chewy or crunchy
Eating catfish, fish sticks, and shrimp

A salty side of French fries
Ketchup, tartar sauce, make it tasty
From the coral reef

To the bottom of the sea
Crunchy skin, chewy insides
A healthy, yummy treat

Oyster, crawfish
New fish to try,
And…to fry

Spicy, mild, salty too
Many fish to eat in the big blue
An alligator nugget will fire you up!
Miguel A. De Hoyos, Grade 4

When Rain Falls

When rain falls,
Gloom and heartache come big and tall.
As I walk through the musty hallway,
Everything is grey.
I feel the taste of tears;
A taste I have always feared.
Tears as thick as shame;
Tears that make me flame.
In the misty haze
I feel it is the end of my days.
I long for hope.
A feeling I can grope.
Then I hear an angel whisper,
I know in time the rain will differ.
I will push through.
In the end, I will not rue.
For if not rain,
The sun would not deserve its name.
Cameron Hajaliloo, Grade 6

Mom

Do you remember that first touch,
That first breath?

Those times of fears,
Where you needed
Someone to help.

When you needed
Someone to push you back up.

In every hard moment of your life
Somebody was always there.
Inigo Redondo, Grade 6

The Art of Baking

I really love baking with all my heart,
and I have always been passionate about it like I am with art,
I always love to eat the dessert I make,
and that's one of the reasons why I love to bake.
I love to bake with my cousins,
and they love to bake too,
We have so much fun together,
and baking, we all do.
When it was my aunt's birthday,
my cousin made a cake for her,
and when it was her dog's birthday,
she made a fake cake of fur.
I once made juice pops on a very sunny day,
and everyone who tried it enjoyed it,
I know that's not really baking,
but neither is a banana split.
Now you know why I love baking,
and why don't you give it a try,
if it doesn't work the first time try it again,
and I promise that soon you will hit the bulls-eye.

Zusanna Villatoro, Grade 4

Olive Green

Olive green is the color of grass
Olive green is the color of beautiful stained glass
Olive green is the color of my crazy socks
Olive green is the color of colorful green rocks
Olive green cannot be seen
Olive green is the color of a yummy lima bean
Olive green is the color of my Christmas sweater
There is no color that is better
Olive green is the color of colorful Christmas holly
That makes you so greatly jolly
It's the color of a crazy frog
That always seems to be jumping on a log
Green is the color of a sour lime
You better hurry you're running out of time
Olive green is the color of my bright marker
Don't forget to make it darker
Someone stole my big green book
Everyone seems to look
Its is the color of my eraser that glows
Olive green is the color of grass you mow

Audrey Lepard, Grade 5

I Am…Isaiah

I am athletic and funny
I wonder if I will play in the NBA
I hear everyone calling my name when I go down the court
I see myself making the winning shot
I like to be funny and for everyone to be my friend

I am athletic and funny
I pretend to be a billionaire
I feel that anything is possible
I touch the basketball in my hand
I worry that I won't make it to the NBA
I cry if my team loses a game

I am athletic and funny
I understand that to do great in school you have to study
I say have faith in yourself
I dream of being a funny actor one day
I try to make funny jokes that I could use in a movie one day
I hope to be a famous actor and everyone will like me
I am athletic and funny

Isaiah Rodell, Grade 4

My Little Baby Brother Jeff

My little baby brother Jeff is so fun to play with
I play with him for a time and width
He wants to go places and I follow him
He likes to play with all the balls
He throws the balls in the hoop
We carry him so he can reach and he is thin!
He picks up balls to go and does it like a swoop
He plucks the violin strings
and dances to piano music
He loves all kinds of silly things
He sees the songs and he will choose it
He's so cute and I love him too
Referring to my family he loves to play with you
Whatever he wants to do
My family sees if it's good to choose
Every day I spend with him
My imaginary mind with a picture and pin
He's the cutest baby brother in my opinion
When he grows up I hope he'll be a good chef
And that is the end of my baby brother Jeff!

Caroline Hsu, Grade 4

Love Is Love

Love is love
Never the same
But you have to remember it could be a game
It could be bad
It could be good
It could even be true love if you would
But still remember
It could be a game
And never the same

Zariah Vela, Grade 4

The Snow Leopard in Love

It's black and white
Like an old fashioned movie
Once you look into its eyes
You fall in love
You hear its desperate cry for love
It may seem heartless but love is yet to come
As it chases its heart
Begging for a hug
From everything that has become and learned to love

Chrislynn Knittel, Grade 6

I'm the Queen of the STAAR

A bunch of new worksheets in our faces, if you
don't pass the STAAR you will disgrace us, fail
the test and you'll regret it, get to work right this minute

look at me I'm the Queen of the STAAR!
suddenly, I'm the teacher's pet
look and see what I get, a
king size candy bar!

shoot for a hundred don't you get lower
stay right on task and stop working slower
Think of me and all that I taught ya, try to
think of all the tricks that I showed ya.

The test is hard so you better study.
Don't mess around and talk to your buddy.
You better read the passages 5 times each, and
underline the information that we teach.
Keep your pencil sharp and your mind too.
Get a good score, its up to you!

Look at me, I'm the Queen of the STAAR.
Suddenly, I'm the teacher's pet.
Look and see what I get, a
king sized candy bar!

Elle Renshaw, Grade 6

Opa

It was the most depressing surprise.
For he was the liveliest of them all.
But his brain went dark, refused to show light.
His boat swam away,
He was unable to catch it.
And for most of us, we never got to say farewell.

I did learn something from him that he gave to me,
without intention.
He taught me that you never know how much you love something,
until you lose it.

Now I am a curious kitten, pawing at the door.
I have been told everything happens for a reason,
What is the reasoning behind this fall?
I wish I knew.

What I hope right now is for him to be,
Flying right above me.
Guiding me my every move,
And telling me when the bridge is not stable.

For he was my dad's father.
My grandpa.
For he was my Opa

Katie Simmons, Grade 6

I Am Gone from the World

I am gone from the world.
I have no idea how.
I am alone in space.
Wait! Is that a cow?

I am gone from the world.
I am near Mars.
I miss my friends right now.
I wish we were in flying cars.

I am gone from the world.
I am drifting towards earth.
I hope it is near Spring.
If so, I get to see new birth!

I am gone from the world.
My space craft is super far.
I hope humans show me how to play golf.
My mom said that I should not try to make a par.

I am landing on Earth now,
As fast as a bull!
I am filling up with determination.
Now I made it to the pool.
Wait! Is that a human child!?

William Betts, Grade 4

If I Were in Charge of The World

If I were in charge of the world,
I'd ban homework and adults' reign,
I'd end vaccines and sicknesses,
I'd even remove horror movies.

If I were in charge of the world,
There'd be no limit to candy,
Dolphins and unicorns would be normal pets.
There'd be fun in everything.

If I were in charge of the world,
You wouldn't have to work.
You wouldn't have consequences.
You wouldn't have bullies.
Or "No iPad for you."
There wouldn't even be any "No's"

If I were in charge of the world,
There'd be a secret portal to a candy land.
Candy and ice cream would count as healthy.
And a person
who sometimes forgets to make her bed,
And sometimes forgets to brush her hair,
Would still be allowed
to be in charge of the world.

Madison Yang, Grade 5

Unicorn Dream
I close my eyes
I fall asleep
And I enter a unicorn dream
I see rainbow fluffy creatures
Their horn is like a golden ice-cream cone
Tipped upside down on their head
Their mane is a bright sunshine
The smell of sugar cubes and cupcakes
Reach my nostrils
I hear them saying
I love you Danielle
And I respond
I love you to
But then something awful happened
I woke up from my
Unicorn dream
Danielle Keller, Grade 4

Green
Green is my friend
It is kind of dark
It is kind of bright
Green is a pretty color
It fits my personality
Green is kind of mean
And kind of nice
Green is like spring
Kind of hot
Kind of cold
Green is the color of good
The color of great
But never perfect
Green is the color of calm
The color of dislike
Green is my friend
Heidi Diaz, Grade 6

Writing
Pencil "check"
Eraser "check"
Writer's notebook "check"
All my supplies
Laid out on the desk
Ready to express my feelings on
paper
Not just any paper
Gold paper
Worth a million dollars
Treasure
That leaves an image in your mind
Writing expresses not just feelings
But meaning
An illusion is made
The characters come alive
Samantha James, Grade 4

Spring Glories
Rain release from puffy, gray clouds
Drip, drop, drip, drop; that's their anthem
Hearing its vibrating sounds
Ready to sprinkle on awaiting blossoms

Florets bloom in the cloudburst
Opening up to see the wonderful hues
Spreading wide to quench their thirst
Waiting for their petals to catch dew

Growing bright and colorful
Blooming in clusters
Oh, so pleasing and delightful!
In the light, the blooms luster

Little youngsters happily guffaw
In the flowers, they prance
Feeling free to let loose chuckles
Through the spring, they dance
Melissa Wang, Grade 5

Mammals
Extraordinary mammals,
Dolphins to bats,
Swimming and gliding
Through
Water and air.

Exquisite mammals,
Elegant leopards
Stalking
Their prey
For survival.

Mammals of colors,
Shapes and
Sizes,
They are
Extraordinary
Animals to the
Core!
William Boyd Collins, Grade 4

The Creature
Lurking in the dark
Waiting for the prey to come
It lives in shadows
He is gonna come one day
Maybe, he is here today.

He is here for you
He is gonna eat you now
You better go run
Because he's gonna catch you
You can run but you can't hide.
Benny Sanchez, Grade 6

Panda!
There is a panda
Eating lots of bamboo
He is very chubby
And that is true

He finishes eating
And goes out to play
He goes under the shade instead
Because it is a very hot day

He lays there
Trying not to get hot
But instead of staying awake
He falls asleep on the spot

When he wakes up
It is not day
It is no longer hot
So he goes out to play

When he comes back to the shade
He is really beat
So then he decides
It is time to eat
Bryce Vu, Grade 5

The Dust Bowl
What's in the storm
it's a
Mouse suffocating in dust,
A house full of dust,
A kid trying to get home through the dust,
A car being buried by the dust,
A cow dying in the dust,
A bird trying to get away from the dust,
that's what's is in the storm.
Maximiliano Finley, Grade 4

Spring Green
Green
is the color
of grass in the
Spring. Green is
the smell of food from
a king. Green is the feeling
while climbing a tree. Green is the
food
from
pods
of a
pea.
Green
is the
Sound
of you and me.
Adriah Blue, Grade 4

Think

When you are hurt,
Your eyes are heavy with tears
You reflect your life in the mind of mirrors
You fall deep down in the sea of memories
Of your faults and broken, taken dreams
To the zone of darkness you will sink
But you need to rise you need to THINK
Eliza Cho, Grade 6

Spring Puddle

Fruit blossoms blooming
Birds chirping in the sunshine
A sprinkle of rain

A sprinkle of rain
It turns into a puddle
The kids splish-splashing
Carolina Murrin, Grade 4

STAR Wars

In a far, far galaxy,
my teacher is teaching
me how to fight.
Hya! Pow! Crush! Ow!
My master has defeated me.
He is well known as
Mr. Yoda Garate.
Jesus Castilleja, Grade 4

Morning and Night

The night air is still.
Fireflies light up the sky
among many stars.

As the sun rises
the sky begins to light up.
The day has begun.
Nicholas Charette, Grade 4

Jazzy

Dog
playful, adorable
running, licking, chasing
poodle, shih tzu, lab, golden retriever
biting, jumping, pouncing
furry, soft
Jazzy
Canyon Mimbs, Grade 5

Santa

S uper cool
A wesomely nice
N ow brings gifts
T aught you not to be naughty
A bsolutely the best
Krish Panchal, Grade 4

Australia

A mazing and peaceful as could be
U nique and extraordinary in every way
S imple place and quiet as
T arantulas crawling around the lawn of grass
R ound and round you'll see them go in
A ustralia, the place you should go
L ook for koalas high in the trees
I n the meadows you'll see roos leap
A nd how extraordinary this place could be where all the wild animals will flee.
Irena Goforth Macritchie, Grade 6

Ode to Chocolate Bluebell Ice Cream

O chocolate ice cream your creamy goodness
O chocolate ice cream a common delight
O chocolate ice cream you take me in when I'm sad
O chocolate ice cream you calm me down when I'm mad
O chocolate ice cream swimming in chocolate syrup and whipped cream
You are the pancakes, I the maple syrup
O chocolate ice cream only one bad thing about you
SPLAT!!!
It sounds like sadness when you hit the floor
Patrick Drez, Grade 4

In a World

In a world full of lies, live us, normal people waiting to be discovered,
in a world full of mischief waits crooked eyes prying
In a world full of beauty waits beauty queens living their majestic life
In a world full of ugliness waits me and my friend hoping to stand out,
Who care about us though
Everyone that it is time to get discovered
Lights, camera, action,
Time has come at last
Saraswathy Amjith, Grade 4

Life with Cerebral Palsy: In My Shoes

I am at the top of the mounting block.
I see my horse pull up.
I stretch my leg over the horse, the pain is unbearable but my leg settles down.
I go to the arena.
I shout "trot mark"
I hear his hooves hit the ground and I go.
I start to become uneasy, but then I smile.
I feel him stop and I can't believe it's over.
Shannon White, Grade 5

A Single Tear

A single tear ran down the sweet little face.
A single tear ran down those little rosy cheeks.
A single tear ran down to meet her lips.
While the world was honking and blinking and speeding and working.
A single tear ran down while no one was watching.
A single tear ran down.
Stella Stompoly, Grade 5

Winter Fun

Waking up from your warm bedding,
And deciding to go driveway sledding,
I have fun when I'm gliding by dry winter trees,
Sitting on my cold winter knees,
Then I start to fear this year's only snow's end is near.

Blake Brown, Grade 4

Maisy

I have a brown dog who is named Maisy
And sometimes she'll race around like she's crazy
My toes are what she'll bite
When she stays up all night
When it's morning she'll pace around hazy

Addy Harney, Grade 5

Cookies

Christmas cookies are yummy in your tummy.
Chocolate chip, peanut butter and vanilla.
They make your mouth water, oh yes they do.
Sugar cookies, snickerdoodles and M and M ones too.
I can bake them, just for you!

Gabrielle Boyd, Grade 4

Sunrise, Sunset

The sun rises and my joy rises as well
The sun sets and my rest is assured
The colors mix and melt and look as soft as felt
May every sunrise bring more promises
And may every sunset bring more peace

Duaa Jamaleddin, Grade 6

Basketball

When you're racing down the court in a hurry
Don't forget to stop and take shots like Curry
Flick the ball off your wrist
Or perform a layup twist
Don't forget to slip on your spirit team jersey

Julian Ritch, Grade 6

Ryan Gustin

Coming down the lane of turns three and four
Huffing and puffing his engine does roar
Dirt flies through the air
Like a shooting flare
Crossing the finish line like a plane does soar

Ryan Lennan, Grade 6

Narwhals

Narwhals are the unicorns of the sea
They have a horn and swim and sing in glee
Their favorite treats are codfish
When they play their tail goes swish
They prefer the water clear and icy

Caitlyn Mills, Grade 6

A Perfect Home

It could be a mansion, an apartment, or a den
Small or tall, big and wide, it doesn't matter what
It is what's inside the house that makes a perfect home
The people in the house you see, make this house a home
The laughs, you see, they fill the walls
Their happy presence coming from in to out
It doesn't have to be a perfect house
To make a perfect home

Kyra Kaya, Grade 6

Galaxy

Our galaxy is vast and wide,
It would be an amazing place to hide.
A game of planet hide and seek,
Could last more than an entire week.
I think that I may visit one day,
Maybe take some friends along the way.
A ton of supplies we would have to take,
But what an interesting story that would make!

Lyba Kahlon, Grade 5

Love

Beneath the hatred there is love
Inside a heart a special feeling grows
Amid the feeling of joy there is also frustration
In your life there are many ups and downs
Love makes you appreciate the people near you
Inside special moments you can feel happy
Above all love keeps the hatred out
Love is life

Timi Corcoran, Grade 5

Jalapeño Dare

My mother dared me to eat a jalapeño
The first bite I gave it felt like it was punching my tongue
Smoke came out my ears, lots and lots of smoke
Lava flowed down my mouth
My fingers melted just by touching it
My face turned so red I thought I was gonna explode
It was all in my imagination
I still ate the jalapeño but with lots of fear

Fernando Rodriguez, Grade 6

Fireworks

Crazy blue fireworks.
Lighting winter fireworks.
Cold fun park.
Cool awesome snow.
Running playing in pants that are like heaters.
Running and throwing fast snowballs that are like baseballs.
sledding winter hill.
crazy blue fireworks.

Parker Barnes, Grade 5

If I'm in Charge of the World

If I were in charge of the world,
I'd make sure there would be no war,
there would be peace,
and there would be no pollution
If I were in charge of the world,
there'd be a cure for cancer,
no illnesses,
and no starvation
If I were in charge of the world,
you wouldn't have to pay taxes.
You wouldn't have to pay for medical issues.
You wouldn't get bankrupt
or you would get poor,
if I were in charge of the world.

Kiana Lu, Grade 6

If I Were…

If I were an animal, I'd be a cheetah.
If I were a car, I'd be a Tahoe.
If I were a island, I'd be the Bahamas.
If I were a river, I'd be the Mississippi River.
If I were a pet, I'd be Obama's dog.
If I were a food, I'd be Orange Leaf's frozen yogurt.
If I were a planet, I'd be Mars.
If I were a board game, I'd be Life.
If I were a building, I'd be the Eiffel Tower.
If I were a famous person, I'd be Taylor Swift.
If I were a sport, I'd be a cheerleader.
If I were a drink, I'd be Dr. Pepper with vanilla and cream.
If I were a flower, I'd be a Bluebonnet.
If I were a month of the year, I'd be July.

Jaycie Holley, Grade 4

Ismael

There once was a boy
Who liked Chips Ahoy
He was an innocent child
Yet very wild
But then one day his wildness faded away
He was taken away that day
I miss his laugh and cry
Thinking about him makes me sigh
Thinking about him makes me sad
Knowing that I will never see him again makes me mad
He will always be the kid who made me smile
Even though it was just for a little while
He will always be in my heart
Till death we will part

Kacey Archuleta, Grade 6

The Orphan

I am a little boy I am sad and lonely
No one is with me I have no help
No friends, but one day I will be happy
With friends, With a family, Someone to play with.

Jacob Rivera, Grade 6

A Journal Is a Litter Box

A journal is a litter box,
If you've got words to say.

You can drop them, shed them, and write them down,
Soon you'll forget them anyway.

Anything you need to do,
Put it down,
Under numbers
1 and
2.

A journal is a litter box,
If you've got something to say.

Besides,
If you don't like what you wrote there,
Scoop it up,
And throw it away.

Sadie Parent, Grade 6

My Dog Ruby

Ruby is my favorite pet in the world
I would do anything for her
and she would do the same
and we do everything together.

Ruby and I have been together since we were five
we did childish things together
but now we got older
I'd still never ignore her, never at all.

We've gotten through a lot together
some rough and some fine.
The hospitals, dentists, and mean dogs
but they all turned out fine.

She would protect me
I'd protect her every time any time
we know when to help and to stay out
we are the best of friends and that will never change

Sean A. Freeman, Grade 4

I Am

I am a flower.
You know me from smelling good.
My mother is nature.
My father is God.
I was born from a seed.
I live outside.
My best friend is grass because I was planted there.
My enemies are bees because they take my pollen.
I fear winter because I will die.
I love spring because it gives me rain.
I wish to be one of the longest living flowers in the world.

Brittany Knack, Grade 6

Spring Fun
Weather, warm, spring fun
5 days off
Sunshine, swimming
Movie, sleeping
Fun time in
Sleep, time out
Nathan Emery, Grade 4

Yellow Is…
Yellow is the sun way up high
Yellow bees flying by
Yellow is a sour lemon in your mouth
Yellow flowers in the south
Yellow lemonade on a hot summer day
Yellow is great, some might say
Ella Klemkow, Grade 4

Dakota
D og-carer, dancer, diver
A verage, American, athletic
K eeper, kind, keen
O utdoorsy, outgoing, one-of-a-kind
T alkative, TV-lover, trustworthy
A ttractive, artistic, acrobatic
Dakota Crabtree, Grade 4

The Dust Bowl
Mysterious darkness,
houses ripped and torn.
Wind ferocious and vicious,
people sorrowful, depressed.
Everything is chaos, and insane
This is the angry Dust Bowl.
Acacia Huang, Grade 4

Christmas Joy
I see the Christmas tree
I smell the Christmas food
I hear jingle bells jingling
I taste Christmas cookies
I touch the Christmas tree
Christmas joy
Isaac Daniel, Grade 4

Ode to Summer
Summer is a sight,
it is also bright and light.
I like the warmness of the sun,
I wish I could stay there all day long.
There are no worries
so summer please don't hurry!
Augusta Thompson, Grade 5

Animals
There are different types of animals around the world,
like, lions, whales, birds, and more,
but they have one thing in common they stand out bright bold.

There are jungle animals, arctic, and marine.
Jungle has lions, arctic has bears, marine has eels that haven't been seen.

Animals are all over the world some are mammals some are not,
they live in cold, warm, or hot.
Some fly, some swim, and some walk.
They understand each other by the way they talk.

All animals are unique in different ways,
By how they look, act, or how they say "hey!"

Most animals look exactly like their parents,
Like zebras, chickens, and most parrots.

Animals are everywhere in the world,
in water, land, and even in the cold.

A lot of animals have four legs,
like dogs that like to beg.
Even though they have different features,
they are all amazing creatures.
Christine Torres, Grade 4

I Am From
I am from Chico
a town full of spirit and in some lush pastures live horses
where cold creeks run through town and some families own farms
where country and city meet

I am from a heritage
where Great Grandpa Tracy was a rancher and he helped found Chico
where Great Grandma Millie was a Rosie the Riveter and Grandpa Funk
served our nation for twenty-two years
where family lives all over the world and meet in Sweetbriar in the summer

I am from a hope
where my ancestors worked for a better tomorrow and I pray for a nicer today
where family wants to see each other and stories are told from all over

I am from a tradition
where God and family come first and football is not to far down the list
and in school we do our best

I am from an apartment
where everything is small and cozy
where the dog gets a lot of attention and I have to share a room
where everybody sits together

I love where I am from!
Rowynn Funk, Grade 5

Disgrace
When they look at my face
All they see is a disgrace
A disgrace to this race
All they want to do is spray me with mace
And put me in a small space

They think I'm a waste
They want to throw me in jail with haste
They may see a disgrace in this face
But what I see is a kid with the Lord's grace
Travis Huey, Grade 6

Nature's Music
Wind swishes through the
trees
Birds chirp through the
sky
The meadow's grass waves
back and forth
Leaves fall gently to the
ground
A little squirrel runs up
a tree
Taylor Walters, Grade 4

Days Go By
Now days go by and I think
Of what it would've been like
To live with dinosaurs
Or to hunt with spears.
Would we get to ride
great prehistoric animals?
Would we get to see
a mammoth?
Now days go by and I'm still thinking
Of what it would've been like.
Jonathan Bonee, Grade 4

Dancing Tornado
Colors dancing one by one
Pointing, turning like a ballerina
Round and round, zigzagging
Crossing back and forth
Big, small
Rough, soft
Roaring like an engine
Points, sides
Themes, music
The dancing tornado
Ella Sablatura, Grade 4

Dusk
Growing more darkness
Astonishing stars going by
Faded, cold, and dark
Sierra Starkman, Grade 4

Autumn
Apple pies being sliced and shared upon the table.
Under the naked trees are piles of leaves dancing when the wind blows.
The scarecrow is a camera watching the cornfields.
Uncovered trees like a flower without its petals.
Monstrous winds blowing the trees "WHOOSH!"
Night falls early and every one is in bed sleeping.
Andres Lopez, Grade 5

Space
Space is dark, but is lit up with the brightness of stars.
It tastes like a giant black licorice ice cream with many, many yellow sprinkles on top.
It sounds like the countdown when a space shuttle is about to take off.
It smells like metal and rotting fruit.
It looks like many aliens smiling at me.
It makes me feel eager to learn so that I can become an astronaut.
Nabila Maazouz, Grade 5

Love
Love, a feeling that triggers the heart,
A feeling so sweet, that you can see it from the tip of your soul,
A feeling so pleasurable, hat your body will be relaxed from head to toe,
Oh love, how you make me honored in every way,
And continue that in each and every day.
Soliana Girlando, Grade 4

People
People can be cruel
Mean as can be
They can be bullies
Can't you see?

People can be weak
Not strong at all
People are people
When they are mean they fall

People can change
Have love in their heart
Be nice to everyone
Right from the start

People are people
Which one will you be?
Mean all the time
Or nice as you see?
Hanna Smith, Grade 6

Dreams and Reality
Dreams
subjective, imaginary
sleeping, dreaming, thinking
fantasy and vision, actuality and real
being, seeing, knowing
authentic, factual
Reality
Maria Lomeli, Grade 4

Ode to Jobs
What would you do without
jobs in life?
I would go crazy,
because you need money to help you
in life!
People would feel useless
like an empty container.
That's why I'm glad we have jobs
today.
Another reason is because
without jobs in life
we would have no home to
sleep in or
food to eat and there would
not be any stores
for meds and healthcare
and other stuff.
That's why I'm glad we
have jobs.
Kalayna Walker, Grade 6

Teacher
Teacher
Nice, funny
Bright, intelligent, caring
Responsible, beautiful, wonderful, wise
Loving, kind, smart
Active, motivating
Ms. Dickinson
Arika Alward, Grade 5

The Shadow

My shadow
My shadow wears all the thoughts I have ever thought
My shadow wears the pain I've felt, yet I never show
My shadow wears the lies I've made without even trying
Her hair is like a bunch of snakes
Deadly and ready to strike
My shadow is a raven
Soaring through the sky
As silent as the night
Never slowing down
She hates the light
For when it comes she's visible
Not being able to hide
Fearing people could see the fears she knows
The stress she has
The pain she's felt
But once midnight strikes she returns
Awake and ready to play
My shadow will always be here with me
She shares all my thoughts, sadness, and fears
My shadow

Isabella Counts, Grade 6

Phantoms

Is our fear our enemy?
Or is it our best friend?
The Phantoms that we see,
Are they just pretend?
Is fear trying to trick us?
Or save us from the evil?
What are the Phantoms that we see?
We may never know.
We just have to know they aren't real.
We have to be brave.
Fear is real, Phantoms are not.
You will see the difference.
Of fake fear and real.
There is nothing to hurt you.
No monsters in the closet.
Or under the bed.
But with real danger,
You have to save yourself
Don't cower in fear.
You can cower from the Phantoms, but not from reality.
No more child's play, Phantoms are not real.

Evan McKee, Grade 6

Texas

Texas is a big state
Red, white and blue make up its flag
North hills and great open fields
In the south are fresh palm trees
The east region of Texas has swamps and lakes
Western land has mountains and plains
The Lone Star State is a good state for me!

John Paul Miranda, Grade 4

I Am…Avery

I am funny and jovial
I wonder if there are cures to cancer
I hear the ocean waves crashing against the seashore
I see what in the future there will be peace
I want a giant tan bear, just for me

I am funny and jovial
I pretend I am performing in Hollywood
I feel happy when people smile
I touch the soft smooth hands of my mom
I worry when I do something wrong, I let people down
I cry when my family is away

I am funny and jovial
I understand when people are disapointed
I say I do not stand for bullying
I dream that everyone has a soft side
I try to do my best on my tests
I hope all my dreams come true
I am funny and jovial

Avery Rose Ward, Grade 4

Baking

Baking is so exciting to do
If you tried it, you'd think that too.
There are many treats that you can make
Any dessert you want to bake.
I wish I could start a bakery of my own
But I wouldn't want to be baking alone.
I hope to be a professional baker
A delightful dessert creation maker.
Baking is always relaxing for me
And making me become the best baker I can be.
If I were old enough, I would bake for a living.
I would bake special desserts for holidays like Thanksgiving.
I can decorate desserts, pretty as a dove
And all of my desserts are full of love.
My baked desserts are all sweet,
And I hope a famous baker will be someone I meet.
I want to learn and improve my baking
I'm so excited about it, I'm shaking.
My baking dreams are what I hope to pursue
And every day, baking is what I'll always do.

Catherine Hsu, Grade 4

Nature at Work

The tree trunks are brown
The caves are dark
The insects are all around
The trees give off air so the animals can survive
The animals hunt
While birds chirp
Rivers run when the lakes stay still
The grass is green
And the rivers are clean

Kalil Sanders, Grade 4

The Park

The park is a place to have fun,
And run, run, run.

I was at the park
And I heard a dog bark.

The dog chased me
Then I got stung by a bee.

I decided to take a ride
On the big slide.

I saw the ice cream truck,
But I only had a buck.
Samantha Avila, Grade 6

Nature

The sun shining as bright as a light
Oh, what a great sight!
All the beautiful flowers dancing
Nature makes me start prancing

The sky is as blue as the ocean
Ocean's waves in motion
Fresh cool breeze blowing through my hair
Puffy white clouds in the air

Grass dancing beneath me
Oh, what a great sight to see!
I enjoy every beautiful thing
Wow, nature how you make me sing
Annya Castro, Grade 6

Light

the
rain
is falling
while the sun
starts to shine
then the clouds fall
into the sky
lights
flicker
BOOM
thunder strikes
sun goes away
the clouds start to darken
it is now night
Serena Bernheisel, Grade 5

My Bed

I love my bed
It is so comfy
The sheets are red
And the pillow is so fluffy
Jathan Garza, Grade 5

Where Is Spring?

It is winter
Where is spring?
When sun shines
And birds will sing

Flowers will bloom
Oh, what a sight
In colors that are
Friendly and bright

It may rain,
But who will care?
It is water
For all to share

But winter is here
What can I say?
I can't wait
For another spring day!
Nicole Nau, Grade 4

Eyes

Eyes sparkle
Eyes shimmer
Eyes see
And eyes look

Eyes speak
Without words
And eyes love
And care

Eyes are beautiful
Eyes are wonderful
Eyes are helpful
And eyes have emotion

Colors swim in your eyes
They are all different
The pigments are unique
And are all special
Finch Williams, Grade 6

Holiday

It's the holidays
It's that time of year
So take that frown off your face
And smile from ear to ear
It's Christmas
Santa Claus stopped by and ate the cookies
He left presents under the tree
For you and me
It's New Year's eve
Tomorrow is a new year
2016 is now here
James Norman, Grade 5

The Dream

Everyone has a dream,
But not everyone lives it.
To accomplish my dreams,
I need more than just love,
I need desire to accomplish my dreams.
I am obsessed with skateboarding;
It is not just love,
It is a burning passion.
I want to land every trick.
I fell more than I landed,
But that brought me to a higher level.
I even broke my wrist,
But I never gave up.
Everyone has a dream,
But not everyone lives it.
Do it so when you are old,
You can say "I lived my dream!"
Aidan McLure, Grade 6

Time to Ski

The bright rays of sun,
Burning through the clouds,
Skis stopping, scraping the snow,
Skis gliding down the mountain,
At top speed,
Turn, turn, turn,
Through the gates,
My damp facemask on my face,
People above on the chairlift chatting,
Slush, slush, slush,
The slushy snow under my skis,
Cold snow,
Landing on my eyelashes,
Bam, stick the landing,
Snowflakes in my hand,
Melting,
Mountain, as tall as the clouds!
Breanna Hester, Grade 5

The Sounds of the Zoo

Lions roaring,
Birds chirping,
These are the sounds of the zoo.

Cameras clicking,
Children talking,
These are the sounds of the zoo.

Jaguars growling,
Feet thumping,
These are the sounds of the zoo.

Rhinos snorting,
Ducks quaking,
These are the sounds of the zoo.
Ward Butler, Grade 4

Cheer

I walk out on a mat of blue.
I see a sparkle on my shoe.

I see the red on the boundary of the mat.
There is no time now to chat.

I smile with a lot of fear.
I Its so loud I can hardly hear.

I see purple on my uniform.
I really hope I don't underperform.

I see the black on the judges' table.
It looks very stable.

I hear the music start.
I hope people will be smart.

My shoes are as white as a cloud.
I just landed my tumbling and now I am very proud.

Sam Warden, Grade 6

It's in the Pencil

Have you heard of a world
where fairies roam and ogres dwell?
It's in the pencil, of course,
and your pen as well!

The magic flows from ink to paper
(lead if you're a pencil fan),
and all it takes for this magic to happen
is to think and imagine and believe that you can!

You can write about anything,
from flying babies to blue monkeys.
Just let the words pour and spill,
rough like carpet or smooth like honey.

The power of words is beyond the world,
past outer space, the galaxy, the stars as well.
And where does this magic come from?

It's in the pencil, of course, and the stories you tell.

Layla Pholsiri, Grade 6

I Am an Owl

I am an owl
Mysterious and elegant
Always gazing into the soft blur of the moon
Deciphering the shining stars that are held within a
polychrome galaxy
I can behold your darkest moments to observe the
last little bit of gleaming light
But in the brightest of days, what dazzling wonders
are there left to ponder?

Thalïa Mulock, Grade 6

A Painting of the Hideous Giddy-Glop-Claws

There once was a beautiful painting
The only one of its kind still remaining
Very unique it was
It painted a picture of the hideous Giddy-Glop-Claws
A monster so very unique
And widely known for its harsh critique

But one day a ruthless man put it in his attic
His name Sticky Static
He stole it from a museum
The Museum of Coliseum
Surely you've heard of it
Known as a place of uttermost wit

After two generations of Statics
Scout Static Jr. found it in his great-great-grandfather's attic
He saw through Giddy-Glop-Claws' revolting eyes, ears, and face
And knew it was a painting of grace

A person who organized fancy events
Sticky Static Jr. proudly presents
An auction for this beautiful painting
The only one of its kind still remaining

Sathya Thiru, Grade 5

What to Write About

What can I write?
How about a frog that turned white?
A bull or a donut?
Maybe a bunny with a big strut?
Or, an owl with a super power?
A Dalmatian on a tower or
A fish on vacation?
George Washington going through immigration?
Maybe I can write about,
Emojis with a reputation.
Or Big Foot with Strep,
A bird with a big bicep, or wait, I know,
An alarm clock with a mohawk!
So many things, I'll be writing forever!

Niamh Collins, Grade 4

The Solar System

S olar panels can absorb the sun's energy
O uter planets are past the asteroid belt
L unar eclipses are a very rare sight to see
A steroids are giant pieces of rock
R overs land on Mars to learn about the planet

S ome people think there are aliens on planets
Y ears depend on how long a planet takes to orbit the sun
S pace is endless and there is so much more out there
T he solar system has a lot in it
E arth is one of many planets in the solar system
M ars has microscopic life forms

Hayden Andrew Mazzola, Grade 5

More Than Just a Counselor

Whenever we have problems, she is always there
No matter what is going on she always cares

When life seems like a dark and gloomy night
She is there to guide us and be our flashlight

She has a heart big enough to fill the whole entire school
And need I mention that she is super cool

She is always there to wipe our tears
And when everything is blurry she makes it all clear

She is more than just a counselor, she is also a friend
Thanks for all that you do Mrs. Martin, we love you
The End
Saniya Locklear, Grade 6

Music

A sound that can be as quiet as a bird.
A sound that can be as loud as a slurp.

A sound that can be as sweet as sugar.
 A sound that can be a sour as a lemon.

A sound that can be as fast as a cheetah.
A sound that can be as slow as a snail.

A sound that can be as emotional as the scream of pain.
A sound that will make you feel like you're in shame.

This sound is a wonderful thing.
Just for you and me.
Music
Alexa Alcaraz, Grade 6

I Am From

I am from a town
Where people roam downtown
Where there are nice restaurants to eat at
And where a college is called Chico State

I am from a house
Where we watch the Warriors game at night
Where we have a traditional chicken curry on special occasions
And where my bumble bee trophy sits in my room

I am from a backyard
Where our pool sits quietly waiting for the summer
Where I play basketball with my dad on a hot sunny day
And where our fruits and vegetables are grown
I love the place where I am from!
Aren Khanna, Grade 5

The Uniqueness of Others

I meet different people every day
Some are nice
Some are the opposite
People whom I don't like:
people who think they are popular
But they aren't
They think that they are the most important
However, I have people that I don't mind:
People who are caring
The ones who are my friends
Most importantly, I love my middle school teachers
And my elementary teachers too
People who care about you
Or people whom you care about
Don't lose them…keep them as long as you can
Kelsey Wong, Grade 6

I Am

I am yellow like sunshine shining down on a field of yellow corn.
I am Christmas with stuffed stockings and yummy cookies.
I am night 12:14 eating popcorn and watching movies.
I am spring with bright and colorful flowers.
I am musicals.
I am books on how-to's.
I am pop music
I am polite.
I am pizza.
I am gym shorts and t-shirts playing tag and games.
I am the mountains with pines trees and fluffy bunnies.
I am birds chirping and singing a tune when I wake up.
I am rain splashing in puddles and getting wet.

I am Anna Rodgers
Anna Rodgers, Grade 4

The Power of Words*

People judge me by the outside.
They just see me shed tears.
No one knows the inside.
I feel invisible.

I cannot talk or walk.
I am in a wheelchair.
No one cares about me.
I am like a door, I just get pushed around.

I am smart.
I can learn.
Everyone is different.
Not the same.
Lexi Baker, Grade 6
*Inspired by "Out of My Mind" by Sharon M. Draper

Last Breath
As I walk down from the plain
I felt so much pain as the rain fell again

As I saw my mom's face I couldn't explain
How sad I was to see her again

As I sat in the car I wanted to roam far
I wanted to get away from this place

There was so much hate like that day
When they those evil men took my last breath
Aaliyah Jefferson, Grade 6

Blue
Blue is the color of the walls in my room
Blue is my favorite color
Blue is the color that makes me feel like jumping into a pool
Blue is the color I think of to make me happy
Blue smells like blueberry cotton candy
Blue tastes like cold blueberries on a hot Summer day
Blue sounds like airplanes in the sky
Blue looks like the morning sky when I wake up
Blue feels like water splashing in my face
Blue makes me want to drink blueberry Kool-Aid
Blue is the color I think is the best
Noor AbouEich, Grade 4

Thunderstorm
The thunderstorm went, "Boom!"
And the lightning went, "Crash!"
The lightning hit the ground and went
"Bam!" thunder went "Roar!" buildings
Went crash as they fell.

The earthquake went "Pow!" Shaking
Buildings went "Creek!" The gas exploded
"Pam!" the ground cracked and made a boom
Sound, the cracks in the ground went
"craaaaack!" as one building went "Bam!!"
Mateo Munoz, Grade 6

Green
Green is disgusting to me like broccoli
Green makes me happy like grass growing in a fresh field
Green is as awesome as I am
Green is the color of my favorite sweater
Green smells like the perfume around Earth
Green tastes like chips going into my mouth
Green sounds like a calm lake, still and quiet
Green looks like beautiful flowers growing tall in a field
Green feels like pillows coming out of the dryer
Green makes me feel happy like a gorilla
Green is my favorite color
Mustafa Muktar, Grade 4

Red
Red is the color of oozing blood of the deer the hunter just shot
Red is the color of a shiny apple that fell from the tree
Red is the color of strawberries from the strawberry bush
Red is the color of my friend's sharpener
Red smells like Kool-Aid I just poured in the cup
Red tastes like a red popsicle I finished eating
Red sounds like a red balloon that just popped
Red looks like Spiderman's costume
Red feels like a war is about to start
Red makes me feel very warm
Red is the color of a tomato
Sulayman Humza, Grade 5

The United States of America
The United States of America
Such a powerful land
We all fight together standing hand in hand
The United States of America
Is not a perfect place
There were a lot of problems in this country we had to face
There was the Civil War and a segregation of black and white
But now we can go anywhere, anytime we like
And that's why this country is special to me
It's big, mighty, amazing, powerful and free
And everyone that lives there is as happy as can be
Isabella Bauer, Grade 5

Green
Green is like seeing the trees moving in the wind
Green is like planting flowers on a crisp autumn day
Green is seeing frogs at a pond at a family picnic
Green is freshly cut grass on an apple orchard
Green smells like apple pie cooking in the oven
Green tastes like mint candy in your mouth
Green sounds like a frog jumping on a lily pad
Green looks like a better earth
Green feels like a fuzzy sweater in the cold winter snow
Green makes me feel very calm, peaceful, and joyful
Green is as beautiful as the ocean
Hana Omrane, Grade 5

I Have Something to Say
If I had a nickel for every time I let you down
I hope I would be even poorer than a hobo.
I do my best to keep you happy and I have one thing to tell you…
"I love you."
I remember when we first met,
Your dazzling eyes and beautiful dress,
You changed my life.
Once we met it was the beginning of a new adventure,
We flew to the moon and back for each other's love
And I have something to say…
"I love you."
Jordon Keener, Grade 6

I Am…Angelique
I am creative and intelligent.
I wonder what the future holds for me.
I hear the wind whistling.
I see the world burst to life.
I want a new art set.

I am creative and intelligent.
I pretend to be a professional artist.
I feel nervous around new people.
I worry my paintings aren't good enough.
I cry when I mess up my artwork.

I am creative and intelligent.
I understand why things happen.
I say everyone is equal.
I dream of another world, full of color.
I try to do my best in everything.
I hope I become someone who changes the world.
I am creative and intelligent.
Angelique Ikner, Grade 4

The Escape
Running toward a new beginning
And leaving everything behind
Children not looking back to homeland
Trying to escape death

Leaping like a swift stallion
Into the clear heavens
They dare to face danger
Looking for a safe home

Flying like a peregrine falcon
Surrounded by dancing clouds
Children feeling hope
As they journey over an open sky

Landing like a soft feather
On a warm and welcoming island
The overjoyed children embrace one another
Ready to begin a new life
Markus Ekstrand, Grade 6

Test Taking
Test taking hand shaking
Don't know what to do.
Am I just making this stuff up out of the blue?
Don't know if what I chose was right or wrong.
Am I going to have to stay here all night long?
Turn it in in 30 minutes
Did I go too fast?
How long is this test even going to last?
Test taking hand shaking
Don't know what to do.
Am I just making this stuff up out of the blue?
Liliana Burns, Grade 4

My Mother
You are my friend
Throughout my life
You're always with me
Through tough and good times.
A tender smile from you
Lights up my day.
You guide my way
So I can find my way.
All that you do,
You being you,
I am proud to say
That you're my mom.
You make all my troubles and worries go away.
My mom is my hero,
She's more than my best friend,
My mom is my life,
Yes that is what she is.
Mom I can honestly call you my best friend forever.
Gisselle Pelaez, Grade 6

Invitation from a Dragon
Fly up higher than the sky, to the mountain caves,
Smell the
Fire
And
Smoke
I
Breathe
Taste the cooked pork I have stolen from the nearby village,
Listen to the boulders rushing down the mountainside
Feel the warmth of magma spewing out of nearby volcanoes,
Erupting with many shakes in the ground,
Wear the scales of a dragoon fierce and bold,
Open your eyes to a world you have never known about

See the
Dragon
Inside
YOU
Lilly Monroe, Grade 4

What Happens to a Dream Deferred?*
What happens to a dream deferred?
Does it soar
like a firework in the night sky?
Or does it pop like a bubble in the harsh wind
and then shatter into pieces
like a demolished piggy bank?
Does it drift away like a balloon in the cloudy, blue sky?
Or does it fade away
like the paint of an old portrait on white canvas?
Maybe it just descends steadily in the calm wind
like a golden leaf in the beginning of autumn.
Or does it vanish away in a deep, dark box of forgotten memories?
Natalie Ozuna-Torres, Grade 6
Inspired by Langston Hughes

Easter Rises
Eggs in a basket
big and small
Hershey's and Kit-Kat
All in all.

Eggs on the tree
Eggs on the floor
Children crowding everywhere
Looking for some more.

For people and children
together as one
Jesus rises
and loves us a ton.

For Jesus is back,
with a whole new story,
and we are together
to give him glory
Catherine Wang, Grade 4

Why
I'm like a lost dog looking for a
new home
Why why why
Why would they do this
I just don't get it
Why would they give me up
All I want to know
Is if they really cared they wouldn't
have left me
they left me suffering
and alone
Why
But soon I'll find
someone who cares
All I want for Christmas is
to find a family that cares
and someone to love
I hope that one of these years on Christmas
There'd be someone to care
Leslie Guereca, Grade 6

With You Till the Very End
I follow, but don't ever touch,
Without the sun, I can't do much.
I run, jump, stride and more,
Dark as a starless night to my very core.

I have no reins,
Yet I'm bound by your chains.
I'm not sure if we are friends,
But I'll stay with you till the very end.
I am you and you are me,
Without you I cannot be.
Birtu Econom, Grade 6

God's Painting
Every evening, I look up high
and see God's painting placed in the sky

With colors of pink, purple, and blue
Sometimes they have a grayish hue

Once again, I looked up high
And saw that painting placed in the sky

With all its colors and grayish hue
Then I saw it fade to blue

It must be getting to night soon,
I thought to myself as I saw the moon

After the moon then came the stars
I might have seen the planet mars
Larissa Wine, Grade 6

If I Were in Charge of the World
If I were in charge of the world,
I'd cancel book reports,
homework, and
everything school related

If I were in charge of the world,
there'd be no curfews
bossing around, and
friendship forever

If I were in charge of the world,
you wouldn't have to eat broccoli,
vegetables, and
food-related healthy food
you could just eat ice cream 24/7

If I were in charge of the world.
Nikhil Hakeem, Grade 6

My Dog
My dog is like a job
She wants to go outside to pee,
I have to turn off the TV.
When she hears some one at the door,
She barks some more.

She likes to eat
Her favorite is meat.
She has a brown cozy fur.
But is no cat to purr.
Every time she hears her box of treats
She comes in one, two, three
She's lazy.
But never goes CRAZY
She's my dog!
Amy Aviles, Grade 6

My Flower
Saguaro Cactus Blossom,
the flower that represents my state,
a,
beautiful welcoming
flower,
that dwells along our cacti,
the queen of all
flowers in our
wonderful Arizona,
home to our friend bees,
my kind
of flower
able to handle our weather,
the
Saguaro Cactus Blossom.
Jiana McDonald, Grade 5

I Want to Live
I want to live
like there's no tomorrow.
I want to dream, like no other
dreamer.
I want to be confident,
with every path I take.
I want to see and be seen,
in the darkest places that you can
possibly imagine.
I want to, I
want to, never I
will. But one
promise that I can keep, is that
I will finish strong,
from what I have started.
Elena Jarnot, Grade 6

Running the Dog
Cold fresh air against my face,
Water flowing in the road's gutters,
Loud panting behind me,
Getting farther away,
Car engines as they roll by,
A slightly wet dog,
Shaking water all over me,
Rough leash in my hand,
But I'm the one pulling!
Warm coat around me,
Dog panting,
Panting,
Panting,
My dog, Cheyenne,
As black as night.
Ruthie Richardson, Grade 5

Band

band is…

loud as a thunderstorm
a chance to learn a new note or song
an opportunity to play your favorite instrument
a place to show friends how to play a song
the secret to playing my saxophone

Luis Damian, Grade 5

Lent

Lent is a time for praise and thanks to the Lord.
We thank God for sending His Son down from heaven
to die and save us from our sins.
We sacrifice our precious things
because Jesus sacrificed His life.
We thank the Lord for saving us from our sins.

David Lindsay, Grade 6

Happiness

Happiness is green and yellow.
It tastes like a chocolate chip cookie.
It sounds hard, loud, and peaceful like music,
and smells like friends around laughing.
It looks like clouds in the sky.
It makes you feel energetic.

Lilia Salinas, Grade 4

Family

F is for family around a big feast.
A is for apple pie equal my cousin a beast.
M is for marvelous brother doing amazing skateboard tricks.
I is for I love my dogs, they give us licks.
L is for laughing to silly jokes.
Y is for yummy food on the grill, I can see the smoke.

Thalia Ramos, Grade 5

Gloomy Leprechaun

"Hi" said the gloomy leprechaun.
I was sitting on a log at the end of the rainbow.
The leprechaun's name was Gloomy.
He lost all his gold as quick as a wink,
His gold was pink in a sink. Someone took it.
That is why his name is Gloomy.

Ella Delucchi, Grade 4

What Is Red?

Lips of love. For cherry, strawberry, raspberry, and more.
You hear a sound go by your house to the fire station.
It is a fire truck down the street
You can smell the burning fire.
Then you can smell the blooming flowers.
At sunset it is red.

Lucas Roberson, Grade 4

I Am From

I am from a house
where there is a statue of Mary
from Nana and pictures of my dad's
parents
where there is a desk that my great grand father made

I am from a neighborhood
where there are basket ball hoops
where Jimmy's red truck sits right in front of his house

I am from relatives
that are fun and yell all the time
where we pray before dinner every night

I am from a living room
where there is a T.V and pictures
of our family
where there is a couch made out
of fabric and covered in grey fabric

I am from a life
where there is a house, neighborhood
and relatives.
I love all the things in my life

Jackson Backus, Grade 5

The Challenges

In life there is always someone better
That's why you have
To try your best
You have to be the greatest
The best of the best

You work hard
To follow your dream
But when you catch it you never let it go
And accomplish the feats you want to be

You'll pass by people you wish
You never did know, but you have to be
Strong with what they say, just go

So try your
Best to do the right thing,
always

Stay on the right path
And never reverse
Your direction,
Go forward
Not back

Alexander Mata, Grade 4

San Buenaventura

S an Buenaventura was founded in 1782.

A lthough in 1795 the church was not completed until 1809.

N amed after Saint Bonaventura.

B uenaventura was the 9th mission founded by Father Serra.

U nlike any other mission of its location

E ven though the first church burned down, they built a second one.

N o one could escape from work.

A fter a period of instruction, which lasted 2 years, the friars would baptize those Indians who wanted to become Christian.

V entura is where it is located.

E xtensive water system at the mission.

N ot only did it have bells, it was the only mission with wooden bells.

T ook the neophytes 16 years to build a new church.

U sed bells for their daily routine.

R eeds and woods were used to make their houses.

A t 6:00 a.m. everyone woke up and went to the mission to pray.

Layla McQuiggan, Grade 4

Teemingly Flowing Forever

Flowing with water every day and every night the sun shines on the water with all it's light
The moon creates tides with all it's strength now the ocean can hit the beach at an unbelievable length

Under the water it's teeming with life but it's dangerous because sea urchins can be as sharp as a knife
Being underwater can make you as cold as 1000 freezers I need to heat up can you get me some Little Caesars

Fish, Sharks, Whales, and Angelfish roam about though I don't want to even mention the creature with a snout
Monstrous basking sharks are bigger than the Great White Shark these grotesque monsters can be as long as a park

Going deeper into the ocean is as scary as the Maze Runner though going underwater is a little more funner
I then feel electricity crackle through my ear eels not shocking I'll see them here

The surface is like a million miles up what hey a creature is ascending to the surface you decide to sway
This magnificent creature is a turtle maybe I'll name him Squirtle

As you reemerge to the surface you feel great and luckily hurt less
This was an adventure you won't ever forget luckily you were able to capture all your pictures in this net

Isaiah Siapno, Grade 6

What Happens to a Dream Deferred?*

What happens to a dream deferred?
Does it hide away like a bat frightened of daylight?
Or does it burn out like an explosion, dying in the night
and then leaving nothing behind but ashes?
Does it hypnotize you to forget everything about it?
Or does it lurk in the dark with fear
like a child hiding from bombs exploding in a war?
Maybe it just erodes
like a piece of coral, smashing into boulders, turning into sand.
Or does it get devoured by other memories, becoming an outcast hiding in the back of your mind?

Lada Abreu, Grade 6
*Inspired by Langston Hughes

Trapped*

Melody is trapped
She can't speak
Nobody understands her

Not being able to talk saddens her
She wants joy
One day her mom has news
She can't wait
To know her mom is having a baby

A smile on her face
She is going to love her sister
Penny is here and Melody is happy

"I will love you because you're my joy
Now I have joy

Kelly Spurger, Grade 6
*Inspired by "Out of My Mind" by Sharon M. Draper

The Civil War

Red and clean is the coat of one side,
for they will crush this insurgency for that is decided.

Blue and dirty is the coat of the other side.
Some think its a lost cause but all will try.

Gold is the trim of the of the drummer boy's drum.
He is only thirteen worried sick is his mom.

Silver and shiny are the bayonets in the sea of red.
Even the horses are scared as they bounce in their velvet red.

White is the knuckles of both sides' hands,
for they just heard the order to start the forward advance.

Swish swish goes the ramming rod as it goes up and down.
All of the men hope today they won't go down.

Seth Gibson, Grade 6

Gold

Gold is my name.
I'm the king among the colors,
The sweet, precious, shiny boss.

I'm alluring and desired by all,
The goal in every game and race.
I'm also a sly trickster.
Don't be deceived by my deceptive
Fool's Gold.

My little brother, Yellow,
Longs to become a priceless mineral like me.
One day, perhaps, he will find his
Extra metallic touch,
And become just as much of a hidden treasure as I am.

Caleb Giroir, Grade 4

I Am…

I am loving and caring
I don't understand why people don't read as much
I hear loud voices all around me
I see my teachers all huddled up when someone is in trouble
I want to be successful
I am loving and caring
I sometimes ignore people when I am mad
I feel the tears on my face when I'm sad
I touch the pages of a empty book ready to be written
I wonder what will happen in the future
I cry when I know I've done something wrong
I am loving and caring
I understand that everyone has their own opinion
I say you van do anything if you want to try
I wonder what I will become in life
I try to do my best at anything that is given to me
I am loving and caring.

Briana Berry, Grade 5

On Writing

Fingers wrap around the plume
Sadly looks the blank page
Finally released from my cage
Like a meadow, the words bloom

A flurry of thoughts, like fresh rain
Explode across the page
The world is my stage
Felt is the joy, forgotten is the pain

The pen moves, has a mind of its own
Paper sings as it's filled with prose
Like a beautiful, blossoming rose
I'm so alive, yet so alone

And then, like all things beautiful and bright
It disappears into the night

Alexander Ashman, Grade 6

The Giant Blue Monster

Its mood goes from light and dark
that thing the air
calm…usually, but can certainly flair

when it's sad it cries
its eyes sparkle in the night
when I see it in the air it's the only thing in sight

that giant blue monster that looks
over my world
with all its emotions so twirled,
that giant blue monster
that flies so high
I think ill now call it by its true name
the sky

Ruben Rojas-Betanzos, Grade 6

Yes That's Me!!!

Yes that's me
Look and you'll see
My hair is blonde
My eyes are blue
My arms are short and hairy
My hands are small
My heart is HUGE
I'm always there for my friends
I never say never
My friends love me
I live with my family
I hope for a good future
I dream big
It's all clear as can be
That's positively, absolutely me
Kambri David, Grade 4

The River

The river,
it flows
down a stream from a mountain top.
Fish,
pebbles, and rocks are found in its
waters.
The sun above makes the beautiful
water gleam
and glow.
Like the
beautiful hair of the sun
flower, Rapunzel.
The stream, it flows,
down,
into an ocean.
Alessandra Villaruel, Grade 6

Night Time

I want to see the sun,
It'll be way more fun.
Oh lord!
I feel so bored
The night sky
May be a treat to the eye,
But I prefer the gold sun
It is way more fun.

I dislike the night
With all my might.
The night feels long,
So I sing a quick song.
The sun is still the best
Than all of the rest.
The night is bad,
And it is driving me mad!
Nathaniel Rios Vazquez, Grade 6

Veterans Day

Return from war in broken glory
Tears stain scarred limbs and broken heart
Whisper into the screaming crowd
As they honor you for a single day

Scream, loud and powerful
Not to be heard
Through those that celebrate themselves
And the break from life you gave them

Remember, free souls
The warriors that sacrifice
An endless burden
So you may live on
And forget them all the more
Catherine Watson, Grade 6

Spring and Winter

Spring
Birds chirp
Flowers bloom
Bees go buzzing
Sunshine shines brightly
Calm trees sway in the wind
Everyone cheers that spring's here
As the days go on, spring is gone
Everyone lights their firewood
Trees all bare sleep in snow
Sunshine shines shorter
Bees go to rest
Flowers rot
Birds flee
Winter

Caitlyn Ho, Grade 6

Success

In this world people are stars,
But I myself am heading to Mars,

I'm getting bigger and better,
Success I will get there,

I am as bright as a spark,
And I'll make sure I make my mark,

Knowledge is the key to success,
And I now know I have to be less careless,

I will get there not soon but,
I am one in a billion,

I now know and adventure has a start,
And it all begins with a single heart.
Ismael Berumen, Grade 6

My Special Garden

The scent of flowers drifting toward me,
Fresh vegetables out of the soil,
The cooling breeze against the leaves,
The sharp scent of a fresh baked apple pie,
Berry hunting,
  Berry hunting,
  Berry hunting,
Shifting branches against the house,
Fruit as big as a cat,
The warm fluffy blanket around me,
The hot mug of hot chocolate,
The gopher laughing as he takes a radish,
The sun setting over the apple orchard,
With its warm pink and orange colors,
Flowers, why are you so colorful?
Madison Andrew, Grade 5

No One Can Change Me

I believe what I believe,
I love what I love,
I am who I am,
And no one can change me.

I believe in many things,
Such as God and peace,
I am who I am,
And no one can change me.

I write my story,
With beliefs,
And things that make me, me,
I am who I am,
And no one can change me.
Maverick Arevalo, Grade 5

Friendships

Today is Happiness
My friends don't have sadness
we have ups and downs

It's fun how we live in the same town
Dance the night away
We all have our ways

Friends don't bump
They jump
we drop and we hit the folks

BFFs always have jokes
We lean and Dabb
And always have fab
Chyiah Holmes, Grade 6

The Old and the New Zoe

I was the youngest from my swell older sister, now I have a younger brother that will grow to be a mister.
I used to live in a tight, little trailer, but now I live in a house with a big dog that's a wailer.
I used to be stuck in a dark lonely shell, but now I have friends and I'm doing quite well.
I used to love to swiftly run, but now I flip on slippery bars just for fun.
I used to think middle school was a shocker, but now I'm excited to get my own locker.
I used to love the shiny, bright color green, but now I love pretty purple wherever it's seen.
I once liked to shop in large malls; now I prefer staying at home watching the cool show Gravity Falls.
Before I was an immature little girl, but now I'm mature and in a big swirl.
I used to cherish spaghetti, but now I love pizza already.
Once I was a little, silent seven year old, but now I'm ten and my words are written in bold.
I used to wander around for long hours, but now I sometimes stop to smell the sweet flowers.
My second favorite animal was a noisy dog, now I prefer to have a silent, jumpy frog.
Long ago I was a tiny baby who used to cry, but now that I'm older I always wonder why.
I used to play fun board games like Clue, instead I'm stuck sometimes wondering what to do.
Back then I liked to go on slippery slides, now I would prefer a long hose to get wet outside.
Before I loved to read tiny picture books, and now I read long books with a lot of good cooks.

Zoe Wade, Grade 5

What I Prefer and I Don't Adore

I used to like huge shiny cars, but now I love collecting football cards.
I used to eat yellow, cheesy pizza but now I eat dark creamy chocolate cake.
I used to prefer colorful hard candy but now I eat crunchy potato chips.
I used to want to be a big strong football player but now I want to go to the Air Force.
I approve of big, smart, strong dogs but now I have small, long, cute dogs.
I used to be good at baseball but now I am good at football too.
I used to not have an X-box 360 but now I do have one.
I loved to work with a partner when I was little kid but now I don't anymore.
Football is a fun, great sport but baseball is more fun than football.
Fruit Rollups are delicious but fruit is even better.
Football cards are great but my X-box is way more engaging
Old cars don't look good but new cars are clean and nice.
I adore cute, soft, and cozy dogs but I prefer the ferocious wolves
better.
I can be mischievous at times, but I can be playful
I like the red planet Mars, but now I prefer the cold tiny Pluto.

Adrian Robles, Grade 5

Music

Music is like a chunk of you that just wants to let loose
and do whatever it wants to do.
The reason I like music is because it is a way to express your self.
Music is also inspiring.
Sometimes when I'm sad and I start listening to upbeat music it cheers me up,
it makes me want to dance and throw my fears away.
Music can be a way of communication for example, in
the time of slavery the slaves would sing follow the drinking gourd as code to escape.
Music can be a way of respect like the "Oh Beautiful America"
is a song honoring the beauty of America.
Music is all around you.   Music can be someone tapping to a beat,
it doesn't have to be with an instrument.
I love listening to music.
Especially by the musicians Fifth Harmony, Ellie Goulding, Adele, Sia, Selena Gomez and Anna Graceman.

Listening to music is a treat for my ears!

Shalom Akinkunmi, Grade 4

Ode to Slacker, My Teddy Bear
Slacker,
my old floppy friend,
you're old and weak,
but you're my little hair ball!

Slacker,
you wait patiently on my bed for me every day.
And, when I'm mad at my hairless brother,
you let me yell in your fur.
Slacker, my Slacker,
while I'm sad you're there for me to cry into.

Slacker,
you're a good friend.
I'm sorry for some things I've done to you,
like getting red paint in your hair,
throwing up on your wife Peanut.
And, I can't forget the time
I got some peanut butter in Peanut's hair,
or got rid of some of your twenty five kids.

I love, love you, Slacker!
We've been together for all these years,
and you're still loyal and loving.
Kyra Gibbons, Grade 4

400 Meter
First call 11 and 12 Girls
First call 11 and 12 Girls
I take a deep breath to calm my nerves
In just a while I'm about to handle these curves

"Take your marks," said the starter as she raised her gun up high
I looked around to check for fear in my competitors eyes
One lap is all it takes to win this 400-meter race
Get set. Bam!! Time to start the chase

My heart starts to burn
I'm trying to pass as many as I can before this last turn
I look beside me to see if anybody's near
Then I raise my hands in victory as I hear the crowd cheer!
Chloe Jordan, Grade 6

Red
Red is the color of the end of your rake or
the flaming candles of your birthday cake.
Red is the smell of smoke from fire or
the smell of a evening sun set.
Red is the feeling of the petals of a rose or
even the feeling of a red candle that glows.
Red is a red popsicle melting in your hand or
A pepper burning in your mouth, like your tongue
being smacked by rubber bands.
Red is the sound of a car blasting down the road.
Red can be so many things.
Trey Jansson, Grade 4

Hogwarts
To enroll to the mystic school of Hogwarts
You will need a heap of hope
That to your house comes a flying envelope
Hold fast to your broomstick as to the school it darts

Now at the school of wizardry
Around the school you're free to roam
As this magic castle is your home
You choose to stay while others try and flee

Home of the magical sport known as Quidditch
Broomsticks fly around the field has as lightning
Violent players are what make the game really frightening
And the seekers task to catch the winged golden ball, the snitch

Hundreds of spells for wizards to learn
Spells and potions to encage others in thick ice
Other spells to summon lightning that will strike more than twice
To learn them all is what most wizards ye
When reaching departure leave in a unicorn drawn wagon
Staying at the school for now a while
Why not leave this place in style
For after all your time at this place was something quite fun
Christian Salazar, Grade 6

If I Were in Charge of the World
If I were in charge of the world
I'd cancel wet dogs,
Gross tasting veggies,
Homework, and moldy cheese.

If I were in charge of the world
There'd be longer weekends,
Cookies for life,
And free ice creams on Sundays.

If I were in charge of the world
You wouldn't have to drink milk.
You wouldn't have to be clean.
You wouldn't have to eat eggs for breakfast.
Or hear "Stop fighting with your brother!"

If I were in charge of the world
An ice cream sandwich would be healthy
And a person,
who sometimes is afraid of spiders,
And sometimes afraid of giant fire breathing snails,
Would still be allowed to be
In charge of the world.
Yuhan Shi, Grade 5

The Lost Hero
The memories of Jason Grace were stolen by the Queen of the Gods
Lost and found at the Wolf House, because our
Hero has to save his memory thief to get his memory back
Varun Menon, Grade 4

The Beach Day

Me and my family went to the beach,
And enjoyed a nice treat,
While observing the waves,
We were so amazed,

We decided to build a castle,
But we changed our mind
because it was going to be too much of a hassle,
So we just played on the sand,
Spending our time on this beautiful land,

We continued to hang around the beach,
And we came across someone that wanted to teach,
About the life of crabs and lobsters,
That looked like a bunch of mobsters,

Their claws grip you so tight,
With all of its might,
Finally, we took a dip,
And we were coming to the end of our trip
The water was so cold,
And we almost froze

Mattiara Brown, Grade 6

Fly

I open the door,
Silence. Peace. Serenity,
I drag myself onto the mattress,
Within seconds, I was gone.
My guardians walk in to see,
Six fuzzy blankets piled on my unconscious body,
My vision was black, until I found myself, in a room,
an odd room, lights off, items everywhere,
The silhouette of a human just staring,
A dim lamp suddenly illuminated the room,
The figure walked forward,
It was a tall man with a bald head,
And a beard as brown as a grizzly's fur,
The man motioned for me to follow him,
Curious, I left, we jumped out the window,
And flew, over the city, through the forest,
and into the mountains, I see…a cabin,
We land, and walk towards it,
Suddenly, my vision blurs,
And I'm in my room again,
Silence. Peace. Serenity.

Greta Helgeson, Grade 5

Dalmatian on Vacation

The Dalmatian on vacation went to the beach.
Instead of getting tanned, he got more bleached.
Then, poor Dalmatian got attacked by a leech.
On his head, the birds went peck, peck, peck.
His friend then pushed him off the deck.
He just wanted to rest, but instead he was a wreck!

Lauren Bryant, Grade 4

The Long Trail Ahead

The suns' first arrival
In the morning sky, as we begin
Jeff King's dogs' fatigue, as I cruise by,
The rich, hot smell of hot chocolate,
Only a few miles away,
Mid-days sun light gleaming,
Snow, Glistening, Glistening, Glistening,
The birds swooping from tree to tree,
The aroma of pine trees,
Throughout the woods,
Soft fur inside my warm gloves,
Keeping me warm,
My Alaskan husky friends barking
As we still keep traveling
The ice cold frosty air
Traveling in and out of my nostrils
Freezing cold sled,
I grasp onto as we glide down the trail,
Across the sparkling snow,
My dogs and I finally arrive in Nome,
We conquered the long, grueling Iditarod Trail!

Breckin Fett, Grade 5

The Beach Is Beautiful

The sand is a squishy sponge,
It's stuck to your feet, then washes away.
The wind icy and breezy, it flows throw your hair.
The seashells crack from footsteps. Smooth, curving
Like the ocean.

The sand is squishy like a sponge,
It's stuck to your feet, then washes away.
The waves splash on the shore.
The sea shells crack from footsteps. Smooth, curving,
Beautiful, like the ocean.
The breeze pushing the waves hard, on the beach.

The breeze pushing the waves hard, on the beach.
The sunset on the horizon delighted by the waves.

Items was up on shore arrive from their journey in the sea.
The wind icy and breezy, it flows throw your hair.
The sunset on the horizon is delighted by the waves.

The beach is beautiful if you just look.

Amelia Harris, Grade 6

About Me

I might be bad but I'm a good kid.
I look like a troublemaker but in real life I'm a really nice kid.
I'm really sensitive to a lot of stuff.
I'm really bad at social life and making friends.
I'm shy because new people can be rude, mess up, and show off.
Making friends can be scary at first,
Then it becomes really cool, then you're not shy anymore.

Isaac Azevedo, Grade 6

From the Fish Bowl

I'm swimming calmly in my bowl
I think I'm under control
The humans are trying to teach me tricks
But in my spot I am fixed

They try to tempt me with food
who do they think I am, a fool?
They finally give up
and put the food back in its cup.

They are watching something called television,
unlike me I don't think they know division.
While they are playing with a flagpole
I'm swimming calmly in my bowl.

Niyati Goswami, Grade 6

If I Were in Charge of the World...

If I were in charge of the world,
I'd make peaches the fruit of Texas,
peace what the world needs, and
no bullying.
If I were in charge of the world,
there'd be a one "for free" day for certain stores,
expensive healthcare for free, and
none would be enemies.
If I were in charge of the world,
you wouldn't bully.
You wouldn't brag.
You wouldn't have a party on weekdays
or sleep super early on weekends.
If I were in charge of the world.

Sarah Hage, Grade 6

Fiji Water Is the Best

Fiji water is the best
Better than the rest
I don't think I can get over its
Soothing taste when it tingles down my throat
Soothing like going to the beach and laying out in the sun
Cooling like the best feeling of my life
I don't think regular water I will drink again
I'd rather be dehydrated and never see the sun
Than to ever again
Drink regular water

Dylan Jackman, Grade 4

I Am Me

I am a random thinker and a dreamer sitting in a chair
dreaming away.
I always wonder if animals appreciate me when I'm around.
I am always up for baby-sitting children and pets.
I love to pretend that I'm the owner of a grand hotel.
I'm the red rose in a meadow of white daisies.
I'm the soft white snow on a cold December morning.
I'm the calm waves on the coast of Dauphin Island.

Evelyn Scaling Brown, Grade 4

Dogs

German shepherds they can be mixed
No matter what dog it is
I think they are the best
Dogs are my favorite because they give me loads of joy
When I see one I say "Oh, boy!"

Dogs are a man's best friend,
They will keep you company till the end
Dogs care for you,
They like to play with you too
Dogs have their own personalities,
That they give their family
Dogs are my favorite type of pet,
But they don't like to get wet

Ivan Luna, Grade 4

Larger Than Life

You can be larger than life,
Your thoughts puncture the Earth like a knife,
You might've never noticed that it's right before your eyes,
We all have our lows and highs,

Step by step your on your way,
To an even brighter day,
It's up to you the door is open wide,
Come on let's take a ride,

Soar through life and fly,
As the stars look upon you from the night sky,
Don't have faith in strife,
Because you are larger than life.

Jose Becerra, Grade 6

Purple

Purple is the color of flowers.
Purple is like a cloud in the sky.
Purple is like a beautiful firework in the sky.
Purple smells like flowers.
Purple tastes like grapes.
Purple sounds like a whisper.
Purple looks like a beautiful shooting star.
Purple feels like a breeze.
Purple makes me want to dance.
Purple is my favorite color.

Maggie Berry, Grade 4

A Mother's Love

A mother's love is very strong
A mother's love is never wrong
A mother's love is very bright
A mother's love is a delight
A mother's love is powerful
A mother's love is wonderful
A mother's love blocks all the obstacles in your way
That is why they have Mother's Day

Khadija Nawabi, Grade 6

I Am From…

I am from a Catholic school
Where we go to mass every Friday
Where elementary students wear white and plaid and the junior high wears khaki and navy
Where we pray every single day.

I am from a kitchen
Where on Christmas day and Sunday mornings we have waffles, scrambled egg, and bacon
Where my dad's homemade pizza is made.

I am from a small house
Where there is always loud noise
Where the fireplace is going while we are sipping hot chocolate and a movie is playing
Where there is joy and laughter.

I am from a backyard
Where a hammock is hung from two trees
Where summer barbecues are held and steaks are sizzling on the grill and ice cold lemonade to drink
Where fruit trees produce apples and oranges
Where Bella rolls around on the fresh mowed grass.

I love where I am from!

Mallory Boyd, Grade 5

Reagan Gerardis Fight for Freedom

I love the sound of freedom, it gives me joy,
to know that people have fought for me to be free.
They fought for all of us to be free,
so that we can live in a land with liberty.
All I want is for the world to be free,
and to feel the feeling of freedom in their hearts,
and we still try today to help everyone get liberty.
They risked their life so that we could have liberty,
and that is what I want to do for all of the of the people that don't have freedom.
I want for every country to have freedom,
like in America. We don't appreciate the people that gave us freedom enough,
so I want us to appreciate them more,
and think about what they did for us on their holiday.
We all want freedom and we are going to have to fight for other people to have freedom too.
Since we are the new generation we can make our own history,
and help all of the other people get freedom too if they don't have freedom at all.
We can't lose faith in each other or anything at all because we need to work together to make this happen.
I think that everyone should love the sound of freedom,
and if they don't have freedom we will help them get freedom. I love that I am free and I want other people to be free too. Like Martin Luther King said, "we should not be judged by the color of our skin but by the content of our character." I think that is inspiring because he was fighting for a cause, like I want to do with my life as well, and to free other people like me.

Reagan Gerardi, Grade 6

My Nightmare of Darkness

I was standing there shocked, just when I thought my nightmare of darkness was over, it came back.
Will I be safe, will the people be safe, will we ever see the clear sky's again?
So many questions in my head.
I feel like I have a wave of consequences coming my way and I can't ignore it, no matter what.
If I die now then I'll know that I died fighting for my life.
Never back…

Julia Romero, Grade 4

Spring

Happiness and joy fills the air in the presence of colors,
Out in a field butterflies and grass in the brightest of greens,
Right after the snow and beauty of winter ends,
To make an attraction that can keep happiness inside us for the rest of the year,
By making everything sprout with colors, happiness, and pleasure.

The eyeful of butterflies and the whimsical colors fill the air with the feeling of joy,
You can feel the happiness and delight just tingling inside of you making you jump,
Pods of milkweed plants are bursting making it look like tiny, playful clouds,
The music of crickets in the night filling you with glee and merriment,
Picking wild flowers to make the best bouquet and flower crown because of the bliss tones.

Picking petals off a flower to throw them in the air to make something so beautiful and kind,
Going to the farm to visit all of the newborn creatures lying in the perfectly heated sun,
Where the only problem is too much exhilaration to hold in that it makes you pop,
At dusk you lay in the grass looking up at the twinkling stars shining ever so bright,
Giving off a cheerful, bubbly, and sparkling vibe to all.

All of the beauty, tones, and joyful feelings all summed up into one word —
Spring.

Brooklynn Esposito, Grade 6

Reflections in the Sea

The reflections I see in the waves is not me,
Yet some ghost of the girl I want to be and emotions and secrets I have had balled up inside of me.
I see the burn in my feet through the moans of the waves, trapped in the usual routine. Up, down, up down, in a few swift movements.
I have been running for too long, I can see it in the ocean.
I see the exhaustion that I feel through the dank, soaked sand sinking beneath my aching feet. The sand is giving up, so am I.
I have stopped running.
I know the pain of the moans of the waves, trapped in the usual routine. Yearning with hate to drown yet another into the depths.
The ocean knows me. It knows what I feel through my reflections in its sea.
I know the exhaustion that it feels in the dank, soaked sand.
The ocean knows me. It knows what I feel through my reflections in its sea.
I know the ocean. I know what it feels and I feel it too through my reflections in the sea.
I know the ocean. I know what it feels. The oceans knows me. It knows what I feel.
The ocean knows me. It knows what I feel through my reflections in it's sea.
As the sun fades, I suddenly see clearer. I see dimmer but clearer.
I know the ocean. I know what it feels. The oceans knows me. It knows what I feel.
I have been running for too long, I can see it in the ocean.
As the sun fades, I see darker, but clearer.
I see clearer my reflection in the sea. It's not me. Just someone I want to be.

Ava Dominguez, Grade 6

Me Myself and I

Here I stand...
On a sad lonely Christmas day
In a place where nobody cares about what I'm feeling on this supposedly very JOYFUL day,
I see families talking happy as can be wishing that could be me
But there's no one here just me myself, and I and people just like me
In this cold frigid weather where I sing to myself in a sweet lullaby.
It's true I lived through it all
LOVE, fear, and now here I am hurt as can be waiting
For loved ones to come and love me
And I know someday I'll see the LIGHT but until then I'll be waiting for my day where I can be HAPPY and free.

Lizbeth Duenas, Grade 6

The Delight Song of Kaycee Robles

I am a pebble in the river, I am a grey wolf that runs in the forest
I am a panther that runs, quietly in the plains
I am the shadow that follows a lone wolf
I am the night, the dark of the world
I am a fox playing with its shadow
I am a bunch of white pebbles
I am the farthest star, I am the cold of the night
I am sound of tears in the dark, I am the glitter of the star
I am the long tears of a scared puppy in the dark
I am a cat of four colors
I am a horse galloping through the plains
I am a field of grass and dead flowers
I am a group of tigers in the jungle
I am the hunger of a wolf
I am the whole world of these things

You see, I am alive, I am alive
I stand in good relation to the world
I stand in good relation to my life
I stand in good relation to the animals
I stand in good relation to the friends
You see, I am alive, I am alive

Kaycee Robles, Grade 6

Too Easy*

As soon as he said it my heart sank
Too easy was wrong,
Too easy…
I worked very hard, but
to him it was too easy.
I'm surprised I got one of the
highest scores out of the class.
"I guess the test was too easy
If Melody passed!!!"
It repeated over and over
In my mind.
Somehow I was out of my mind.
If it was so easy then
everyone should have
passed it with flying colors!, but they didn't
So I guess they are just
DUMB!
Because it was to easy for Melody.
Not only was that unfair
but also the most
very wrong idea.

Maleigh-Saige Feldhauser, Grade 6
*Inspired by "Out of My Mind" by Sharon M. Draper

The Apple Tree

If I were an apple tree with great big strong roots,
I'd have ripe delicious sweet fruits.
They'd be red, the brightest red you've ever seen.

I'd let you climb my great big branches;
I'd let you shake my great big trunk.
I'd give you all the fruit I've got.

I'd keep you alive, I'd help you thrive.
I'd make you strong,
The strongest anyone has ever seen.

I'll watch you grow up to be
The greatest there has ever been.
And when you get old, I'd let you take my branches.
And build your house.
I'd watch you
And hope you will teach your children to grow up strong.
Strong and bright.
Yes that's right.
That's what I'd do
If I were a great big apple tree.

Hanna Lyna Montague, Grade 4

The Delight Song

I am a cat on the tree branch
I am a tan lion that lurks on the savanna of Africa
I am a shark that protects itself in the bottom of the sea
I am an owl that follows the Parliament
I am the knight, the dark knight of the world
I am a lion playing with the cubs, I am a cluster of great friends
I am the farthest tree, I am the cold of the snow
I am the roar of the lion, I am the glitter on the snow
I am the long mall of stores in San Francisco
I am a book full of four colors
I am a bird that flies through the night
I am a field of crops and flowers
I am the pack of wolves on a hunt in the mountains
I am the hunger of a homeless man
I am the whole human of these things

You see, I am alive, I am alive
I stand in good relationship to my brother
I stand in good relationship to my sister
I stand in good relationship to my parents
I stand in good relationship to my loved ones
You see, I am alive, I am alive

Daniel Villasenor, Grade 6

Dust Bowl

The sand blows hard and the houses aren't safe
It blows down the houses and kills people
It happens where the trees were cut down and soil isn't steady
The wind picks up tons of dust and carries it every where
The wind stops and the new trees grow, it finally stops

Tyler Toups, Grade 4

Myrrh

There was a girl named Jenny who lived in Big Sur,
Whose mother owned a bottle of myrrh.
She wanted to see this oil that was blessed,
But spilled it and made a big mess,
And *Boy* was her mother mad at her!

Clara Kaisersatt, Grade 5

Happy Christmas

Watching other kids get
Adopted before Christmas
Makes me feel happy for them
But I feel lonely inside.
I woke up and it was Christmas
Lots of parents come to adopt kids
And I haven't gotten chosen
A married couple come with a little baby boy
And I go in line with the two bullies
The parents have a tough decision
So they let their baby boy choose
I thought that was crazy
but the baby picked me
But then the other kid
Then he went back to me and said, "Him"
This was the best day of my life
I finally have a family to spend time with

Nethan Acevedo, Grade 6

The Amazing Continent

South America the amazing continent
is very unique
it is filled with desert and rain that says splash
when it falls on the ground

South America the amazing continent
with people that get along together
even though they have different religions

South America the amazing continent
so many wonderful sites
like waterfalls mountains continent

South America the amazing continent
so mighty so bright
will always be
a part of me

Thomas Cunyus, Grade 4

The Sunset

The sky is a fiery scarlet, a crimson red
As the sun settles down, curling up in its bed.

It relishes the time it eats into the dark,
Savoring each moment, as a killer whale would a shark.

It dreads the moment it would have to rise again,
Starting its journey to give warmth to women and men.

It shines in all its glory, as should a sun,
Before it dives again into the horizon.

The sky will stay dark for a long, long, time,
But when that time ends, the sun will shine.

The sky is a fiery scarlet, a crimson red,
As the sun settles down, curling up in its bed.

Srivi Balaji, Grade 6

What Spring Brings!

Spring comes with many wonderful things,
Trees, flowers, blossoms and buds it brings,
Quick squirrels and rabbits are rapidly chasing,
The yellow hot sun is also blazing.

Loud birds are chirping to a tune,
On the ground, the rain is pouring,
The grass is very pure green,
There comes sprouting beans.

Red, yellow, and orange leaves from fall all turn green,
Although the mighty pines each season you have seen,
They always stay one color, which is green,
Blossoms only sprout in spring.

Spring brings all kinds of organisms,
Trees, fruits, flowers, blossoms and other things it brings.

Ganesh Sankar, Grade 5

Welcoming the Sunrise

Children in the unforgiving, rocky terrain
They have been waiting for this moment for years
Sleeping through soggy showers from mother nature
Lonely forever in their dead stone habitat
The beating of the drum wakes your hearts up
The tribe of youth will gather together with every beat
Dart up that hill, my children! Feel the joy and passion!
Release all of the pleasure that has been building up all of your life!
Soaring through the air, overlooking the cold, blue sea
Children hugging the deep blue sky
Little boy, have courage
Run up to that cliff!
Fly over the bleached sea foam
The new generation has fulfilled their lifelong dream
Welcoming the sunrise

Eric Yoon, Grade 5

Getting Off the Roller Coaster!

I just got off the roller coaster.
It was so cool-er coaster!
I'm starting to feel a little nauseous.
It's probably because before the ride I ate a whole rhinoceros.
I quickly run to the bathroom and let it all out.
Then my mother gave a shout.
"Come out, come out, come out, my dear!"
"I can't, I can't, I'm sick in here."
Once I'm done letting it out,
My mother gave me one more shout.
"You good, you good, you good my dear?"
"I'm fine, I'm fine, I'm fine in here.
I'm just finishing up, my mommy dear!"
I went outside and learned something new today.
You don't eat a whole rhinoceros before you play.

Avery Elkins, Grade 4

The Wind

When the wind is strong.
The ocean is an angry exploding tornado.
When the wind is strong.
A flood comes out.
When the wind is strong.
It is destruction everywhere.

Mark Lincoln, Grade 5

One Inch

If you were only one inch tall
The carpet would be a forest
An ocean could not be crossed
A fire would be invincible
And yet there is always adventure
If you were only one inch tall

Caden Seaholm, Grade 6

Thankful People

T hankful for my older sister
H aving a home
A ble to have the best family
N eighbors letting me play
K ind people
S miling for joy

Rithik Bhardwaj, Grade 4

Mission Santa Cruz

Charming and small,
The big white tower is very tall.
The Ohlone neophytes once lived here,
At mission Santa Cruz the love is clear.
When you leave Santa Cruz,
You will get the blues.

Ava Arriaga, Grade 4

Danger

D ramatic break up
A nger and rage rushing in the body
N ever-ending destruction
G oing insane
E motions taking over the body
R isking failure

Katie Nguyen, Grade 6

Thankful

T hankful for family
H aving great moments
A lways loving
N ever-ending fun
K aede as a sister
S adness is gone

Alexis Chung, Grade 5

Ebony Black

Ebony black is darker than the shadows, it is deeper than the ocean shallows.
The color of ink, it is sure to make you blink.
The color of cloth, the cloth makes you feel like a cozy sloth.
Ebony black is very dull, it's the only color that makes me mull.
It is like a cat that is black, not much luck but lots of slack.
It is like most lead, I found a lot of it in my shed.
It is the color of my tablet, playing it becomes a big habit.
It's also like a phone, while playing it you shouldn't break a bone.
It's like the night sky, very dark which people glorify.
It's like paint, that liquid is never faint.
It's like a black rug, it can be large or small but always snug.
Ebony black is the color of sadness, yet it's still prettier than badness.
It's like a horse, big and has plenty of force.
It's like outer space, there is way more than one place.
It is like jelly, it's hard to catch because it's in my belly.
It is like the end that is not hard to comprehend.

Lucas Hamacher, Grade 5

Untitled

The sand has a story within every grain
I wonder how long it took to become so tiny and insignificant
The sand was crushed and pulled apart time after time
Yet the sand unwillingly sits there waiting for the sea to make its next move

The puddles have something to tell you with their swaying whisper
It wants to show you the other side, unwitnessed, the fragment of rage you have
They want you to notice your flaws again and again like you're a grain of sand
You fall apart,

You can't harm the water because it only ripples it away what you had given it

The horizon has something to show you
It wants to show you the line that defines sky and sea
It always tells the sky and the sea what it isn't and is
But what is the horizon, sky or sea?

Sabina Hall, Grade 6

Red Flower

Red flower standing in the barren wasteland
No man's land the soldiers call it
nothing but gray ground and broken trees
both sides are dug up in trenches
waiting for the all charge signal
while the red poppy just stays there.
Not a sound to be heard…the flower just waving in the wind
when suddenly a loud whistle is heard echoing
through the land
Suddenly, screams of soldiers with bayonets charging towards the other
while poppy is now not the only one who is red.
The end of the battle is bloody with stabbing people getting blown up
it is all horrifying. At the end people come to clean the bodies
the flower is still standing there
after all these years
and I know it saw everything.

Paul Harriman, Grade 6

Earth-Binders

Feet thrum on soft earth
A march of pain
Feet dance in shoes of leather
On hard tile floors
Feet are soft and kissed by mothers
Tiny inside the bassinet
Feet run
Feet are paws
Feet are claws
Feet are what connects us with our home
The Earth
Feet are running
Feet are walking
Marching
Singing
Thorns and grass
Ocean and sky
Fire and water
Feet hold us down so we don't fall into the air
Feet bind us to our soul
Feet carry us wherever we need to go

Audrey Gutierrez, Grade 6

I Am...Jovan

I am intelligent and brave
I wonder if everybody can be nice
I hear happy jolly voices everywhere I go
I see people having fun with families and friends
I want to be in the NFL and NBA when I get older

I am intelligent and brave
I pretend that I am a quarterback for the Carolina Panthers
I feel the cold air in the stadium
I touch the top of the rim in my reams like I am doing a dunk
I worry that my mom won't be at my games when I get older
I cry about doing badly in school

I am intelligent and brave
I understand that I have to get good grades in school
I say I will be the first person to be in two major league sports
I dream that I will have a dream like every other kid
I try to do my best in school
I hope my family lives forever
I am intelligent and brave

Jovan Jester, Grade 4

Sunrise

Sight, looks like dark skies
Brightening with hues of
Pink and orange

Taste, tastes like my morning coffee
Touch, feels like the nice morning breeze
Smell, smells like nice fresh air
Sound, sounds like the music that I play every morning

Antonio Biancaniello, Grade 6

Wendy My Pet Dog

I am very passionate about my pet dog
She was very kind and very sweet
Wendy never hurt anyone
And when an neighbor came by she wouldn't let them pet her

She liked to walk out of the garage
And walk down the street
She liked to see my neighbor's cars "beep"

As she grew older
She couldn't be as bold
And that made me sad

As she got weak
She didn't do much
But on one day my life changed

When I went to school
My dog crossed the street
And a car came and ran her over

Now all I have left is a turtle in a cage
And my heart is scarred forever that's all I can say

Allan Urban, Grade 4

My Little Sister

Natasha is sweet honeydew
She smells as good as daffodil flowers
Her favorite color is blue
We play together for many hours

She can be very funny
She doesn't care about people's looks
Her favorite animal is a bunny
She really enjoys reading books

Her hair is as long as spaghetti
She expresses a lot of emotion
Her best friend's name is Betty
Her eyes make you feel like you're in the ocean

David Madadian, Grade 6

Jellybean

If I were a jellybean
I would taste sweet.
I would be full of fruit flavors.
I would like to be eaten by a famous person.
I would want to be eaten by George Lucas.

If I were a jellybean,
I would be happy to be in a full jar.
I would wish to be human-sized.
I would love to be a magic jellybean.
I would listen for someone licking their lips.
I would be a delicious orange jellybean.

Andrew Vallance, Grade 4

Sun and Moon

I love the moon, I love the sun
The sun is bright and lights up the day
The moon is bright and lights up the night
Two wonderful creations by God
So similar, but so different at the same time
With the sun I conquer the day
With the moon I sleep at night
I love the moon, I love the night
I love the sun, I love the day

Amira Helmy, Grade 6

Fishing

Person humming
Fish bubbling
These are the sounds of fishing
Fish striking
Person reeling
These are the sounds of fishing
Fish jumping
Person cheering
These are the sounds of fishing

Jonathan Marcincuk, Grade 4

Summer

Summer, Summer,
almost here
Let's give Summer
a big fat cheer
Of this fact
I'm surly clear
Summer is my
favorite time
of year

Christi Hames, Grade 4

They Don't Know Me

On the inside
They don't know me
The real me
The girl who wants to run
The girl that wants to be heard
The girl who's feeling get hurt

They don't know me
I just want to be like them

James Benton, Grade 6

Up and Down

Up
High, cold
Flying, climbing, sky-diving
Ceiling, sky, ground, basement
scuba-diving, mining, digging
deep, hot
Down

Iago Ansede De Veylder, Grade 4

Hope

What do you see when you look up to the night sky?
The clouds?
The stars?
The moon?
Or that only beam of moonlight that pierces the dark veil of night?
Just remember, THERE IS HOPE

What do you feel when you are injured?
The pain?
The reality?
The doubt of what they'll say?
Or the thought that you'll be okay, like the sun after a storm?
Just remember, THERE IS HOPE

What do you realize when all hope is lost?
The truth?
The forceful impact of reality?
The guilt?
Or the realization of what hope really is, like fireworks exploding in the obsidian sky?
Just remember, THERE IS HOPE

Just remember, THERE IS ALWAYS LIGHT.
THERE IS ALWAYS LOVE AND FREEDOM.
THERE WILL BE HOPE.

Franchesca Untalan, Grade 5

Sacrifice Trees

The trees, all around us, seeing all, hearing all, giving all.
Receiving nothing.

Out in a forest of trees, sits the best of all, its branches strong,
its trunk big, its leaves bright green.

The tree.
The powerful. The confident. The fearless. The sacrificing.
Tree.

The tree.
Giving, sacrificing all. Receiving nothing. Giving oxygen, giving paper,
Giving fruit, Giving beautifulness. Receiving nothing.
Nothing at all.

The tree, standing straight. Nothing to hide. Standing still. Nothing to lose.
For soon, it will give all. They begin to cut it down.
The tree looks straight ahead, it has nothing to fear, for fear does not exist in its roots.
No fear, all to give.
As it hits the floor, its leaves fall, and there is a loud sound. The sound of sacrifice.
The sound of life. Soon it will be giving all, all to life.
All for us, us who take all, but give nothing.
These are one of the true heroes, of this world, the power trees.
The sacrifice trees.

Cynthia Govea, Grade 6

I Am…Carlton
I am intelligent and humble
I wonder about the scientific research of dinosaurs
I hear the roar of an Indominus Rex
I see a raptor on the S.W.A.T. team
I want to be a professional basketball player

I am intelligent and humble
I pretend that I am Stephen Curry
I feel the fur of a lion's mane
I touch people's hearts by my poetry
I worry about my family and siblings
I cry inside at a funeral

I am intelligent and humble
I understand everyone's beliefs should be respected
I say we should stop bullying
I dream of being the best I can be
I try to impress my parents with good grades
I hope the world will be a better place
I am intelligent and humble
Carlton James Sullivan Jr., Grade 4

Trapped
46 miners trapped underground
Water and food going round and round,
While the vultures caw endlessly.

38 miners trapped underground
Little food and water going around,
While the vultures wait relentlessly.

23 miners trapped underground
Barely enough food and water to go around,
While the vultures pierce the rock.

9 miners trapped underground
All battling for a crumb,
While the vultures wait.

1 miner, all alone
Black blurring his vision
He breathes his last breath and,
The vultures caw endlessly.
Samitha Nemirajaiah, Grade 6

A Day at My Aunt's
I went to visit my aunt.
We went out to the yard.
Then we planted plants.
The stool I was sitting on was hard.

My cousin came and I played with her.
We were pretending we were in a jet.
"Time to come in," my dad said. I said, "Yes, sir."
He had a surprise, it was a new pet.
Sarah Clements, Grade 4

The American Dream
A dream,
Promising success but shining only on some
Shining, like a midnight moonbeam
We are promised equality,
If we work hard
We are promised success,
If we work hard
Then why are we not equal in this world of regrets?

We were together in the beginning,
So why not in the end?
What happened in the middle,
What has brought us to this downward descent?
Stop this downhill slope!
Stop before we reach a bitter end!

Someday we will be together,
Someday we will figure out this twisting kaleidoscope,
And all hands will be interlocked
"The American Dream": A dream, a fantasy, a hope.
Violet Jean, Grade 5

The Crab
Down the beach scuttled a crab,
Click, click, click, click, click.
I've heard that sound before,
Clack, clack, clack, clack, clack.
That friendly sound, that friendly sound,
Click, clack, click, clack, click.
It brings back vivid memories,
Clack, click, clack, click, clack.
Of crashing waves and a gentle breeze,
Click, click, click, click, click.
Of that towel as soft as a cloud,
Clack, clack, clack, clack, clack.
I close my eyes and enjoy that sound,
Click, clack, click, clack, click.
It feels like a million years have gone by,
Clack, click, clack, click, clack.
When listening to that soothing noise until…
Pop!
Back into its hole hops the crab,
And silence is paradise.
Rayen Lin, Grade 6

Dust Bowl
D eadly storm started
U nable to do anything about it
S ickness spread, people died
T he buildings, everything even hope was destroyed

B ig clouds of dust coming our way
O h, I wonder will it ever end
W ater was not a reliable source those days
L ast 5 years the most devastating in different ways
Camila Guevara, Grade 4

Where I Belong

I'm from a family who stands tall with pride;
I'm from the family who hopes for faith and strength.
I am the one who shows kindness and love to others around me.
The family who dreams for everyone to love each other.

Where the street I'm from with a marvelous park;
Where the birds chirp and the kids laugh.
Where the people go off to work and the cars gobble up the road.
The street that people go to eat.

Hope for what you hope for
Dream for what your dream for
Believe for what you believe for;
Live for what you live for
and never stop giving up.

Hope for what you dream is going to happen in life;
Believe for it and live for it and never give up.

Addai Vazquez, Grade 6

School

First grade, the most exciting year
It's when all the tests appear
The beginning of your career
The days go by so fast
And then at last
The year has past
Second grade, you wonder what's in store
If it's fun or homework galore
But into the second week you're already bored
Wanting to be on the first floor
Playing a game called war
Finally you can say no more
And go play with your friends next door
Then there's third, fourth, fifth and all the rest
And then the final year the one that's the best
Yes there are a lot of hard tests
And you leave the mother's nest
But then you get to rest.

Nadege Pelletier, Grade 6

What Happens to a Dream Deferred?*

What happens to a dream deferred?
Does it fade
like all of the color on an old telly screen?
Or does it blossom like a blood-red rose
and then wilt at dawn?
Does it singe
like a wildfire?
Or does it vanish
like the sun descending over the horizon?
Maybe it just effaces from your mind
like the stars in the morning sky?
Or does it collapse from existence like a spirit?

Samantha Huff, Grade 6
*Inspired by Langston Hughes

Nature

As the sun peeks
Through the trees

The wet tall grass
Starts to shine

Suddenly the wind
Starts to blow

Then the birds
Begin to sing

The animals
Begin to play

Nature a beautiful
Thing that is
Around us

The most beautiful
Thing in the world.

Diego Antonio Allende Hernandez, Grade 4

Earth

Earth
Our home —
Beautiful sunsets
in the night.
Clouds soaring in the sky,
forest roaming the land,
as far as the eye can see —
A wonderful, peaceful
Place.
Earth
Our home —
Earth
Our home —
War starting and ending
Men dying
Countries destroying each other,
Innocent people are being put to their death
until the Earth,
is alas not our home.
Earth
Our home —

Benjamin Eyer, Grade 6

Sharks

Sharks are amazing creatures with lots to do.
They are constantly hunting for things to devour.
They migrate long distances for a warm ocean.
Many sharks are frightening but some are cute.
They mistake us for prey while surfing or diving.
Sharks don't kill for fun, they re just looking for food.
Sharks are mistaken for what they aren't.

Michael Owen, Grade 4

If I Were in Charge of the World

If I were in charge of the world,
Donald Trump couldn't run for president.
I'd make school a fun place to go,
and ice cream wouldn't make you fat or sick.
If I were in charge of the world,
there'd be no bullies or annoying people,
and you wouldn't wear pink unless it's a breast cancer shirt or hat.
You wouldn't have math or Social Studies.
Instead you would have recess or Kickstart.
You wouldn't ever go to gym, only Kickstart.
You wouldn't have bedtime,
if I were in charge of the world.

Keagan Huff, Grade 6

A Chance to Change the World

I care about if people like me and not
I can change the whole world
With just one thought
Poof! Like magic I can make a change
I can end world hunger
Or stop violence
For children who are younger
I can give the whole world a second chance
I could even cure cancer
With ideas as sharp as knives
I will have the answer
Wow! Me making a change will open people's eyes

Jaliyah Brooks, Grade 6

A Trip to Colorado

We're taking a long car trip
To go to Colorado
Leaving Texas' July weather behind
For the cool, fresh mountains of Breckenridge.
First thing we do is ride the cold, fast rapids
Of the Arkansas River.
We soared above the clouds on a hot air balloon
Climbing up the mountain inside a swaying cable gondola
Whooshing down a fast bobsled rail coaster
A lot of shopping, eating, and walking in between.
Time to load up and head back home.
Hoping that we could go back again!

Mason Bates, Grade 6

What Am I?

I am a cheetah
    running fast across the plain.
I am an apple
    hanging on a tree with all the other fruits.
I am a bunny
    hopping strongly out of the snow.
I am a stone
    lying lazily across the floor.
I am a lion
    standing proudly on a rock.

Ethan Capen, Grade 4

Dust Bowl

what I see is that a black cloud of storms is coming
what they see is more than that
our lives must mean something
that's what I see but…
what they see is more than that
a big black monster coming this way
that's what I see but…
what they see is more than that
a big black monster coming this way
our lives must mean something
what they see is more than that
what I see is that a black cloud of storms coming

Daniel Huynh, Grade 4

A Tear Drop

When your kneeling upon
you realize she's forever gone
Wonderful memories will never be forgotten
A hole in the heart that'll always be rotten
A beautiful picture behind me, I begin to cry
You look above and know it's a goodbye
A billion tears brings back the pain
My room is flooding filling a drain
In my dreams I see her smile
Cherishing the moment for a while
Feeling as if she were in Alabama
This lady who I truly miss is my grandma

Melanie Cruz, Grade 6

Blue

Blueberries are good for you
    and that is my most favorite fruit
Oceans are blue…I love the
    ocean and the ocean loves you
Bruises can be blue sometimes when
    you trip from your shoe
I hate bruises and so should you
    I like blue
        Bins but not bruises on your shins
I like blue lines especially the
    the ones that shine
As you can **see** I love blue and it loves you.

Braeson La Vergne, Grade 4

Dust Bowl

I remember a big black cloud
I remember it following me when I was running.
I remember birds flying with fear
And screams from people.
I remember animals in the air because of the wind
I remember people crying through cuts on their face.
I remember people looking for cover.
Even after being scared I lived.
I remember that big black cloud.
But my favorite memory's yet to come

Joel Lagrenade, Grade 4

How Much I Love You

I can't tell you how much you mean to me.
There is so much that I love about you.
If I were to write it all down I'd need more paper.
My life would never be the same without you.
I love you!

Luz Arzarte, Grade 6

Molly

There once was a dog named Molly
Whose owner thought she was quite jolly
She met a handsome pug
Who was rolling on the rug
Which she liked until she saw the lovely Collie

Rilee Nunez, Grade 5

Ice Cream

I like ice cream a lot
It taste good when days are hot
Vanilla, chocolate, or strawberry are the best
And if you disagree
I will put you to a taste test.

Angel Johnston, Grade 4

Dancing

The ballet dancer is very flexible and limber.
She gracefully turns and leaps.
Her dancing technique is beautiful yet lonely.
Dancing in the moonlight, longing for company.
She dances in her dreams.

Tu Han Huynh, Grade 4

Observations of a Sibling

Sissy, sissy, oh, that girl
Kind, caring
but crazy still.

She's got fingernails a half inch long
That don't bother her
not at all.

Nine years old, she's my best friend
She's still waiting
for her nails to extend!

Got some shirt she never wears
She's got Tinkerbell
on her underwear!

A little bit wacko, but still kind
I'm so glad
that she's mine.

Sissy, sissy, oh that girl
My favorite sister
the only one still!

Bree Hill, Grade 5

The World That We Call Home

You are born into this world,
This world we so call home,
Where people roam the streets,
Always on their phone,

Walking by,
With a silent whisper,
Acting like they don't know anyone

You ask me why?
I do not know,
We are in this world
This world that we call home.

Life seems pleasant all is good,
All you know is perfect

Just until you realize,
Who is living on this Earth

You begin to see,
all the tension,
all the poverty,
And then you ask me why?

I already told you
It's just the world that we call home.

Lexi Laymon, Grade 6

Golden Gate

Here is life in finest form,
The sun of Heaven with rays so warm.
To think and wonder, live and dream,
Thoughts are flowing in a crystal stream.

Here I see not but joyous face
Man and women of every race.
Here where all suffering is away for good,
Away from Earth I've understood.

Yet there are beggars at the Golden Gate
Weighed down by chains of strife and hate.
In Purgatory stilled in stance
Eyes are begging for a glance.

They are lucky, we are blessed,
Yet there's a place for all the rest.
They lie in pain in fiery pit
In evil world of flame and grit.

Knowing now all their wrongs,
While we may here the angel's song.
Now aware of Earthly choices,
Following the angel's voices
To reach the Golden Gate.

Nathan Delatorre, Grade 6

Friendship and Love

At first you were the person who was simply smart,
the person who I didn't know had a heart.
You aced every test you ever took,
day after day, you had a book.
Grades were the things that brought us together,
maybe we would be comparing them forever.
You became more than just an enemy,
I knew that you and I would share some memories.
Day after day, you made me laugh,
it was like you were my other half.
Friendship and love are the best things I got out of you,
if I hadn't said that one sentence, I wouldn't have knew.

Kailee Kee, Grade 6

What Happens to a Dream Deferred?*

What happens to a dream deferred?
Does it descend
like a snowflake from the sky?
Or burn
and then disappear?
Does it transform into stone to never be revealed?
Or decompose
like bad fruit?
Maybe it just drifts away
like a leaf in the wind.
Or does it fade like color from a movie?

Gabriel Etchamendy, Grade 6
*Inspired by Langston Hughes

What Happens to a Dream Deferred?*

What happens to a dream deferred?
Does it burn
like a crackling fire on a cold winter's night?
Or peel off like an old brown banana peel
and then get thrown away and forgotten about?
Does it turn into a shiny bubble and then POP?
Or die from old age
like a human longing for the afterlife?
Maybe it just sneaks out of your head in search for a new human
like an orphan in search of a home?
Or does it lurk in your head and hide away until you find it?

Emma Jones, Grade 6
*Inspired by Langston Hughes

I Wish I Had a Family

I wish I had a family to play with in the snow
I wish I had a family to have fun with,
to play games with
I look outside and see all the other kids
Playing with their parents,
but I feel like a baby dog left out all alone
I just wish I had a family
I wish
I wish
I had a family to do fun things with

Makala Ingram, Grade 6

Thieves

I'm here building with some blocks,
Starting to wish there were chests with locks.

So other players wouldn't steal from me,
These items are mine and they're not free!

They do it while I'm not looking and behind my back,
I have to chose a time to attack!

I'll teach and show them how it feels,
It's like they'll be shocked by some eels.

On beautiful days, they rob me blind,
Oh I'm gonna give them a piece of my mind!

I'm going to steal all their stuff,
And show them that's about enough.

Khamani Ward, Grade 6

The Love of a Cat

Every day and every night, I wonder what it is like for them
Then I know it must be better
Oh, the loneliness I felt then
The emptiness I felt then
For almost a year I lived in this
I lived like that
Without that love from a cat
But it changed
My life changed
It was whole again
And just like then
Just like that
I was filled with joy and the love of a cat
Now my life does not feel lonely anymore
But when I look in the air I see four smiling faces, way up there
Just like that
The love of a cat

Molly Barley, Grade 6

What Is Pink?

Pink is when you dye your hair pink for the first time,
a sunset after a long day,
when a dog laps water,
and when spring blossoms after a long winter.

Pink smells like a rose blooming,
when you blow a bubble of bubble gum,
and the smell of fresh cotton candy.

Pink is when your face blushes when you first fall in love.

It is strawberries before they are red.

Pink sounds like a baby pig oinking
for the first time and flowers blooming.

Allivia Butler, Grade 4

Navy Blue

Navy blue is the color of the ocean — very stunning and full of commotion
Navy blue is the color of blueberries — much less sour than raspberries
Navy blue is the color of a car — very nice and can go exquisitely far
Navy blue is the color wiggly playful Jell-O — very wobbly and I don't think it will say hello
It is the color of colorful jelly beans — sweet and the best flavor to see
Navy blue is the color of a school crayon — pretty but it wasn't made for eons
Navy blue is the color of a moist cake — very delicious but not fun to bake
It can be soap — full of bubbles and it gives you hope
Its the color of a delicate and free butterfly — flapping its beautiful wings high in the sky
Navy blue is the color of this enormous fish — scaly and is very so rich
Navy blue can be the color of flowers — their petals are pretty but they don't grow in an hour
It's the color of a beautiful gem — very shiny and you're not going to find it in a gloomy dark den
It's the color of a rich smoothie — very thick and good to see a scary movie
Navy blue is the color of jewelry beads — you can make them into seasonal wreaths
The color of ink — dries fast, and thank goodness it doesn't stink
Navy blue of the color of sports shoes — very fashionable and so comfortable you can even peacefully snooze
Messiah Nieto, Grade 5

The Ocean and the Sunset

The gorgeous, churning, flowing ocean.
The bright orange of the sunset reflecting off the glass clear sea.
Life beneath the ocean waves seems to be peaceful, at least for now.
Nothing seems to be going wrong in this world, an almost exact copy of our own.
It's just the ocean and the sunset. Nothing else seems to be there at all.
Just the gentle ocean water, and the slowly setting sun.
Turning away is close to impossible. It is captivating how the slightly churning waters reflect the light of the sun turning the rolling waves into dancing flames.
The moon is rising, the scene is leaving.

The moon has risen fully now.
Turning away is only a matter of time.
Still it is hard. The sunset was beautiful and the ocean was stunning. The reflection in the water was captivating.
Nothing as gorgeous can be seen on a camera.
Without seeing the real beauty, a picture is just an image, a copy on a device or paper meant to capture something's beauty.
What you will really want to keep is the memory of the gorgeous image, that you can interpret your own way.
McKenzie Honish, Grade 6

I Remember

I remember when it was okay to not be okay.
I remember when no one let society get in our way
I remember when people used to not think about the bad times.
And I even remember when there really were no lies, people just told you the truth
I remember when everyone used to be by your side
But no, society made everyone be "fake"
Society made it okay for people to call you names, that you wouldn't appreciate.
Society made everyone think that if you're not keeping up on trend, everyone would dislike you.
When people ask you the question, "are you okay?"
The other person expects you to say you are okay.
They want you to be okay, because if you had a total breakdown of tears
They would say to stay strong, but they don't understand what's happening
Because they could care less
Society made everyone not care about others.
They expect you to be happy even when the worst thing is happening to you.
Society. Oh gosh, what are we going to do with society?
Ginna Marin, Grade 6

Shark's Teeth

The thing about a shark is its teeth.
One row above, one row beneath.

Take a good look.
You will find another row behind.

Still closer here, I'll hold your hat
it has the third row behind that?
Kevin Aguilar, Grade 6

I Wish

I wish I was fast
Like a cheetah
And I dream I could fly
I am very creative
I used to think of what I could make
But now I make things out of Legos
I seem to make amazing things
But I'm really awesome
Logan Williams, Grade 6

The Ocean

The wind blows
as the ocean water flows
In the deep blue sea
the green seaweed grows on ground sea
When I open my ears I hear
the ocean's splashing waves
I end my day
with a good wave
Camila Vargas, Grade 4

Football

F ans screaming
O vertime when the game is tied
O n the field playing
T ouchdown to get points
B all over the end zone
A ll players like to play
L owering the rope for the field goal
L ast name on the back of the jersey
Israel Blackwell, Grade 5

Night

fog
cold, still
night, moon, light
sun, shine, good night
shine up, light up
night up
wake
up
Ezra Tomlinson, Grade 5

Stray Cat

Over the stream
Under the waterfall
Into the cave
Out of the city
Turning to night
Toward the wilderness
Away the wind flows
During the night
Toward the home
Until she remembers
In her dreams
About the home she doesn't have
Apart from her friends
Since the days
When thunder came
Before her friends went
Out of sight
Inside the prison
Before they betrayed her
Under the shadows
During the night she cried
Annette Dillihunt, Grade 4

The Alamo

The Alamo
holds great
history
Many men died
on this sorrowful night
this challenging night
has gone for a long time

Still stands for 200 years
will never fall

Travis making it secure
first to fall
on the presidio wall

Bonham on the chapel
with a 8 pounder cannon
firing the most as possible
the only victory was Spanish rights
that's all the history the Alamo can
handle
Campbell Moncrief, Grade 4

Happiness / Sadness

Happiness
Cheerful, joyful
Smiling, cheering, enjoying
Gladness, delight — gloom, worry
Depressed, distressed, anguished
Awful, hopeless
Sadness
Sharlene Valdivia, Grade 4

Soccer Player

Runs with the ball
As swift as the wind
Dodging the other players
Passing the ball
Asking his teammate
To pass the ball back to him
Dodging the defenders
And makes a goal
Helping his team
To win the game
Hasan Abdurrahman, Grade 6

Running Horses

Clip, clop, clip, clop, neigh!
Horses run by
Clip, clop
Running so fast
Neigh! Neigh!
Strong and mighty
Clip, clop, neigh! Neigh!
Their manes fly
Clip, clip
As they run by
Isabelle Schiller, Grade 4

Fox

Hook as sharp as a spear
Red as roses
A loving pirate
A caring fox
Eyes yellow as the sunshine
Fur soft as a bunny's
Teeth as sharp as titanium knives
Tail as bushy as a squirrels'
Foxy the Pirate Fox
Brianna Montoya, Grade 6

The Sun

It wakes me up so I can go
to school, shines so bright
So I can go outside and play
when it leaves at the end
of the day I get sad
when the moon shines I
go to sleep and when I
wake up I'm happy
Again!
Alexis Sanchez, Grade 5

Rip!

There once was a clumsy boy named Darris
Whom no one could ever embarrass
Until at lunch he did trip
And we all heard a rip
But I won't tell you where the tear is
Joseph Waked, Grade 5

I Am
I am unique and kind
I wonder what God is like
I hear birds singing
I want peace in the world

I am unique and kind
I pretend to be a photographer
I feel my mom's kisses
I touch the blue water
I worry what will happen in the future
I cry when people fight

I am unique and kind
I understand life's path
I say, "Keep trying!"
I dream I will accomplish my goals
I try to learn new things
I hope for no war

I am unique and kind
Bianca Garcia, Grade 4

Cowboy's Winter
Early in the morning
All the snow crisp and white
All the cattle looking like snowballs
Like little dots in the field
The cow boss gathers his men
Brave cowboys on strong horses
To gather the snow-covered field

They ride out in the snow
Frost on their cold hats
Like bandits of the West
The cowboys push the cattle
All sitting on hard saddles
All frostbitten and frozen
The cattle are brought back home

All the horses are fed
All the cows are roaming
But the cowboys are getting ready
For tomorrow's ride out in the snow
John Riordan, Grade 6

Horses
Eyes are innocent
Gentle as a soft breeze
Curious they are
They prance across the winter snow
Then they proudly stand

Strong beasts
Amazing creatures
That's what some horses are
Madison Rockwell, Grade 4

Craze
Water and Waves
I hear the ocean
Time to have fun on the waves
Surf's up! Here I come!

The Gentle Grass
Spring comes with sun fun!
Spring's gentle breeze passes by
Birds chirp up the sky

Galaxy Gaze
You are like the Sun
You-heart of the Milky Way
You help us survive
Sharanya Nemane, Grade 4

My Fear of Heights
I know I am a pretty tall kid but
I have a huge fear if heights
because when I go very high up
my stomach doesn't agree!
I like going on roller coasters
but I think they go too high,
if it gets too high and too loopy.

My name is Alexandra Paige Thomas,
and I am really scared of going high.
When I'm with my friends at school
I really try to hide it, but every time
I close my eyes it simply goes away!
Never of course on a roller coaster!
Alexandra Thomas, Grade 4

If I Could Fly
If I could fly over humankind
It would be a blessing in my mind
I would do tricks like a butterfly would
For an hour or even six, if I could

If I could fly around the sun
I would fly until the day is gone.
I would fly as far as the moon
I won't be back anytime soon

I will come back to Earth
The planet of my birth
I am sleepy, so I will go to bed
Then, I will fly again in my head
Taylor Horton Raymond, Grade 4

Superheroes
They are strong
They also fight
Sometimes they are wrong
And mostly come out at night
Bryan Cantu, Grade 5

What Is Blue?
What is blue?
Blue is the ocean
The great Pacific

Blue is a thunderstorm
In a sad movie
With rain and sorrow

Blue is a Blue Jay
A Peacock and a
Poison Dart Frog too

Blue is a symbol
A symbol for people and animals
What is blue to you?
Ben Hamilton, Grade 4

Love My Life!
I want to live my life
Because it is mine.
Not one person can tell me
Who I can't be.
I want to love my family
Because it is mine.
How much I love them
Cannot be a surprise.
I love them too much to explain.
I want to love my life.
My dreams will come true
Because they are mine to control.
My dreams are my future.
My future is my life.
I want to love my life!
Hannah Sanchez, Grade 6

Christmas Night
'Twas Christmas Eve
The candles shone bright
The outside was like a white blanket
Glistening in the night

The time drew near
The clock struck nine
The mice ran by
Which was quite divine

For me to know
What happened then
It is up to you
To figure out
Christmas night
Priyanka Soe, Grade 5

Santa Cruz

The sun shining,
Bare feet marking
In the sand,
The sandy wind
Blowing overhead.
The waves crashing
In the breeze.
The feeling of love
Through the air
Touching me
Deep in.

The evening sun
Shining into the
Ocean with a
Gossamer touch.
The laughs upon faces.

The warmth of the
Loving hugs, the
Sand bugs nibbling
At your bare skin.
That's Santa Cruz to me.
Hanna Fong, Grade 4

Math Class

In the withering environment
Of school education,
Where the voice of silence roams,
Where only
The scratching of pencils is heard,
I bring a book,
In a place where we cannot read.
I bring a journal,
In a place where we cannot write.
I bring a brain,
In a place where we cannot think.

Things thought before,
Discovered before,
Proven before
On a test
Things said before,
Quoted before,
Lectured before
On the wall.

Why do classes
Have to be so bitter?
Brandon Nguyen, Grade 6

Strong Frogs

Frogs jumping on pads
With their powerful strong legs
They try to eat flies
Ryan Alonso, Grade 4

Rejection

A feeling of dread crept
over my mind
an arrow of pain shot through my heart.

It hurt
why would you hurt me like that?
My world felt like it was coming to an end.
I wanted to crawl into a hole and cry.

It hurt
never wanting to trust again.
I have one question
Why?
Why would you hurt me?
Why would you do this?
It hurt
Hadley Hallmark, Grade 5

Cancun

Windy skies
Crashing
Crashing
Waves, warm waves
Sandy feet
Swimming
Swimming
Fish, small fish
With the dolphins
Riding
Riding
The beauties that roam the seas
One more treat
Kissing
Kissing
The manatees
Olivia Pigram, Grade 5

Monday

You wake up on a Sunday starting
a new week,
But then you realize as the day goes on
tomorrow is Monday.
School is coming.
It gets you by surprise.
Waking up early again
doing the same routine.
You go to sleep early as told,
and you have to wake up early for five days.
School goes by quite fast
you then realize
it is Friday tomorrow!!!
The weekend at last, what a fun week.
Oh no?!
Tomorrow is Monday.
Joanne Nguyen, Grade 6

A Winter Night

Unostentatious as a mouse
The blanket of white lies over the house
The vista untouched by man
You will know what nature can
What a great sight
On that winter night
As once you awaken
You will see that all you've seen has shaken
Things you've seen
Cease to exist
As children pour out to play
On that snowy winter day
Srinath Nandigam, Grade 6

Problem

I really feel guilty when I talk BACK
or SCREAM at my parents.
When I get really MAD at them,
I don't even notice when I get ANGRY,
And I start c r y i n g
Then I reflect that I was
Being really RUDE
I notice that I have done
Something bad because they
Tell me to STOP!
I kind of have ANGER problems
But, I don't know.
Angeles Mendez, Grade 6

Orphan

I am sick
I am cold
And no one is told.

If they seek
For the weak
Then it is me they will greet.

So if you meet me
Then you will see
That this sad child
Is me.
Levi Wilkins, Grade 6

Water Park

W ater is crystal clear
A ctive kids jump in and out
T eachers teach them to swim
E nergized all day
R ushing water flows past

P eople like to swim
A lways with a smile on their face
R acing to the towering slide
K ids go crazy wild.
Roselyn Caldera, Grade 6

Writer's Winter Night
The night did come,
A blanket over the lively world.
The sun goes down,
The moon takes its turn.
The wind blows in the dry winter night.
Colorful lights flicker on.
The candle on the windowsill
Bright as day.
I sniff,
My nose runs.
I blink,
My eyes sting.
I think,
My head pounds
I write,
My hands sweat.
The light of the reading lamp
Casts shadows over the carpeted ground.
I glance at the clock.
10:45…p.m.
I think that should be all for tonight.
Amanda Reid, Grade 6

Friends
A friend
Is happy
Is funny
A friend makes you smile

A friend
Is helpful
Is a boy or a girl
A friend never leaves you alone

A friend
Is loving
Is calm
A friend is someone you can share

A friend
Is kind
Is brave
A friend considerate about your emotions
A friend
Is Rosibel and Keren
Daisy Garcia, Grade 6

Cat
The important thing about a cat is
that it can purr.
They are multicolored.
They can leap, run, and can hide.
Cats feel soft and smell like fish.
But the important thing about a cat is
that they can purr.
Landon Ontiveros, Grade 4

Untitled
Once I saw
A little boy
Who, alone, outside
Played with a toy
In the wild
He smiled
He saw his blue shoes
And that gave him a clue
So, he swung on a rope
He sure liked to swing
And he walked
And he talked
Until he felt like a king
Dakota Williams, Grade 4

Animals
Animals that live in the wild
they eat, they hunt, they swim,
and they run.
The world is filled with lots of creatures
that are fast, and slow,
that jump and leap.
Animals can go anywhere they want
but it's hard to survive
out there in the snow,
desert and forest.
To survive, you need a den, food and water
every single day
being an animal is not easy
Leslie Gutierrez, Grade 4

If I Were to Be in Charge of Ethiopia
Things are never fair
For the Oromos
Who live in Ethiopia
They get killed
For being Oromo
I don't understand why
The more they kill
The more people who start protesting
I am Oromo
And I care for my family
If I were in charge
I would treat everyone equally
And let no violence happen
Lensa Negassa, Grade 6

The Dolphin
D ashing
O ver
L ovely
P od
H eavenly
I mage
N ature
Kailey Holden, Grade 4

The Eiffel Tower
it's standing tall
touching the clouds
over a massive sea of people

his friends are
the ultraviolet rays of
the scorching sun

when people get on top of him
there's no sorrow on their face
instead there's a joyful smile
The Eiffel Tower is a soothing place

as he stands there
each and every year
he will help make the world
a more beautiful place
Silvana Pescador, Grade 4

Diamond
In the dirt you shall hide,
When I find you on the side.

Where you twinkle as bright,
As the sun's light.

When you wink at me on my ring,
It makes my heart want to sing.

You're prettier than jade,
And that well never fade.

You come in many different colors,
Definitely worth more than a few dollars.

You'll always be my friend,
Even past the end.
Julianna Smith, Grade 6

The Meaning of Big
Here I stand
Big as ever
I'm a cow with marks all over,
a fat cat with no legs,
a bald man with
a shine on the top of
his glistening head.
I'm up and down
and all around
with dust in the air.
Big and wide for
TEN
to carry me.
I block the views of most and can't move,
for I am the meaning of Big.
Leeah Chang, Grade 6

Ponies

Across the desert
Ponies riding along with faith
Going to Texas
Jacquelynn Nopp, Grade 4

True Human

If I were an ant, I would work hard
By saving food for the rainy day!

If I were a honey bee, I would provide delicious fruits
By pollinating the flowers!

If I were an earthworm, I would help the farmers
By making the soil ready for the tender roots!

If I were a frog I would make the world a less itchy place
By eating bothering bugs!

If I were a hen, I would make the world a healthier place
By laying protein rich eggs!

If I were a vulture, I would keep the Earth clean
By scavenging on dead animals!

If I were a sheep, I would keep you cozy in the winter
By sharing my warm wool!

If I were a cow, I would make kids strong
By providing nutritious milk!

If I were a tiger, I would protect the jungle
By scaring evil humans away!

If I were a true human, I would help the world
By preserving these amazing creatures for the future!
Akhil Vellaturi, Grade 4

Coffee

"Oh no! Can you pick that up please."
Said my mom.
"Ok" I said. I touched the thing and it
Smelled chocolatey and that's when I realized
That it was coffee
Then it feels like I am in
HEAVEN
Then memories
Start to run through my
Brain.
I remember one time I was in
Starbucks and smelled like coffee and the
Coffee tasted even better!
Tadely! Tadely! TADELY!
"What" I said.
"Pick the coffee up" my mom said
Then I smelled it again.
Tadely Flores, Grade 6

Maple Leaf

A maple leaf goes
Dancing with the autumn breeze
Stopping on a branch
Yarazet Martinez, Grade 4

Reading

I look at the selection and see only green.
I need something that is not very mean.

Looking for magic, wands, and fairies,
But looking at this is making me very wary.

I look and look but can't find a book.
The series is near, but I still have to look.

I finally found my favorite book!
I sit down instead and open and look.

I read for an hour or two or three.
Rereading is my favorite thing!

Soon it is time to close the building.
I should check out before the clearing.

I walked down the street with my nose in the book.
I don't even notice the man and the crook.

The crook takes off and runs towards me.
I smack him with my book and stop him thankfully.

The man runs up and thanks me again.
The police arrest him and gives me a bin.

I accept it quickly and think what it is.
I open and look for it is a new book!
Kylie Brennan, Grade 6

Sand Castle Ruin

A place on a beach where the waves don't go,
There lies a castle that is broad and tall.
Or it used to be; now, it's a ruin low.
It has been cursed with pride that makes one stall.

The first one to be infected with pride
"Helped" the others to fall into the trap.
The castle was doomed; the king had just died,
And there was no heir — no time for a nap

The people now thought, "Oh, what have I done!"
They started to repent and think again.
And the people over greed have now won,
But the castle was never seen again.

But then again, how could they think or stand,
For they were only statues made of sand.
Martin Saenz, Grade 5

Scribble to Story

They start slowly, like a child learning how to walk.
Like tiny birds flapping their wings in desperate attempts to fly.
They start, pause, and then start again, slowly throwing themselves out on to the crinkled piece of old paper.
Scribble after scrabble.

The words come faster now, like a boy running towards his mother in a joyous reunion.
Each word tumbles after another, and the intended shape begins to take place.
The letters flow like a river, line after line after line.
Scribble after scrabble.
Letter after letter.

They soar across the paper, creating splotches and stains of ink until the paper can no longer hold their weight.
With a great flourish another one is produced, just as wrinkled and smelly as the previous paper.
Faster and faster they go, until the human's hands get tired, and he almost stops. Almost. Then he starts again.
Scribble after scrabble.
Letter after letter.
Word after word.

Slowly, the they begin to lessen in intensity, now flowing like a stream on a pleasant autumn day.
Like a cool breeze to keep the humans cool when the sun unleashes its rage.
Like the slow song that a mother sings to her child at night.
Scribble after scrabble.
Letter after letter.
Word after word.

Akhila Gunturu, Grade 6

A Wonderful Life

Let's get started on a wonderful life.
First off, 5 and 6 year olds, eat your veggies when your mom tells you to.
Trust me; you won't even get dessert if you don't...you don't want that to happen, do you?
Be nice to your mom and dad; they are the ones who gave you life, for goodness' sake!
Oh, and try not to cry too much; it really annoys people.
When you get to be about 10 or 11 years old, do your best in every event.
Obey your teachers and coaches, and pay attention if you want to get good grades.
Respect your peers if you want to keep your friends.
With friends, you an always have fun
By jumping on trampolines or playing pranks on your brothers or sisters!
Teenagers...I know it starts getting a little crazy, but don't take drugs.
No matter what, make good decisions...you know what I mean.
Young adults, it is so important to get an education, and get a job.
Young parents, I know a baby is a big responsibility, but don't be afraid to make rules.
Be wise about how you raise your children, and send them to a great school.
Your children will grow up so fast, so savor every moment.
All you middle aged people, it's never too late to try something new, so do not have a mid-life crisis!
Please don't stay so stressed out, you still have life to live!
Those of you who are getting up there, just hang in there, fight through it, and stay healthy.
Look back at all the wonderful life you've lived and be grateful.
At any age, do your best, and live the best life you can live.

Charlie McMullen, Grade 4

The Oak Tree

We plant the seed its leaves turn green, oh how we love the oak tree
The squirrels and birds have found a home and how they love to roam, all throughout the oak tree
The leaves turn brown, they cover the ground, all around the oak tree
The limbs are bare, there's snow everywhere, it's so fun to see the four seasons of the oak tree

Whitley Jeffcoat, Grade 4

Watermelon

Watermelon in the summer
sun enjoying the fresh air in
his sun-drenched patch. He is
the refrigerator cooling, like a cactus
getting watered, finally. He
arises from the ground
on his leafy, green vines.

He provides vitamins A (in the form of carotenoids), B1,
B6, and C. He provides
a good source of pantothemic
acid, copper, biotin, and
magnesium. He gives
people nutrients, and
hydration.

The sweet smile is
the first thing you see
when you cut open his
oval-shaped head. His sweet
smile is the happiest expression.
He rolls over like a dog
following commands for a treat.

Zoe Jenkins, Grade 4

Love

Love is endless, love is free,
It's everywhere to those who see,
You let that one person know how special you feel,
Love is like this world, unreal.

Swoosh, with your affection you enchanted me,
By conquering me in totality,
Your love flows through my veins like the current of a river,
Whenever she calls, I flee towards thee.

This love is a dove,
It flies through the breezy wind that extends,
With our soft emotions that never ends,
Now in my mind I have found love.

Tyree Wilson, Grade 6

The Feeling

Have you ever felt that feeling
where your heart is going to beat out of your chest,
or like you are going to faint?
You can't stop smiling or being happy!
You suddenly hear a voice,
a voice that you have been longing to hear.

You turn and there he is,
your crush
you try to speak
but you are overpowered by...
THE FEELING!

Puma Wright, Grade 6

Family

It's almost Christmas
My parents have been fighting
About the presents they're going to get us
My dad lost his job in downtown area
My mom doesn't have a lot of money to spend
My little sister is crying for not getting Christmas gift
And me I just want my family to have a good Christmas.

Josue Fuentes, Grade 6

Moonlight

The moon looks like an ivory ball,
The vast universe makes it seem small.
In truth, it has a very wide berth,
But not as wide as the Earth.
Orbiting our planet like a satellite,
Shining down on us, exceptionally bright.
Dear Moon, I thank you for what you give at night.

Safwan Al-Amin, Grade 6

Sadness

Sadness seems dark blue
Like the roaring ocean.
I see tears of sorrow.
I hear screams of madness and cries of the wind.
I smell nightmares of blood.
I touch the dread in rosy red hearts.
I taste the wet salty tears of terror.

Juniper Reynolds, Grade 4

Raining from the Heavens

The storm is loud. My comfy home is quiet.
Oh how loud the thunder. Oh how soft the rain.
Oh how bright the lightning that strikes in the dark sky.
Oh how that is not the devil that is not a fallen angel.
It is answer of many prayers.
So come rain come faster than ever.
The good you do, rain, the good you do.

Sydney Holder, Grade 6

Anger

Anger seems dark red
Like the volcano in Hawaii.
I see boiling hot lava.
I hear people screaming for help.
I smell smoke drifting from burning houses.
I touch heat from the cracking ground.
I taste madness.

Zackary Gennette, Grade 4

Dust Bowl

it arrives when tons of dirt were swept
it fills houses with dirt and hurts people
blowing from Great Plains
when it picks up lose dirt it creates a black blizzard
when the wind slows down it leaves

Jason Garcia, Grade 4

The World in My Hands

If I was in charge of the world,
I would have everyone own a small garden
Make sure only certain trees were cut down
No one would be allowed to frown
only when a loved one is gone

If I was in charge of the world,
I would have all Fridays off at school
Funday, the day between Saturday and Sunday
No homework on Wednesday
and a free soda machine in every classroom

If I was in charge of the world,
Donald Trump goes to jail
Obama gets to stay in the White House
Hilary Clinton becomes President
and Bernie Sanders the next four years after that

If I was in charge of the world,
no more guns
Isis would end
no more dangerous knives
and say goodbye to bullying forever

Lola Miertschin, Grade 6

I Am the Sun

I'm something so bright I make you squint
When I go down the moon comes out
In the summer I stay out later
The planes fly over me
I make you live
I make the plants grow tall
When you draw a picture I am always in it
I make you happy
I make you glad
I make you sweaty
I am the colors of yellow and orange
No matter what you say I will always be there
I am the sun

Jazmynn Muzquiz, Grade 6

If I Were in Charge of the World

If I were in charge of the world,
I'd make sure there was no homework on the weekends,
no projects during a break, and
no studying during the summer.
If I were in charge of the world,
there'd be a land you could go to,
called Free For All, and you could get five things for free.
If I were in charge of the world,
you wouldn't have to do chores;
you wouldn't have to go to boring places with your parents.
You wouldn't have to walk to places,
or have to go to work on the weekends.
If I were in charge of the world.

Brianna Solis, Grade 6

The Earthquake

The Earth shook under my bed,
My dresser came down with a clang,
I woke up and my face was red,
My house came down with a crash,
I realized that I had hit my head,
And my books hit the ground with a smash,
I sure hoped that I wasn't dead!

I couldn't see anything through all of the rubble,
The only sound was the stairs with a creak,
I looked to see if I was in trouble,
But my brother then hit me with a whack,
And I couldn't believe my eyes,
My roof had just fallen with a crack,
And there were floating pies!

I saw French fries strewn across the floor,
I just tripped over a piece of wood and fell with a bash,
And I just realized that I didn't have a door,
My bed flew up into the air and hit the ground with a boom,
I couldn't think of anything to do but scream,
And I ran away as fast as I could with a zoom,
But this was very odd, because, it had all been a dream!

Renee Wing, Grade 6

A Walk to School When I Ruled the World

One day I will rule the world
and when I do, I'd make the world bright and clean!
It would be so nice that every day it would turn your mood around
and, when you look around, everything just looks perfect
If I ruled the world
you'd have your own personal minions
and sweets would be considered "vegetables"
If I ruled the world
you wouldn't see any bullies
you wouldn't have to worry about forgetting homework
you wouldn't have to wait for lunch
and finally school would be short
But only if I ruled the world

Aleeza Wajeehullah, Grade 6

I Am…

I am all colors like a rainbow.
I am Christmas giving gifts.
I am spring watching the flowers bloom.
I am midnight seeing the stars shine bright all night.
I am a book about legends with people wondering if it's true or not.
I am a comedy with people laughing.
I am heavy metal music with people screaming.
I am calamari with people saying "yummy".
I am integrity always telling the truth.
I am t-shirts and shorts on hot days.
I am music with people dancing.
I am a kitten sleeping all day.
I am Leena loving rainbows.

Leena Keylani, Grade 4

Piano

Piano keys can be flat and sharp
The music that it makes sounds like a harp
Some keys will be black as night
The white keys will be white as light

The tiny hammer hits the string for less than a second
I guess the sound really is pleasant
I had heard nothing of its kind
The piano was a river, an angel, and I find,

There comes a place called a rest
And that place is always best
The piano, a melodic carpet ride
A heavenly journey where my heart can hide

Alannah Witte, Grade 6

Civil Engineering

When I grow up and get really old
I would like to be a civil engineer
I really want to go to Yale and get a doctorate degree.
I want to own a company but if I can't that is fine with me.

I could invent a bridge that goes to 400,000 miles
Or I could build a skyscraper that has all the colors
This goes to my head can't you see
But if I can't build anything that is fine with me.

I want everyone to say "congrats!" and have a party
I would like everyone to live their lives
I can correct this world you see
But if I can't that it NOT fine with me

Laila Mouton, Grade 4

Who Am I? Who Are You?

I used to not understand
But now everything is clearer
I always feel emotions, both good and bad
But I never want them to stop
I was once someone different
But now, I've changed for the better or worse
If I could heal the scars emotionally and physically
I would dedicate my life to help heal them all
I never would want to be a bad person
But sometimes I can act like it
I can't always be who I want to be
But I can be myself
And that's who I am
Who are you?

Leyna Nguyen, Grade 6

Mars

M is for moons of which Mars has two
A is for atmosphere where Mars does not have enough oxygen
R is for red, the color of Mars' soil
S is for Sojourner, a probe on Mars

Trevor Lee, Grade 5

If I Were in Charge of the World

If I were in charge of the world,
I'd make school only be on Saturday and Sunday,
July 18th a worldwide holiday called Mint Day,
and books available everywhere.
If I were in charge of the world,
there'd be root beer fountains,
Burger King everywhere,
and smoothies available at every drive through.
If I were in charge of the world,
you wouldn't have a set bed time.
You wouldn't have to eat brussel sprouts.
You wouldn't have any homework
or have to do chores.
If I were in charge of the world.

Maxwell Lopez, Grade 6

Our Earth

Unique is our Earth
It's beauty is rare,
The wrangling sound of rivers
Attracts all to stare
The down and dust here
Become charming with the sparrow's twitter,
The crows crowing on parapet
Bringing news of welfare of the dear
Unique is our Earth in the world
With green and charming meadows,
The passers by heave sigh
Of relief
Under the green trees'
Shadows

Kareena Kamal, Grade 5

My Majestic Cat

My majestic cat is something I've always dreamt of.
My majestic cat is something I will always love.

My majestic cat will always be there.
My majestic cat acts like it's big strong bear.

My majestic cat is a little bit crazy.
I hope not today another day it docsn't lcavc mc.

I know I have not known him for a very long time.
I know that I will love him for a long time.

My majestic cats is the best thing to me.
My majestic cat is now part of my family.

Rammy Sameen, Grade 4

Nature

Grass gleaming in the rain
All the trees as tall as giants
How I wonder what is out there
How I would love it if the sun would come out

Reed Banning, Grade 4

The Star

There once was a star
That traveled so far
It was so rare
That you had to stare
Then run grab a jar and catch that star!
Aryanna Mendoza, Grade 5

Turtles

Turtles are green
Turtles are slow
Turtles live outside
Turtles dig many holes
Turtles
Adam Stokes, Grade 4

Brooke

There was a girl named Brooke
Who was always taking my book
I took it back
She did not attack
So I gave her a friendly look
Jennifer Torres, Grade 5

Basketball

Sport
Fun, exciting
Running, bouncing, scoring
It's fun to play.
Basketball
Kristiano Plata, Grade 4

The Black Blizzard

It begins with a thunderous boom
Tears down hope
In the valley of farmers
It takes piece by piece until its all gone
It leaves roughly but its all over
Daniel Akapo, Grade 4

Summer

Summer
Red, yellow
Tanning, swimming, sunshine
Always makes me tan
Awesome
Alejandro Mares, Grade 4

River

River is going
Going to the ocean blue
Moving us apart
Taking all my love for you
I have a small broken heart
Emily Phan, Grade 4

The Miracle

Here is a beautiful Melody.
Flowing through everyone's ears.
Some accept while others deny.
And that makes the Melody cry.

Some use it for fame.
Others try to help but can't.
The Melody remember every success and mistake.
Sometimes the Melody thinks it's the mistake.
BOOM!
A Miracle.
Machine.
Of Joy.
And laughter ahoy.
Now the Melody sing.
To all the girls and boys now her confidence has risen above the void.
Finally the Melody of its dreams and joys.
Andrew Rolland, Grade 6

Light

Light,
Is what shines faintly on a firefly's backside
It pours out of flashlights to guide you to safety
To increase your knowledge, light helps you observe
When you walk into a room, it dances merrily on your skin.
It nurtures all life and reaches to the depths of the shadows,
To lend a helping hand to those in need.

Back in the dark times,
The night once clawed his way to the center of the world,
And before the light touched the top of the crust,
The black infected the core with evil, causing darkness
The only way to stop the darkness was if the sun cured the evil pits
She banished the dark to only come out at the time she needed to rest
Whenever the daylight leaves, the wicked darkness tries to once again overrule the world,
Just as it gets to the core,
The rays of hope smile over the world banishing the dark for another night
Alissa Zenero, Grade 6

Happiness

It's the feeling that everything is right
When life opens its doors.
It's the good in life.
Happiness is anything that makes a person smile.
Whether it's sports, reading, or having a good laugh.
Everyone has something that is unique and personal that makes them happy.
Happiness is the little things in life.
It can be putting a smile on the face of a distressed person,
Or it can be hanging out with friends
Everyone needs these little things to feel happiness.
All of the little things add up to joy.
It doesn't matter what people think;
It only matters what good friends and loved ones think.
Life is good.
Be happy.
Maxwell Campbell, Grade 6

Beautiful View

Wow! What a beautiful view!
Now I can see it through.
Cool how life can change,
From a different perspective of age.

When it rains it is beautiful.
When the sun shines it is wonderful.
Life is a roller coaster, up and down,
But a view like this can turn a frown upside down.

It might be simple to you,
But not for a million-dollar view,
Of a world God created
That many artists have painted.

Nature is beautiful to me.
Oh how I wish you could see!

Camryn Korbitz, Grade 5

Something Nice to Know

Before, I wanted a cute, funny turtle,
But now I have a special tiny, perfect puppy.
I used to love all types of delicious chocolate,
But juicy, mouth-watering bacon is cooler.
I had a bunch of little Kung Zhu's,
Now I collect wonderful cars.
I used to be a silly, young baby,
But now I am a smart, young man.
I used to cherish awesome carrots,
But now I devour perfect potatoes instead.
I used to have a colorful fish,
But now I have a cute baby sis.
I used to not enjoy cursive,
But now I write it very well.
I used to have no friends,
But now I have some nice, wonderful ones.

Brandon Toto, Grade 5

Outside of Civilization

The short green grass flows in the wind
The trees spiral up into the sky
Like long staircases shooting into the air
Looking down upon all who cross their path
And the blue lake filled with reeds silently ripples
Everything is at peace
And everything is quiet
You can only hear the wind
Birds chirping, and squirrels rustling the trees
Refuge, unlike the commotion of the city
Where cars and talking fill the air with noise
Never a moment of complete silence
It is a storm, filled with lightning and thunder
Never a moment of the serenity and quiet
Of Alpine Meadows
Engulfed by nature and surrounded by peace

Max Schaller, Grade 6

Mom and Dad

Mom and Dad you are wonderful
Dad and Mom you are caring
Mom and Dad you are loving
Dad and Mom you are funny

Mom and Dad your the best parents
Dad and Mom you are fun
Dad and Mom you are my favorite people
Mom and Dad you are all I need

Dad and Mom you are awesome
Mom and Dad you are my life
Dad and Mom you are most of my heart
Mom and Dad I love you

Aaliyah Stewart, Grade 6

If I'm in Charge of the World

If I were in charge of the world,
I'd have a magical pet,
a lot of money, and
eat an infinite supply of gelato ice cream.
If I were in charge of the world,
there'd be world peace,
more privileges for students, and
freedom to all
If I were in charge of the world,
you wouldn't be in school right now.
You wouldn't be bossed around by teachers.
You wouldn't be restricted from games because of height issues
or of your age
if I were in charge of the world.

Jessica Vu, Grade 6

If I'm in Charge of the World

If I were in charge of the world,
I'd make the world a republic,
get rid of communism, and
make everybody have equal rights.
If I were in charge of the world,
there'd be human cloning,
a super computer AI, and
a virtual-reality video game.
If I were in charge of the world,
you wouldn't have to sleep at 9:30, and
you wouldn't have to go to school for 7 hours.
You wouldn't have to take the STAAR test
or take the final exam,
if I were in charge of the world.

Anthony Hoang, Grade 6

Baby Blue

I am quiet in class like the color baby blue
I am soft and kind like the color baby blue
I am great like everyone and like the color baby blue
Baby blue describes me

Terry Martinez, Grade 6

Hummingbird

Hummingbird why so swift and agile?
As you move from one flower to another,
Getting your daily nutrition for use in your energy.
Why so vivid?
With blues and greens covering you from head to tail tip,
Your wings creating a rainbow of color.
How do you make your soothing, humming sound?
As you fly so high going anywhere you need and know.
Why so still?
But your wings still moving so fast as you swiftly move,
From flower to flower,
Sucking sweet nectar.
Why so small but brave?
As you protect your offspring from danger approaching,
With your long fierce beak.
Hummingbird why so unique?
With your agility and colors,
A bird like no other,
The Hummingbird.

Ahuitzilin Enrique, Grade 4

I Am

I am creative an caring
I wonder what my name is in different languages
I hear the wind howling
I see a beach with beautiful white sand
I want to turn back time and create a happier future

I am creative and caring
I pretend I can touch the stars
I feel cold saltwater between my toes
I touch the soft fur of a fox
I cry when someone I love passes away

I am creative and caring
I say, "As long as you keep smiling, you'll be okay"
I dream about my friends staying by my side
I try to keep my grades up
I hope the people I love still remember me

I am creative and caring

Anabella Estrella, Grade 4

Fantasies

Daydreaming
A wish waiting to happen
a misty fog hiding my dreams
ocean waves sparkle and crash
Winter snow softly brushes against my cheeks
Giggles echo around me
a happy wonderland
a place I can escape to
where I desire crazy things
a wish
waiting to happen

Julia Vanoli, Grade 6

I Am

I am only a child
I wonder what it is like to be an adult
I hear it is very stressful
I want to stay young forever

I am only a child
I pretend I am grown up
I feel so small in such a big world
I touch the surface of my abilities
I worry I will never be as good as my parents

I am only a child
I understand there are some things I cannot do
I say I am old enough to make my own decisions
I dream of being the richest man in the world
I try my hardest in all I do
I hope to be the best soccer player ever

I am only a child

Riley Good, Grade 6

I Am From

I am from a house
where every meal is enjoyed with family
where my favorite soft grey couch is
where a bookshelf full of books is
where all seven rooms are filled with excitement and joy

I am from a backyard
where plants are fed with love and cared for
where chickens please us and dogs wrestle each other
where I love to sway in my swinging chair

I am from a tradition
where family and God comes first
where we work together and never give up
where every summer is spent at a different place but brings us closer
where all friends become family

This is who I am
and I love where I am from

Annalise Greenlee, Grade 5

Can You Hear Me

Mom
Dad
Listen
Can you hear me
Look at me and see.
You're busy
With money and bills, my soul
kills when my words are ignored,
I wish the mornings and afternoons could switch
Mornings are full but afternoons are
E   M   P   T   Y

Karina Moreno, Grade 6

Fish

O fish O fish
How you bubble
How you swish
How you splash
I Love You
Just the way
God made you
Jeshuah Davis, Grade 4

Flames and Ice

Flames
Powerful, shiny
Burning, swooshing, killing
Fire, embers, snow, hail
Freezing, cracking, slipping
Clear, reflective
Ice
Solange Barbier, Grade 4

Anger

Anger seems bright red
Like the erupting volcano.
I see the smoke that comes out of the fire.
I hear the rocks colliding.
I smell smoke from the fire.
I touch the 360 lava.
I taste fear coming to you.
Dylan Tun, Grade 4

Summer vs Winter

Summer
Hot, fun
Playing, growing, shining
Fields, kids, lakes, hockey
Ice skating, slipping, falling
Cold, slippery
Winter
Jordyn Juette, Grade 6

Fear

Fear seems dark black
Like the shadows that lurk in the night
I see black, liquidated blood
I hear screams of terror
I smell trash being burned
I touch black, hairy spiders
I taste a burnt cookie
Robert Rodriguez, Grade 4

Rain

Raining
Helps the plants grow
Rain makes a ton of mud
Absolutely fascinating
Pouring
Tim Greynerovich, Grade 6

Baking

Entertainment, sweets and goodies
Everyone eating and sometime pets too
With yummy treats and frosting like glue
Yummy treats on display
It almost makes me want to shout "Yay"
From scratch to boxes both are good
But to be a professional baker, oh I wish I could
To have a bakery all on my own
I'm too excited I might turn to stone
When my mom bakes I love the kitchen smell
My mom is quite a professional and her treats make me swell
It's very fun but waiting for treats to bake and cool down
Not being able to eat my treats will make me frown
I love to bake but I'm not the best
And my dad says "Learning from mistakes is the way to learn the rest"
No matter what you bake people will like
But eating too much will send you on a hike
Everyone will love it as long as it tastes yummy
But not if it's not fully ready like not cooled gummy
Overall baking is the best
And without it I can't get any rest
Jennifer Lam, Grade 4

I Am From...

I am from a small town…
Where you will meet a friend just around the corner
Where you will never feel lonely
Where you will never have a bad day

I am from a yellow house…
Where you can hear us from miles away
Where you are free to be yourself
Where you are never judged by clothes

I am from a green backyard…
Where you can climb fruit trees as high as the endless blue sky
Where you will be able to build a magical castle
Where you will be able to rule your enchanted kingdom fearlessly

I am from old traditions…
Where we sit around the warm burning fire on Christmas Eve
Where we look for black bears in the summer at Lake Tahoe
Where we bask in the sun at the sandy beach in LA

I am from people and places that form me to make me the me that I am
Ella Riccomini, Grade 5

Joy

Joy seems fluorescent yellow
Like the happy dandelions in the prairie fields.
I see children skipping through the valley.
I hear bubbling laughter climbing up and down the hills.
I smell the sweet aroma of cherry red roses.
I touch the soft fur of a little puppy sleeping without a care in the world.
I taste the sugary lollipops lined up like trees in a forest.
Madison Tull, Grade 4

The River
I'm close
so very close, yet so far away.
I've crossed deserts and oceans to reach my destination.
Look! In the distance! The tree!
The orange leafed tree! The mile marker!
And…could it be? The River of Erised!
The river that grants any mortal eternal life just by swimming in it!
But I fear it's too late,
my body is too weak
I'm giving out…goodbye…goodbye…
Hayden Baldwin, Grade 6

Green
Green is grass on a summer day.
Green is leaves swaying in the wind.
Green is in a forest.
Green smells like a green apple.
Green tastes like a sour apple.
Green sounds like a forest.
Green looks like my grandmother's eyes.
Green feels like grass.
Green makes me want to lay on a soft patch of grass.
Green is my grandmother's favorite color.
Zoe Robison, Grade 4

Who Am I?
I am pink like the color of a pink tutu,
I'm an adventure book like Indiana Jones,
I'm a comedy for fun and laughable moments,
I'm a country song like the ones Blake Shelton croons,
I'm pajamas that fit comfortable and loose,
I'm Norell perfume that smells like a fresh cup of hot chocolate.

Who am I?
I am Claire Matyastik
Claire Matyastik, Grade 4

Winter Breeze
My hair flowing through the winter breeze.
I realize I'm about to freeze.
My thoughts are frozen in ice,
although it feels nice.
My soul is being swallowed by the dark night,
but not everything is in plain sight.
As I walk in the meadow that is snow covered,
I couldn't believe what I discovered.
Payton Naylor, Grade 5

Easter
E aster is a time of joy.
A fter death rose again.
S tarting at lent we rise to Easter
T errified were the Apostles when they saw Jesus
E ternal life in heaven is a gift from God.
R ejoicing at Easter is something we all do.
Lainey Clark, Grade 6

I Am
I am smart and curious
I wonder how people use longitude and latitude
I hear the sounds of nice angels
I see the kind hearts in kids
I want to stop law breakers
I am smart and curious

I pretend that I'm a spy
I feel the opportunity to learn
I touch new ideas
I worry that everyone will hate me in the future
I cry when people fight and kill other people
I am smart and curious

I understand people who have a hard time
I say that there is no reason for war
I dream for world peace
I try to do well in school
I hope I can make a difference in the world
I am smart and curious
Da'Marcus Hill, Grade 5

I Am
I am sweet and silly
I wonder how California Indians got their names
I hear the sound of angels singing
I see my old pets
I want kindness in the world

I am sweet and silly
I pretend I am a famous artist
I feel snow on a sunny day
I touch colors of a rainbow
I worry about the safety of my family

I am sweet and silly
I understand why people are different
I say, "As long as I live I am kind"
I dream about my friends and family thinking of me
I try my best to support my friends and family
I hope for better people in the world

I am sweet and silly
Caitlyn West, Grade 4

The End
Everything will be crashing down.
All will die.
We will wait for our next life.
We will not see, all will be dark, sad, and hopeless.
Until you see a bright light.
Then you see him.
He said, "You are home."
We walk to the light.
We feel loved, hope, and happiness.
Mia Espino, Grade 6

I Am…Jericho
I am athletic and thoughtful.
I wonder if there are aliens in the galaxy.
I hear people cheering for me.
I see the future in which nobody will fight.
I want to be a famous football player.

I am athletic and thoughtful.
I pretend to be a grownup sometimes.
I feel the wind blowing around me.
I touch the souls of my family members that left me.
I worry that my brothers will get hurt.
I cry when someone hurts my feelings.

I am athletic and thoughtful.
I understand my dreams won't always come true.
I say people shouldn't kill animals.
I dream everybody will live in harmony.
I try to get all A's on my tests.
I hope for people to help the homeless.
I am athletic and thoughtful.
Jericho Williams, Grade 4

My World Concern
My concern for the world is that water pollution will
Make every person and animal sick and ill.
It is killing coral in the water,
And also killing innocent baby otters.
Unwanted trash goes down the drain to a bay
Sending bay porpoises very far away
Oil pollution in the water can kill fish
Leaving them dead with a swish.
What is the cause to all this happening?
It leaves many people wondering.
The answer is simple and very clear.
We are making the ocean have dark black smears.
Can we fix our mistakes?
Yes we can so we just don't take
Picking up trash and cleaning up creeks.
Getting rid of oil spills so they don't reek.
So let's keep all of our water clean.
So animals and people don't get quarantined
We will stay alive and have seafood
And that will put some people in a good mood.
Melina Johnston, Grade 5

The Sunset
The lord of the day is about to descend
Beyond the hills different colors blend
In the sky appears a sunset
Where the sun and the horizon have just met.

Birds flap their wings and fly home
Crickets chirp, and in the grass they roam
Rabbits munch carrots and they jump into their holes
Natures grandeur fills and uplifts the souls.
Neel Gajare, Grade 5

Someday
A tree in the winter, branches bare to the bone
A sunset in the dead of night, shining on us alone
Someday in the future there won't be a sun
Someday in the future the winter will have won

Take a chance while you have it, take a chance while it lasts
You won't have it forever
This life goes by fast
The life that we're given
This life that we have
It's a beacon of hope
One we must grasp quickly
For it will slip away, while the winter is still nippy

Some things we don't know and some things are too far
They remain out of reach on that one lonely star
The winter will win
Or the sun down in flames
The things bigger than us will decide on their own
They may cause great pains
But this hope
This hope still remains
Someday, Someday
Logan Dorothy Falkel, Grade 6

Softball
Batter up, WHACK!
Ball out of the park
Running towards first
Base coach yelling
Umpire yelling STRIKE ONE! STRIKE TWO!
BOOM! The girl hits the ball with her bat
Flying through the air, it lands
First base, second base, third base, heading home
Everybody yells, "HOME RUN!"
Girls jump and yell in excitement
Finally, they get the ball, throwing it through the air
SMACK! Right in the glove
Game over!
Taylor Lookabaugh, Grade 5

If I'm in Charge of the World
If I were in charge of the world,
I'd make sure everyone is happy,
I would make sure no one is being rude to anyone else, and
I would make sure that everyone would be treated fairly.
If I were in charge of the world,
There'd be peace,
more charities and homes for the homeless, and justice.
If I were in charge of the world,
you wouldn't have any type of segregation.
You wouldn't have violence.
You wouldn't have bullies
or terrorism,
if I were in charge of the world.
Michelle Varghese, Grade 6

Fire and water
Water,
cool, soothing,
splashing, swishing, wet,
cold, calming, hot, violent,
flaring, smoking, dry,
warm, frightening,
Fire.
Ayiana Prevost, Grade 5

Dance
dance
graceful, gentle
moving, flowing, spinning
solo, duo, trio, group
leaping, pointing, stretching
beautiful, stunning
Ballet
Margo Barton, Grade 5

Changes!
Night
Dark, grayish
Sleeping, sitting, laying
Home, rest, read, warm
Talking, walking, playing
Shiny, hot
Day
Samantha Rivera Vences, Grade 6

Gray
Sadness seems stormy gray
Like the darkness.
I see lightning strike.
I hear pouring rain.
I smell the whiff of a storm.
I touch the soaking mist.
I taste the dingy cloud.
Jenesis Scott, Grade 4

Emotion
Tears
Sad, unhappy
Crying, sobbing, mourning
I am not happy at all
Laughing, singing, dreaming
Happy, joyful
Smile
Kori Banks, Grade 6

Embarrassed Darris
Once there was a young boy named Darris
Who always felt kind of embarrassed
Until one day he floated away
And no one found him that day
And he still may be in the sunny bays
Gavin Wallon, Grade 5

Yellow Feeling
I will reach my tendrils into your mind,
My limbs into your soul,
Our minds will collide, and then you will be happy.
You will have to trust me, as I have trusted you.
You will have to smile
Don't listen to the gray skies of blue.
I may be small, just a drop in the sea, but you are smaller.
You don't know how to smile.
Listen to me.
My voice will be heard over the loud din of red
And the disappointments of green, and black, color of dread.
You have not yet explored the Hills of Joy.
You are content (though not really)
To stay in a Valley of Them where you don't matter,
Where you are a toy.
So clasp your hand in mine and you will find someplace most divine.
Where you can be just that: You.
A place where all is good and true.
But first, you must listen to this something I propose:
Come with me, be happy
For I am Yellow Rose.
Rebekah WolfsonKilayko, Grade 5

I Am From…
I am from a farm
Where ladies roam around free and happy
Where we have Toulouse geese as guard animals instead of a dog
Where Mable jumps and plays in the fresh green grass
Where beef cows are kept as pets and Dotty the pig is a local celebrity
Where peach juice drips down my chin in the summer
Where walnut trees sway and blow in the wind in fall

I am from a large family
Where cousins come in all ages from 1-13
Where boys are outnumbered by girls
Where everyone likes country
Where uncles stay up late in the night playing games
Where we all gather at Oma's house on holidays

I am from a farmhouse
Where cowboy boots stand against the walls and mud is everywhere
Where food is always homemade
Where books line the walls
Where the wood stove heats the house in the winter
Where we all sit on the brown leather couch and read
Katherine Matthews, Grade 5

Ode to Horses
Horses are beautiful, and so majestic.
They are made from the soul of an angel, and the beauty of the Earth.
You can't tame their freedom, and you never should.
When you ride a horse you borrow the freedom they were born to have forever.
Horses aren't meant to be bought and sold.
They are meant to be loved.
Hannah DeMaio, Grade 6

Moving Day

Driving on what feels like an endless road,
As the wind whips out over the white clouds.
You, in your cramped car, drive away from the home that has been forgotten,
But a new life and a new home will be found
Somewhere in this new, strange world.
Once you arrive, you'll feel like an alien thrown onto a new planet.
Unsure scared, and confused about the new home and place that you will have to adapt to, but
You will grow, thrive and find beauty in this new world away from the world that you have forgotten and left behind.

Allison Hampton, Grade 6

Happiness

If happiness were a color, it would be as colorful as five different crayons.
If happiness were a taste, it would taste like pizza with sausage.
If happiness were a feeling, it would feel like catching a firefly, setting it free.
If happiness were a smell, it would smell like morning and evening, daytime and nighttime, too.
If happiness were a sound, it would sound like knowing a secret.

Natalie Nations, Grade 6

Swim Team Race

Take one huge cup of freezing water and pour it in a natatorium.
Take some perfect dives and mix them until they glide into the water.
Take perfect, fast postures in strokes and smoothly cut them into the water perfectly like a knife.
Keep mixing them together down the pool and back.
You will know you are done when you win the race.

Aidan Harman, Grade 6

The Raven

Here I lay with a Great Depression in my heart as I tug for the sound of a raven in the woods where I shall claim my death.
Upon this lone grave in the woods, finally I hear the screech of a raven.
As I hear the terrifying sounds of death.
I scream at the lone grave in the darkening woods as I die slowly with a fear stricken heart,
in the undeniably creepy and lonely woods.

Levi Smith, Grade 4

My Last Tail

Here I am just a spirit I howl as I see my owner weep in the tiny window in her room, although the sun which makes everyone happy shines brightly in her room she still weeps at the loss of her once beloved dog Cookie that is me. When I was put down it ripped my owner to pieces to see me die. I tried to make her feel better but I could not get her attention. She thought I was gone forever but I was right there with her, I will always be there with her. I want to come inside to come see her but she might get frightened so I shall wait, I shall just wait until she is older.

Sophia Rodriguez, Grade 4

I Wish

I wish I could see her but I will never meet her
There are so many things in my heart that I see in you to where your music makes me feel free
I have many things in my heart that I dream from day to night
Roses are red and violets are blue I love you to where I hug you to death
Sometimes I maybe wrong but of course I'll never give up on you

Reuben Barnes, Grade 6

Dust Bowl

The dust was in the air, my dad said the world will end, all the townsfolk agreed, so then some ran for their lives, some ran in houses, and my family was one of them, the rest stand outside screaming their lungs out 15 minutes in the storm their voice stopped, my heart sank at the end, cattle on the ground, dead people on the ground, my parents started to cry and me too.

Antonio Finley, Grade 4

San Francisco de Solano

S an Francisco de Solano was built in 1823.
A merican people were in charge.
N ever did the girls hunt.

F riar Jose Altimira founded it.
R ivers were near by.
A ztecs came to this mission.
N earby was a jail.
C attle were also nearby.
I t is located in the town Sonoma.
S onoma is a native word that means valley of the moon.
C oast Miwok lived there.
O nly one of the California missions for eleven years.

D oes have a garden.
E ven has a small hospital.

S oldier housing is close by, too.
O riginal bell is still in front.
L ots of Native American Indians died from an illness.
A lso does have seven rooms in it.
N one of the American people died from the illness.
O rchards are there also.

Bridgette Andersson, Grade 4

Swimming

Sweet water, splish, splash,
like a witch stirring her pot.
Oh my,
all those sweet children laughing
and splashing water at each other.
The sound of father and coach screaming at me
"You can do it sweetie,
swim as if a shark is chasing you!"
My hands touch the gutter
the most amazing feeling!
The announcer screams my name
telling the people in the crowd
that I am the winner.
I'm overjoyed.

Pharren Porter, Grade 5

Aurora Borealis

Indigo, emerald, magenta, a flash of white
Colors, spiraling, twisting, contorting,
Billowing outwards in an everlasting caper,
Across the majestic expanse of stars,
The colors never stop dancing, do they?
They frolic across the black of the night forever,
Bringing hope to those who have lost their way,
They flash across the sky,
Illuminating the vast landscape,
Indigo, emerald, magenta, a flash of white

*Try reading this poem from bottom to top.

Alice Xu, Grade 6

The Things That Are Green

Green is the emerald on a necklace just waiting to be worn,
And comes from the camouflage on army men.
It comes from an olive in a martini glass,
And the luck
Of a four leaf clover.
Green is the color of
Sweet grapes on a warm day,
And comes from
That queasy feeling when you are sick.
It comes from the mossy rocks,
And the shallow water
On a white Hawaiian beach.
Green is the color of land,
On Earth.

Kimberly DeBarger-Gestring, Grade 6

Ode to Keyboard

O'keyboard, with your sounds a-clicking,
Typing words across the bright, smooth screen,
Writing all my wildest, sweetest dreams,
While sitting at my desk.

O'keyboard, with your buttons many,
Doing innumerable various things,
Coming back up, just like springs,
Still resting upon my desk.

O'keyboard, you control my laptop,
Games and apps and music abound,
But soon, alas, your light fades out,
Now sleeping on my desk.

Brooke Gieselmann, Grade 6

I Am

I am the purple in the TCU logo.
I am Flag Day, my birthday.
I am the dark night on a warm summer day.
I am the pop in music.
I am the fun in funny.
I am the cheese in cheeseburger.
My DREAMLAND is Rosemary Beach.

I am Will.

Will Davidson, Grade 4

My Friends

Friends are my life.
Run with them late at night.
In the little store we go for fun.
Enter the door with a big smile and say
Nothing like another day with my best friends.
Dancing around in the last day of school
Sadness comes in the last minute too.
I WILL MISS YOU
ALL

Leslie Hernandez, Grade 6

Free

A girl is playing in the sand, her skin the color of mud,
Then out of the trees come men, and take her to another land

In this land they hit her, whip her, scold her, hurt her
A rough, cold hand smoothes dirty ragged hair away from her face
She cries wet tears that fall down her cheeks, a soothing voice sings her to sleep on the rug
The girl with the skin the color of mud

A gun is fired, people scream, she clutches her child close
Fighting men outside yell for freedom, their skin the color of mud

She picks up an envelope, yellow like the sun
Tears wet he edges of her eyes as she reads, she cries; her dear husband has died

Huddled by a grave, three people stand, one white, two black
The mother clutches her child's hand, her skin the color of brown sand
The white man walks away, the child starts to cry, the mother holds her close and she screams
"Oh why, oh why'd You take him from my hands?", they walk away, their skin the color of brown sand

Blood has shed, tears have fled, people fight, battles rage, vows have been made
Her daughter, all grown now with children of her own stopped knitting in her chair
"Mama," she says "What's wrong?" — "Darling Darla, my sweet child, it's time for me to go."
Her daughter clutches her hand, their skin the color of dark sand

In a bed of hay lies a woman, wrinkles on her face, six people huddle around her
As she gasps for her final breath she says, "I'm free at last! I am free!"
And falls into an endless sleep

Taylor Foster, Grade 5

The Color of Your Skin

In a world not too long ago
One thing would decide your entire life
Some would fight
Some would hide
Some would reach great heights
Some who stood up to change things died

In this world people could be cruel,
Things could be unfair
And people could be thought of as fools
Some would be spared, but that does not compare
To those who were not

In this world people are treated unequal
One thing decides your destiny
And whether your life be full or sullen
Whether your thoughts be full of hatred or overflowing with sympathy
The color of your skin is what defines you

Until one day when this world will come to an end
And One will come who is mightier
The One whose words will live on through time, who said, "I have a dream"
The One who will not rest until the age comes when the color of your skin does not confine you
The day when the person you are inside defines you.

Melanie Charron, Grade 6

Imperfection

They want to live in a world of perfection,
In a world where the light always shines,
Where everything is fine —
But it's not

Where the poor were rich,
Where the sick were healthy,
Where color matters not
Nor did the views on what is right or wrong
But that is a mere wish,
Just out of our reach,
As we try to grasp the feeling of perfection

Why can't it be perfect?
Where misery, and pain don't exist
A place where there's no soft part in your heart
Why do they have to wish?

They want a world where they can dream
And never face the true reality
Where your dream is your world,
But it can't be.
They want riches, and ponies, and a mysterious love you may see,
But I am forgetting the one who wants, is me
Cameron Zytkewicz-Ray, Grade 6

Ode to Art

Art,
you are the subject of creativity
your colors stand out like fireworks in the sky
you are a story expressed on a canvas
you are the subject of creativity

You are the subject of imagination
any thought I have turns into you
anything I've seen turns into you
you can look like anything
you are the subject of imagination

You are the subject of fantasies
you can take any form from large paintings on a canvas
to drawings on a window made by someone's breath
you are the subject of fantasies

You are the subject of creativity
you are the subject of imagination
and you are the subject of fantasies
All I want is for people to notice you
to appreciate you
to treasure you

Art, all I want is for you to never change
Olivia Kadosh, Grade 6

Dance

Letting your body take you wherever
Feeling a pounding beat in your heart
Dance isn't just dance. It's a work of art

Finding a character deep inside
Countless hours practicing
Getting sore but wanting to keep on going
24/7 day and night; never stopping

Some call it a hobby. I call it a lifestyle

Never having enough time to hang out with friends,
It all pays off in the end
Blood, sweat, tears
You learn to face your fears

I can't, I have dance

Bruises and soreness
Dancing since I was 3,
Pink tutus and competitions

Letting your body take you wherever
Feeling a pounding beat in your heart
Dance isn't just dance. It's a work of art
Sabrina Esteban, Grade 6

Luke Skywalker the Boy That Got a Green Lightsaber

I wanted a green glowing lightsaber
Because it should be mine
My daddy's Darth Vader
I'll make him pay the fine

So I asked my powerful daddy
If I could get a lightsaber
And he said, "Of course we can, You're my son
and I'm the great Darth Vader."

I was really happy on that day
For what my daddy said.
So we gathered tools and started building,
and were careful not to hit our heads.

When the lightsaber was finished,
It looked super super cool.
My daddy Darth Vader then put down his tool.
I said, "We did it, now let's try it out,
the size is perfect without a doubt."

At first it was sort of heavy
So I got black gloves to keep it steady.
When I pressed the button
It came out green, it looked amazing, it was just like I dreamed.
Michael Chandler, Grade 5

I Am a Soccer Ball

You know me for getting kicked around in a game.
My mother is a field of green grass.
My father is the goal post.
I was born in a ball-making factory.
I live in a store called Soccer Corner.
My best friend is an Adidas ball because we are always talking.
We like to be in a goal and watch the players celebrate after making a goal.
My enemies are the other balls in the store that aren't my friends because they get bought before me.
I fear of popping during a game because then nobody can use me and I die.
I love the players and coaches because they are the people that take me to the field.
I dream of being used in the World Cup final of the 2018 World Cup.

Jonathan Gomez, Grade 6

Love

A single tear runs down my face as you walk away. Inside me, my heart is stopping, breaking.
You hear sirens as an ambulance rushes by. The rain pelts down as my hair clings to my face.
I cry out and you come back. I see you standing there, just far enough so that I can't touch your pale face.
As I slowly move closer, you back away. You turn and run as I stare into the distance. I drop to the ground crying.
I hear footsteps. When I look up, there you are with your mop of unruly brown hair, your laughing eyes, your daunting smile.
You help me up and I don't let go of your hand as you walk me home.
When we reach my warm and glowing doorstep, we hang back in the shadows.
I look into your eyes and I see that twinkle that I first fell in love with.
As we wrap each other in the tightest embrace that we can manage, my mother calls my name.
When I break away, you slip a note into my hand that I will treasure forever.

Ada Greve, Grade 5

Remember the Times

I remember the days we went swimming
I remember when you needed my help
I remember when we went to the movies
And you got scared and you needed me to be next to you
I remember when we went to the park and you needed pushing on the swing and I was there to help you
I remember when we were in school and you fell down, I was there to pick you up
I remember when you would always get bullied I was there to help you
Even when you would get in the bad times or have bad days I will always be there for you
I remember when we became best friends it was the best day of my life
But my favorite memory's yet to come

Linda Corriz, Grade 6

Amazing Amineh

Amineh
Kind, caring, loving
Sister of Maya and Yaqoub
Lover of California Adventure, pumpkin patches, and jewelry
Who feels shy around adults, nervous about misunderstanding directions, and happy when playing with her little brother
Who fears bad people, getting low grades, and being in the hospital
Who would like to visit Disney World, see the most beautiful sunset, and become a doctor.
Resident of Tigard
Zakarneh

Amineh Zakarneh, Grade 4

Lighthouse

I am turned on, all the people leave. I am alone. I have no house no home. I am going round and round sad. When my light shines on the night sky, stars disappear when I go by. I keep boats protected from rocks and the unknown. I hear the hawks as they pass by. It's their hello and goodbye. I am a lighthouse lonely as can be. So lonely just the stars and me.

Claire Allen, Grade 6

If I Were in Charge of the World

If I were in charge of the world,
equality would be our priority.
Gender and racial stereotypes would be abolished,
and affirmative action would be a must.

If I were in charge of the world,
school wouldn't be stressful.
Education would be given
but not to the extent of an exhausting life.

If I were in charge of the world, you wouldn't have wage gaps.
You wouldn't have tired feet.
You wouldn't have dampened souls or any single, "You can't."
You wouldn't even have doubters.

The theory: if "a equals b," and "b also equals c,"
then "a equals c," would be remembered.

If I were in charge of the world,
an Asian wouldn't always have to be smart.
All races would be homo sapiens,
and everyone would get at least one standing ovation.

And a human who sometimes forgot
that five plus five equals ten, but so does six plus four,
would still be allowed to be in charge of the world.

Katy Lin, Grade 6

The Dog

The dog sits,
in front of the tree.
He protects his house,
and his owner.

The dogs sits,
never to move
from his spot,
unbothered.

The dog protects
his owner from
the rest of the World.
Never to move.

Yet, the dog is happy.
He runs and plays with his owner,
He tugs at rope,
and squeaks his toys.

The dog plays,
The dog runs,
The dog and his owner
Are HAPPY.

Emily Sotelo, Grade 6

My Soccer Team, She-Hulks

She-Hulks is our name
Soccer is our game
Undefeated in 143 and 11k is our title
Trying our best is absolutely vital
First in the league is our team
Going to states was our dream
Our uniforms are black and green
Coach Jojo made us soccer machines
She-Hulks is our name
But we are not all the same
Lisa and Sydnee play midfield
They are like a giant shield
With Paige, Vinny, Ashtyn, and Ashley on defense
Everything just makes sense
Valarie, Grace, Bob, and Aneka are offense
When games are tough we all get tense
Cambria, Ashley, and Grace
Us goalies aren't afraid to take it to the face
Our coach made us the best
We have beaten all the rest

Ashley Wolf, Grade 5

Homework

Why, oh why, does homework exist?
It always just feels that I'm breaking my wrist!

It bores and annoys
And I can't play with my toys

I'd rip it, smash it, and throw it away
Most people would hit the hay, wouldn't you say?

Homework is like a brick wall
You just can't get past it at all!

It wastes so much time
And pops in my head without a chime!

Boom! It's how fast it's received!
But it's nothing a regular student wouldn't believe

I know I'm acting a bit childish
But homework has caught me like a wild fish!

Ethan Suharto, Grade 6

My Sister

Take some baby dolls, Barbies, and stuffed animals
Put sugar, spice, and sweetness in a pink bowl
Mix in a glimmering blender
Add in some big pink bows
Cook in an oven at 350 degrees
You can tell it's done when she hugs you until you can't breathe
Let stand until you hear giggles
Add sparkly pink shoes
Taste a sweet little sister!

Madeline Sikes, Grade 6

Ode to My Mother

My mother, dear mother,
Kind and wholehearted,
I would cry if we parted.

Oh mother, dear mother,
So perfect and reliable,
So beautiful,
And never deniable.

Mother, dear mother,
Oh, so graceful and true,
I would never,
Just never leave you.

Mother, dearest mother,
You are just the perfect mother,
I just hope that we
Will always have each other.
Julia Engel, Grade 5

Not Perfect

I'm just sitting
in this chair
watching
them scream
and yell.
Him and her
will never
STOP fighting
until the world
will end. The
only thing I hear
is thunder and
raining all over
the house,
but the only thing
I want is for
the sun to
come out.
Alejandra Castillo, Grade 6

Eclipse

Flickering flames engulf the moon,
It's clasping something no one can tame.
An enchanting light too bright to see,
It tantalizes the sky.
The cross between life and death,
Join together as one.
Midnight shadows dance across the ground.
Far below the fire,
A whole world watches in wonder.
They are hypnotized by the glory.
Flickering flames engulf the moon,
It's clasping...
It's clasping.
Catherine Mahowald, Grade 6

Outside

I like playing outside
With my mom with my dog
I throw a ball to my dog
And a Frisbee to my mom

My mom throws back the Frisbee
And my dog the same with a ball
I ride my bike down the street
And back to my house

Then we go to the park
And race down the slides
I climb up the rocks
While my mom swings on the swings
Landen Clark, Grade 5

My Cowboy Life

I'm out in the field
Riding my horse
looking for cattle
Out in the brush

Out in the distance
I gather the cattle
For five hours or so
So I can bring them to the ranch

I'm at my ranch
With my cattle
I put them in the corral
My work is done
Braxton Oros, Grade 6

Nature

Grass at my feet
Breeze blowing sweet
Gophers scampering
Trees swaying in the breeze
The trees will sway
Leaves blow away
It smells so sweet
Spring springing
The damp air
Gophers pop up
Watching their young
Birds singing, tweeting
Playing so happily
The rain on my face
Ana Gilbert, Grade 4

Beautiful Forest

When you see leaves on the ground
And lots of trees to hide behind
You look up
There is a shadowy figure in the treetops
It's me in my favorite place
My forest.
As you walk through the forest
The sunlight peeks through the trees
At midday.
But when the day is done
And the world goes to sleep
I say goodnight to my
Beautiful Forest.
Lilly Brittain, Grade 4

Starlight

Star bright
I wish I may
I wish I might
have this wish
I wish tonight
From the stars starlight
to a diamonds bright shine
Make my wish all mine
Tomorrow at dawn
my wish will come alive,
and everything will be all right
Starlight,
star bright
Sara Barboza, Grade 6

A Special Girl

My heart is pumping for air
as my friends and I play
Truth or Dare.
As they go on,
I see this girl
wearing a pearl.
When I see her,
I start to freeze,
as her hair has a breeze.
When I see her I ask,
"Do you want to play?"
And as we walk I think
everything is going my way.
Oscar Flores, Grade 4

Summer and Winter

Summer
Hot, sunny
Swimming, tanning, camping
Pools, beach, ice-cream, vacations
Skiing, snowing, playing
Cold, fun
Winter
Catherine Huang, Grade 6

The Adventure for the Children

The boy, looking out into a sea of blue
The drum by his side, telling him I can see you
The boy knows that his drum is a sign for freedom
Walking, waiting, wishing, wondering, of wisdom

As the pounding starts. the children began to appear
After the sound, the wolf walks with no fear
The gathering begins like churches
Holding hands historically hinders hardships

The group sleeps on the hardness of the rocks
Like the rocks are telling them to sleep on their backs
The group is resting so soundly as if they were dead
Trying truthfully trusting treacherous tread

As the group leaves the edge of the cliff and float into the sky
The air begins to hug them while they fly
The group moves through the air like birds
Lifting leaving loving lifting letting go

Jace Rhee, Grade 5

Keep on Going

Being black was hard.
Countless slaves,
Escaping from the plantation's yard —
Like a tree's leaves on a windy day.

Countless obstacles blocked their way.
Yet they tried —
And they kept on going,
With the North Star as their guide

They could've turned back,
But held "Keep on going" as their only thought.
So they went on —
It was their only shot.

Countless enemies and few supporters —
And barely more than one white friend —
But they believed in themselves,
And thus they made it to the end.

Maria Oxyzolou, Grade 6

The Sparkling Flower

The flower in the night,
Didn't look quite right,
So I splashed some color,
And made it bright.
I added some red, some green and some pink,
Then I added some sparkles,
So it could shine like a diamond on a ring.
Like the stars in the sky it shone through the night
I looked at the flower and it was just right,
I stood there mesmerized by it,
It smiled back at me with delight!

Sharon Asariah, Grade 6

Jackson's Psalm

God,
You comfort me like my mom
You comfort me when I am hurt.
You gently bandage my scrapes
And help me to stay calm.
You help me build things
The way my dad builds toy houses with me.
You provide the tools I need
To build something cool.
You are like my brother
Playing baseball and swimming with me.
You are always active and ready to play.
You are my granddad and grandma.
Helping me play hide and seek with my cousins in their barn.
I might hide from my cousins
But I could never hide from you, God.
You are my family.
You are the best!

Jackson Farragut, Grade 4

Blessing of Life

I used to be fearful of the dangers in the world.
But now I cherish the blessing of life with great joy.
I always have doubts in my self about the future.
But I never have uncertainty about the present.
I once treated life as an inferior and daunting boon.
But now I treat it as a stupefying prerogative.
If I could share my erudition of life.
I would inculcate all people on how life is an incredible entitlement.
I never tolerate inhumane grievance towards life.
But I might sympathize those who quibble towards
nefarious monstrosities in life.
I can't comprehend why immortality must belong in the world.
But I can decipher that the world is nowhere near immaculate.
I won't conjecture that world peace is feasible.
But I might believe the world can ameliorate through toil and effort.
I used to have a hard time expressing my feelings.
But now I have learned of its helpfulness.

Kelvin Phung, Grade 6

The Snowy Giant

I am the mountain, not big, but great
Overseeing the eyes of the human race
Recording the sounds of footsteps and strong winds
Feeling climbers jab and stab me in the chin
Sniffing and snuffing the thick and frosty air
Knowing that the way they know me is very fair
Swallowing the rain as it seeps into my mouth
Also confirming that the kids are very loud
Breathing the odors of humans here and there
Hearing camera clicks as they walk up stairs
Noticing my own rocky terrain
However, organized by the human ways
Towering and chill, snowy and vast
This is who I am, and I am the mountain

Kelvin Nguyen, Grade 6

Summer
Super hot!
Hot sun nice breezes.
Let's go to the beach.
Let's go surf.
Let's go to Hawaii.
Let's go swim.
Gage Harriman, Grade 5

Computer
I use you for homework
I use you for typing
I use you for clicking
I use you for seeing pictures
I use you for watching videos
I use you for doing everything
Brittany Villarreal, Grade 4

The Stars
Oh stars! you're so bright.
You make me happy at night.
Sometimes I look up in the sky,
I wish I could fly.
I wish I could be you,
Looking so new.
Azalhea Guerrero, Grade 5

The Mustang
A Mustang is my favorite kind of car.
The car goes very far.
It's rubber sticks to the street
And can make a great beat.
It will roar and win the race
And come to home base.
Ryan Higueros, Grade 5

Milky Way
If a cow went to the
moon
And you asked him why
I bet he would
tell you
"To find the Milky Way"
Lena Bishop, Grade 4

Spiders!
Spiders! They're sneaky.
But also very creepy.
They also try
to eat the poor fly.
They also bite.
They'll give you a fright.
Jorge H. Martinez, Jr., Grade 5

Mia and Patience
God has a path for everyone, for my family a part of our path was having to say goodbye to my little sister Mia.
I remember her very clearly, she was very chubby, cute, always had her eyebrows sticking up, and always had a smile.
I wonder what she would look like? Would she be tall? Would she be short? All I know is she would be the best little sister in the world to me. (Even if we would have some fights.)
I love my little sister Mia she will always be in our hearts forever.
Even though my brother never saw her it feels like he knew her a long time I just don't know why?
She was born in September 11, 205 and died on February 27, 2006 and only five months old.
It was hard on everyone, especially my mom.
Every time I go to her grave I cry because I miss too much for words to say.
My family will wait until the return of Christ's coming to see her again.
MaKien Wolcott, Grade 6

I Am Andrew
I am purple like the TCU Horned Frogs.
I am April Fool's Day with pranks and funny jokes.
I am winter when the NFL Super Bowl comes.
I am 2:34p.m. when I ask my dad to have a friend spend the night.
I am reading a survival book under my covers at night.
I am watching a funny movie on Friday night.
I am listening to rock music on my way to band practice.
I am trustworthy.
I am eating a 20 pound steak at Railhead.
I am choosing what Nike Elite socks to wear in the morning.
I am sitting in my room playing XBOX.
I am at a Texas Rangers game hearing the crack of the bat.
I am sitting around the fire at my grandparent's house smelling the smoke of the fire.
I am Andrew.
Andrew Edwards, Grade 4

The Red Car
There once was a red car that couldn't drive so far
It tried and tried but its motor always died
Soon it gave up driving there was nothing left thriving
He then forgot about the bad and remembered the glad

Then the race bell rang he was off with a bang
He now knows life is a journey and that he should not worry
He was happy as a kid on Christmas and knew he could make the distance

He then jumped up into the air
and knew happiness was near.

Jude Haughton, Grade 6

Soccer Field
My family is like a soccer field.
My dad is the goalkeeper that blocks all the bad things happening,
My mom is the defender that tries to help the goalkeeper.
My big brother is the midfielder that goes back and forth to keep us safe,
My little sister is the referee that blows the whistle and gets me in trouble.
And I'm the striker that always takes all the chances.
Christian Gomez, Grade 6

The Hunt
The sun descends low
The creatures come out lurking
The moon starts to glow

It shines very bright
Filling the night with it's light
Soon, the ground rumbles

The people tread through
The animals go to hide
The owl calls, hoo hoo

They load all the guns
Shots left and right, killing tons
The hunt is now over
Isaac Geng, Grade 6

Texas
The land where cattle roam,
and beams of sunlight shone,
on every flowing field of wheat,
horse barn, and Main Street.

The land where cowboys rode,
and tradition overflows,
onto every sunny mile,
ranch house, and hay pile.

The land of the Mexican War,
I feel like I've been here before.
On the dark red soil I stand,
looking out at the fields so grand.
Colin Scruggs, Grade 6

If I Were in Charge of the World
If I were in charge of the world,
I'd cancel out tangled earphones,
itchy mosquito bites, and
pimples.
If I were in charge of the world,
there'd be no world hunger,
gun violence, and
natural disasters.
If I were in charge of the world,
you wouldn't have to be afraid of anything.
You wouldn't have stinky breath.
You wouldn't have bullies,
or diseases,
if I were in charge of the world.
Cristine Liang, Grade 6

Volcano
Boiling lava
Will erupt when furious
Hawaiian beauty
Muskaan Schievink, Grade 4

Earth, It's Your Day!
Hello world,
Today's your day
You've had trash
From the desert to the bay
Hello world,
We're here to help you shine
Today's your birthday
We want to make it divine
We want to make you look pretty
From the North to South poles
We'll get ready
Let's grab our supplies and let's go
Clarissa Holguin, Grade 5

What Happens to a Dream Deferred?*
What happens to a dream deferred?
Does it drift off
like a white dove into the heavens?
Or does it levitate into the clouds
and then fade away?
Does it reverse into a new dream?
Or multiply into many different dreams
like a clone machine?
Maybe it just sparks and then goes away
like a lightning bolt.
Or does it erase forever?
Maliyah Ross, Grade 6
*Inspired by Langston Hughes

The Sun
The sunny sun
Grew brighter
When she tried
To wake us up
A light high
In the air

She has her moods sometimes
And is kidnapped by the rain
But found again
High and bright
In the sky
Safiya Sayd, Grade 6

Why Does This Happen?
I do not understand
…why we get mad,
…why we can't all be free,
…why me and Kylee fight so much.
But most of all I do not understand
…why people can own guns,
…because they kill people!
What I understand most
…is that I am loved,
…because that's what counts.
Clayton Calloway, Grade 5

I Used To
I used to crawl
But now I walk
I always talk
But I never lie
I once cried
But now I face life
If I could do anything
I would not change a single thing
I never thought about it
But I might become the president
I can't see the future
But I can fix the present
I won't stop fighting for what's right
But I might get tired
I used to give up
But now I will persevere
Irsa Moeez, Grade 6

The Dark
At night I see
Nothing but black
Owls in flight
I can only hear
A small cat or mouse

Imagining things
Sometimes scary
The dark
The curtains closed
I am scared
Of the dark

The dark is gone
Nothing but light
Relieved
Gianna Casentini, Grade 4

Deep in the Seas
Deep in the seas,
There lies a creature
Never seen before

It's like a human
But isn't.
It thinks like a human
Looks like a human
But has no legs.
Instead it has a tail

It swims really fast
But gets tired easily.
I dream of becoming one.

To become a mermaid.
Arabella Ravnell, Grade 6

A Brighter Place

I broke the barriers of racism —
I broke into a world of equality,
Where all things were fair
Where people could run freely
Without the shackles of despair
No longer fettered —
by judgments of hatred
That pulled me back,
But soon enough faded
Strength —
The strength that guided me,
Through thick and thin
Made my world much brighter,
Like the sun rising at dawn
Starting at the dark of the night,
Ending with the radiance of the sun —
Help me make the world a brighter place —
A world where everyone has a voice

Daniella Goldrich, Grade 5

Umbrella

Rain
Drop, Drop, Drop
The rain is tumbling down
It is cold outside splash, splash
Rain comes tumbling down faster, and faster
I go down the road running and jumping around
J
U
M
P
O
V
E
R
P
U
D
D L E S

Daylee Driggs, Grade 5

Christmas

Christmas
Is coming
Lonely no family
To celebrate with
Ready to
get picked. No one picks me
lonely again. Parents ready to pick
I'm the only one left finally get picked,
Family finally
Ready to celebrate Christmas with family,
Meet brothers and sisters, not lonely anymore
FAMILY

Edwin Coronado, Grade 6

My Healthy Family

My dad is the band aid, he is strong and helpful.
My mom is the tweezers, she picks and pokes.
My sister is the candy, she's sweet but sour.
My dog is the cotton ball, fluffy and soft.
I am the ice pack that helps and loves them.

Rosemary Ashley Merino, Grade 6

To Judge a Game

I once bought a game off Steam
It was on sale for a good deal or so it deemed
When I installed the game
I found out it was lame
I just got ripped off now I want to scream

Aidden Sibayan, Grade 6

Into the Storm

With a cluster and a blow of the wind.
The storm was fearsome.
Many died and animals too.
No food nor crops.
I just wish that my life won't get taken from me too.

Jasmine Bazemore, Grade 4

Life

What is life all about?
I would like to know all of life's secrets.
It would be great to know what life means.
Could life mean nothing at all?
It would be great to find out what life is about.

Rossteen Kheder, Grade 4

Dust Storm

It rolls across the land like an avalanche
Filling houses with dirt and despair
Blowing across the Great Plains
Picking up loose dirt from the ground
The wind's speed decreases and the dust falls.

Braxton Riggs, Grade 4

A Road to Iowa

Texas, Arkansas, Missouri, and finally Iowa.
The states seem to fly by.
But, at last, I come to the place I've always wanted to go.
Peaceful cornfields, cheerful farmhouses, and small towns.
This is the place for me.

Travis Davidson, Grade 4

If We Were Fish

What if we were fish, swimming in the sea.
Gliding through the sunken ships.
With gills on our cheeks.
Having tails and fins would be a wacky thing.
To swim underneath the ocean sea.

Daegon Gorre, Grade 5

For You, Tree
You shelter me from the sun's rays,
you give me air to breathe on all days.
Happy or sad, angry or mad,
You'll always be there and I'll always be glad,
For you, Tree.

Your beautiful leaves of beautiful color
will never, ever make may days duller.
You're tall, strong and always bold,
and I'd turn down any offer of gold,
For you, Tree.

But day and day your kind is being cut down.
Your soul and spirit, being sunk and drown.
Killing your symbol, it's just what they do,
but you must be strong and know I'll always love you
For you, Tree.
Paulete Perez-Haiek, Grade 6

I Am…Gavin
I am helpful and athletic
I wonder how they make baseballs
I hear images of sound in the jungle
I see people being kind to each other
I want the world to be peaceful

I am helpful and athletic
I pretend that I am a fast swimmer
I feel one day I will be a success
I am scared I will not get into a good college
I get sad when family members die

I am helpful and athletic
I understand people will not always like me
I say hamburgers are American food
I dream that I will make it to the NBA
I am helpful and athletic
Gavin Hollins-Law, Grade 4

Vacation
When the winter birds arrive, the seasons follow.
The smell of spring draws nearer.
For the hundreds of days we've been in school, but
Spring will make it worth the wait.
The smell of flowers arrives;
Spring has nearly sprung.
The time to feast will come.
When I look outside, the wind is screaming.
I know that spring has come.
I can't hear the big bunny
Placing eggs in hidden havens
Signaling spring is here.
I'm anxious to uncover what will reside.
School will end soon
And the treasure of summer awaits me.
Liam Miller, Grade 6

How I Change Over Years
I used to enjoy Flaming Hot Cheetos
But now I desire sweet smooth chocolate
I used to adore shine purple
But now I love a bright wonderful red
I used to choose tiny puppies
But now I prefer big dogs
I used to be good at rough soccer
But now I want to be an active basket ball player
I used to like tasty spaghetti
But now I love tacos
I used to desire sweet candy
But now enjoy smooth crunch chips
I used to like drinking water
But now I love drinking soda
Before I used to read little kid books
Now I read challenging chapter books
I now like to play outside
Tamia Lopez Burkley, Grade 5

Stormy Night
I looked out the window on a cold winter night
What I saw gave me a huge fright
Blue ribbons danced across the twilight sky
I was afraid that if I touched one I would die
The screaming lightning sounded a loud bang
But in my little head I thought that it sang
I wished the clanging lightning would stop
Because if the booming continued my ears would pop

That was when I started to hear the rain
Oh how I tried to stop the noise in vain
The endless thuds coming from my roof
Made me want to disappear in a poof
I then saw that there was still lightning
Except now it wasn't as half as frightening
Now that the rumble of thunder started again
I thought that it was louder than the chime of Big Ben
Avash Adhikari, Grade 6

Snow
I look out the window
what I expect to see is not there
no longer a dead and dry place
but rather I see a blanket of ice

Snow I say the word aloud
Snow is better than barren land
Snow is not just ice it's a work of art

Each snowflake is individual
not one has the same pattern or look
snowflakes are just like us

Not one is the same!
Each and every one of us is special in our own way.
Ben Jones, Grade 6

The Donut Hog

Lurking in the corner near the Krispy Kream
The beast smacks its lips in hunger
Gazing at the numerous flavors and fillings
She asks: "I'll get four boxes of this, that
and a generous handful of donut holes!"
She snatches the collections of artificial treats and just leaves.
"We appreciate tips, ya know!" said the man running the stand.
She comes back home and sets the boxes on the table.
I reach for the remaining pastry and she shouts:
"Did you really have to eat the last donut!"
Be careful with the donut hog, for she is a vicious creature.

Walter Dufour, Grade 6

Near the Tree

Near the tree
laughter and joy,
but all I think of is my dad,
I wish he'd be here next to the tree,
here, with me.
Now it's only mom, sister, brother and me,
it's not the holidays, there's no laughter, no joy, in me.
I am like a car without gasoline. I am super sad.
Mad.
All I can think of is my dad, No laughter, No joy, for me.

Kiara Ramirez, Grade 6

My Curiosity

My curiosity,
My hopes, my dreams,
All fill up with tears, that can fill up an ocean,
An ocean of my sadness, my pain,
Almost all I had, what I believed in is gone…
But hopefully what's left of me,
Can become a great big ocean,
So that my hopes, my dreams, my curiosity,
Can keep flowing into a great big…
Ocean.

Jocelyn Chavez, Grade 6

Hello Goodbye

When I say hello that is the day I'm never letting go
I won't go through the storm without you
when I say goodbye
that's the day that I'll die
So I wont be able to hold your hand anymore
GOODBYE

Anthony Smith, Grade 6

No Family

I have no family nor home
sometimes I wish but I don't.
I see those happy families giving and getting
but jealousy doesn't get me any.
One day I will have a family to laugh and giggle,
to hug and share memories that will never be forgetful.

Arleth Suarez, Grade 6

Piano

Making your mind, heart and soul fly freely
Making music
From your heart very deeply

The sound bouncing off the walls repeating
Over and over again you closing your eyes
Just playing out all your feelings
Sad, happy, angry

The only beam of light on you and your piano
Making a code only you know
And only you can tell it
Perfectly

You're letting your hands freely play out how your tender heart feels
You feel as if you're the only person in the world
Just you and your piano

Then the applause comes and it's all over
But your mind won't let go
So you play on
Playing more beauty, hope and possibility

Dagney Leigh Duggan, Grade 4

The Old Yellow Swing

Silence,
silence for 23 hours,
you wait,
and wait.
Nothing for 23 hours.
you get used, 60 minutes a day.
you love going high,
high, into the sky like an angel,
sweeping through the clouds.

Then, the silence breaks in.
You love the silence, and the sun,
but you hate the dark, and the wind howling,
your rusty yellow Friend disappeared.
Now it's only you, and your old blue bud
next to you,
alone,
Lonely and quiet,
23
hours
a
day.

Serafin Stauch, Grade 6

4th of July

Beautiful fireworks in the middle of the night
Barbeque being grilled for supper
Laughing children playing with firework sticks
Grilled BBQ steaming in my tongue
The warmth of my laughter as I laugh along with the others

Alina Kim, Grade 5

Ode to Peppermint York Patty
York
Oh York,
In that
Silver wrapper
You look like a wheel of chocolate
You make me feel better when I'm
Sad
With your minty flavor when
It hits my tongue

Life would be poor
Without you
My family and I love you
You can fit
ANYWHERE

When you melt I cry

When I get you
You're on the
Shelf
Where I last saw you
To buy to eat
Tomorrow
Piper Baine, Grade 4

Words Will Never Hurt Me
Sticks and stones
May break my bones,
But words will never hurt me.
As long as the real me is shown.

Your feelings could get hurt,
But you
have to fight through, I know…
I can…so can you, too.

When life gets tough,
And your feelings get crushed,
Go to a friend because it
Has happened to all of us.

You don't know why
A bully is a bully so…
Go talk to them, be their friend.
What can happen…? You never know.

Words will never hurt us,
But sometimes they do.
So pretend they don't,
And love will come to you.
Jaya Johnson, Grade 5

A Pony Tail
There are many kinds of ponies
black, white, and brown.

But no one has seen a unicorn
with a golden crown.

It will lead to the key
that will solve the mystery.
Ella Sledd, Grade 6

Drums
The drums go Bang!
And the cymbals go Crash!
I can hear it from here!
I can here the drums bash!
The snare goes tat!
And the bass goes boom!
I can feel the room rumble!
They are loud I assume!
Logan Gladden, Grade 6

Dreams
When thoughts close and memories open,
You can fly without knowing how,
You can run faster than the wind,
You can walk over oceans.
If only it would last forever,
But when dark fades and skies brighten,
Thoughts open and memories close,
And it is time to leave.
Emma Stanek, Grade 6

The Freeze
The season is winter
ice shimmers as the earth freezes
The ocean is not affected
like a pause in time
Life,
bleary as the air in a snowstorm
As a shooting star goes by
I wish it all would end
John Hoffman, Grade 6

Infinity
Infinity means forever
But not that it will last
If you are really clever
then you know not to ask
There are a lot of consequences
and you will miss the big perspective
Be careful what you wish
It might not be as blissful, as you think
Brianna Salazar, Grade 6

Ocean House
A house by the ocean
A sight to see
Nothing greater than thee

The life by the sea
Grab your swimsuit
And jump in with me
Once we are done
We will watch the sun

The sparkling blue water
Fireworks at night
Sure to light up your life
The trees shimmer and show
The green leaves aglow

My house by the ocean
The life for me
Nothing greater than thee
Andrew Caver, Grade 4

Baseball
Baseball is my life
Playing all day and night
Working as a team
Giving other teams a fight.

The game is about having fun
But it's also a mental game
With lots of things to learn
I want to achieve fame.

We wear our jerseys
And love the smell of gloves
We race to the park to play
Because this is the game we love.

We dream of making it big
Growing up to be a star
Sharing the love of the game
And hoping we all go far.
Anthony Almes, Grade 5

A Shining Star
There once was a star in the blue sky,
if you look at it, it is very high.

It shined so bright,
it did it with all its might.

The view was so nice,
that you can't even put a price.

Even though you see it usually,
it will always shine so beautifully.
Gianine Umali, Grade 6

Puppies
Puppies
Golden, brown
Playing, eating, sleeping
Always playing with you
Retriever
Abigail Howell, Grade 4

Lloyd
There once was a guy named Lloyd
Who, at night, got paranoid
So he climbed up high
Straight up into the sky
Then he got sucked into the void
Conner McNatt, Grade 4

Basketball
basketball
swish, three
shooting, running, dribbling
basketball is for everyone
win!!!
Kline Mayo, Grade 4

Lion King
A lion's roar is so mighty loud
Even birds can hear them in a cloud
It sleeps all day
Hunts when light's away
As king of the jungle he is so proud
Luisa Hernandez, Grade 6

My Sister
Sister
Sweet, pretty
Caring, smiling, loving
Always making people happy
Keli
Leiah Graham, Grade 4

Dog
dog
growls, barks
playing, chewing, licking
she is a lab
My dog's name is Sister
Landri Payne, Grade 4

Sister
sister
awesome, pretty
loving, giggling, playing
she loves chocolate cake
Kamdyn!
Kassidy Marin, Grade 4

The Delight Song
I am a cloud in the blue sky
I am a brown bear that sleeps in the forest
I am the swan that swims, swiftly in the pond
I am the sun that follows the moon
I am the night, the dark of the valley, I am the dog playing with a ball
I am a bunch of shimmering stars
I am the farthest mountain, I am the cold of the blizzard
I am the chirp of a bluebird, I am the glitter of the diamond
I am the long giraffe of the jungle ground
I am a rainbow of four colors
I am a fox running away in the woods
I am a field of flowers and grass
I am a pack of wolves on the grass mountain
I am the hunger of a famished tiger
I am the whole world of these things

You see, I am alive, I am alive
I stand in good relation to my parents
I stand in good relation to my friends
I stand in good relation to my family
I stand in good relation to my environment
You see, I am alive, I am alive
Brianna Guting, Grade 6

I Am From
I am from a city
Where pollution is high and aggressiveness is low
Where the friendliest place is the local Catholic school
Where you don't go downtown unless you have guts
Where the Fresno Grizzlies make their city proud

I am from a school
Where teachers proudly roam halls
Where children triumph and play on soft grass fields
Where 4th, 3rd, 2nd, and 1st grade play on the bright blue and gold playground

I am from a barn
Where horses gallop free in pastures
Where champions are born
Where friendships are made

I am from a white estate
Where family came together almost every holiday
Where I was brought home in a small basket
Where we always had great food

I love where I am from!
Jesika Pajouh, Grade 5

Invitation from a Bird
Come up in the trees and watch the other trees sway in the breeze.
You can swoop down and grab some worms,
Take a bath in a lake and chirp all day long and play.
Have little races smell the green leaves and see the blue lakes and oceans,
Wrap yourself in a blanket of twigs.
Aydan Pinckney, Grade 4

Green
Gloriously fresh
Stretching and growing to the sky
Rolling in my grass
Alive
Abby Novak, Grade 6

Nothing Will Change
All the orphans are sad
the caretaker was mean
waiting in my bed wishing
someone would take me
Justin Tovar, Grade 6

Fire
As the fire starts
Sparks glowing, and flames flying
Then it slowly dims
Davis Marks, Grade 4

Extraordinary Flowers
blooming in the grass
colorful, gorgeous, fragrant
breathtaking, pretty
Julia Waldman, Grade 4

Flowers
Blooming in the Spring
Bees and butterflies love them
Have lovely fragrance
Hannah Carbunaru, Grade 4

Flowers
They are everywhere
Roses, lilies, daffodils
They bloom during spring
Andrea Bautista, Grade 6

Caterpillar
It crawls up a leaf,
and he eats holes as he goes,
growing long and strong.
Matthew Leone, Grade 4

Rainbows
Rain clouds here and there
After a rainy shower
Rainbows everywhere
TyLeigh Dayton, Grade 4

Beach
Waves crash at the beach
The salty breeze hits my face
Soft sand at my feet
Madison Crosby, Grade 5

The Happiest Place on Earth
The opening day of the Happiest Place on Earth
Was clearly happiness' birth.

I'm overflowing with joy from when I pass Downtown Disney's red flower fountain
To the last drop on Splash Mountain.

My, oh my, beauty spans from Pizza Port to the Hungry Bear,
Or from Fantasyland to New Orleans Square.

Your beauty reaches Sleeping Beauty's Castle's highest tower
And is as great as Maleficent's power.

Dazzling parades in the night shine bright
With the theme "Light Up the Night".

Following comes grand fireworks
That are so grand, unnecessary are perks.

I adore you like Winnie adores honey.
Nothing can between our love, not even money.

When it's time for the festive Haunted Mansions Holiday,
This is where I'd rather stay.

When I'm away, bitter tears stream,
Making me like the Queen of Hearts and scream.

At the end of a magical day,
I wish to never go away.
Thomas Correa, Grade 6

Ode to My Blanket
Oh blanket
You have been with me since I was little.
You are both medium and large.
I want to wrap you around my shoulders for the soothing comfort.

Oh blanket
You have a rectangle shape with the colors of light green, purple, pink.
You were made with the softest yarn there could be.
When you get washed you smell like the ocean breeze
That is when I fall asleep with you around me.
You feel like the lightest cloud in the sky when you are with me.

Oh blanket
When I cannot be with you
I will keep you tucked in my bed, all warm and safe.
If you were not in my life I would be a blank piece of paper
With no writing at all.
We have a very special relationship.
You are not common at all
That is one reason you are so special to me.
Oh blanket
You make me happy when I am sad
Thank you for all the things you do.
Elle Snyder, Grade 4

The Boy in the Block Till the End of May

The new boy in the block
I've seen throwing rocks
He looked at me
Staring with glee.

Surely that boy was mysterious
But I'm very curious
If he will ever be my friend
Maybe a note or a message I could send
The next day, I decided to write a letter
Surely a reply would be good,
Or even a smile would be better.

I went to the post office
And there he was,
With a letter that showed my name
He stood with a smile that was the same
The next day we played all day
Until the end of May.

Kim Hoang, Grade 4

What Skateboarding Means to Me

I am insane about skateboarding,
Skateboarding is nothing like any other sport
It makes you feel free
In any type of way

You have no lanes
No courts
We don't have to rely on a team
Or anyone

There will always be those will do more
It's not a competition with anyone
It's a battle against yourself
to just keep getting better

Every where I go you will see me with my board
At any where
And anytime
I will be skating

Izzac Zavalza, Grade 6

Dandelion

A seed full of hope
that no one can seem to cope
swept away by wind and air a journey to which no one can compare
wind settled into a low breeze
then it could fall gently at ease
covered by dirt and gravel
it ended in a successful travel
once again to grow white and soft
to be wished upon and set aloft
a fully grown dandelion spread out everywhere
to help everyone that is in despair

Meliya Russom, Grade 6

An Unexpected Finish

It was an unexpected finish,
they actually won!
No one would've guessed it, victory for the underdog!

Many were injured,
they had a lot less men,
But when they got the win, I was the happiest person alive,

I didn't really care,
coming into the game,
but when they kept the game close, my eyes were glued to the TV,

I was in disbelief,
that they had a chance,
but as the game went on, it became more real,

When they got a big lead,
I could finally relax,
and I knew this season was a big success!

Sam Dusek, Grade 6

I Am…Damani

I am helpful and loyal
I wonder what I will look like in the future
I hear race cars zooming around the track
I see a knight in shining armor
I want a hover board

I am helpful and loyal
I pretend I live in a mansion
I feel like an angel in the sky
I worry when I'm all by myself
I cry when somebody dies

I am helpful and loyal
I understand long division
I say I believe in Santa Claus
I dream I have a crystal chandelier
I try to work harder
I hope I have a beautiful family when I grow up
I am helpful and loyal.

Damani Lamar Gamble, Grade 4

Am I Alice?

The bright blue butterfly flutters its wing.
When seen, your heart wants to sing.

I feel like Alice in this "wonderland"
As I look in astonishment at the bizarre colored sand.

The beautiful, iridescent water may not seem like much,
But it can do great things with its healing touch.

Some creatures even seem to show malice.
I then ask myself, "Am I Alice?"

Natalee Martinez, Grade 6

Christmas

On Christmas I see wrapped presents.
I smell delicious baked cookies.
I hear jingle bells.
I taste Christmas cake and cookies.
I touch the Christmas tree and presents.
Christmas

Brianna Flores, Grade 4

Rocks Explore

Rocks explore in a twisting turning way
Drop and splash
draw with the environment
In unique patterns of figure 8s
They swim
And are having fun.

Cooper Tully, Grade 4

Nature

Looks like the rain
Smells like lavender
Sounds like the song of every bird
Tastes like fresh bell peppers
Feels like a lizard
Nature

Elliot Johnson, Grade 4

Horses

Horses are brown like a brownie
They taste like wind in your face
They sound like a happy stomp
They smell like hay every day
They look like a big warm hug
They make me feel like a happy heart

Faith Gulick, Grade 5

Happiness

Happiness is a family's love around you
It sounds like the laughter of a child
It smells like flowers in the spring
It taste like ice cream on a hot day
It feels like your mothers love when
She gives you a hug

Paulina Ortega, Grade 5

Space

Around the world
Beyond space
Underneath the stars
By Venus
Near the sun
In the shuttle

Samantha Torres, Grade 4

For People Who Are in Mourning

Trapped at the bottom of this dreary ocean of misery,
The chains confining me here have grown ever so strong
After the last beacon of hope faded.
While everyone around me seemed to be smiling,
I stood there and crumbled into nothing but foam and salt.

A new light emerges, utterly destroying the merciless devil
That has held me captive here for so long.
As the color of my thoughts and words cut through the chains of loss and mourning,
I fly.

I fly as free as the dolphins in the sea of dreams,
So near me yet always so far.
I float until I find my grandfather's eyes on the sandy white beach.

With a shaky breath, I stand up, grabbing a handful of moist sand.
Tears encircle my heart and soul as I run back to the city I knew and loved.
Hugging the parents I thought I'd never see again
While I was trapped in the confines of my ocean of sadness.

I rest under the banyan tree,
Watching the beautiful dance of the hummingbird
Showing off the beauty of its feathers to its beloved mate.

And I know this is happiness.

Noa Ledor, Grade 5

Life

Life is a journey,
A journey full of mysteries.
Life is an equation that even Einstein couldn't figure out!
Life is a circle that doesn't have an end.
Life is joy and life is misery.

When you're a baby, you figure out life is a clutter of mysteries.
When you're a child, you realize that you have the ability to solve them.
When you're an adult, you try to solve them.
But when your end is coming near,
The answer hits you like a flashing lightning bolt.
The answer to the big mystery was you.

Life is like a company,
A company you have to manage.
Life is a trophy,
A trophy you have to earn.
But the biggest thing in life is you.

When you learn to be yourself,
To never hide your talents,
To let your inner beauty shine bright,
Then you have learned to live
A life.

Tanvi Sud, Grade 5

Center of the Earth
What will you find in the center of the earth?
A pond of eternal life?
Satan's wife?
A giant wielding a knife?
What will you find in a dormant volcano?
A magical moon pool?
A new diamond tool?
Two knights having a dual?
What will you find in an ant hill?
A miniature wind mill?
A frozen cockroach to give you a chill?
An ant with more than one gill?
What will you find in a termite home?
A piece of a honey comb?
Wasps outside the home?
Some kind of weird green foam?
What will you find?
Is it an adventure for mankind?
Will it show you that you're not blind?
Will you find that you are very kind?
What will you find?
Kaitlyn Carter, Grade 5

What Am I?
Cold as night
The color of fright
Why?
Or is it something difference
Clouding your mind
This is the color of freedom
Not so
This is the color of nightmares
Void of space
This is the color of sorcery
And evil's leader
I differ
This is the color that spawned it all, an Alpha
The color in which you find comfort
Christened evil but is it
Not so
This is the absence
This hates the light
Hates fate
Hates happiness
What am I?
Darsh Shah, Grade 6

Drumbeat
The drum is there
From the first, it is there.
It is always there.
It merrily marches over the hills,
The steady beat of countless feet,
Calling, "Wait for me!" like an echo
Repeating, repeating
Unlocking the locked room of loneliness
But that is only the beginning.

The others are voices in the symphony of unity
Solitude has kept them at bay,
But when they hear their music, they awaken
"Wait for me!" they exclaim, and their music joins the band
They laugh together, they grow together,
Until they are not many but one
The drum is carrying them through the world
And it is still there when they reach their end
They are at peace together, and that is why
The drum still beats when they fall
Towards their deliverance and their doom.
Olivia Chung, Grade 5

San Francisco de Asis
S an Francisco de Asis was established in 1776.
A lot of livestock was raised here.
N o one at the mission was disrespectful to God.

F ray Junipero Serra was one of the founders.
R ivera was also one of the founders.
A merican Indians were treated unfairly.
N eophytes at the mission ate grain.
C hristian is the religion of the Ohlone Indians.
I ndians wore less clothing.
S an Francisco de Asis' nickname is Dolores.
C oast is the region where Dolores is located.
O hlone Indians' diets included acorns since they were easy to find.

D ifferent is a word that describes the Ohlone Indians.
E uropeans thought they were better than the Indians.

A merican is the nation that Dolores is in.
S panish thought the Indians were savages.
I ndians had a lot of jobs at the mission.
S pain sent several explorers to the new world.
Olivia Bell, Grade 4

When I'm Not Home
When I'm not home, my TV turns on
When I'm not home, my remote works on
When I'm not home, my clock ticks on and on
When I'm not home, my cuddlies play on
When I get home
They think I don't know
But I do know
Hannah Fain, Grade 4

A Horse Named Tug
There once was a friendly, gray horse named Tug
Of course he is much faster than a slug.

He snorts or he neighs
And prances or plays.

After a great race, his rider gives him a hug.
Milla Van Maren, Grade 5

The Nightingale's Song

There once was a nightingale, soaring,
soaring, through the sky, delivering songs,
if only the bird, the nightingale missed the mountain;

Its heartbreaking call of death, striking fear into all,
yet as it plummeted, it sang, sang its last song,
And as it sang, it saw the world, all at once;

If the bird could only fly, but it could not,
its time had come, but it refused,
the nightingale wanted to see the world again,
it wanted to see its friends, family, home.

It shed its last tear, its final song,
it would not let go, but it knew it was time,
so it embraced death with a smile,
and let go of everything, and hoped to be remembered.

With its song, "The Nightingale's Song".
Eduardo Silva, Grade 6

I Am…Ryan

I am creative and funny
I wonder if there will be flying vehicles some day
I see that I will invent mechanical robots
I want a car that is very fast

I am funny and creative
I pretend that I have a super hero family
I feel like I will be awesome on my test
I touch flying jets and planes in my dreams
I worry that there will be chaos all over the world
I cry when I get laughed at

I am creative and funny
I understand that my parents love me very much
I say that electronics are cool
I dream that I can run very fast
I try to do better in school every day
I hope that my parents get together again
I am creative and funny
Ryan Fowler, Grade 4

I Am a Lily Pad

I am a lily pad.
You know me for sitting above the water.
My mother is the stem.
My father is the roots.
I was born in water and dirt.
I live in a pond.
My best friend is water surrounding me because it holds me up.
My enemy is a frog because it sits on me.
I fear the wind because it blows me away.
I love flowers because they lay softly upon me.
I dream of being the prettiest lily pad in the world.
Kaitlyn Makens, Grade 6

Lost

O' my dear lost friend,
Where dost thou lie.

Many a day do I think of your eyes,
Do I miss your scent.

In the morning, dewdrops on a web.
Does it remind you of the diamonds we wore?

And when we are not together,
Do you think of me when you gaze into the sky?

To my mother, you are known as "Teddy".
But not to me Theodore, not to me.
Cameron Kwok, Grade 6

Guardian Angel

Take a bucket love,
a pinch of gold,
and a pair of wings,
add a spoon full of Heaven.
Then put it into a golden bowl.
Mix with a sparkle whisk,
until you hear singing and see bright rays of light.
Pour it into a cookie pan and smooth out the top.
Bake in the oven at 350°,
until you see white wings on the pan.
You can tell when it is done when you see a golden halo above it.
Let cool until you see sparkles on the top.
Then sprinkle some white pearls.
You should have an amazing guardian angel!
Emma Staid, Grade 6

Ice Cream

Creamy and sweet
Something you can eat
With all different flavors
That you can now savor
There's cherry, coconut, and cinnamon bun
So you should make your sundae fun
You can have one scoop or two scoops and even top them
But you need to try not to drop them
It makes you smile and beam
When you eat ice cream
Eliza Fay, Grade 4

Solar System

Asteroids come in shapes and sizes
Thousand stars in the sky
Comets shooting one by one
Mercury, Venus, Earth, and Mars are near the sun
Some planets are hot and cold
Jupiter, Saturn, Uranus, and Neptune are old
Did I just see a shooting star?
Why are dwarf planets so far?
Ashley Nguyen, Grade 5

The True Melody*

The girl on the inside
When told has no meaning
Face scrunches and starts steaming
Even though can't say a word
That won't stop her life on earth
Melody is the best of them all
But even though she has to be pushed around
That won't stop her from playing on the playground
The girl on the inside is smart
But some people judge the outside and say she is not a work of art
Even though Melody goes to room H5
She sometimes thinks they treat them like they're 5
Melody wants in real classes and to be treated right not have fright
She wants real friends who stick up for her not leave her in the dirt
Melody is strong, tough and smart
She is the best and wants to be like the rest.
Just like the rest.

Cade Carter, Grade 6
*Inspired by "Out of My Mind" by Sharon M. Draper

When I Am Old with You

When I am old with you,
We will gather crumbs
And go to the lake
And feed the ducks all day long.

We will bring our fishing gear
If we get bored.
We will play croquet in your front yard,
And we will not care who wins.

We will sit by the fire and tell jokes.
We will draw until our hands get tired,
And we are hungry.
We will sit outside and listen, with open ears,
To the birds sing in the breezy afternoon air.

We will watch the leaves fall, a colorful shower,
And we will do it all again.

Reed Hightower, Grade 6

Calling

Waiting by the ocean for the call of the drum
walking away from the sea's end
to a place where children play
a place where dreams can be free
and a place where children can be bold
gathering kids along the way
to conquer the night
a fox to mask the person behind
each stage a different page
fire to lead the rebellion
drumming to the sound of the waves
running from what they lost
flying free off the cliff's edge

Danielle Copeland, Grade 5

Cyber Grape

Cyber Grape you know him,
The royalty of all colors.

The purple cool one,
He just hangs on the spectrum vine.

Did you know, if you put red and blue together,
They make grape?

Cyber Grape,
You're the bravest warrior of all the colors.

No one can squeeze you.
You're so strong!

You're a TCU Horned Frog in the night,
And a LSU Tiger in the day.

You're the star,
The coolest crayon in the box.

Cyber Grape,
A network of knowledge, a vision of reality.

Dylan Davis, Grade 4

I Am From...

I am from a town large and rumbling
Where people are rushing to sports games to cheer
Where buildings tower above
Where people are occupied with modern day electronics

I am from a small family
Where aunts, uncles, and cousins come to feast
Where we meet each other by the mountains in the summer
And come by to help each other out

I am from a house large and narrow
Where a pool sits as kids splash around
Where there is a gas fire place under a mantle
Where there is a room full of games big and small
Where rooms line every edge of the house

I am from a Catholic school
Where smiles in every hallway are bright
Where students rush past to get to classes
Where kids run free and shout at recess
And where I'm motivated to keep my grades high

I like where I am from!

Noah Ferguson, Grade 5

Song of the Sea

Silence. It's all you hear.
The pulsing sound of nothing.
Swimming through the cold, dark water.
You open your eyes, introduced to the colors of the sea,
Colored fish, playing on the coral reef, their playground.
You gracefully glide throughout the reefs, reaching out to the fish.
As you kick past the shallow waters, twirling until you're dizzy.
Then you realize you've swam too far.
You look down into the utter darkness of the sea,
You look above to see the light of land.
Yet you swim deeper.
Whales swim past you, singing.
Singing the song of the sea.
Then you sit up. You're in your bedroom.
It was only a dream.
Only a dream…

Alessandra Adkins, Grade 6

Ocean Waves

When a breeze picks up near an ocean
I head over to it without causing a commotion
When I reach the beach
I sit near the ocean
And think of everything that went away
Including my dog Codi, that wasn't a stray
Now these waves speak to me and say
That no matter what she'll be back someday
Now I sit near this ocean
That isn't ever causing a commotion
And then when I head home
I lay to rest and say goodnight
And sleep without a groan
Saying to myself it will be all right
I know I won't always be alone

Erik Wold, Grade 5

I Am a Star

I am a star.
You know me for being bright in the night sky.
My mother is a shooting star.
My father is the sun.
I was born in outer space.
I live in the universe.
My best friend is an astronaut,
because he studies me.
My enemy is an asteroid,
because he runs into me.
I fear running into planets,
because I could explode.
I love watching planets orbit around the sun,
because it makes me feel like I am moving too.
I always wish to be studied by astronomers someday.

Maggie Quinn, Grade 6

Could You Imagine…

Could you imagine me by myself
With no food, no family, no shelter, anything!
I see other kids being with
Their mom and dad,

Could you imagine?
How would you feel
If you were me what would you do?

Cristal Tapia, Grade 6

Almost to Freedom

Tired, scared
Hungry, thirsty
Almost there
Hear howls in the distance
Might be successful
Alone in the dark
See a safe house with a quilt
I go towards the porch and the door opens slightly!

Lauren Ragan, Grade 4

The Day of Joy

My parents shout
when they think no one is around
My sisters and brothers slam doors on each other
When today is the day of joy
Why be sobbing
and being angry
when you can just say,
I'M SORRY.

Eduardo Hernandez, Grade 6

Sarena

It means awesome, nice and kind
It is like having no school for 3 years
It is the memory of my friends
It is the memory of the number one person
Who taught me how to be the best friend I can be
When she is the best friend I can ask for
My name is Sarena
It means to be the best friend you can be

Sarena Hart, Grade 6

You Are Strong

Don't waste your time
You can go out and get an education
Write a book or direct a movie
You can travel the world
Show that you can do things on your own
You are as strong as any man
Show the world that you can do it by yourself
Not with the help of a man

Tyler Graffis, Grade 5

Pizza

I love Pizza Hut
I can eat pizza all day
Pizza is yummy
Andres Diosdado, Grade 5

Trees

A home to many,
covered in brown and verde,
giants standing still.
Alexis Bielinski, Grade 5

The Water Drop

Little water drop,
Sounds like a slishity slosh
Little drop falling
Rachel Poycattle, Grade 5

Movies

Movies are the best
I watch movies all the time
I like watching them
Brasia Anderson, Grade 5

Softball

I like to play sports
Softball is my favorite one
We get to work together
Kylie Valderez, Grade 5

Trees

The long trees so high
With green leaves up in the sky
The land to the birds
Kenza Hanafi, Grade 5

Snow

Frigid flakes falling
Coating everything it touches
Painting the world white.
Madie Huynh, Grade 6

Fruit

My name starts with A,
It has the name of a fruit.
Yes I am an apple.
Daniela Canada, Grade 6

Rose

A rose is pretty
It is the color of blood
A rose is for love
Jasmin Rodriguez, Grade 6

I Rule the World!

If I were in charge of the world,
I'd help out the homeless,
let kids who can't go to school go to school, and
school will focus mostly on studying instead of sports.
If I were in charge of the world,
there would be cleaner neighborhoods,
there would be taco Tuesday, and
everyone would have a lot of happy memories instead of sad memories.
If I were in charge of the world,
you wouldn't have low grades.
You wouldn't be lonely.
You wouldn't be stressed out all the time.
Or, you would be able to spend time with your family,
if I were in charge of the world.
Rebekah Tran, Grade 6

The Horse

Horse, horse, with coat so slick
In the pasture green and thick
Oh, how you run graceful and quick.
Why do your nostrils flare? Why do your ears prick?
I know you're eager to see the other side.
Why do you run like you have to hide?
Perhaps you see the truth,
Or perhaps you're trying to lose the fear of the animal you left behind.
Run, run quick horse.
Run in the pasture with grass so thick.
Run with your nostrils flaring and ears pricked.
Run to the other side.
Go to the forest to hide.
The cougar will not find you there
Dylan Walters, Grade 6

I Remember…

I remember when I went to Mexico and shot fireworks.
I remember when I slept at my uncle's house by myself.
I remember when I went to Disneyland and saw fireworks.
I remember when I went to Las Vegas and went in the pool.
I remember I went on the Disney cruise and did activities.
I remember when I went camping and did activities.
I remember my baptism when my uncle Bob and my uncle Horacio baptized me.
I remember when I went on a boat with my grandpa and played games.
I remember my grandma used to take care of me and we played games.
I remember preschool and we would go outside to play.
Nicolas Valdovinos, Grade 4

Trouble

Troubles are pitch black, puzzled days
They taste like a recipe that just went false
They sound like children weeping for help as the tears tremble down their cheeks
They smell like moldy cheese in the back of the mistaken refrigerator
They look like a war beginning to start
They make me feel alone, and to be hidden in an area
They make me want to run out, confused and hopeless,
Toward the world and see where the path takes me as I begin to settle down
Ameera Eshtewi, Grade 5

Wait for You

I was waiting for you
I stood just as I said I would
In the rain on a cloudy day.

I was waiting for you
Right in front of the woods
hope to see you soon
but I guess I knew
deep inside you wouldn't be there soon
wouldn't you

I took one more look
Before I took off into the night sky
Out of sight of the human eye
When I hear you say
"Sorry I was late
For our date"
Ella Burnes, Grade 5

White Water Rafting

My family reunion – here I am again.
The rushing water,
flowing with power beneath my raft.
Giant boulders blocking our path.
My raft flips to the side
my cousin and I fall in the rapids together.
It feels like I am under water forever.
Finally,
I'm rescued back into my raft.
We head down the rapids again.
We pass by a dam and it calls to us.
"Come on up here!"
So we climb the top of the dam –
and we jump!
The water is clear and cold.
Together, we build memories.
Together, my family and I.
Carly Campbell, Grade 6

Black

Black prefers the darkness
It never cedes to light
Black is trouble, hatred, horror
A mystery unsolved
Black is the world behind the stars
And the depths of a cave
Black is a bat in the darkened night
Soaring amongst the stars
Black is the color of cruelty
Black is the absence of good
Black is a loved one, gone
It is the space between the realms
Black is when you're falling
Down…, down…, down…
Black
Annika Holmstrom, Grade 4

I Am Free

I am free to be a Catholic girl,
I am free to be me.

I am free to believe in any God,
I am free to be me.

I am free to choose my own religion,
I am free to be me.

I am free to pray to the Virgin Mary,
I am free to be me.

I am free to go to church any day I want,
I am free to be me,
a Hispanic, Catholic girl, who is ready to
be FREE.
Luzgabriela Zermeno, Grade 5

The Lost Puppies

The brown and lost puppies
    were in the middle of the parking lot.
        sad and lonely.
We took them to the beach.
It was pure joy!
Lily and Cinnamon Rolls,
    special names for OUR new puppies —
        or so we hoped.
Three nights passed,
    and then we had to give them away.
Back to the beach we went…
    without the puppies.
At least the puppies went to a good home.
We swam,
    and listened to the waves crashing.
The sun was shining.
Cassie Fleck, Grade 4

The Lion Cub

The little lion, playing now
Will hop and play and eat.
Little does the little one know
That one day, one night, one morning
Mother and Father will be no more.
He will have to commence the hunt
So his own cubs may eat.
His parents will not be the kings
Neither will his neighbors, enemies or prey.
He alone will rule the kingdom
With no help except for another lioness.
In the meantime,
Mother and Father will teach the cub
To hunt, to care, to share.
That way he will not fail to feed his family
And the family will not perish.
Kennedy Cargo, Grade 6

What Scares Me

Deep waters that are dark,
The shocking failure "F" mark,
The roaring lion at the zoo,
My twin brother when he says "boo,"
After school detention,
Having two weeks of suspension,
Doctors with syringe needles,
Crawling spiders and beetles,
Monsters underneath the bed,
Blood that is dark red,
Diseases that kill,
Having to listen to a will,
The inevitable math test,
Eating what mother says is "best,"
Frightening, swimming sharks,
The guard dog that always barks,
Small, confined places,
And clowns with creepy faces.
Alana Lim, Grade 5

Nature's Fury

Tornadoes chasing,
Earthquakes shaking,
Do you have your shelter?
Tsunamis rising above the shore,
Landslides falling to the earth,
Are you out of the way?
Floods come fast,
So take cover,
Flash floods are even worse!
Are you high above ground?
Hailstorms crack,
Rockslides clash,
Are you hurt?
Typhoons are big,
Cyclones are monsters,
Take cover,
Whew! Now it's over,
And here lies the aftermath.
Aiden Baldwin, Grade 5

The Lonely Lighthouse

I am a lighthouse
People do not like lighthouses
For I am different
I can light the world
I can glow happily
But no, they like the dark
So, I am just a lonely lighthouse
One day, someone will appreciate my glow
Oh, that wonderful day when they realize
The light is better than the dark
Darkness, darkness
Light, light
One day they will see
Mary Spencer, Grade 6

Dogs

Dogs are so fun
They walk to the park
Dogs like to run
And they like to bark
Gustavo Perez, Grade 5

Shiloh

Shiloh, my dog, is dead,
Which is very sad.
I always loved playing with him instead
Of being bored and mad.
Justin Chapa, Grade 5

Life

L iving things
I n every shape and size
F ind their way across
E very type of landscape imaginable
Grace Lewis, Grade 6

Mustangs

Mustangs are very fast.
Mustangs are very loud!
Mustangs are from the past.
Mustangs can bring in a crowd!
Guimel Sanchez, Grade 5

Minecraft

A game of peace, skills, and survival
Surviving the night
Fighting monsters
Waiting for the day to arrive
Caleb Molina, Grade 4

The Ugly Duckling

Waiting for someone to see his potential,
To see how much he can be.
One day, one night
Someone will truly see what I see in thee.
Saara Bidiwala, Grade 6

Dust Bowl

Disaster came upon the sky
I wonder how and I wonder why?
Dust was the thing that was ruining
A lot of people and a lot of dreams
Sia Mistry, Grade 4

Thunder Struck

Everyone screamed, when thunder struck.
Everyone jumped, when thunder struck.
Everyone cried, when thunder
Follows Mr. Lightning down the sky.
Isaac Hendricks, Grade 4

The Mountain

One day the leader awoke, a plethora of thoughts on his mind
But there was one special object that he wanted to find
It was a mountain, but not an ordinary one
A mountain, its tip glimmering in the shining sun
He looked out onto the waves, the water dancing on the sand
There was also a fireball, its orange hue being quite grand.
The boy thought long and hard, trying to figure out the way to that hill
He pondered for hours and hours, but his mind was still,
Suddenly a poem waltzed into his brain,
Every night his parents would sing this refrain:
Look not in the world for the magical mountain you seek,
Instead meander through your mystical dreams for that majestic peak.
"The key has been found!" He triumphantly said,
And full of excitement he retired to his bed.
Sound asleep, in his dream eyes' view,
He looked around, and immediately knew,
That the mountain was nigh, and his fervor grew,
He had found his quarry at last, and up it he flew
Gavin Goldsmith, Grade 5

Colors*

Under an oak, I look down on my feet
Slowly, I push off my shoes
I feel the grass, the earth underneath my cold wet feet
Right on top of the grass, feeling the breeze of letting go of the past and relief,
I finally can sleep without any crying because my brother can sleep, is safe
I get out a sketchbook and draw
I said in a whisper, I'm going to draw the whole complete picture
I look at the sky, it's blue like the sea, the clouds like pillows in the air
I smile and begin, thinking…
If everyone cared and nobody cried
If everyone loved and nobody lied
If everyone shared and swallowed their pride
Then we'd see the day when nobody died
I said, "Devon" and "I'll miss you, Devon.
Big brother
I fall asleep.

Angelina Rodriguez, Grade 6
*Inspired by the book "Mockingbird" by Kathryn Erskine

Peaceful Aquamarine

Peaceful aquamarine is the color of joy when a kid gets a new toy.
The color of the bottom of a tall waterfall as high as a hotel wall.
A pretty blanket that a baby holds when it gets cold.
Aquamarine is the color of a poison frog that just jumped off a mossy log.
The color of a bright tiny sea horse that found its right course.
The color of mint ice-cream that makes you smile with glee.
Aquamarine is the color of hope that makes no one say nope.
Aquamarine is the color of a turtle's belly and that turtle's name is Shelly.
It's the color of flowers that are beautiful all hours.
Aquamarine is the color of a cat's collar that only cost a single dollar.
A superhero's blue and a baby's too.
Aquamarine is the color of nail polish that looks so perfectly flawless.
The color of peace together just like beautiful sunny weather.
Peaceful aquamarine the color of a clear sky you are never to pass by.
Jeslyn Lightfoot, Grade 5

The 9th Planet
So close to Venus
Bright blue shining in your eyes
Where were you hiding?
Sammy Skulsky, Grade 4

Leaves
Leaves are big and green
they fall off a tree and die
they are colorful
Zachary Oros, Grade 4

Neptune
Smallest gas giant
One of the outer planets
Furthest from the sun
Chloe Pham, Grade 5

Rain
Rain on the house, rain on the trees
Rain on the birds, but not
On me!
Olivia Fletcher, Grade 4

A Spider
With silky strings a
Spider will haunt us all day
And kill bugs and flies
Joseph Riordan, Grade 4

Butterfly
Yellow, blue, red, green
Beautiful in the high sky
Butterfly flies high
Andrew Dollarhide, Grade 5

Stars
Stars are very bright
Stars shine at night in the sky
Sometimes you see them
Marilyn Jimenez, Grade 5

Water
Sweet sounds of water
Its soft drops fall to the ground
So calm and so quiet
Joshua Ordoyne, Grade 5

Sports
I like to play sports
Baseball is my favorite sport
I like soccer too
Ty Lawless, Grade 5

I'm Happy
The beautiful diamonds shining in my sister's eyes;
The joy in my brother's laughter
Hearing the cheerful sound of my mother's voice when I get home;
And getting a text message or a phone call from my father every morning before work
I'm happy

My teachers assisting me in school;
My friends letting me borrow a pencil for the day
My bus driver dropping me off at my house when it's raining or cold;
The Nurses taking care of me when I don't feel good
I'm happy

Giving gifts to family and friends on their birthday or for the holidays;
Or baking sweet treats for my family just because
Making people feel good about themselves;
And helping others with questions on their homework for school
I'm happy

Seeing family and friends everyday
Family, friends, and teachers helping me, giving back, and making them happy
Putting a smile on others' faces —

These things make me Happy
Devyn Mehrtens, Grade 6

My Brief Poetic Account of the Red Tree Painting by Thomas Locker
Summits fading beyond autumn reddened leaves,
a darkened sky that once parted for the fingers of this lone tree,
leave no parting as they swiftly glide passed the forgotten tree,
ghostly colored leaves part like shrapnel in the darkened sky,
once spring green grass now wears autumn's scars,
an autumn laden horizon falls into a fiery valley stream,
in the midst of winter's freeze, the land lays low under the horizon,
all life seems frozen beyond this solitary tree,
autumn passing, the world is in the shadows of winter,
beyond the peach tinted stream lives a lone house,
behind a lone tree,
in a lone valley,
all seems forgotten in this world,
though this tree is but a lone soul
Bryce Kanowsky, Grade 4

Wonder
I'm a rainbow gazing over a city.
I am a present in the back of Santa's sleigh.
I am white snow on a cold winter day.
I am the beat of a drum in a parade.
I am the sweet sound of a violin's strings
I am a number in a math problem.
I am a star in the night sky.
I am a free spirit on a summer day.
I wonder who I'll grow up to be.
I dream of being a basketball player dunking a ball in front of a thousand people,
or a hero saving millions of lives.
I'm Paulo.
Paulo Engelhardt, Grade 4

Trixie
Trixie
Funny, furry
Playing, chasing, barking
Trixie is really goofy
Boxer
Layken Cagle, Grade 4

Beautiful Tree
beautiful tree,
outside our house,
swaying branches in the breeze,
as it finds a way to produce photosynthesis,
trees
Owen Wimmer, Grade 5

Mouse House
There once was a little mouse named Boo.
Who lived in a smelly old work shoe.
One day he wanted cheese,
So he asked the cat "please".
Later that day, he started to chew.
Hailey Roeder, Grade 5

Melon
Melon,
Red juiciness,
Splatters everywhere,
As it disappears in my stomach,
Sadness
Daniel Tomt, Grade 5

Life
Life is short
It passes by
So many things I can do
in a short time
So I'll do what I can
Jose Diaz, Grade 4

French Poodle
French poodle
Friendly, playful
Playing, running, sleeping
Loving, nice, doesn't bite, no barking
Dog
Connor Bell, Grade 4

Love vs. Hate
Love is powerful:
A sweet emotion,
That makes people attract to its beautiful effects,
This charming and attractive emotion makes many people moonstruck.
This emotion makes us do lovable things instead of awful and nasty feats.
And gives us the power to end violence

Hatred is powerful:
A cold, lukewarm sensation that lasts forever.
It has so much power that it can make you do hateful things;
make us change things.
It is born from anger,
And makes us forget about the whole world.
It makes all other feelings except for the need for revenge disappear,
Allowing great enmity.
Hate is perfect just the way it is,
But it is still love in disguise.
Lakshya Nagal, Grade 6

I Remember
I remember the nursery rhymes painted on my wall.
I remember drinking the honey from the honeysuckles with my mom.
I remember pretending after dance class.
Each class made me feel as though I was in a movie.
I remember Sunday school, and I loved
Coloring different pictures of Jesus.
I remember walking my sister to preschool every day
Just because I missed it in every way.
I remember choosing a different stuffed animal every night,
So that no animal would feel bad.
I remember staying up as late as I could the night before Thanksgiving,
Just so I could make pies with my aunt.
I remember dad saying, "I will pay you 20 dollars
If you stay up until midnight on New Year's Eve."
Everyone knew I'd fall asleep before midnight.
I remember getting tucked in every night and feeling so safe.
Childhood is amazing.
Madelyn Campbell, Grade 6

Wonderful Winter
Snowballs whiz past you,
As you make a snowman with a hat that's fairly new. Sledding, skating
And snowboarding too. Winter fun, there is
So much to do!
Sit by the fireplace, with hot cocoa in
Your hands. Surrounded by family and friends
And a love that withstands.
Christmas is here! The most joyful time
Of the year. When presents are found under the tree,
You shout with never-ending glee.
When winter passes and spring comes, you wonder where all the heat came from.
Winter is the best, winter is fun,
And sometimes you think, why does winter have to be done?
And then you realize,
That winter will again arrive…
Rishika Porandla, Grade 4

Black and Red Ned
There once was a boy named Ned,
Who had stripes of black and red.
He went to the nurse,
It was just a curse,
They were gone when he went to bed.
Emma Hanko-Williams, Grade 4

Larry the Coyote
There once was a coyote named Larry,
Who loved to eat lots of cherries.
He wished upon a star,
And got cherries in a jar.
But all the cherries made Larry hairy.
Emmi Kolyszko, Grade 4

Dancing Green Cow
There once was a dancing green cow
When people walked by he would bow
He danced in a tutu
Which amused a few
However the people would just say, "Ciao."
Lily Beaver, Grade 4

Cats
Cats
furry creatures
they purr softly
cats don't like water
animal
Alison Davis, Grade 5

Storm
Splash, the water went.
Boom, the waves crashed.
Zoom, the lightning roared.
Whistle the wind sang.
The storm took everything!
Treyce Tiemann, Grade 6

Chinese Zodiac
Dragons
Monstrous, scaly
Scorches, terrorizes, soaring
Fierce, beautiful but deadly
Basilisks
Caleb Compton, Grade 6

Track
Running
Faster, faster
Down the track running quick
We race farther, and farther down
The track
Kelsey Cessna, Grade 5

Freedom
Freedom is such a word, because it is not what it means
You think freedom is talk how you want, independence of color, freedom of pain
But it is much more than that —
You think freedom is free?
Do you think freedom is just given?
Freedom is not free, and freedom is not just given;
Freedom means years of warring countries, riots, and prison bars
Freedom means taxes and hard labor
Freedom means lives being lost, and knives being sharpened
People are free because other individuals pay for them
People die for others, kill for others, live for others
But freedom is a beautiful thing, even with all the suffering in it
Suffering, pain, money and work, make up what is freedom
We take it for granted, just walking down the streets without a curfew is freedom to us
Freedom has many meanings
But the outcome is beautiful
And because we work for it, we get it
The amazing word, the cry for it,
Freedom.
Isabel Ner, Grade 6

I Am…Mackenzie
I am adventurous and considerate.
I wonder if aliens will appear and rule the Earth.
I hear beautiful angels sing when I am calm.
I see a future of world peace.
I want to be the first woman president.

I am adventurous and considerate.
I pretend I am a doctor performing surgery.
I feel that I can do anything.
I touch beautiful silky clouds when I am calm.
I worry when my brother is worried.
I cry when my family is upset.

I am adventurous and considerate.
I understand I can't have everything I ask for.
I say, "Good things come to those who wait not to those who wait too late."
I dream of a world of ice cream and cookies.
I try to be the best I can be.
I am adventurous and considerate.
Mackenzie Alise Young, Grade 4

Wild Horse
I am a horse.
You know me for galloping across the plains.
My mother is the leader.
My father is the protector.
I was born in the meadows.
I live near the mountains.
My best friend is my sister because we like to gallop across the land.
My enemies are mountain lions because they hunt us and stalk us at night.
I fear of being captured because they will break my wild spirit.
I love the open plains because I get to have more room to run.
I dream to be wild forever and never get captured.
Belle Siripanyo, Grade 6

The Deer
A clearing at midnight
Pale shadows of the moon coming to rest where you sit
You wait in silence
And it greets you with a gift
She prances out of the darkness
And for a split second
Her warm brown eyes meet your cold blue ones
In that moment you see what life is,
or what it's supposed to be
You see the flowers, the trees, the sun,
And the memories you chose to put away
But that moment is gone now
She turns, runs away from you into the lights that strike too fast
and your heart stops beating
You look at her, cold eyes flashing with sorrow,
But instead you find nothing
Nothing except a red footprint
On the other side of the road
Hope Paschall, Grade 6

Spring
Spring has sprung
I asked to go out and Daddy said yup
Plants whose heads were hung down
Are growing up, up and UP
The rain is coming down in a big schlup
Wetting the leaves and fur on a pup

Spring has sprung
The birds tweet and fly on to the street
As the mud collides with my shoes
Oh pooh! I am stuck!
My foot after strain comes out with great pain

Spring has sprung
I am home now
Mabel the cow is milked
George the dog is fed
Time to go to bed
Nikhil Sampath, Grade 4

What Happens to a Dream Deferred?*
What happens to a dream deferred?
Does it drift off into space
like a star in the black void of your mind?
Or does it go extinct
like the dinosaurs
and then get a new beginning by other people?
Does it come and go as people young and old?
Or does it disintegrate
like the paint on the Terra-cotta Warriors?
Maybe it just fades
like a warm day to a cold winter's night.
Or does it wait to be remembered like an old friend?
Aidan McCoy, Grade 6
*Inspired by Langston Hughes

If I Were in Charge of the World
If I were in charge of the world,
I'd cancel bedtimes,
darkness, and
scary movies.
If I were in charge of the world,
there'd be ice cream everywhere,
no doing chores, and
no school.
If I were in charge of the world,
you wouldn't feel pain.
You wouldn't be scared,
you wouldn't have homework
or mean parents.
If I were in charge of the world,
there would be no groundings,
no mowing the lawn, and
no bullying.
If I were in charge of the world,
you would be allowed to chew gum in school,
have tons of presents on your birthday, and
you wouldn't have to read when your teacher tells you.
Colton Green, Grade 6

Someone There for Me
Something in my heart
that wasn't there before,
a light guiding the way.
Setting a fire of light
that guided my life
she's here and here to stay.
A sister for me
who came when I was lonely
for years I was looking for her.
She's here for me I'm here for her
together we're inseparable.
They can't pull us apart
because she's here in my heart
she won't leave me,
I won't leave her.
She sparked me with her love
that felt like it was from the angels above
she came when I needed her most.
Without her I wouldn't make it here
She is my one and only.
She set a fire of love in me, it's still there, and forever will be.
Phoenix Ng, Grade 4

Just a Kid

I am just a kid
Just a kid
I NEED someone to care
I lost a special someone
The one I cared the most for.
All I have
Is hope.
But soon…
I won't be alone
Sad no more
Hungry won't exist.
For me
A family.
I always wanted.
A home.
A new start
A new beginning
Only.
Time will tell
Only time.
"I will see you soon. New family."
Joanna Mora, Grade 6

Once Upon a Time

What a phrase,
what a phrase.
Who could possibly think
of such a phrase.
When said, such a phrase
promises are made.
Promises of danger, excitement,
enchanted forests, beautiful castles,
magical fairies, daring princes,
and evil trolls.
When said such a phrase —
the blood runs cold,
the heartbeat accelerates;
fear for the prince,
and his brave steed
as they battle and conquer
the rampaging dragon.
No other such phrase
could enchant such as it.
Once upon a time.
What a phrase.
Sara Mackenzie, Grade 6

Grass/Soil

Grass
Green, scratchy
Pointy, bright, neon
Dry, cheerful, wet, non-cheerful
Flat, dark, sticky
Brown, rough
Soil
Jacob Pack, Grade 4

Playstation

There is happiness
when I switch on
the Playstation;
there is glory
when I find
something new.
There is rush when
I'm on the battlefield.
I enjoy the feeling of power and
my head is adorned with a crown.
I relish the grip of the sword
in my sweaty hand.
This is fun,
this laugher
is all part
of play.
Ryker Strong, Grade 6

War

A time of sorrow,
A time of need,
When heroes are made,
Innocent fall.
A time of sorrow,
A time of greed,
War causes trepidation,
In the hearts of all civilization.
From ancient to present,
People fight.
A time of sorrow,
A time of decree,
When some thrive,
Many die.
This isn't right.
This is war.
Sam Hajaliloo, Grade 6

A Winter in Russia

A winter in Russia
Is a cold one indeed.
Everyone is dressed
In their warmest winter clothes
Topped with ushankas.
Everyday,
Workers come to clear the road of snow
So people can drive.
A winter in Russia is a hard one,
But there's snow to play with
And snowmen waiting to be built.
If you've got skates,
Then you can ice skate
On Crimea River.
A winter in Russia is hard.
But at least it's fun!
Boriana Spassov, Grade 5

Beauty of Snow

I glimpse outside and
See clouds of gray and
Silver trees covered with sparkles
I step outside
And feel the sparks of frost
Touch my skin
I look beneath my feet
And see my footprints
Leave their mark
The frigid air forces
Me away back
Still, I stand to
See the stunning
Portrait of winter
My heart is filled
With the joy of
This heavenly world
As I step back into my cozy cottage
Khadeeja Mian, Grade 6

Riding

The feeling,
The feeling of
Wind in my
Hair and the horse trotting
To the end makes me realize
I should never give up.
As I fix
My reigns to
Take control,
I kick harder
And go faster.
We stop suddenly
And look around
On this dusky day.
We run.
Where?
We don't care,
We are free.
Marley Mills, Grade 6

Metacognition

M onitoring your skill
E ncouraging
T hinking about thinking
A ccelerating
C hallenge
O ften works
G reat scores
N ever fail your tests
I ntelligence
T ests your abilities
I mportant to have in life
O pposing to some
N ever use anything else!
Carly Childress, Grade 6

Who Am I?
Who Am I?

Am I the odd one in the back?
Maybe the quiet one in the book?
Possibly the weird one, who laughs a lot?
Maybe I'm all of them.

Might I be the one who's polite?
The one who hides?
The one who's scared?
The one who tries?
Maybe I'm all of them.

Maybe I'm the mature one?
Maybe I'm the childish one?
Maybe I'm both.

Who am I?
This
Is

Who I Am.
Arya Pathak, Grade 6

Animals My Mom Doesn't Like
My mom despises cats,
She also hates the rats.
Every time they come,
She would…RUN!!

My mom rejects dogs,
She says, "A better pet would be a LOG!"
Another pet would be…
Me,
Fishes,
A fake dog that would 'give her wishes,'
A drying board,
A cooking lord,
A magic pony of the light,
A gust of wind in the night.
But
She would love me
As her pet
The most

(More than my sister!!)
Michelle Zeng, Grade 6

Thunder
Thunder comes in howling
Sending shivers up and down my spine
Like skittering spiders
Through the plains of Texas
And livens up the sky
Horrifying
Cecily Sandoval, Grade 4

The Cow
One day, there was a bundle of hay.
It was a day in May.
The bundle of hay in this day of May,
Sat there where it lay.
Then a cow came along singing a song.
Bingling bong singing his song.
He was tired for he had walked so long.
He noticed a little bundle of hay.
The cow walked over there on this day.
He got over there and started to lay.
He ate and he ate, but it was getting late,
So he walked over to the gate.
There he slept, dreaming of his fate.
The next morning he woke up.
Then he saw a little pup.
On the collar of the pup, it read Gup.
The pup and the cow started to play.
They were so happy and gay.
Then they started to walk away
From that little bundle of hay.
John Machtolff, Grade 6

White
Clouds,
High in the sky,
Daisies,
Moving with the wind,
Beluga Whales,
Bobbing on the surface,
Of the ocean.
Stones,
Moving with the current,
Of the river.
Snowflakes,
Falling from the sky.
Bones,
Underground at a cemetery,
Hailstones,
Hitting the car door windows,
Marshmallows,
Being eaten at a campfire.
Wolves,
Crying out to the full, white moon!
Sophia Nagl-Mermelstein, Grade 5

Flying
white and blue,
cold and breezy,
swaying back and forth,
birds beside you,
time has stopped,
don't have to worry about the ticking clock,
having fun,
you don't have to run,
heading towards the rising sun.
Alannah Jahn, Grade 5

I Am
I am nice and creative
I wonder how the human race began
I hear monsters lurking in the night
I see a shadow
I want power to turn the world to peace

I am nice and creative
I pretend to be a robot
I feel glory in the future
I touch a cloud one million miles away
I worry that I might get bit by a spider
I cry when someone suffers

I am nice and creative
I say, "I'm fast!"
I dream for a better life
I try to make my dreams come true
I hope my family is safe

I am nice and creative
Isak Bradley, Grade 4

The Beach
The breeze you can feel
And the waves you can hear
The kids are yelling and
Running to the ocean
But they forgot to put on lotion
The kids are gathering sand
With their own little hand
To make something crazy
That they will never see again
Because they forgot all about it
Some people had a board
And surf on waves
The coach is looking if you are drowning
The day is getting dark
But no one was scared when it got dark
But they were scared of sharks
When it is night they can't see anything
So then they just go home and sleep
Until a new day comes
They go back to the beach
William Ha, Grade 4

Baby Animals
Animals are interesting,
Especially in the spring.
Babies run and play,
That is their way.

Some are really slow,
Even when it blows.
They are very hungry,
For food they always plea.
Kambrie Chadwick, Grade 4

Spring Break Is Almost Here

Spring break where are you?
Oh wait, you're almost here!
Don't stop coming.
It's becoming clear!

I don't know what I'll do.
I hope it's fun.
Maybe go eat.
Or go on a run.

Maybe go into town.
We will do a few things.
I don't know…
Maybe buy a ring.

We could go swimming,
Or play a game.
Either way,
I know it won't be lame!

So grab your passport.
Let's hit the road.
And we'll get into,
The spring break mode.
Madison Musil, Grade 5

HW Excuse

I started my HW
But my pen ran out of ink
I started up my PC
It shut down like a blink

So I brought it to the library
With a great big frown
All of a sudden
It was abducted by a clown

He said it would cost infinity
I said "no way"
So he pulled a plane from his pocket
And flew far, far away

At that point it wasn't worth it
So I went home
And I got ambushed
By an army of lawn gnomes

My escape was an adventure
I cannot say what I did
The thing is, I don't have my HW
So ask some other kid
Derek Chen, Grade 6

A Poison Powderpuff

A Poison Powderpuff on the ground
an umbrella in the forest for
the small, little bugs
These mushrooms small as a teacup
are the stepping stones in a river of grass
With a cap with a light brown center
and ivory and white everywhere else
they form stools like chairs
and they have round caps like jellyfish
they grow on the ground
and are usually found near trees
some of their kind grow on the
trunk of a tree
forming the steps
up to the low branches
they bring death to those who eat them
A Poison Powderpuff on the ground
Alexandra Park, Grade 5

Stranded

Lost in the woods,
hoping to come out good.

Silent night,
provokes a little fright.

Rustling through the leaves,
always alert for thieves.

Hunting for food,
to get a little barbecued.

Spend the night on the dirt,
to wake up soar and hurt.

Now the sun illuminates the way,
wishing them a better day.
Briana Garibay, Grade 6

Rain

flowing though rocks and sand
animals drinking plants adsorbing
rich fertile soil being created
then heat strikes to make it boil
steam rises and touch's the sky

while it soars through the sky
to crate shade for all to enjoy
then suddenly light stops
thunder comes down in a bright light

when it all calms down
the bright vivid sun comes out
theirs an object seen in the sky
its a rainbow with all its beautiful 7 colors
Richard Camacho, Grade 6

All Alone

I'm always all alone
Sitting on my bed crying
I always seem to be on my own
Because I am quite different from others

I begin to close my eyes
And dream about my lonely life
Wishing I lived a different lie
Though it won't ever happen

When I show up at school
Everyone is laughing at me
Because they think I'm not cool
So now I'm in the bathroom crying again

I don't think this will ever end
Because of the rumors going around
So I come home and cry on my bed
Because I'm always all alone
Kaitlyn Jones, Grade 6

Friendship

Friends are like tools
they help you.
Accomplish anything? They
will be there too.
Friendship is one important
thing in life.
Without it you will go
through strife.
Friends may be big friends may
be small.
Some friends might not be human
at all.
Yes animals can be friends too.
They can be friends
with you.
Friends will help through thick and thin
and be there if you win.
And help through all the times that are sad
and help in life which is not bad.
Viro Arioboma, Grade 4

Purple

Purple is the smell of delicious
blackberry juice on a spring day.
Purple is the smell of grape
juice when violets open in the
spring. Purple is the sound of
spray paint on scissors. Feelings
of purple are exciting feelings with
your new purple jacket. Crayons
we color with have happy emotions.
Blackberries, snow cones, and purple
gummy worms, all have purple.
Evelynn Reed, Grade 4

Just One Match

Crack! All at once I start crackling
As if I were thunder breaking the silent night.
She sits by me, unafraid of my cackling
As the shadows dance with my light.

Over the holidays I make the room cozy
As if I were the sun keeping her warm.
She wouldn't care if there was a frenzy
She wouldn't care if there was a thunderstorm.

At night she sits by me
Reading her favorite book.
I really enjoy her company.
She also draws in her sketchbook.

By one another we feel like companions
She watches my flames dance for hours.
Her eyes gleam like stars by the millions.
With one match, many hearts I empower.

Heloise Hoffmann, Grade 6

Ready?

Are you READY?
Those words made my knees unsteady.
I smile at my family, my team
And together we scream!

Eight minutes to prove we belong!
These other teams don't know we are strong!
We have worked hard all year
Just to make it here!

Destination Imagination,
A time for out of this world CREATION.
Are you ready? You ask!
Yeah! we're ready to tackle this task!

Time to enjoy all my team has done
To become ONE!
Together we have achieved more
Than anyone at my school has done before

Curiana Flores, Grade 5

Summer's Eve

Summer's eve
The sun goes
Up, rushing through the
House yelling. It's two o'clock
Bathing suit on grabbed a towel
Ran to the pool I put one foot in. I
Quickly felt the ice cold arctic water run up my
Legs, my hands started shaking they looked pale
Like frost bite. My lips turned dead purple the warm and
blazing sun hit the crystal clear water reflecting like glitter on
My bathing suit that's my summer's eve.

Anahi Silva, Grade 6

I Know You Know

I know you know
What is creeping up my spine
What is keeping me awake at night
I know you know how
The shining lights blind me
The piercing silence burns through my ears like a wildfire
I know you see
My dreams
Good or bad
My secrets tucked away at night
I know you hear
My thoughts
My emotions flaming or soothing
I know you feel
My passion fiery and radiant
My pain or pleasure
Fear or love
I know you know in spite of all
We all come together and share the love of life

Reverie Sisco Kearns, Grade 6

Vietnam

I thought Vietnam was just swell.
All my relatives were doing well.
They treated me like I was the richest man on Earth.
They had never bossed me around.
I could eat what I wanted when I wanted it.

The flowers there were so pretty.
They planted flowers on top of a hill
Making them spell words.
The beaches were a breathtaking sight.
There was also a lot of waves action going up and down.

The food was all so good.
Both the taste and the sight of it
Made my mouth water.
Some of the food there
I haven't had in a long time!
Some day I want to
Return there.

Aidan Ly, Grade 4

Happiness

If happiness was a color,
it would be pink,
as soft as a bunny's nose.
If happiness was a taste,
it would be fresh baked cookies.
If happiness was a feeling,
it would be as joyful as a little baby.
If happiness was a smell,
it would be blooming flowers.
If happiness was an animal,
it would be a newborn puppy lying in your lap.

Grace Kight, Grade 6

Delight

I am a shark in the deep ocean
I am a black panther that lies in the tall grass
I am a horse that gallops through the plains
I am the kid that follows a dream
I am night, the dark of the river
I am a tiger playing with a mouse
I am a cluster of tiny fish, I am the farthest planet
I am the cold of the snow
I am the whistle of the wind
I am the glitter of the rain
I am the long fin of the shark in the deep ocean
I am a rainbow of four colors
I am a cat that runs away through the wild
I am a field of wheat and grass
I am a pack of wolves in a dark cave
You see, I am alive, I am alive
I stand in good relation to my family
I stand in good relation to my friends
I stand in good relation to my pets
I stand in good relation to my beliefs
You see, I am alive, I am alive

Lauren Watanabe, Grade 6

The Delight Song

I am the feather on a graceful peacock
I am a brown dog that runs in the prairie
I am the dolphin that jumps gracefully in the ocean
I am the cat that follows the owner
I am a cluster of graceful gazelles
I am the farthest moon
I am the cold of the Arctic
I am the howl of the wolf
I am the glitter of the sea
I am the long stem of the flower in the field
I am the season of four colors
I am the field of grass and roses
I am the pack of wolves on the quiet mountain
I am the hunger of a grazing cow

You see, I am alive, I am alive
I stand in good relation to my parents
I stand in good relation to my sister
I stand in good relation to my brother
I stand in good relation to the Lord
You see, I am alive, I am alive

Kristine Villalpando, Grade 6

Spring

The birds lay their eggs in the spring sky blue,
The air is filled with magic and the weather is warm too,
The downy, feathery, snow was fun to watch and play in,
But I couldn't go outside and my school grounds were frozen,
Now that the season is spring,
I feel like I can do most anything.

The trees are pink as they blossom and bloom,
They will become edible wonders anytime soon,
The migrating birds fly back to their home,
It's a magical sight to watch the butterflies roam,
Now that the season is spring,
I feel like I can do most anything.

The sleeping grass awakens from its snooze,
The birds' sweet song makes us amused,
Ladybugs flutter from flower to flower,
Baby bunnies munch on their leaves,
In the gentle spring shower,
Now that the season is spring,
I feel like I can do most anything.

Ananya Nair, Grade 4

Follow Your Dreams

Incomes low but hearts high
They grew up together
Looking up at the sky
Dreaming at night until the stars aligned
Singing stupendously until it came time
to go to the man that makes things right
Inspiration fills their joyful songs
when they sang the whole world hummed
Reaching for the North Star
to guide them on their way
Following a path that will stretch farther than today
Their lives must change from here on out
As people start to scream and shout
She goes out on her own and makes a stand
And if we fall she will give us her hand
Rising together the music is grand
It plays a soulful tune lifting light like air
It is like the ocean saying goodbye heart in hand
to all that feels bad
A woman with heart and feeling
One who will change for the better of others.

Charlie Belciano, Grade 6

Santa Ines Mission

Santa Ines Mission, a tall mission,
It stands an outer mission across this land.
The 19th mission out of a trail, a tradition.
Santa Ines Mission, its bells gleam in the sun,
And as the children around are having much fun.
A ring of a bell might be quite swell.
That's how Santa Ines Mission goes!

Tommy Fealy, Grade 4

Besties

B esties for life
E ndless relationship
S isters that are forever true
T rue friends that spend an eternity together
I s a trusted and loyal companion
E ncouraging when feeling down
S tays together

Dayana Sepulveda, Grade 6

Kittens

A kitten is cute and fluffy,
The kitten meows and is a feline.
They love to play and play all day,
I hope all kittens are fine.

When they are born their eyes are shut,
And they can barely walk.
They can be colors from black to orange,
The kittens then squeak and talk.

Kittens love to scratch things,
Sometimes even carpet.
They're cute until they mess things up,
I wonder how much trouble they get.

When they are older,
They'll hunt very well.
They'll catch birds and mice,
I think all cats are swell.
Dakota Vierig, Grade 4

Batman

His parents were killed when he was young.
The butler helped him make a suit.
In the night from the shadows he sprung.
Stopping robbers from getting loot.

Upside down the robbers hang.
Waiting for the police to come.
No longer a robber gang.
The police can't run from.

Quickly hopping in his car.
He speeds away to his home.
Coming back home with no scar.
His butler had just gone to Rome.

Going down to the bat cave.
Batman finds his next task.
To stop a giant tidal wave.
So he took his tools out of a cask.
Isaac Halls, Grade 4

Creator of Everything

Do you know who I am?
I am the creator of everything
I create the flowers that grow
In the fields
I create the people who walk on the Earth
I create the trees who protect you from
The summer sun
I create the wild and non-wild animals
I created your emotions
But you're the one who created your path
In life
Gizelle Landeros, Grade 5

Moment to Shine

Being afraid at first
feeling spiders crawling up your throat
dancing like your nothing
singing songs so loud
performing in front of people
it feels like your dream is on a cloud
finishing the show with a smile
going out to dinner that's a mile
the night running like it's wild
going to sleep feeling special
waking up in the morning singing
living a life like a star
Abigail Diaz, Grade 6

Those Icy Blue Eyes

Their eyes as round as Earth.
Their eyes an icy blue.
Their eyes have so much worth.
I wish I had them too.
Eyes bluer than the sky.
Eyes filled of hope and joy.
Those eyes though, my oh my.
I want them so, oh boy.
Eyes deeper than the ocean.
Those sensitive blue eyes.
I shall wait till then.
I wish I had blue eyes.
Tatum Dickson, Grade 6

A Funny Coincidence

In the shadows,
there's chattering in the air.
Alone in the
deep, deep, dark
I scream and hide.

My heart is beating
faster and faster.

All of a sudden
something scratches me.
It was my cat.
Luis Nunez, Grade 4

Thorns

Roses are red
Violets are blue
You are evil
And I am good
You bathe in
Blood
I in
Gold
You are no match for me
For I live for infinity
Claudia Salas, Grade 6

No One Knows

No one knows what I know
But me
I can see colors listening to music
But no one knows
That there are many things I wish to say
But I can't
No one knows
But me
Many things fill my mind
That I want to say aloud
But they're all stuck inside
So no one knows
But me
Maybe if someone tried
They could know me
But no one has
No one knows
The girl on the inside
Olivia Stith, Grade 6

Painting

Oh, how the paintbrush feels,
gliding across the canvas
As the elegant colors mix,
the calming sound of painting goes.
"Swish, swish, swish!"
Dip the brush in water,
then swipe it across a towel
Yellow, red, blue
Gasp! The magnificent colors
A tree? A bird? A whole forest, yes!
You could paint anything
as long as you have a paintbrush
Watch the color dance
beckoning, "I'm great at tinting!"
or, "The water is a place for me,"
Oh, how the paintbrush feels
finishing your painting with —
a signature.
Sophia Deaver, Grade 4

Reaching for the Stars

Reaching for the stars
Is an amazing experience
To find the inner you
So dreams can come true
Reaching for the stars
May be hard and rough
And sometimes you will fall
But it is easy to get back up
If you believe on crossing that finish line
Of hope and love
Reaching for the stars
Will be the biggest accomplishment
You overcome
Maya Gill, Grade 5

Harriet Tubman

Harriet was born in Maryland
She is the child of Mr. Ross and Mrs. Ross
She lived in Dorchester County
She studied how to read
She overcame slavery
She worked as a slave
She was challenged by discrimination
Her personal traits were working hard as a nurse and being fearless
She always helped people
She never left people behind
She is best known for her underground railroads
Harriet was an amazing person

Mariana Damian, Grade 4

Something

Oh I wish there was something to do right now!?!
I could ride a pig or even a cow.
Or I can go to Hogwarts and be a wizard,
But also, I might cause a huge blizzard.
I can fight crime and defeat evil,
But the problem is I might go medieval.
I can start a super team of super heroes,
But also be one of the number one zeroes.
Or rather read a nice cookbook,
But I'm not the guy with the challenge to cook.
But then again I might get the flu.
Oh I wish there was something to do?!?!?

Sebastian Reyes, Grade 6

Inspiration

One day I met you,
you brightened the world of black and white,
shaped the line to something extraordinary,
turned my world upside down,
transformed the known to even more.

And I gave you,
light in the darkness,
sound in the silence,
a word on that blank page,
a mind that never stops pondering,
you are my inspiration.

Makayla Phea, Grade 6

Invitation from Rabbit

I am inviting you to the woods, dig

in the ground with me and find insects with me.
Smell fresh carrots and pull them out with me,
then taste them with me.

Please come in my burrow and
wrap yourself in green nature.

Please come in my burrow.

Ezekiel Anderson, Grade 4

Roller Coaster

Craaannk!
Click
My heart's pounding
As the coaster makes its way to the very top…

WOOSH!
The coaster is going down so fast
You couldn't breath even if you wore an oxygen mask
it swings vigorously

SCREEEECH!
As it comes to a stop a smile crawls onto my face
And I say
let's do that again!

Samuel Jeppson, Grade 4

Cats

Cats are funny, kind and cute.
I think I've seen one fly a parachute.
Some are orange, some are black.
Some are mean and give you a scratch.
They sometimes leap, sometimes pounce.
Sometimes they even weirdly bounce.
They give lots and lots of love.
They also give you kisses and hugs.
Some cats meow, some cats cry.
Some make you not want to say goodbye.
So we should all remember, that cats are our special friends.
And never let that bond break until the very end.

Marie Fontaine, Grade 4

Field of Home Turf

Fans cheering for the home team,
Announcers cackling the lineup,
The scent of hot turf,
A comfy sports jersey against my skin,
My feet vibrate from the fans loud cheers,
Sun beaming down through the stadium windows,
Fans cheering,
 Fans cheering,
  Fans cheering,
Players as strong as an iron wall,
There is not better place to be,
Than at the soccer stadium.

Brady Rufner, Grade 5

Yellow

Yellow feels like the sun streaming down on you and me.
Yellow sounds like a bumble bee buzzing around my body.
Yellow is the sticky feeling of honey on my fingers.
Yellow tastes like lemonade on a hot summer day.
Yellow tastes like freshly cut pineapple.
Yellow is a sunflower standing tall in my yard.
Yellow is the taste of corn on the cob on Christmas Eve.
Yellow is the taste of sour lemon heads melting in my mouth.

Donna E. Campbell, Grade 4

Roller Coaster

As life moves on
It twists and turns with drops and bumps along the way
As life moves on like a roller coaster

As time passes
There are ups and downs as things grow and shrink —
excitement along the way
As time passes it is like a roller coaster

As books progress
All the way through from start to end,
With sudden drops and sharp corners from beginning to end
As books progress like a roller coaster

As music is made
With highs and lows, loops and strange combinations
As music is made like a roller coaster

As things happen
All things have twists and turns, starts and stops, highs and lows
If life is flat just wait —
excitement is just around the corner
As things happen like a roller coaster

Isaac Gibbens, Grade 6

Traveling the World

So many places, the places I'll go!
Africa, Antarctica, can't miss the snow!
American deer, where's mother doe?
The world has so many places to go!
Until the sun comes up

In South America, birds will cry
The baby croc earned its fishy prize
He needs to eat something bigger than his size
So he can grow and maximize
Until the sun comes up

In Europe, the pastries await
The Mona Lisa is there always
The Great Wall of China, oh so very long
Maybe it can reach all the way to Hong Kong
Until the sun comes up

Kangaroos, koalas, Australia's the place!
If you want to start a whole country race
Tarantulas will show "Pick up the pace!"
The kangaroo is the one that will ace
Until the next day arrives.

Chikanyima Brown-Nkemdirim, Grade 4

White Beach Chair

From my favorite white beach chair,
I watched the waves wash wildly on the sandy beach.
Wiggling my toes into the shore,
The sun enclosed me in a warm embrace,
While the breeze tickled me gently and rustled my hair.

I got up from my favorite white beach chair,
And raced faster and faster into the salty sea.
The water felt as cold as my freezer.
Shaking the imaginary icicles off my back,
I swam a bit farther.
Coming from below, I cleared the water from my eyes,
And saw a dolphin next to me.
Our eyes met as if we were old friends.

I popped out of the salty ocean water, enjoyed the sunset,
And ran back to my favorite white beach chair,
To see the sun sink into the horizon.

Julia Nickl, Grade 6

Pearl Harbor

Boom — Boom
Go the explosions of
Terror
Screaming
Planes endless in the air
Like bees if you disturb them
The humming sound
Then awakened
Hundreds of men running out of their barracks
Getting their weapons ready for
Defending Pearl Harbor

Boom — Boom
Terror
Filled the air
On that
Treacherous day at
Pearl Harbor

Ty McMahon, Grade 4

Hungry Dreams

Coffee fills my dreams tonight
Along with crazy bagels
Demonic potatoes danced with highlighters
And cheeseburgers wrote a song.
All of a sudden, a doughnut ate the stars
And sprinkles filled the sky.
Cookies tried to rhyme
While glue bottles shook their heads.
Nacho cheese volcanoes towered behind
With psycho marshmallows jumping in.
A wild gummy bear sat in a bush
While a hat ate a tree.
Never go to bed hungry, or you'll end up like me.

Hope Foote, Grade 6

The Pencil

I am a pencil.
You know me for writing.
My mother is an eraser.
My father is a pen.
I was born in a classroom.
My best friend is an eraser.
He is so nice we like to write.
My enemy is a sharpener.
Because it takes my skin off.
I fear of getting snapped.
Because it would hurt.
I love an eraser.
Because it is always behind me.
I dream to be written by someone famous.
Brayden Zimmerman, Grade 6

Ode to Sister

Sister, Sister
So cute and sweet
I love you so much
You make my heart beat

Sister, Sister
I love you so
You are my shimmering star
You are my high to my low

Sister, Sister
How you are so nice
You make me smile
You are my life
Evelyn Mundt, Grade 5

Ode to the Wright Brothers

Wilbur and Orville
You flew the first airplane
Your plane was magnificent
You guys have brains

Wilbur and Orville
You guys failed a lot
But you pulled through
Some wondered if you ever fought

Wilbur and Orville
You invented the Wright Flyer
It worked the last few times
It flew higher
Toby Giroux, Grade 5

Strong

I am strong
Not built nor tough
Not athletic but strong

Your words
Cruel words, hurtful
Buried inside me
words

I am strong
Not built nor tough
Not athletic but strong

In ways you will never be

I am strong
Not built nor tough
Not athletic but strong

I hold it all on my shoulders
You hold nothing which makes me strong
Not built nor tough
Not athletic but strong
Minza Mirza, Grade 6

My Final Exam

My heart is beating full of fear
For my final exam is almost here
Though I may not pass this test
I will do my very best

My heart is beating full of fear
For my final exam is almost here
Education is the key
For all these tests that come to me
I will pray right out loud
Make my parents very proud

My heart is cooling down a bit
I am brave enough
And I start to sit on my seat
I am ready to start
I am not scared
I have a change of heart

My heart's not beating full of fear
Because I am happy
That my final exam is almost here
Marwa Salem, Grade 6

All Alone

I want to know the day it went bad
To go back and not be sad
Everyday that goes by gets worse
I think I might have a curse
This curse is ruining my spirit
No on makes an appearance
I need to find the way out
The road is not doubt
The way out is happiness
But all I have in unhappiness
There is no sign of the road
So I guess I will have this load
Angela Villa, Grade 6

JFK

Born in Boston, MA
Child of Joe Kennedy
Lived in Boston his whole life
Studies politics
Overcame haters of the world
Worked as President of the USA
Challenged by Soviet Union and Cuba
Nice, caring
Always there
Never disrespectful
Best known for being a great President
Preston McCaffrey, Grade 4

My Dog

My dog is better than your dog
She hunts bears all day
Her breakfast is a snake
While her dinner is raw steak
My dog is better than your dog
She runs 50 miles per hour
While playing basketball
With some great power
She taught herself to drive a car
Along with sparing
And guitar
Connor Fitzgerald, Grade 5

Snowy Days

Snow fights
Cold nights
City lights
Snowy boots
Owls hoots
Fast blinks
Skating rinks
Yummy snow
Happy glow
Dirty dogs
Fire logs
Radha Vallurupalli, Grade 4

Sad Little Orphan

I'm just an orphan
Sad…
Alone…

I…

Cried so much it made the ocean
With no family to be with
I'm just an orphan with
nothing to get
Instead of getting presents
I Just want a family to spend
the holidays with
Soon…
Soon I will get a family that
loves me and cares about me
But in the future it will be
different I will have a family
and brothers and sisters.
I hope…

Paola Gutierrez, Grade 6

The River

A stream to wherever it leads me
never ending
quiet and peaceful
then loud, uncontrollable
thrashing, screaming, winding along its icy path
then calm once more, a gentle giant
like a dream leading to fantasies
showing me the way
it has always been here, it will always be here
gleaming blue under the moonlight sky
it sings a beautiful lullaby
mysteries waiting to unfold
swift but soft
like a morning dew
cleaning me of my guilt
each new day is a new dream
a new life
The River
a stream to wherever it leads me
never ending

Kensington Nelson, Grade 6

Friends

Friends don't betray
Friends are companions
Some friends are furry
Some friends have skin
Friends don't hurt you
Friends help you
My friends have my back
My friends are forgiving
Friends are loyal companions whether furry or human

Linden Loos, Grade 4

Spike

SMACK! CRACK!
I look down at my burning arms,
redness spreading through them.
The ball hits the ground with a thud.
Satisfied, I return to ready position
arms apart, knees bent, feet shoulder width apart
I smile,
seeing the ball fly across
to the opponents side.
I wait, getting prepared for a spike from the opponents.
WHAM, the spike sails across to the bumper,
CRACK, the setter reaches for the ball and hits it,
up, up, over right to me.
Time slows. I know this is my chance.
I start my steps,
left, right, left.
I jump up, hoping to hit the ball
I swing my arm back and…
WHAM…it hits the court!
SPIKE!

Lucy Hynes, Grade 6

I Am…Anthony

I am curious and intelligent
I wonder are there animals in the world to be discovered
I hear people in the world getting along
I see myself recreating a dinosaur
I want all wars in the world to end

I am curious and intelligent
I pretend to be a great football player
I feel myself graduating from UCLA
I touch the first recreated dinosaur
I worry that most of our animals will become extinct
I cry when a family member gets hurt

I am curious and intelligent
I understand that some people can't get along
I say the ocean isn't completely discovered
I dream I will discover a new animal
I try to be the best person I could be
I hope I will have a great life
I am curious and intelligent

Anthony Duenez, Grade 4

Easter Morning

On Easter morning, I get out of bed
Knowing that Jesus has risen from the dead!
Easter is a time for fun
With family and friends to celebrate the son!
Even though Lent is gone, we must strive,
Because He is alive,
To be better than we were.
Jesus is so good to us; look at what He did.
He died for everyone, even the smallest kid!

Fey Jung, Grade 6

Shining Stars

Some light bulbs shine as bright
As the sun and some just shine
Like ordinary stars

The country has a million
Beautiful stars above
Some shining bright and some shining dull

Laying down under a tree staring at
The sky gazing
The shining stars on the reflection of my eye

This image will always keep an
Indelible moment
In my heart
Stars have an image in my mind that makes me
Feel like I can do anything
Stars can give me power to everything

Natalia Guerra, Grade 4

I Am

I am imaginative and creative
I wonder what mysterious things hide in the horizon
I hear angels singing in my ear
I see them walking with me
I want peace in the world
I am imaginative, and creative
I pretend to be special
I touch the angel's soft wings
I'm sad when they leave
I worry about what's happening up there
I cry when I see animals die
I am imaginative, and creative
I understand that God can't save everyone
I say that everything has a purpose
I dream of peace
I try to do my very best
I hope that I will become someone important
I am imaginative, and creative.

Leah Hasberry, Grade 4

Heaven

There is a mystic place where everybody wishes to go;
A place only certain people can visit.
Nobody owns this place.
It's not a country, not a state, nor a continent.

It is a place where everybody is free and treated equally.
There is no hatred, no evilness, only kindness and friendliness.
It's a place where wishes come true.

A place of wisdom,
This place of wishes,
Is above the sky.
It is my ultimate goal.

It's my resting place.
It's my eternity.
It's my nirvana.
Your nirvana.

Brody Liebl, Grade 6

Grace

She said I broke the lamp
No I didn't!
She said I pushed her down
She just fell
She said I was being mean to her
She started it!
She said I ruined her project
Her fault not mine
She said they'll be ok
But they weren't
She said she wouldn't have an attitude
Yea, that wasn't true
She said she wanted to play with me
Ok, so I let her
She said that she had fun
That's nice to hear
She said that she was sorry for blaming everything on me
I said it was ok because I love you anyway

Bryce Clayton, Grade 6

Mission Soledad

Mission Soledad so lonely and old.
In the summer so hot, in the winter, so cold.
In 1791, this mission was made.
It was so small and of so low grade.
The padres and Indians thought it was a disgrace.
They worked hard and made it a better place.
A couple years later three floods came.
It ruined the mission three times like a game.
As a result of the floods it could barely stand.
It was sad to see 'cause it was oh so grand.
It now stands proud and tall with its old big bell.
Whom, I think have both aged so well.

John Hayward, Grade 4

Colors of the Ocean

Oh, the COLORS of the ocean!

The BLUE has a flash,
The green will always be a splash.

The PINK in the coral,
So many colors it looks FLORAL.

The colors of the squid-DARK as night,
The flashlight fish will give you some LIGHT.

Oh, the COLORS of the ocean!

Emme Dallmeyer, Grade 4

My Best Friend

Cody
Fun, adventurous
Running, playing, barking
Crazy dog, best friend
Eating, sleeping, begging
Lover, Chihuahua
Cody
Ryan Weinstock, Grade 5

Cold/Hot

Cold
Winter, snow
Frigid, freezing, cool
Rain, white, fire, red
Warm, burning, boiling
Summer, sun
Hot
Kalahikiola Kagawa, Grade 6

Jack

There's a black and white cat named Jack
Who likes to find toys to attack

He hops and he bounces,
He skips and he pounces

Energy he will never lack
Elizabeth Arnolds, Grade 5

Heights

We are going on an airplane today.
I'm scared of heights…really bad.
It is not ordinary like a kite.
I think I might throw up.
The only thing to stop me now is if
the flight gets cancelled.
Here I go…to face my fear.
Daniel Olvera, Grade 4

Veterans Day

V igilant soldiers fight.
E very soldier is good.
T ons of soldiers miss their family.
E very soldier is good.
R est in peace loyal solider.
A lot of soldiers hate the wars.
N one of the soldiers are unworthy.
Gage Peck, Grade 5

May

There was once a girl named May
Who went down to the bay
But then she was bit
By a tiny little kit
And she fell in, by the way!
Natalie Tunnell, Grade 5

Easter

Jesus sacrificed his own life for our sins.
That is what Easter is for.
Easter is about Jesus' ascension into heaven.
After Jesus was crucified,
the disciples had Jesus buried in a tomb
and guarded by Roman soldiers.
One night, the soldiers were guarding the tomb,
and there was a bright light coming from inside of the tomb.
Then the door blew open,
and an angel came down from the sky.
Jesus walked out of the tomb and went up into heaven with the angel.
The next day, one of the disciples went to check on the tomb
and saw the door blown open.
The disciple went back to the house where the others were
and saw Jesus speaking with them.
One of the disciples didn't believe it was truly Jesus
unless he put his hands on his wounds.
Jesus let him put his hands through the holes in his wrists,
and He let the disciple touch the wound on his waist.
Easter should be celebrated,
and we should be grateful for Jesus' sacrifice.
John Tewksbury, Grade 6

Link My Dog

Link who is mighty and strong
And was never wrong
When it comes to smell and danger
We bring him everywhere to camp and to the park
It brings memories of him when I'm at camp
He's fast and big and in the grass he leaves marks
In the mud, he plays, and goes back inside where he's muddy and damp
He was always happy with his tail held up high
Running gracefully through my front lawn
Listening to hear my voice when he's lost
Not being shy and greeting many people

Link always follows directions
Waiting patiently for food to eat
Lives in the house with a nice little bed
Getting a walk, and thirsting for water
Link with black and white fur
And nice blue eyes shining at night
Fluffy fur I lie on at night
Crunching on food, and scaring birds off
In memory of Link

Steven Vo, Grade 4

Ode to Earth

Earth, oh, Earth. Your perfect tilt takes my breath away.
What is more, you are home to the wondrous pandas!
You give life to all humans and wildlife. No other planet could replace you.
They cannot give life to humans easily, whether it's in water, oxygen, or food.
You have many wonders inside of you. Tell me, please, oh, tell me,
do you think other planets can provide the necessities Earth gives for us humans?
That is why Earth is so astonishing.
Abigail Melendez, Grade 6

Horseback Riding

I want to become a horse rider because
Horseback riding is very unique
You have to know how to control
You have to really be into horses to want to ride
You have to be ok with getting dirty
You have to be able to get hurt
You have to be aware

You really need to know if you want to ride
Because horses are very expensive!
There are a lot of expenses
Their check ups, getting them groomed, and food
All of those things are expensive
You also have to buy saddles and a stick
Horses are like people they are expensive

Horse riding is fun and exciting
You can experience different trails
Different horses
You can see new sites
You can connect with nature
You can practice with your horse
You can also ride in races

Kourtni Giladney, Grade 4

Baseball

The batter stepped up to the plate
He got into position
He hit a home run!
It went as high as the sky

When the next batter came up
He hit the ball with a big "clink!"
The ball went to the beautiful, emerald green grass in the outfield
He ran so fast
He is a cheetah

The crowd went wild!
They wouldn't stop!
We won the game!

Daisy Sanchez, Grade 6

Nature

Nature is everywhere
From bugs, animals, and flowers that are so rare
We can camp and eat S'mores all night
And then find some stars that glow with a lot of light
Wake up the next day to hear a bird
Chirping so loud that it can always be heard
Look! I see and eagle nest!
The feathery bird is giving itself a rest
Now that it's nighttime, let's go on a star walk
Soon, we will go to bed, can you look at the clock?
Now it's time to go home
From the place where animals roam

Hau Nguyen, Grade 5

Who Am I

Who am I?

I am blue,
Like the calm floating skies.
I am Christmas,
Full of happiness, laughter, and presents.
I am winter,
Like the cold snowflakes drifting down from the sky.
I am afternoon,
The time of day when you get out of school on a warm sunny day.
I am a nonfiction read,
Like the "I Survived" and "Who Was?" books.
I am Inside Out,
Like the strange and weird people in your head.
I am a pop singer,
Like Rachel Platten and Taylor Swift.

Who am I?
I am Sadie Paul

Sadie Paul, Grade 4

Fairy Tales

We all know them,
Fairy tales,
Lulling you to sleep,
Transporting you to another world,
A better world,
Shaping your young and innocent mind,
Making your life better in every way,
Until you outgrow them,
No more escaping from an unfortunate day,
Running away and hiding with your make-believe friends,
Imagining the most impossible scenarios,
No more,
But it should not be this way,
No longer should they turn into forgotten books decorating shelves,
Only reminding you of your childhood every blue moon,
They should be clinging to your heart and mind,
The best barnacle,
If only we would understand how much better our lives would be

Jordan Stock, Grade 6

The Storm

Flash.
The ground shakes.
Boom!
A tree two feet away crashes through the house.
Bam! Lights flicker then out.
Splash. Splash as wet as can be.
Knock, knock.
Neighbor answers.
Warm soup on the stove.
Night falls.
Blink. Blink.
I look through the window. Destruction is all you see.

Laura Boge, Grade 5

Come with Us

My thoughts were jumbled
Into a crumpled ball of uncertainty
I did not want to go with them
The freedom that I now wish I had taken
Did not matter

The water licks my limbs
The water is pulling me into its tight embrace
I wish I had just done what they said
Jump off the cliff, child.
Come with us.

I can still hear them laughing as I fell
Smiling at my confused face
The sea floor underneath me comes closer
The seaweed sways gently, whispering
Everything is fading
Come with us.
The seaweed sways
Jump off the cliff.
The water pulls
Blackness engulfs me and this strange sea
Come with us.

Asha Haley, Grade 5

I Am

I am green like a frog
I am Christmas with presents galore
I am winter reading a book snuggled in a blanket
I am night with critters a crawling
I am fantasy with wizards and spells
I am a sci-fi movie with lots of action and mysterious aliens
I am pop music to get you up and dancing
I am rice with soy sauce, yum!
I am respect, treating your parents with kindness
I am a tuxedo to make you look cool
I am the sound of a piano that is so smooth
I am vanilla ice-cream that is so sweet
I am Marco a friendly person indeed

Marco Olmos, Grade 4

Natural Brightness

Nature is a secret heaven, a place
of beauty and love. The gentle woods,
the rushing steam, the fox and pure white dove.

A time of stress, a time of fear,
it's time to leave the house.
Go outside for relaxing peace,
and run in the light green grass.

Summer, spring, winter, fall,
the seasons of the year.
Be in the bright, beautiful air,
and never shed a tear.

Audrey Payne, Grade 6

Disneyland

You walk into Disneyland
All of a sudden you hear SCREECH!
Screeches of people riding roller coasters,
Screeches of little kids,
Screeches of almost everyone!
You're riding Space Mountain SCREECH!
You're riding California Screaming SCREECH!

Getting on the haunted mansion,
The ride starts and your seat goes,
"Bump, bump, crash, bang!"
With all the sound effects
You see laughing heads, zombies, mummies, and grave tombs!
All moaning, and crying out to you!
COME…JOIN US.

You just got off your favorite ride
Your stomach starts to growl.
You see every person at the food courts,
Going CRUNCH. CRUNCH. CRUNCH!
You want to go on other rides
But what about lunch?
Maybe a churro would be something great to MUNCH!

Emma Gaines, Grade 6

Guitar Performance

White are my hands as I hold the neck.
Black are my shoes and black is my dress.

Red is my face as I walk on stage.
Dark is the theater in which they wait.

Grey is the strap as I put it on.
Brown is the neck that I set my hand upon.

Blue is the pick as I begin the downstrum.
Copper are the strings as they begin to hum.

Purple are my nails on my hands that form chords.
Louder and louder become the screams and roars.

Rebecca Hurt, Grade 6

Boys

I don't understand boys
Why they can be confused
Why they act all goofy
Why they wear much cologne
But most of all they can be stupid sometimes
Why they say sometimes then they say something
Why they can lie to you
Why they can act all smart
What I understand most is they can be funny sometimes
Why boys fall off something
Why they can act all bad and they mess up
Why they can act all buff but they aren't

Elizabeth Samson, Grade 6

Future
Is there really a future?
Or, are we really going backwards?
The numbers may be going forward,
But we might be going back.
If you look closely things are going back like they used to be,
Racism, violence, wrongdoing leaders,
Misrepresentation, true colors, and discrimination
I thought that we were past this!
Doesn't anybody learn?
History is here to help us remember,
We do not want to be like that anymore.
It is sad, this is how dictators come to power.
People are brainwashed,
you may think they are perfect and can make things great again.
I disagree,
Get it together and look closer
because you have fallen asleep and can't get up.
The day I can walk around naked, black, white, tan, mixed,
Just when EVERYTHING will stop, I will finally actually be content,
Hopefully, I will live long enough to experience such happiness and,
I hope you will, too.
Laïssa Mbiene, Grade 6

Take Part
I want them to hear, I want them to see
Why pandas are so important to me
These black spotted creatures, with so many features
Are endangered, they don't get angered
But I do, I assure you
They did nothing to us, the poachers will cuss
If I continue
They are getting sold, for money I'm told
you care about dogs, but pandas are logs
These people have to stop, or I will pop
For they are ruining His miracles
They kill them instead, right in the head
But you don't care, this is not fair
We can do something, like spreading the word
For people to stop
Their place is a menace
To them I see, so please join me
Say halt to the poachers, their guns are like motors
They kill them instead of making their bed
So spread my word, we shall be heard
We shall succeed, that's what they need.
Nadine Bandek, Grade 6

Earthquakes
On a peaceful Tuesday, hot as an oven bake.
There was an earthquake!
It made my entire block shake.

I almost died that day.
After that my mom said, "We are moving today."
It really scared me, what can I say?
Carlos Magaña, Grade 6

An Open Door
A rabbit hopped
and hopped some more
looking for an open door
he hopped in this room
and then in that
but all he found was a big fat cat
the cat said "meow!"
and the rabbit said "holy cow!"

And he hopped and hopped
and hopped again
this time he found a little hen
the hen was pecking on the ground
the rabbit didn't make a sound

Then he hopped and hopped some more
and then he found an open door
he hopped and hopped as fast as he could
but then he went outside and it felt really good
the sun was shining nice and bright
but then it was time to say goodnight
Milana Bonilla, Grade 4

The Land of Colors
In a land no one has ever seen
Everything was the color green.
And many people tried to free
The curse on the land that was the color green.
From sticks to bricks everything was green.
Carrots, oranges, and even the beans.
The people really hated this
Even though the witch was full of bliss.
Then the witch gave a wink
And everything was the color pink.
People were sure mad now
When the witch changed the color from pink to brown.
And the people said wow.
The people gave up soon
So the witch changed the color to maroon.
Then the color came back to green
The people wished she wasn't so mean.
They had had enough of this and that.
That she would fly away like a bat.
But in the end of the land of green
The curse was reversed and the witch wasn't mean.
Lauren McNulty, Grade 4

What Is Orange?
Orange is the color of the amazing sunset at night, pencils
A tiger's warm fur, magma under the earth,
the sun high in the sky, and flames dancing in the dark
It is the smell of a tiger lily and an orchard of ripe orange,
orange makes you feel energized and happy,
It is oranges and creamsicles,
orange is the sound of a crackling campfire…orange is light.
Landon Fink, Grade 4

Homeless

It's cold and I don't have a blanket
I'm broke.
I'm starving no one cares about me
I'm hungry
I ask for money no one gives
I'm sad
I ask for food but they just ignore
I'm stressed
I wander around for shelter
There's a house for sale but I have no money
I have nothing
I'm looking around to see what I can find
Nothing only three pieces of crumbs
Nothing to find
I see kids laughing and playing
I'm just sitting here crying
I'm depressed and tired I look and look but,
There is nothing.
Jazmine Rodriguez and Danielle Badillo, Grade 6

Ode to Mangoes

Mangoes are very sweet
like a summer treat
the delicious cool taste in your mouth
waterfall in your mouth
when you take out the mango from the fridge

The mango
peeled or not
still amazingly delicious
mangoes will always be on your mind
daydreaming night dreaming

there are mangoes everywhere
I see them in stores
I see them in your fridge
I see them on a mango tree
mangoes are love
mangoes are life.

Alexander Rupp, Grade 6

My Daddy

You held my hand when I was a little girl
You were always by my side
You laughed, you joked, we played all day
I wish that you would have never gone away
I know that you are in heaven
And Kyle says that you are in a better place
I just wish that I could have one last chance
To see your smiling face
I sing for you today Daddy
And know that I will never stop
I know that you are singing with me
From the heavens up on top
Kaia King, Grade 4

The Lonely Orphan

THE LONELY ORPHAN
I am ALONE
I am SAD
I see kids happy but I AM NOT ONE OF THEM,
THEY have parents but I DON'T
THEY have a family
But I DON'T
I have nobody to talk to
I CAN'T express my feelings,
I pray for a miracle TO HAVE a family
I am a kid that DOES NOT have NOBODY
I HOPE one day I can be like a normal child,
I WISH to have a home were they bring me joy to my lonely life
BUT FOR NOW
I feel like…
I DON'T BELONG.
Aylin Ortega, Grade 6

Cancer

We must find an answer,
to try and cure cancer.

Something to at least make you feel better
so please help people with cancer.

Cancer really stinks at least I think.
So let someone know if you have cancer.

If you start to feel sick don't think it's a trick
go to your doctor and get some help.

Your friends and family will give you support
so don't be such a worry wart.
If people are more aware
we can save lives every day.
Mikey DeWitt, Grade 5

Feel

Why did I turn out like this
Everyone is always making fun of me
Is it because I'm different
Or just because I can't talk
Or the fact I am in a wheelchair
Just because I can't talk or move
That does not mean they can judge me
No one likes to be bullied or picked on
So why am I the one the only one that is always getting bullied
It is not fair to me I'm trying to fit in
But I can't talk or move so that's a challenge
When I get the Medi Talker one day
I can type what I want to say now
But it takes a while to type
I can only move one finger at a time
Which makes me sad
Bryce Olsen, Grade 6

Softball
Softball
on the field
down the base
hit the ball
down I go
for my team
toward home base
now I'm up ready to win the game
Kristina Beamon, Grade 4

Hatchy
My baby is so smart
He has fun all day
No run, but dart
He sits and stays, you'll say hooray
His body is small with fluff on his neck
He's such a rascal, you'll want to scream
Never leave him alone or he will wreck
But the two of us are always a team
Ximena Falcon, Grade 5

Jesus
Jesus saves
Jesus loves

Jesus keeps us safe
Like are parents

Jesus watches over us
We love Jesus and Jesus loves us
Arianna Hoffpauir, Grade 6

Softball
S coring points makes you happy
O ften makes you a better player
F aster and faster the better you'll do
T eaching others helps you learn
B etter and better you know you can do
A wesome is what you can be
L aughter is what can help you
L ove will inspire you to play harder
Ini Sokoya, Grade 4

Edith
Smart, caring, hardworking, lovable,
Sibling of Gissella and Laura,
Lover of pets and family,
who fears to be unloved,
Who needs to be cared for,
who gives pride for love,
who would like to see heart,
Flores
Edith Flores and Sol Antuna, Grade 4

Jealousy
The blackbird,
Shadow of a dove
Comes swooping in,
Beady eyes,
Feathers black as night
Sure to swallow love
Elegantly, mysteriously,
Hiding in the above
Spending all of it's days isolated,
High up in the thunder clouds,
Wearing a smirk, hiding a frown.
Using all of its strength hiding a wish,
A dream,
One that will never come true
And yet the dove still wears the crown.
Why, the black bird is like me and you,
When jealousy overcrowds.
Helena Fuller, Grade 6

Guitar
I love to play guitar
It's really fun you'll see
I have one that's electric
With a medium sized bar
I think you should have more than one.
But that's probably just me.

You get to learn some riffs
You get to learn some chords
You get to learn minors and strings
you get to learn all sorts of things.

It'll take a lot of time
But when you finally learn
You'll see it's worth the while
And when you finally finish
With passion your heart will burn.
Cole Verow, Grade 4

Sleep
Sleep is lying down
in bed, resting your head
on a cool pillow.

Sleep is snuggling
down deep into soft warm
sheets at the end of the day.

Sleep is relaxing in
peace and quiet after a
stressful day.

Sleep is clothing your
eyes and dreaming, dreaming
of tomorrow
Jose Lopez, Grade 6

Spider's Web
Spider, spider spinning a web,
running out of hope with dread.
Every day and every night
the web is destroyed in great spite.

Working without losing a hair,
always ready when insects land there.
Dawn light wakes up in the night,
now the spider has its first bite.
Celina Stodder, Grade 4

Sounds of Lacrosse
Pads crashing
Sticks banging
These are the sounds of lacrosse
Teammates cheering
Helmets buckling
These are the sounds of lacrosse
Coaches telling
People yelling
These are the sounds of lacrosse
Teeg Crumley, Grade 4

Ocean
The pink sky,
Crabs walking by,
Seashells on the shore,
Fish I catch,
Wind in my ears,
Surfing in my view,
Laughter fills the air,
Stars in the sky,
It's time to say goodnight.
Teresa Luak, Grade 5

Upset and in Pain
Just because
my eyes don't tear
doesn't mean
my heart doesn't cry,

Just because
I come off strong
doesn't mean
there's nothing wrong.
Eva Taylor, Grade 5

Sunrise/Sunset
Sunrise
Waking, lighting
School, playtime, clothes
Rising, working, chilling, setting
Home, bedtime, pajamas
Sleeping, dimming
Sunset
Nadia G. Jack, Grade 4

I Am

I am a cat
   prancing around.
I am a bug
   looking up at you.
I am pages of a book
   making you wonder what will happen next.
I am love
   contentedly spreading.
I am a sunflower
   always blooming.

Mady Kubiak, Grade 4

Poem

Poems are little diaries
each one holds an emotion like a brain.
Poems are little rule breakers
Poems are an imagination stations
Poems are your friend you can tell anything to
Poems are boredom busters
Poems are crosswords
and you need to figure out a way to understand it
Poems are...
EVERYTHING

Aastha Agrawal, Grade 6

The Snowflake Ball

Once I was watching the snowflakes fall,
And I saw flakes going to the snowflake ball.
In the back were the women-flakes with dresses of tiniest thread,
But first came the men-flakes dancing ahead.
They danced and they danced in the waltz of the breeze,
Until they got tired and lay in the fallen leaves.
But more kept on dancing and dancing away,
I watched them for hours, 'til the end of the day.
Next time that snowflakes swirl and fall,
I'll watch them again as they dance at the ball.

Elise Giles, Grade 5

My Father

I love my father, someone I always trust
He was there to help me, when my day was a bust
We spend time together, I love it very much
We go to different restaurants, Red Lobster and such
Don't tell anyone he's my favorite family member
I love him very much, and I'll cherish him forever

Maslah Jama, Grade 6

Beautiful Butterflies

Butterflies how graceful when they fly in
the sky their colorful wings reflect on the sky.

When they land on my shoulder and tickle my ear and
when they burst from a cocoon and full of flame.

They drink from a flower so they make the whole day perfect.

Kelsie McGee, Grade 4

White Is Everywhere

White is for soft, puffy clouds,
Floating through the sky.
And flying airplanes,
In the collage of colors above ground.
And from whiteboards that get covered up,
From the thinking of inquisitive kids.
White is for white-out that takes away,
Silly or hard mistakes made on paper.
And spacesuits that help astronauts,
Explore the moon that illuminates the night,
When it turns the color of the Underworld.
It come from soft, titillating whipped cream,
teaming up with pancakes to make a scrumptious meal,
Covering up your mouth,
Making you crave for more.
And delectable, luscious eggs you can make exquisite,
Foods out of,
White is for the tiny,
High-pitched squeak of a furry mouse,
And most importantly, the sensitive sclera,
Helping you relish the wonders of the resplendent world!

Ashmit Gaba, Grade 6

Jackson

J okester, he tells funny jokes
A wesome in many different ways
C omedian, he makes everybody laugh
K ind kid is what he is
S illy as a goose
O ne fun student
N ever backs down

C ontagious smile
A fable boy
R eady for anything
T en years old
E nthusiastic guy
R espectful

M indful youngster, always happy
C aring and loving
S tars and planet lover
T ask doer
A ble to solve math problems at the speed of light
Y earning to be every body's friend

Thomas Canfield, Grade 5

Waterfall

It falls,
It drops,
But whatever it does it never stops,
Like puffed marshmallows,
Like whipped cream,
Though you can never mistake it for a stream,
So there it is a waterfall so bright, so tall.

Ardel Wilkinson, Grade 5

Happiness

Happiness seems pink
Like the fur of unicorns.
I see gleaming rainbows.
I hear singing unicorns.
I smell fresh daisies.
I touch fluffy, white clouds.
I taste rainbow cupcakes.
Paige Ravsten, Grade 4

Joy

Joy seems like rainbow colors
Like the smile of a baby.
I see a blue motorcycle.
I hear a giggling woman.
I smell watermelon chapstick.
I touch a pink flamingo.
I taste red gobbling gum.
Emely Ramirez, Grade 4

What Can I Do to Help?

You hear the leaves rustling
You see the leaves blow
You think to yourself, what can I do to help?
I can water the plants to make them grow
I can cover them up when it starts to snow
Now I know, I did my part
For I am a naturalist at heart
Jayda Bright, Grade 4

Snow

Snow, Snow, Snow, snow, snow, snow
I see you fall to the ground,
Snow, snow, Snow, snow, Snow, snow
I watch you as you glitter all around
Snow, Snow, snow, Snow, Snow
I learn every day that you have been brown
Snow, SNOW, Snow, SNOW!
Jenna Kasper, Grade 5

My Easter This Year

This year for Easter
I went to visit my family.
We went Easter egg hunting.
A helicopter dropped 5,000 eggs,
but we all know the true meaning of Easter,
Christ's death and resurrection.
Overall we had a very fun time this Easter.
Hunter Frantzen, Grade 6

Ocean Joys

I feel the sea scented breeze touch me with a tender embrace
I close my eyes and cherish the many gifts the wind has given me
I close my eyes and feel the breeze
but only I am there
my spirit is dancing across the waves leaping with joy in the pearly white foam
I walk across the sandy shores
every grain a work of art
each step an opportunity
the rocks are scattered and painted with a mural full of colors magic can you see it?
the mist flying can you feel it?
the waves are crashing can you hear it?
this is magic lets share it
dance with me leap with me celebrate the beauty ocean joys
Ayla Power, Grade 4

I Am From

I am from a neighborhood,
    where the street has potholes that no one is willing to fill,
    where empty land is always available but never in use,
    where I walk the streets alone.
I am from a family,
    where we decide together on decisions,
    where I learn things most other people never understood,
    where I can choose freely without someone telling me what to say.
I am from a place,
    where we all say the same pledge,
    where my family fought for what they thought was right,
    where we all laugh at the dark wooden dinner table.
I love the place I am from!
Weston Mitchell, Grade 5

Spring

Spring is for fun and playing
Outside and eating popsicle in the warm sun.
Inviting friends to come and play and to be happy with all sorts of fun.
And go lay in the grass and admire the flowers
and have some fun with jumps and twirls.
Have some fun and be outside
Today is your day to shine.

Go have fun and drink some Icee's
go swim and have some fun.
Play with your friends all day long.
And wear shorts and play outside.
Have a happy spring time.

Jeannine Perez, Grade 4

Accident

The blue and red of the lights shine bright.
The metallic taste of blood fills my mouth.
The sirens scream like a hungry baby in my ears.
The bitter smell of smoke fills the air.
The accident plays out like a scene in a movie.
The sight of death makes me feel like curling up in a ball and never leaving.
Kendall Wetter, Grade 6

Sam We Won!

Sam tied his cleats and brushed his hair.
He tucked in his shirt and ate a pear.
"Ready for the big game?" Sam's dad called.
"Yeah," Sam said, but he tried to stall.

Sam's mom was excited,
For Sam was supposed to bat.
Sam said, "Drat,
We're going to lose."
Sam's mom asked, "Do you have your shoes?"
Sam said, "Yes," and managed a brief smile.
"I'll get tired after a while."
"Well you can still try and try and try," Sam's dad said.
"I will," Sam said, like nothing was a thrill.

That day Sam's team was on a roll,
Then Sam came up to bat.
Drat, Sam thought and he straightened his hat.
He looked down and rubbed the dirt with his shoes.
"I hope I hit this or I'll be feeling blue."

Sam got into a stance,
He readied his bat,
And he whacked the ball,
It flew out of the park.
Sam smiled, he ran around the bases and did a dance.
"Sam, we won!" everyone cheered.

Delaney Orma, Grade 4

Together We Thrive

Thick, gloomy, grey clouds sit on top of the misty sky
The ocean is the only light left in a barren landscape

Low booms of the drum echo through the land,
The sound calls to his followers and a leader is born
Footsteps follow the drum's vibrations

The bright sunshine laughs
in the breezy grasses of love and friendship

The oil spills and the torch is lit
The fire is close

The space between yesterday and tomorrow
is a walk across the road

On rocks as light as clouds and as soft as pillows,
they dreamed of their dreams

New light shines upon a once gloomy land
The drum beats to the rhythm of their hearts

The children's hair waving goodbye in the wind,
The cliff approaches,
They jump…

Donya Ghassemieh, Grade 5

Yin-Yang

A memory carved into the mind
Forever etched into
The fabric of our time

The meaning of life
The knowledge beholden to our ancestors
Vanquished not even with a knife

The love, the life, the magic within
A power beyond anything known
Free from sin

Powerful energy of the Yin-Yang
The thin line between good and evil
So very fine

To learn both exist within you is to learn the truth
A coming-of-age
A step away from the lies of youth

The dark and light magic force
They are actions, thoughts, words
Ones occurring in life's course

Life
A thin line surrounded by gray areas
Let thine actions shine

Hilary Nguyen, Grade 5

A Golden Memory

I was a boat adrift, lost in the sea.
The water surrounded me.
Waves were calm, but it would change.

The wind whispered,
Stay smooth.
A frozen hush stood silent, silence.

A parade of angry waves
Clashed fiercely on the shore.
Tearing my heart away.
Rage met sadness.

Storm clouds,
Powerful and thick, tears brought
Waves clashing with even more force.
Then, the waves froze, silence.

Another crest of waves rushed,
But this time, the waves waned in anger,
In a parade of pride.

A golden memory cannot be broken
We won, and I was riding the wave,
Because no matter what happened, everything would be all right.

Andrea Tsai, Grade 6

Friendship

Friendship is what keeps the World together, If we did not have Friendship We would not have Allegiance
We did not have Friendship In massive battles Even if you are just One person you need at least one Friend,
Otherwise you won't be joyful You will be… Lonely, maybe angry, or even melancholy If someone does not have a Friend
Help them find one or be their Friend

Kylie R. Stuart, Grade 4

Panthers

A panther's strong tail is like a snake
So you don't want to make a mistake
Just like the night
It gives you a fright
So, don't make a sound for your own sake

Larry Roberts, Grade 5

Bad Hair Day

There once was a teddy bear, who loved to brush her hair
one day she forgot, it got tangled in knots
and gave people quite a scare

Isabella Scuderi, Grade 4

The World

The world is a colorful place.
It is right in front of your face.
There's red, orange, yellow, green, blue, indigo, violet.

Joseph Ramirez, Grade 6

Happiness

Happiness seems golden yellow
Like the clouds smiling.
I see the sun smiling brightly.
I hear cheer all around.
I smell chicken pot pie fresh out of the oven.
I touch the feathery ducks.
I taste joy.

Samantha Moore, Grade 4

My Dog Daniel

I love my tan dog
We like to jog
He likes to bark
And sleeps in the dark

Carlos De la Cruz, Grade 5

Puppies

Puppies and puddles
Licks and hugs
Soft and cuddle-able
Just like pugs

Katie Mendoza, Grade 5

Snowflakes

Snowflakes
Gently tumble
To the ground carefully
They are like angels in the sky
Gorgeous

Dominic Campos, Grade 5

The Kite

Riley
With a kite
Then her kite
Flew.

Lizbeth Morales, Grade 4

Index by Author

Index by School

Interested in Writing More Poetry?

Each of the poetry forms below has an easy-to-follow template.
An (*) by the title means it is an editor's favorite!

ABC Poem
Acrostic
All About Me
*Animal Poem
Best Friend Simile Poem
Biography Poem
Bio(logical) Poem
Cinquain
Color Poem
Concrete Poem
Diamonte
*Emotional Animal Poem
Famous Biography Poem
Five W Poem
Haiku
*Hold On Poem
Holiday Poem
I Am Poem
I Don't Understand Poem
*I Remember
I Used To...
If I'm In Charge of the World
Lament
Lantern Poem

Limerick
List Poem
Lune
Mask Poem
My Shadow Poem
Name Poem
*Nature Personified
*Noun Adjective Phrase Poem
*Ocotopoem
One Inch Tall Poem
*Pantoum
*Pensee
Phone Number Poem
Quatrain
Quinzaine
Sedoka
Senryu
Septet
Tanka
*Title Poem
*Triolet
Verb Verse
What If Poem
Yes, That's Me...

It's easy, free, and you can do it from anywhere!
Create your next poem for one of our contests,
or have fun exploring and creating poetry!

Author Autograph Page

Author Autograph Page

Author Autograph Page

Author Autograph Page

Author Autograph Page

Author Autograph Page